# TERMINAT

### FOR REASONS OF TASTE

# TERMINATED

## FOR REASONS OF TASTE

Other Ways to Hear Essential

and Inessential Music

## Chuck Eddy

DUKE UNIVERSITY PRESS *Durham and London* 2016

Library of Congress Cataloging-in-Publication Data
Names: Eddy, Chuck, editor.
Title: Terminated for reasons of taste : other ways to hear
essential and inessential music / Chuck Eddy.
Description: Durham : Duke University Press, 2016. |
Includes index.
Identifiers: LCCN 2016002413
ISBN 9780822361893 (hardcover : alk. paper)
ISBN 9780822362258 (pbk. : alk. paper)
ISBN 9780822373896 (e-book)
Subjects: LCSH: Rock music—History and criticism. |
Popular music—History and criticism.
Classification: LCC ML3534.E293 2016 | DDC 781.6409—dc23
LC record available at http://lccn.loc.gov/2016002413

Cover design by Skillet Gilmore.

TO ALL CHUCK'S CHILDREN

# Contents

# Acknowledgments

To conserve space, it seems prudent to start this off by honoring two huge *groups* of people, namely (1) everybody I thanked in each of my three previous books, all written in eras overlapping my writing in this one; (2) any and all friends on Facebook (more or less 570 these days—I'm *kind of* selective) who no doubt inspired me somehow and somewhere. If you're in either of those categories, consider yourself appreciated; if not, feel free to look and see who is.

Before there were "social networks," there were social networks. Also after. So if I ever agreed or argued with you at *Why Music Sucks*, *Radio On*, ilxor .com, or *Singles Jukebox*; or ever worked with you at the *Village Voice* or *Billboard*; or ever spent every noon CST Tuesday for years on a Rhapsody conference call with you, we should probably go out for a beer sometime.

Editors who first printed these pieces (and frequently improved them) include but are by no means limited to Milo Miles at the *Boston Phoenix*; Jim Walsh at *City Pages*; Rob Kenner at *Complex*; Dave DiMartino, Bill Holdship, and John Kordosh at *Creem*; Greg Boyd and Bill Reynolds at *Eye Weekly*; Chris Chang at *Film Comment*; Siobhan O'Connor at GOOD; Alastair Sutherland at *Graffiti*; Maura Johnston at *Idolator*; John Payne at *L.A. Weekly*; Jessica Suarez at *MTV Hive*; Phil Dellio (who also mailed me a Matchbox 20 photo I used in here somewhere, and whose own recent collection *Interrupting My Train of Thought* belongs on your reading list as well) at *Radio On*; Keith Moerer at *Request*; Garrett Kamps, Sam Chennault, Rob Harvilla, and Stephanie Benson at Rhapsody; Nick Catucci at rollingstone.com; William Swygart at *Singles Jukebox*; Sue Rollinger at the *Spectrum*; Simon Reynolds, Charles Aaron, and Chris Weingarten at *Spin*; Will Fulford-Jones at *Time Out London*; Doug Simmons and Harvilla at the *Village Voice*; and J. Edward Keyes and Jayson Greene at *Wondering Sound* (called eMusic at the time).

(Some related legal stuff: MTV's "September 11: Country Music's Response"

The headline "Past Expiry Hard Rock Dollar Bin" was partly swiped from the title of a recurring I Love Music thread initiated in 2009 by George Smith, who I probably borrowed a riff or two from as well. George, Gina Arnold, J. D. Considine, Stephen Thomas Erlewine, Tom Ewing, Tim Finney, Joshua Kortbein, Glenn McDonald, David Cooper Moore, Ned Raggett, Mark Richardson, Philip Sherburne, Steve Smith, Jannon Sonja Stein, and Annie Zaleski, among others, provided valuable recollections on a Facebook thread I summarize herein about the origins of music writing on the Internet. Jody Rosen, who also knows more about turn-of-the-20th-century music than I do, gave "bro-country" its name. And it's impossible to gauge how much my thinking and writing have been inspired over the years, and continue to be, by colleagues like Jacob Alrich, Kevin Bozelka, Dan Brockman, David Cantwell, Jon Caramanica, Robert Christgau, Matt Cibula, Leila Cobo, Anthony Easton, Justin Farrar, Michael Freedberg, Jeanne Fury, Keith Harris, Jewly Hight, Christian Hoard, Charles Hughes, Edd Hurt, Maura Johnston, Josh Langhoff, Greil Marcus, Michaelangelo Matos, Chris Molanphy, Daddy B. Nice, Martin Popoff, Ann Powers, Mosi Reeves, Metal Mike Saunders, Rob Sheffield, Sara Sherr, Alfred Soto, Jack Thompson, Barry Walters, Eric Weisbard, Dan Weiss, Carl Wilson, Scott Woods, Ron Wynn, and above all Frank Kogan and Scott Seward . . . seriously, I could go on forever.

And then there's Lalena, whose husband I am, who deserves thanks for putting up with me and line-editing all the chapter intros, and Annika, Cordelia, Sherman, and William, whose dad I am, who deserve thanks for keeping me halfway grounded and teaching me about jiu-jitsu, TERFs, graffiti, and yurts. And Ken Wissoker, Elizabeth Ault, and Danielle Szulczewski Houtz at Duke, who let me do this thing again and walked me through it, tolerating my obsessive-compulsive logistical questions as if they weren't the mark of a troubled mind. And finally, whoever buys, reads, or writes about this book. I'm so lucky y'all are out there. Thank you falettinme be mice elf agin.

# Introduction
## Sold a Decade at a Time

When people meet me and find out what I do for a living, they inevitably ask me what kind of music I listen to and write about. I never know how to answer the question—never have—so usually I just kind of fumble and stutter a lot. If I told them how I really felt, they'd probably just think I was weird: namely, that pop music is bigger, more multidimensional, endlessly compelling in more directions, than they ever imagined. So it's kinda hard to pin the stuff down.

If it helps, though, when I used to moonlight as a bar DJ late Saturday nights while living in New York City at the start of the 21st century, here's how I advertised my genre leanings: "DJ Edelweiss spins a danceable and drinkable ALL-VINYL selection of proto-Eurodisco bongo-rock, German reggae, danceable prog, hair-extension metal, Gregorian garage, boogie-oogied country, stoner glam, industrial bubblegum, popping-and-locking Zulu wildstyle space-cowboy hip hop bommi bop, and drunken frat-soul with parties going on in the background. Plus zillions of ancient Top 40 songs you'd forgotten—until now." Okay, maybe that doesn't help so much.

Still, here's the thing: I see music history repeating itself, revolving again and again in strange, intriguing, disturbing, revealing, often hilarious ways. In the more than three decades during which I wrote the pieces in this book, popular music itself, music criticism, the music industry, communication media, and America have all changed immeasurably. So this book aims to plug into a whole bunch of those changes as they occurred, and somehow tie them together.

Though it might look at first like an unnavigable dump, there is rather meticulous method to my madness—a logic, or several overlapping logics. There are trapdoors and secret passages connecting it all; if you want, you can make a game of it. Yet all the material comprises just a fraction of my music writing—or rather, *another* fraction, after the 100 or so pieces compiled in my previous Duke collection, 2011's *Rock and Roll Always Forgets* (which followed 1997's *The Accidental Evolution of Rock'n'Roll*, which followed my 1991 heavy metal album guide *Stairway to Hell*, which I updated and expanded in 1998). So yes, I am milking my once-prolific career as a rock critic for all it's worth! There's even a short piece I wrote for my high school newspaper, back in the '70s. But though I was contributing a decade later to *Rolling Stone* and still do, I've included no pieces from that magazine, unless a Kanye West live review that only ran on their website counts. None of the hundreds of reviews I've written over the years for *Entertainment Weekly* or *Blender* or *Billboard* (where I worked as an editor) are in here, either.

Even more than its predecessor, *Terminated for Reasons of Taste* includes plenty of writing I didn't even get paid for—much of which first appeared in Xeroxed fanzines, on Internet discussion boards, on nebulous websites that came and went. Two full-length "reviews"—of '60s folk artist Niela Miller and a 2009 Bruce Springsteen album—are actually pieced together from extended off-the-cuff posts on the I Love Music board; for whatever reason, I think they captured more of my voice than most reviews that actually paid my bills. Occasionally, especially with selections from more amateur outlets like that one, I've since self-edited pieces from their original rambling-off-the-top-of-my-head state or folded adjacent posts together for reasons of clarity, coherency, and accuracy and to avoid redundancy and dumb typos; a few pieces have also been condensed somewhat, so as not to waste precious space, or reverted to pre-editor-remixed form when I was convinced they'd lost something in translation. I've also retooled certain headlines if the originals weren't doing their job, or made no sense in retrospect. But throughout, I tried to select work that somehow holds up for me—believe me, a "worst of Chuck Eddy" compilation would be way thicker than this one.

I started writing professionally, if you can call it that, in early 1984, and the book divides itself into five chronological sections, revolving around music from the 1980s, 1990s, 2000s, 2010s, and—in the first one, facetiously titled "B.C."—all of history Before I was a Critic. Under each of those umbrellas, I tried to organize pieces like a playlist or mixtape or good radio set, to transition logically into each other—to set each other up, answer each other's questions, carry on an internal conversation or debate. So pieces on similar genres or by related artists or with intersecting themes or geography tend to be grouped together when feasible, with cusps between genres (rap-rock, say) sometimes serving as mortar. This allows styles to evolve through the pages. For instance, I trace country music's mutations from the '20s all the way to the present, in part via five batches of song reviews first published on the mostly hip-hop-oriented website Complex in 2012. In another thread that keeps popping back up, you get to watch me fall in and out of and back in love with heavy metal. Even folk revivals, never my specialty, recur now and then throughout—from Niela Miller and Catholic folk masses all the way to Mumford and Sons.

Other serial threads recur as well, including a few from *Spin*'s post-print-era website: two pieces on country rap; three Sonic Taxonomy columns exploring essential albums in unexplored (and, in the case of "Fake New Wave," maybe imaginary) genres; three titled with arrows (→ or ←) where I discuss a current artist alongside one from decades before. There are also two assemblages of real-time single-song reviews from the '90s fanzine *Radio On*, sequeled in subsequent decades by similar collections from the *Village Voice* and the Singles Jukebox site.

Some extramusical threads no doubt run through, too, and I'm not even sure I could name those myself. But I do plenty of explaining, in too much detail maybe, in all five section introductions. So I'll terminate this now, and hope you find some of what follows to your taste.

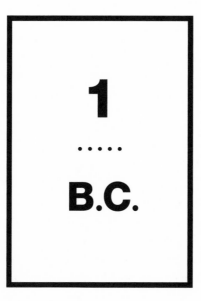

**1**

· · · · ·

**B.C.**

**THIS SECTION** covers more or less a half-century of music, which is obviously ridiculous. It's also nothing: the Ronald L. Davis *History of Music in American Life* volume I've been wading through lately runs 1620 to 1865. And back in the early '90s, Robert Christgau put together a "Prehistory of Rock 'n' Roll" timeline for *Details* that started with courtly loving *jongleurs* of 1227, jumped to colonialist British explorers praising Gambian drum rhythms in 1623 and then to Viennese waltzers dancing as couples in 1815, and advanced forward from there. Interviewed by Michaelangelo Matos two centuries after those waltzes, Christgau explained that in teaching music history at the Clive Davis Institute of Recorded Music, he now reads "one of the oldest pieces of prose known to exist—4,500-odd years old," an order from "the boy-king named King Pepi to 'bring a pygmy dancer to the court.'" By comparison, my own B.C. begins almost yesterday: in 1930, with a slightly abridged version of one of several "50 Best Songs of Whatever Year" pieces that accompanied playlists I programmed for the streaming website Rhapsody in the past half-decade. I dip back into the 19th century here and there on subsequent pages, but only momentarily.

So basically, here's where I put my writing about music made before I wrote about music. Where subsequent sections increasingly go heavy on real-time criticism, "B.C." necessarily comprises pieces written almost entirely in hindsight, mostly in a recent era of so-called Internet "listicles" that had websites trying to maximize page clicks and monetize eyeballs—which was also, as it happens, an era in which downloads and the so-called cloud theoretically made all of recorded musical history available at will. So editors were increasingly open to critics writing about archival music, if frequently as bite-size blurbs rather than at length.

A disclaimer: I do not in any way consider myself a historian. The oldest baseball card I owned growing up was a 1949 Vernon Bickford on Bowman, so if some music I'm writing about seems like ancient history, you're not alone. The further back I go, the more of a tenderfoot I am. And while I grow ever more fascinated tracing that backward path, I also realize I'm extremely selective about which route I take. You'll find nothing here about Jenny Lind or John Philip Sousa, jubilee singers or parlor piano players, trilingual-at-the-same-time late 1910s drum-whistle-rattle Dada power trios at Zurich's Cabaret Voltaire or the tragic but titillating whore songs of 1920s Berlin literary cabaret. And though I touch at least a few times on the intriguing if unsavory legacy of 19th-century minstrel shows, especially as they prefigure southern artists ultimately marketed as hillbilly music, anybody whose curiosity I spike should seriously consider seeking out the work of authors and academics whose expertise on the topic (and concurrent music from before the World Wars) puts mine to shame—a short list might include Amiri Baraka, David Cockrell, Ken Emerson, Karl Hagstrom Miller, Paul Oliver, Nick Tosches, Elijah Wald, David Wondrich, David A. Jasen and Gene Jones, and Yuval Taylor and Jack Austen, for starters. (Fill up your library card—I did!)

I know I'm treading on potentially dangerous ground here. I'm a middle-aged white guy, and much of what I write about early country music takes into account race—always a lingering issue in a South that, 150 years down the line, still hasn't gotten over losing the Civil War or let go of its collective amnesia about slavery, the rollback of Reconstruction, the Ku Klux Klan, or Jim Crow. In 2009 I moved to Texas, where a year later the governor was still arguing for "states' rights" and where you couldn't miss the ominous Confederate flags along U.S. Route 290 long before Dylann Roof massacred nine black people in a historic South Carolina church. The Sambo and golliwog caricatures and dialect lampoons fostered by minstrelsy's "Negro delineators," nostalgia for antebellum plantation life, and razor-toting "coon songs" of the 1890s are inextricable from centuries of racial oppression and violence that still make the front page.

But paradox or not, remnants of those offensive ancient shticks lent verve and humor to more 20th-century music than we'll ever know—examples referenced in pages ahead barely skim the surface. There was, for instance, Jack Benny–associated midcentury band leader and "The Thing"–maker (among other things) Phil Harris, whose "singing style is basically a sort of rhythmic talk coated with the glib overtones of the circus barker," explained the liner notes to 1958's *That's What I Like About the South*—so basically, he rapped—with "an obviously deep admiration for the work of the great Negro comedian Bert Williams, who, like Harris, talked his songs." On 1974's *Stone Mountain Wobble*, Ohio's Hotmud Family were still passing off chestnuts like "Georgia Camp Meeting" and "Bully of the Town" as "country ragtime," complete with a Mr. Bones stand-in known as Mr. Spoons. Even four decades later, you could still go to a Civil War reenactment and observe outfits like the Second South Carolina String Band play Dan Emmett songs about "darkies," and blackface Otellos were commonplace at opera houses well into the early 21st century. Less blatantly, lines could be drawn through the talking blues, Hoagy Carmichael, and Dean Martin's 1955 *Swingin' Down Yonder* all the way to Old Crow Medicine Show, Pokey LaFarge's 2011 cover of Fiddlin' Arthur Smith's 1936 "Chittlin' Cooking Time in Cheatham County," or casually wistful references to fried chicken, watermelon, and the flood-and-race-riot-prone river juncture town "Cairo, Illinois" on 2015's *Something in the Water*, and even today's hick-hopping "bro country." Some aesthetics never go away.

So while I don't want to be insensitive to evils of the era that spawned the stereotyping, and while I acknowledge that exercising entitlement as a person of non-color means I risk being complicit in the original sin, I also don't want to deny that a willing misconstruction of African American culture helped give white artists—minstrels to string bands to rockabillies to Kid Rock— a freedom to let their music be loose, raunchy, funky, and funny in ways it clearly wouldn't have been otherwise. No amount of deserved moral outrage is going to stop me getting off on it. Much of it remains reprehensible, but at very least you might benefit from knowing it's out there.

Anyway, that's not all this section is about, and maybe some background is in order. I was born in 1960 in Detroit, and didn't pay all that much attention to music for the first 18 or so years of my life. I was vaguely aware of Paul-is-Dead clues on Beatles album covers because classmates talked about them, but the most I've ever written about the band since was five blurbs on Ringo solo songs for rollingstone.com in 2015. A guy named Jim Tierney, signing my senior yearbook, claimed I quoted Frank Zappa once, which is odd because I don't remember listening to any Zappa albums until the late '80s. I learned about the band Styx when some hilarious vandals painted "Welcome to the Grand Illusion" across the front of West Bloomfield High School once, and I'm pretty sure the closest thing I read to rock criticism at the time was when some other graffiti artist and perhaps fellow busboy scrawled a rant on a back kitchen wall at Maple House pancake restaurant about how rock was on the skids now because the New York Dolls were long gone and Kiss weren't making good albums anymore and something else about Ted Nugent and Aerosmith. Yet more smart-asses from school had a band called Luke Mucus and the Phlegm that I mainly remember as a talent show parody (other members: Runny Buttz, Lew Putrid, Yid McForeskin, Burrito, har har; songs about "fartin' in a pool" and sniffin' Sheila Young's bicycle seat), and when they finally compiled their 1979–'80 recordings and those of their more Romantics-commercial 1980–'81 incarnation Luke Warm (local 45 "hit": "Jesus Chrysler") on two archival LPs in 2013, I was amazed how much the *Cracked* / *Creem* / Ron Sweed / Alice Cooper / Dictators / B.T.O.-riffs-as-faux-punk sound and sensibilities prefigured (even shaped?) the Midwest-suburban wisenheimer critical stance I not much later made public.

Wouldn't be surprised if those guys were as cynical about John Denver-loving "granolas" as I was, or at least pretended to be in the one ancient piece I've included that I actually wrote for West Bloomfield's student newspaper. Or maybe I was just self-consciously obsessed with taxonomical peer classification in general. I'm not quite sure where I would have categorized myself, clique-wise, though I was geeky enough to be on the debate team both my freshman and senior years, taking sides on resolutions to overhaul the presidential election system and instigate national health care. One of my favorite books as a teenager was *What Really Happened to the Class Of '65?* by David Wallechinsky and Michael Medved, the latter of whom went on to become a hardline Zionist right-wing talk radio host. The Palisades High student in the book I most identified with back then was Jamie Kelso, a brainy little neurotic who later resurfaced as a prominent white supremacist. Funny—neither seemed like a budding neo-fascist at the time.

Then again, neither did Ted Nugent. Long before he started palling around with Texas governors, and back before I became fluent in the lingo of genre, I assumed he and Bob Seger epitomized what my classmates meant when they talked about "hard rock"—a kind of music that I also assumed I didn't like. But you never know with Detroiters. Seger seems fairly progressive politically these days (2014's *Ride Out* included protesty global warming and gun control songs), but let's just say Nugent plugs into a long tradition. As a little kid I collected toy VW Beetles, but assembly-line mass production and the techno music it ultimately inspired aren't all that Michigan and Germany have in common. Chip Berlet and Matthew Lyons's *Right-Wing Populism in America* names some names: Henry Ford, Father Coughlin, Charles Lindbergh, plus Joe McCarthy just one state west, where the John Birch Society now has its headquarters. The upper midwest is also where class-resenting rock fans set disco records on fire in the late '70s. Sometimes I even wonder how much the suspicion of elitist northeastern intellectuals certain skeptics detected in my early music criticism owed to my hailing from that neck of the Rust Belt.

What I didn't know until recently is that I had ancestors surnamed Steinberg on my dad's mom's mom's side who came to Michigan around 1880 "from someplace near Posen," which Germany had just taken control of nine years earlier but which belonged to Prussia before that and Poland later. August Steinberg "never revealed his background except to assert he was German, a devout Catholic, and a hard worker," my great-aunt Ethel Wooden wrote in the late '70s, four decades after she'd started a vocational trade school for young women in Toledo. August's son Frank sang mean ditties at family reunions about not having "one drop of Polish blood," unlike lots of guys he worked with as a Grand Rapids mason; Frank's artistically inclined son George designed camouflage during World War I then later got a job at a specialty shop in New York only by showing up with his blonde hair and proving he wasn't Jewish. Eventually he changed his name to Stonehill, and when a heart attack killed him at 53 his wife trashed all his paintings. Also, according to Aunt Ethel, "one of the men could play the small accordion and all were expert with the polka." Which seems relevant here, for some reason.

So uh . . . where was I? Oh yeah, the '70s. Halfway through, this section takes a crazy leap forward in time, barely touching on '50s or '60s music except for meager helpings of country and folk, completely ignoring mortality-minded late-'60s L.A. jug-jig-and-jive raga-hoedown tricksters Kaleidoscope even though they're just about my favorite band ever right now, then diving whole hog into '70s hard rock that's been buried by history and hence provides excellent blind alleys to wander down. The tone of my writing maybe switches, too, since I'm perfectly comfortable making fun of white guys rocking hard, seeing how that's demographically close enough to making fun of myself. From there, I get a bit old-man-yells-at-cloud about how modern-day alt-indie is no match for new wave back in the day (magnet on my refrigerator, dad to son, sorry: "It's not that I'm old, your music really does suck!"), praise some darts that coked-up record execs threw at the wall and missed while flush from profits of *Frampton Comes Alive* and *Saturday Night Fever* and *Rumours*, and sneak into the '80s defending also-rans who couldn't decide if they wanted to wear skinny ties or not.

Mainstream hard rock was endangered by then—or so some hoped. "Will the marginal fans of boogie and heavy metal decide they're tired of all that calculated spontaneity and putative self-expression? Will they turn from those big, thick cushions of loudness and decorative licks of musicianship?," Robert Christgau wondered in late October 1977, in a long *Village Voice* essay about the future of a scene he was still calling "Avant-Punk." He picked the Stranglers, Dead Boys, and Eddie and the Hot Rods as good bets to make it with loud-guitar-loving American teens, though none of them ever really did. The same special section had Richard Meltzer writing about his new joke-punk combo Vom and predicting punk would soon "splinter off into Beatnik Rock and College Rock—rockers vs. the mods all over again!" Simon Frith, meanwhile, had just attended a "Music for Socialism" fest in London where all the folkies and avant-gardists in the workshops dismissed punk as "the most reactionary fascist trend in popular culture today." A few ads in the *Voice* section in question: Rick Derringer, Ram Jam, Karla Bonoff, E-Z Wider rolling papers, Sam Ash, "Korvette Salutes the NEW WAVE of music on SIRE RECORDS."

So, yeah—'twas a long time ago. Though not as long ago as the times before that. But how about you step into Mr. Peabody's WABAC machine with me, and see where it takes us?

# The Best Songs of 1930

. . . . .

Given that the stock market had crashed just two months before New Year's, it's maybe no surprise that so many of the most notable songs of 1930—or at least the ones that historians, collectors, collective memory, cinema, and the *Anthology of American Folk Music* have assisted toward the surface 84 years later—comment on the economy. What's more surprising is how many of them find dark humor in it: old-timey North Carolina banjo man Charlie Poole being booted by his landlord for lack of rent payment in "It's Moving Day" (revived a mere half-century ago by the Holy Modal Rounders); Gene Autry, still more hillbilly bluesman than Hollywood cowboy, sweeping motel floors in "Dust Pan Blues" just as the Dust Bowl was starting to rev up; string bands the Carolina Tar Heels ("Got the Farm Land Blues") and Buster Carter and Preston Young ("A Lazy Farmer Boy") counting corn crops wither away; mysterious proto-blues-style medicine-show hokum songster Lil McClintock losing his bed and frying pan to a debt collector in "Furniture Man"; minstrel-throwback country ancestor Uncle Dave Macon watching banks collapse and the infrastructure pork barrel run dry in "Wreck of the Tennessee Gravy Train." "Of all the times I've ever seen, we're sure up against it now," Uncle Dave rambles, but on some level, people seem to have been *laughing* about such misfortune.

Cannon's Jug Stompers in "Bring It with You When You Come" and Jimmie Rodgers, backed by Louis Armstrong's trumpet and Lil Hardin Armstrong's piano in "Blue Yodel No. 9," played the parts of hobos and bums, Rodgers smarting off to a cop that his name could be found on his shirttail. In "High Water Everywhere," Delta blues founder Charlie Patton was still reeling from a 1927 flood. And guess what? Every performer I've named so far came from below the Mason-Dixon. Uncle Dave Macon had been fathered by a Confederate officer in Tennessee in 1870, five years after the war ended. In 1930, the year Congress established the Federal Bureau of Narcotics, other southerners both black and white sang about coping with Depression (and depression) via illegal substances: "Prohibition has killed more folks than Sherman ever seen," since boozeless folks were turning to morphine and coke, warned solo Skillet Licker Clayton McMichen's delirium-tremens yodeler "Prohibition Blues"; in Memphis Jug Band's "Cocaine Habit Blues," Hattie Hart confirmed that she preferred white powder even over whiskey and gin.

Up north and beyond, things were maybe more sophisticated, even optimistic, if not so reliable about it. Think of sons of Russian Jewish immigrants Ben Selvin (leading his orchestra through future FDR campaign song "Happy Days Are Here Again") and Harry Richman (enraptured by snobs, swells, "lulubelles," and "high browns" parading through Harlem in top hats and spats in Irving Berlin's "Puttin' On the Ritz"). Ruth Etting complained of taxi-dancing for dimes with "bowlegged tailors" and "rats from the harbors" in "Ten Cents a Dance." But even that wasn't nearly as decadent as Lotte Lenya back in Berlin as the Weimar waned, hunting down the next whiskey bar and little boy in Brecht-Weill's newly penned "Alabama Song." In London's East End right about then, 78-year-old (born 1852!) music hall dinosaur Charles Coborn was slurring about striking it rich in "The Man Who Broke the Bank at Monte Carlo."

Lots of excellent songs by Johnsons that year: Mississippi Delta blues woman Louise Johnson's piano-pumped "All Night Long Blues," with her alleged boyfriends Charlie Patton and Son House raising hell in the background, barrelhousing like its title promises; Jersey stride-piano composer James P. Johnson's post-ragtime "You've Got to Be Modernistic"; Louisiana-to-Missouri jazz / blues guitarist and clear Bob Dylan vocal inspiration Lonnie Johnson's hilariously nihilistic "Got the Blues for Murder Only" (partly about people in Mexico eating rattlesnakes and drinking gunpowder!); Texas gospel/blues guitarist Blind Willie Johnson's ferociously gruff and menacing (and much-covered) biblical prophecy "John the Revelator," which must rank as one of the greatest songs ever about an author (John the Apostle).

Eleja Choir's proto-juju "Jubilee Anthem," performed by an African Methodist choir in Nigeria; Evstratios Kalogeridou's "Malevitziotikos Horos," a fiddle-dance jam from Crete; and King Nawahi's steel-guitared Hawaiian train rhythm blues "Honolulu Bound" all make perfect sense in the context of music coming out of Appalachia and America's Deep South at the time. But "Fatal Flower Garden" by Nelstone's Hawaiians is just some Alabama guys who've *learned* Hawaiian steel guitar, albeit performing (get this) an American adaptation of a tragic British traditional ballad about ritual child murder that dates back six centuries or so, and originally qualified as blood libel before the Jewish antagonist was changed to a gypsy lady.

Welcome to Old Weird America. Tom Darby's "Frankie Dean," the Carter Family's "John Hardy Was a Desperate Little Man," and Texas cowhand Edward L. Crain's "Bandit Cole Younger" meanwhile reported on more recent killings, bank robberies, and mishaps of a fugitive nature that begat legends on American soil. In New York, D.C.-born Duke Ellington and Georgia-born Fletcher Henderson may have been getting ready to ring in swing, but the South was still knee-deep in barn dances and hoedowns—old times. Not to mention hard times, obviously. But African American string band the Mississippi Sheiks were "Sitting on Top of the World" regardless, or at least their hit said so. And North Carolinans Hendley-Whitter-Small insisted "A Pretty Gal's Love" was all they needed, because "I'd rather be happy than rich." Wonder if they continued to feel that way, as the Great Depression dragged on.

—rhapsody.com, 26 February 2014

## Depression Music

· · · · ·

When *American Graffiti*, revolving around a 1962 radio station's "oldies weekend," hit theaters in 1973, the pop hits of the '50s—all newer then than the first Beastie Boys album is now—seemed ancient, as if dropped from some alternate universe. But over the past quarter-century, as songs of the 20th century's early decades have rematerialized first on vinyl reissues, and then on CD box sets, and have eventually become ubiquitous everywhere from movie soundtracks to Starbucks to MP3s available at split-second notice, the music has managed to lose its remoteness. Somehow, technology has the effect of compressing time. So maybe it shouldn't come as a shock that now, as we scarily slump our way into an economic downturn destined to put Carter/Reagan-era stagflation to shame, music that came out around the Great Depression is feeling curiously current. In 1998, the venerable reissue label Yazoo Records compiled 46 songs of bank failure, credit collapse, rent inflation, joblessness, and panhandling, on a two-volume set entitled *Hard Times Come Again No More*; five years later, the Sony/RCA imprint Bluebird Jazz gathered up 24 such performances on a disc called *Poor Man's Heaven*. When these collections were released, they didn't receive much media attention, maybe partly because their themes still seemed distant. But since then, history has flipped—and now, it's impossible to hear these old 78s without thinking about what you read in the business section this morning.

What's weirder still is that it's hard to think of any new music released in recent years that you can say that about. The best 2008 examples might be mere coincidences of title, like Young Jeezy's keep-on-grinding hip-hop cycle

*The Recession* and Jamey Johnson's druglife-recovery country dirge "The High Cost of Living"; "Spend Spend Spend," a miraculous and universally ignored '08 track by Brit metal matrons Girlschool, comes closer ("Getting hard to borrow, pay the bills tomorrow"), but it's technically about England. Shouldn't working-class hero Kid Rock have done something on Detroit's autopocalypse by now? Especially when *Poor Man's Heaven* opens with a monologue called "Eddie Cantor's Tips on the Stock Market" where the old Borscht Belter jokes about everybody getting a bad break but his uncle, who died in September: "Poor fellow had diabetes at 45. That's nothing, I had Chrysler at 110." Ba-dum bum.

The Cantor routine is actually one of two *Poor's Man Heaven* tracks that aren't songs; the other, a lilting church sermon from Atlanta Baptist preacher and sometime gospel vocalist Rev. J. M. Gates, is called "President Roosevelt Is Everybody's Friend"—but this year, when you hear Gates praise "*our* president," FDR might not be the one who comes to mind. The rest of the compilation starts at surprisingly swingy vaudeville and Tin Pan Alley, then moves through rawer fiddle hoedowns, jug-band hokum, calypso, and explicit agit-prop from folkies like Woody Guthrie. For the urbane stage-musical selections toward the beginning, the most successful formula pits upbeat rhythms against downbeat melodies and sets them to darkly comic words about lost prosperity; that's certainly what's going on in Leo Reisman's epochal rendition of "Brother Can You Spare a Dime?" and George Hall's similarly themed "Remember My Forgotten Man"—the latter recorded for *Gold Diggers of 1933* and seemingly referencing World War I vets demonstrating in D.C. in 1932. "Poor Man's Heaven" itself, credited to country duo Bud Billings and Carson Robison, goes so far as to fantasize violent revolution: "We'll own all the banks / And shoot all the cranks / And won't give a durn who we hurt." Later, a Texan named Joe Pullum does a high-pitched piano blues about how Roosevelt's Civil Works Administration helped him not need his woman anymore. The oldest song, and one of the most familiar, is hobo-turned-labor-organizer Harry "Mac" McClintock's work-spurning "Hallelujah, I'm a Bum," a revamped public-domain ditty published by the Wobblies in 1908 but revived as the title song of an Al Jolson movie in '33.

Unlike the frequently upper-class-slumming *Poor Man's Heaven*, the often deliriously raucous "early American rural songs of hard times and hardship" on Yazoo's *Hard Times Come Again No More* almost exclusively reside along an as-yet-undemarcated crossroads between impending blues and hillbilly music, occasionally reaching back to minstrel shows and Celtic ballads for inspiration. Certain specifics—boll weevils destroying crops, dust storms blowing Okies west, train-hopping tramps killed on the rails, tenant farmers bleeding sharecroppers dry—are necessarily tied to their time; Jules Allen's "Little Old Sod Shanty" and Edward L. Crain's wonderfully titled "Starving to Death on a Government Claim" are both basically cowboy songs about whether homesteading on the open prairie is worth the considerable trouble. But "Wreck of the Tennessee Gravy Train" by Uncle Dave Macon and Sam McGee directly addresses a catastrophic 1930 bank failure, hardly an esoteric situation in this season of bankruptcies and bailouts. And the songs' overriding preoccupations—middle classes losing their footing, loans and eventually meals getting tougher to come by—are as pertinent now as when the lyrics were written, or soon will be.

Several titles actually contain the phrase "Hard Times"; it's no wonder the late Studs Terkel gave that name to his indispensable 1970 oral history of the Depression. But here's something just as interesting: a half-century after the 1929 Wall Street crash, as an oil-shock recession dragged the '70s into the '80s and hip-hop was first mapping out its place in the world, Kurtis Blow did a "Hard Times" rap, then Run-D.M.C. kicked off their first album covering it. Country neo-traditionalist John Anderson opened his 1980 debut LP "Havin' Hard Times" as well. So where are the hard-times songs now?

—www.GOOD.is, 2 May 2009


## Country Rap Prehistory

. . . . .

If you really explore the prehistory of country rap, you will wind up wandering down some unsettling abandoned corridors, leading back to a time long before not only rap, but even country, existed—a time when the racism in American popular music was anything but accidental.

To get there, though, you'll need to start with the talking blues—a rhythmic, rhyming, humorously yarn-spinning talked vocal style you've heard if you've heard much early Bob Dylan, or Johnny Cash's 1969 "A Boy Named Sue," or C. W. McCall's pop-chart-topping 1975 CB radio novelty "Convoy." Talking blues were all over country, and frequently crossed over to pop, in the '60s and '70s: "Hot Rod Lincoln" for Johnny Bond in 1960 and Commander Cody in 1972; "Big Bad John" for Jimmy Dean in 1961; "Ringo" for *Bonanza* actor Lorne Greene in 1964; "My Uncle Used to Love Me but She Died"—as absurdist as anything by Beck—for Roger Miller in 1966. Ex-Dylan sideman Charlie Daniels made a career of them, though he never sounded rappier than in his first charting single, the uncharacteristically left-leaning "Uneasy Rider," which went Top 10 pop in 1973 then seemingly went on to inspire the cadence that southern soul artist turned X-rated proto-rapper (and "Convoy" parodist) Blowfly flew with in his 1980 single "Blowfly's Rapp."

Dylan may have nicked his own rap flow from mid-'40s Woody Guthrie or early '50s Arthur "Guitar Boogie" Smith, but talking blues officially date back to 1927, when mandolin-wielding South Carolina car mechanic Chris Bouchillon was recording in Atlanta, and an A&R director found his singing skills lacking, so he suggested Bouchillon just talk the words instead. Countless "Talking Blues" imitators ensued: usually white (Coley Jones and "Talking" Billy Anderson were rare black exceptions) and generally "not really blues at all, except in name," Nick Tosches argues in *Where Dead Voices Gather*, his 2001 book about the hugely influential second-quarter-of-20th-century blackface minstrel Emmett Miller (who I'll return to). One of the style's few blues-based practitioners, Tosches says, was one Herschel Brown, who followed his own 1928 "New Talking Blues" (which, like Bouchillon's, confusingly discussed not needing to work hard when one has "a gal in the white folks' yard") with two records that added a nasty N-word to the title. Which might not be surprising, given where talking blues came from: the form had "likely been around, in songster tradition and on the minstrel circuit, longer than could ever be known," Tosches writes. "Its age might be measured in centuries."

"The impulse to chant with a rhythmic background is probably as old as human culture," Don Kent's notes to the 1996 Yazoo Records compilation *The Roots of Rap: Classic Recordings from the 1920's and 30's* reiterate, citing church sermons and work songs as well as vaudeville and medicine shows as relevant in rap's evolution. But minstrel is key: frequently fast-talking country guitarist Jerry Reed's funkiest hit, "Uptown Poker Club" from 1974, was actually a revival of black Bahamas-born blackface superstar Bert Williams's atypically razor-toting 1914 "Darktown Poker Club"; Reed's Top 10 pop 1971 country rap "When You're Hot You're Hot" concludes with offensive muttered asides about welfare checks and Cadillacs, just a year after Guy Drake hit the Hot 100 with a disturbingly stereotyped talking blues *called* "Welfare Cadillac." Conversely, African American Memphis funk pioneer and Rabbit Foot Minstrels veteran Rufus Thomas's #49 pop 1964 rap progenitor "Jump Back" revived rhymes that date back to white blackface originator Thomas "Daddy" Rice's 1828

"Jump Jim Crow," the opening shot of the minstrel era. And in 1936, Emmett Miller dueted with Gene Cobb in "The Gypsy," and the way they trade off lines sounds as much like rap music, proper, as nearly anything waxed before 1979. Even decades after America had swept minstrel's burnt cork under the rug, aging hillbillies like Harmonica Frank and Cowboy Copas were making hay with talk-rhyme routines that, consciously or not, clearly channeled rhythms and most likely shticks from the Great Depression, if not the 19th century.

None of which is to suggest that country rap is inherently racist, just that navigating its origins is a daunting obstacle course. Black precedents are even more elusive, since most white ones were ostensibly mimicking black music in the first place, but maybe these qualify: ska toaster Prince Buster galloping into Dallas in 1964's "Texas Hold-Up"; Parliament yodeling and yelling through 1970's "Little Ole Country Boy"; jazz-funk bassist Bad Bascomb tossing square dance calls in 1972's "Black Grass"; Clarence "Gatemouth" Brown bluesifying Jerry Reed's raging-Cajun smash "Amos Moses" in 1975; Isaac Hayes and Solomon Burke introducing their respective covers of "By the Time I Get to Phoenix" and "I Can't Stop Loving You" with soul monologues—in fact, in years leading up to "Rapper's Delight," plenty of R&B artists (Shirley Brown, Millie Jackson, Swamp Dogg, Joe Tex, Bobby Womack) dabbled in both soul-rapping and country, if usually not simultaneously. And those are only the names we know. Back in the ancient unrecorded crevices of time, there are country rappers—black and white—we never will.

—spin.com, 30 April 2013

## Country Songs I

· · · · ·

### Charlie Poole and the North Carolina Ramblers: "White House Blues" (1926)

Country music just a few years into its record-making existence, already fixated on the distant past: a string trio led by the banjo—African instrument, barely used anymore by African Americans—chronicles the news of exactly a quarter-century before. Namely, a president's assassination in 1901 by a second-generation Prussian/Polish anarchist from Alpena, Michigan, and his replacement riding the train from Buffalo, where he took the oath of office, to Washington: "Roosevelt's in the White House, he's doing his best / McKinley's in the graveyard, he's taking his rest." Then, a threat from an ex–First Lady widow with a gun. Poole, in his middle 30s but just five years away from his own death, has what sounds to us like an old man's voice, but he sings and plays with a young man's energy—a hard liver, he'd mangled his banjo-playing hand in a drunken baseball accident. His music is "old-timey" in the sense of "that's the way we always done it around these parts," as David Wondrich put it (in his 2003 book *Stomp and Swerve: American Music Gets Hot 1843–1924*) about 1870-born banjo banger Uncle Dave Macon, who had started recording just two years before. Poole's sound could actually charge more furiously elsewhere, but "White House Blues" is the song that Tom T. Hall harked back to in 1973 on a non-LP B-side called "Watergate Blues"; the song John Mellencamp, pissed off about hanging-chad recounts in Florida, recast as "To Washington" in 2004.

### Emmett Miller and His Georgia Crackers:
### "Lovesick Blues" (1928)

A throwback blackface minstrel backed by jazz musicians—including Tommy Dorsey on trombone and Jimmy Dorsey on clarinet and alto sax—starts out with a comedy dialogue, offensively parodying dialect Uncle Remus–style: "Birds singin' in de trees and de sun am shinin', you shouldn't have no blues." "I know I shouldn't have 'em, but, but . . . I got it. Every *known* indication of bein' in *that* condition." "What's the matter, did they lock up your bootlegger?" Nope, Emmett explains, it's his girl—she "done caught air." Then, to some loud but teary-eyed brass chords, he starts singing, showing generations of later country singers how it's done, many of whom mimicked his over-the-top phrasing outright: Jimmie Rodgers; Hank Williams, who theoretically made this song his own in 1940; Bob Wills; Jerry Lee Lewis, who covered it in 1958; Merle Haggard, who paid tribute to Miller on 1973's *I Love Dixie Blues*. The secret is in the impossibly crazed and stretched-out—often "yodeled," but not the way sheepherders in the Alps yodeled—hangdog high notes, probably not what the Russian-born Jewish American Irving Mills had in mind when he'd copyrighted the words back in 1922: "I'm in love, ah—HIIIIME—in love," "I got a feeling for the blue—WHOOO—*ooz*," "She calls me sweet DA-AA-AA-DEE." Other notes get lowdown—the "refuse" in "I TRIED and I TRIED but she just *refuse*," an "*Oh Lawd*" that all but altered the earth's axis. And this wasn't even Miller's most audacious vocal: check out the insane, almost klezmer-like

Allen Brothers: *The Chattanooga Boys* (Old Timey, 1973)

prohibition speakeasy tongues of "Anytime," recorded two months later. Or maybe 1936's "The Gypsy"—a full-fledged rap record, 43 years before "Rapper's Delight."

### Allen Brothers:
### "Maybe Next Week Sometime" (1929)

Two Chattanooga siblings—Lee on guitar, Austin on banjo, both on vocals—spin wobbly yarns around the pickle barrel, sounding simultaneously lazy, melancholy, comical, maybe even drunk (though not nearly as drunk as they sounded in 1934's "Drunk and Nutty Blues," which largely consisted of them laughing and crying hysterically). Also, at least to other white folks of the time, they sounded black—so much so that they once sued their record label for releasing one of their singles as part of its "race" series. Here, though, they might well have assisted that perception, and not just by echoing jug bands: "Y'know, I was goin' down the street with lowdown blues. Shineboy said look heah nigga, let me shine up them shoes." That ugly word returns later, too, tossed off in a disturbingly casual way; country music hasn't learned yet to even try to hide its roots in 19th-century minstrel shows. Anyway, the Allens decline the shoeshine offer for today, leaving the following week's engagement calendar open—same thing they do later in the song to the looney Birmingham gal who pulls down the shades, the ghost chasing them who suggests they stop to rest, the buddy they're throwing a "spree" with who requests another drink, and the horny gal in the parlor who turns down the lights: "Ya husband might come home, I'm scared." Strings provide rhythmic accompaniment for the recitation throughout; between some verses, Lee's high flatulent kazoo serves the yodel role.

### Roy Newman and His Boys:
### "Sadie Green (Vamp of New Orleans)" (1935)

When Texans first started western swinging, they were really more western Dixielanding, truth be told. (In 1935, swing had only just begun.) And this Dallas ensemble, numbering up to 10 members revolving around trumpet / guitars / fiddle / standup bass / drums, was certainly on the pre-swing end of the spectrum. Their most high-profile vinyl reissue is on a record label called Original Jazz, and the rhythm here—starting with a generous instrumental lead-in—could almost pass as a smoking Charleston. The words concern a popular young woman named Sadie, who's "got more beaus than the Navy's got Marines," and "big brown eyes and teeth [!?] to match," and (look out) "when she starts to love, oh gosh / All over my Mackintosh." Or maybe (as some clearer enunciators than Roy Newman have covered it) *Mama burn my Mackintosh,*" but still—how did these guys know about Apple computer sex way back in the '30s? Unless Roy's Mackintosh was a British raincoat, and Sadie peep-show entertainment. Either way, what's certain is that a group called the Five Harmaniacs had recorded the same title way back in 1926, and the all-black Memphis Jug Band had done the related "Everybody's Talking about Sadie Green" in 1930: "Everything about her is tight like that," "wears her dresses above her knees, lets folks say what they please," "uses powder, uses paint, it makes her look like what she ain't," "lets you ride her . . . in her car." Must have been quite some lady.

### Milton Brown and His Brownies:
### "Texas Hambone Blues" (1936)

An ex–cigar salesman from Fort Worth lets his western swing band stomp and swerve: the fiddler, pianist, and guitar player all take hot solos; the latter, Bob Dunn, was electric and amplified before anybody else in his vocation. Who knew an instrument from Hawaii could change the world? Meanwhile, Milton Brown gets dirty. "I'm goin' down to Cowtown, to get my hambone boiled / 'Cause the New York women done made my hambone spoiled." (You've heard of Cowtown, right? Big balls there, western swingsters always claimed. AC/DC would understand.) He's got groupies in Houston and San Antone, too (hoes in many area codes!), and a "Dallas gal make a good man leave his home," not to mention—you figure it out—"a black-headed gal make a tadpole hug a whale." At the time, this team was not only better, but also more popular, than the one led by Brown's former fiddle bandmate Bob Wills. But their reign would end later that year, when Brown was killed in a car crash at 32—possibly asleep at the wheel, legend has it, and with a teenage girl in the passenger seat.

### Smokey Wood and the Modern Mountaineers:
### "Everybody's Truckin'" (1937)

The Modern Mountaineers were, just maybe, America's first adolescent punk band. No better way to put it: 17- and 18-year-old white boys, big Fats Waller and Count Basie fans, and at least as big marijuana fans—or at least Arkansas-born / Oklahoma-raised pianist Smokey Wood was; according to liner notes of the 1982 reissue *The Houston Hipster: Western Swing 1937*, he used to raise 20-plus stalks between signboards near Houston's Main Street. Also, they *played* like adolescent punks: sax and clarinet fart-honking fully down into the dirt, Smokey and southpaw guitarist Lefty Grove yelling choruses way too loud when the boogie-woogie piano kicks in. Sensitive souls averse to racist horse-shit might want to cover their ears now: "Down in Harlem on the street! You can hear them dancin' feet! See them darkies everywhere they go! You can hear 'em singin' hidey-hidey-ho!" So yeah, they apparently knew their Cab Callo-way too; he'd put out "Minnie the Moocher" in 1931, and another, maybe even higher-temperature, Modern Mountaineers track, "Keep On Truckin'," is an homage to gongs being kicked around. And, oh wait, left out the most punk-rock part: Everybody's not just "singin' and truckin'." They're also "swingin' and fuckin'." Repeatedly.

### Moon Mullican:
### "Pipeline Blues" (1940)

Sort of the white rural equivalent of Louis Jordan–era jump blues, hillbilly boogie was the missing link between western swing and rockabilly. Histori-

Moon Mullican: *Sings His All-Time Hits* (King, 1958)

ans usually peg 1940 as the year it started, thanks to a record called "Boogie Woogie" by Johnny Barfield, but Moon Mullican was boogie's main hillbilly, and 1940 was also the year he initially laid down "Pipeline Blues." He'd record the song again and again well into the '50s—eventually shaking it up more and more, like Jerry Lee Lewis, who his ivory pounding laid the groundwork for, but also eventually watering down its lyrics. For instance, early on, he'd sing, "I'm an old pipeliner, and I lay my pipe all day / I got four, five women waitin' to draw my pay," which sounds a whole lot raunchier than his later "four, five young'uns." Also, "the meanest gal in town" reforms, in later years, to "the sweetest gal in town." Didn't really work, though—by the '50s, he looked too old for rock'n'roll's new teenyboppers to care, and to this day, YouTube commenters know what his manual labor was really about: "It's true: wine dine pipeline," observes one. Dude was pimpin', either way. (Also worth hearing: the 1983 cover by usually chaste family bluegrass/gospel group the Whites, sung atypically by patriarch Buck: "Every time I see you, you're always on the street / You hang around the corner just like a policeman on the beat." But Buck still swears he'd walk 130 miles—"Dallas clear into Wichita Falls, Texas"—to see her.)

## Bob Wills and His Texas Playboys:
## "I'm a Ding Dong Daddy" (1946)

The Texas Playboys were the Beatles of western swing, and Bob Wills was the Bob Marley maybe, in the sense of towering—in terms of sheer historical visibility—over his musical genre. Thing is, compared to lots of western swingsters, if not necessarily compared to nostalgists from Asleep at the Wheel to George Strait to Hot Club of Cowtown who've attempted to revive the sound since, there was something too doggone *polite* about the Playboys. In his 2003 book *Southwest Shuffle: Pioneers of Honky-Tonk, Western Swing, and Country Jazz*, Rich Kienzle even dismisses them as "a mediocre band led by an ex-Light Crust Doughboy." Maybe it's just the price of superstardom—when you're the record company's meal ticket, you might have to rein your sound in now and then, if not always. But these guys had a smart way to circumvent that. Wills had been making records for well over a decade when, in 1946 and 1947—fortunately, right around the time Lester Barnard started letting his electric guitar distort—the band recorded 370 "Tiffany Transcription" tracks onto noncommercial 16-inch discs for play on a syndicated radio show. These recordings let them get loose in ways that Vocalion/OKeh, MGM, Columbia, and the like wouldn't. Rhino Records finally issued several collections of them in the '80s; volume 3, called *Basin Street Blues*, focused on the Playboys' "swing, blues, and jazz side," and is probably the best for it. My pick-hit from that disc, "I'm a Ding Dong Daddy," done 16 years after Louis Armstrong did it, bounces all over the dancefloor, with new recruit Roy Honeycut ("that's that boy, his name is Roy") taking a sweet steel guitar solo, and Tommy Duncan sounding both slurred and assured on top, boasting about being a "wild Poppa from polecat holler, I don't wanna get rough," threatening to shoot some little dame down with his Thompson gun nonetheless, and granting y'all permission to shake it and break it and hang it on the wall—just like Delta blues founder Charley Patton had done in *his* catchiest song, from 1929.


## Delmore Brothers:
## "Freight Train Boogie" (1946)

Respectable tenant farmers' sons from Alabama, their close family harmonies once reverently rooted in gospel and Appalachian folk music, learn to rock'n'roll—a decade too early, but don't hold that against them. By 1946, the Delmores had accrued a full band: bass, mandolin, steel guitar, fiddle, guitars. Electric guitar and drums wouldn't be added until a year later, apparently, but they already had the beat down. And that beat sounded like valve gears, high whistles, smokestack lightning: on the 1975 vinyl Gusto set *Best of the Delmore Brothers*, emphasizing their boogie period, three songs out of 10 are train songs—"Pan American Boogie," "Tennessee Choo Choo," and this one, which is the most propulsive, jazzy breakdown and blues harmonica tooting from Wayne Raney on down.

### Arthur "Guitar Boogie" Smith:
### "Who Shot Willie" (1951)

Eight years before George Jones's wild rockabilly side "Who Shot Sam," a comparably cooking wise-ass murder mystery that's no mystery at all: pretty Maxine's groom gets shot on their wedding day, and Smith knows the culprit but he's pleading the Fifth: "Who could it be? I ain't gonna tell 'cause they'd hang me." "I'm a country boy," he admits, "but I know this much—to keep my eyes wide open and my big mouth shut." Smith came up playing Dixieland jazz and got his nickname from an early hit; he also allegedly (1) composed "Dueling Banjos"; (2) hosted the first nationally syndicated country music radio show; and (3) ran the North Carolina recording studio where James Brown recorded "Papa's Got a Brand New Bag." And judging from his vocal cadences and sense of humor in early '50s ditties like "Just Lookin'" and "Don't Look for Trouble," he probably taught Bob Dylan a thing or two, too.

### Harmonica Frank Floyd:
### "Rockin' Chair Daddy" (1954)

Born in Mississippi in 1908 and showing off his two-harmonicas-at-a-time (one with his nose!) and singing-while-playing-harmonica-out-the-corner-of-mouth tricks in carnivals and medicine shows for decades thereafter (only competition, maybe: Peg Leg Sam Jackson, who seems to have kept alive a similar vaudeville-minstrel shtick), traveling hobo Harmonica Frank Floyd didn't record until well into his 40s. But once he did, holy shit: there was "Swamp Root," a slobber-scatted talking blues where you'd best get out of saliva range every time a word starts with *b* or *p* (most dangerous, appropriately: "PPPimm-PPPle"); there was "The Great Medical Menagerist," an American historical tent-show tall tale about concoctions that grow hair on doorknobs, among other miracles; decades later there was "Shampoo," dang near obscene enough to make Blowfly blush. And there was the slavering, deranged, distorted, and frequently incomprehensible proto-rockabilly single "Rockin' Chair Daddy," which feels downright primitive, and just as mean—the most outrageously nasal white-man falsettos and asides since Emmett Miller ("awwww shucks—BOOT it now!"), subversive boasts about being an unschooled fool, lines half-recalled from old Jimmie Rodgers records ("Told her my name was on the tail of my shirt / Rockin' chair daddy don't *have* to work"), all amid noise that's an uncanny forecast of Captain Beefheart. If that ain't country, he'll kiss your bbbig bbbullfrog.

*—Complex*, 5 June 2012

## Niela Miller: *Songs of Leaving*

· · · · ·

Got sent this vinyl LP two days ago called *Songs of Leaving* on a Chicago label called Numerophon by this girl folk singer named Niela Miller, recorded in 1962 in NYC—or, really, by 2009 (even 1981, if not 1962) standards more like a vinyl EP, since it seems to clock in around 20 minutes for about 10 songs. The thing is on 150-gram vinyl, really thick and heavy; label looks like it would have been plastered on some old 78. Record cover cardboard is also super-thick, made to look like some Folkways album from the '50s. Clever (and actually quite beautiful) marketing concept, I gotta admit—maybe even smart, on an extremely small scale, since the idea I guess is to make physical product collectible in the age of MP3s. (Apparently this album is the first of a series on the label. Though I have no idea what it would cost to *put out* a record that looks like this one in 2009, with vinyl pressing plants supposedly shutting down and all. Also, though the thing looks real classy on one hand, it's also obviously kind of ridiculous, which may or may not be part of the point.)

Thing is, there's also music on the thing, and it's just . . . okay. Niela sings her (apparently mostly if not all original) blues-folk in a tone that strikes me as really proper and cautious, maybe a precursor of Joan Baez–type singing (maybe proto–Janis Ian too?)—basically, it's how you'd expect those ironed-haired private-girls-school rich chicks in *Animal House* (also set in 1962) to sing. Played it back-to-back this morning with a couple of New Christy Minstrels LPs from around the same period, and Miller sounded completely strained and constrained and unenergetic and humorless in comparison (and

Niela Miller: *Songs of Leaving* (Numerophon, 2009)

the New Christy Minstrels didn't seem as good as the Kingston Trio or Lime-liters, all of whom I'm guessing Miller's milieu would have dismissed as pho-nies and sellouts).

Still, I like the record okay—especially "Goodbye New York," which has a tune and some bite to it plus a lyric I identify with right now, as my apartment fills up with boxes packed for my move. And (apparently the main justifica-tion for the reissue), there's also this song called "Baby Don't Go to Town" which the (Folkways-like) liner notes peg as a prototype of "Hey Joe"—or, at least the song that was allegedly combined with Carl Smith's 1953 country hit "Hey Joe" to get the song that Hendrix and the Byrds and Leaves and Deep Purple and Cher later did. (Aside: Back at University of Missouri in the early '80s, I knew a guy—otherwise a major fan of the Jam—who collected on cas-sette tapes all the versions of "Hey Joe" he could get ahold of.) Supposedly Niela Miller's "unstable boyfriend" Billy Roberts stole her version and had it copyrighted, and the rest is history. I'm skeptical about all of this, but it's a good story, either way. And there is a certain proto-garage-punk (post-blues) punch to the guitars in Miller's song. Or at least I imagine there is, so I can keep her cool-looking record.

Then again, probably the proto-garage part of how "Baby Don't Go to Town" sounds is just its guitar *progression*. And the liner notes zero in on

Amaj (not that I'd know). And Niela might be as proto-"freak-folk" (or proto-the tuneless kind of '60s folkies that freak-folkers gravitate toward now) as proto-Baez. And by "Miller's milieu," I guess I basically mean Dylan's—she supposedly attended his West Village debut. But her backstory doesn't make her sound "authentic" at all: learned about folk music at summer camp in the Catskills while on vacation from the High School of Music and Art in '48, became the promoter of folk music at "liberal Antioch College" in '52, dated a "black, Jewish and Communist folk singer," wrote "Too Long Blues" after an early boyfriend snubbed her for another gal at a Weavers gig in '53. I swear, the whole plot reads like a parody to me. I half expect the Beastie Boys to come out and start rapping about beatnik chicks just wearing their smocks.

But though I never thought of the folk revival this way before, it also all means that she was learning about the blues around the same time that all the (white) early rock'n'rollers were. Which is kind of cool, even if she wasn't nearly as good at it (and even if ignoring rock'n'roll then makes her a total geek). Also makes me wonder how much audience crossover there was between early '60s rock'n'roll and early '60s folk—there must have been frat bros who bought both Beach Boys and Kingston Trio LPs at least, right? Both groups even kinda dressed alike!

—I Love Music, 8 February 2009


## '60s Catholic Folk Mass

. . . . .

To Catholics and lapsed Catholics of a certain age, it might seem like a dream: for a few years starting in the mid-'60s, maybe while a formal high mass was being celebrated upstairs, church basements filled with fabric fish cutouts and folding chairs provided a habitat for clean-cut college beatniks—and even pretty young nuns wearing casual clothes!—to strum songs like the Youngbloods' "Get Together" on acoustic guitars, perhaps with bongo accompaniment. Overnight, a solemn medieval ritual, unchanged for centuries, made way for a hootenanny.

Ken Canedo, in his slim 2009 history *Keep the Fire Burning*, analyzes the "folk mass" as the upshot of a few concurrent events: Pope Paul VI's late 1963 Second Vatican Council encouragement of vernacular non-Latin liturgical language; young Catholics' growing focus on social justice in the wake of JFK's assassination; those same young people's growing Kingston Trio and Joan Baez collections; and the predicament that, when English-language Catholic hymns were suddenly allowed, not many existed. Which led to the use of certain secular pop hits, and old spirituals like "Kumbaya" and "Michael Row the Boat Ashore" resurrected during the '50s folk revival, but more importantly led to a cottage industry of original songs—an industry directly anticipating the largely Protestant genre of Contemporary Christian Music.

In fact, Ray Repp—whose 1966 *Mass for Young Americans*, generally considered the first folk mass recording, predated the '70s Jesus Movement by half a decade—is proclaimed "the earliest of all [CCM] pioneers" in Mark Allan Powell's encyclopedia of the genre (which Canedo quotes). Paul Quinlan, the Dameans, Joe Wise, John Fischer were prolific composers in their own right, and familiar songs from the Byrds' "Turn! Turn! Turn!" to "Day by Day" from *Godspell* snuck into church through the early '70s, when bishops reined the rebels in.

—rhapsody.com, 13 August 2013

## Country Songs II

. . . . .

### Cowboy Copas:
### "Alabam" (1960)

A living fossil in the age of rock'n'roll, Cowboy Copas had a career that dated back to '20s string bands, then had a Top 5 country hit in 1946. "Alabam," which topped the country chart and got to #63 pop in *Billboard* when he was 47, partook in a rhythm unmistakably echoing those bygone eras. And it wasn't even the last of its kind—Guy Drake (1970's race-baiting "Welfare Cadillac"), Jerry Reed, obese *Hee Haw* sideshow Junior Samples, and "Convoy" trucker-rapper C. W. McCall all made music at times harking back, somehow, to the white talking country blues of the Great Depression, long after most anybody remembered what was being harked back to. "Alabam" itself consists primarily of warmly recited couplets that, for all we know, could've survived on stages or in barn dances since Reconstruction days—about people down the street eating like wild geese, tramps in the cornfield, Sal with worn-down shoes tied onto her feet. Who knows anymore whether it was heard as a novelty,

Dick Curless: *Tombstone Every Mile* (Capitol, 1972)

or whether its sound had simply retained backwoods currency over the decades? Not Cowboy Copas, that's for sure—he died three years later, in the same plane that killed Patsy Cline.

### Dick Curless:
### "Tombstone Every Mile" (1965)

From a strong silent type who looks as robust as the men he sings about, brass-knuckled and burly-baritoned Country & Northern about truckers navigating an ice-ribbon stretch of highway in Maine ("Route 2A between Houlton and Macwahoc," say John Morthland's liner notes to 1998's *The Drag 'Em off the Interstate Sock It to 'Em Hits of Dick Curless*)—about as masculine as music ever gets, with momentum like an 18-wheeler sliding down the mountainside. Curless, born on Maine's Canadian border himself in 1932, has an eyepatch over his right eye, and sounds like it. "You've got it made if you're hauling goods any place on earth but those Hainesville Woods"—so the mile-spaced gravestones come from imagining how the landscape would look if all the truckers lost there had been buried there. A #5 country hit, framed in sub-Arctic wind sounds that feel like specters.

## Hank Thompson:
## "Smoky the Bar" (1968)

Whiskey-smooth, corny-punned, buy-another-round two-step relaxation honky-tonk about, well, a smoky bar, from an amiable Texan who mined several decades worth of country hits (from a #2 in 1948 to a #32 in 1980) out of balancing the good times and bad times in drinking establishments after dark, and who managed to keep western swing and hillbilly boogie halfway viable years after their sell-by date to boot. On the *Smoky the Bar* album, for instance, "Let's Get Drunk and Be Somebody" beats Toby Keith to that title by several decades, and has a nifty alliterative part about "a gushing goblet goads my ghostly gloom"; "Drunkard's Blues" updates "St. James Infirmary Blues" and sounds like a goth jazz dirge; "I See Them Everywhere" jokes about seeing pink elephants and other creatures crawling up walls; "Girl in the Night" considers a sad beauty who soaks in the nightlife every night to kill some past pain the singer hasn't quite figured out (popular glam rock theme too); "New Records on the Jukebox" hopes somebody will play them because all the old ones choke Hank up too much. Most of the songs are tragic, but hardly any are slow, and most have a beat. Also, Hank's voice sounds surprisingly gentle, somehow, even when he's rowdy—a trick Toby Keith managed to pull off decades later, but not many others have. Thompson's 1966 *Six Pack to Go* LP with the Brazos Valley Boys ("a program of their biggest beer-drinkin' hits!") actually had *two* songs with "hangover" in the title—how often does that happen? *Smoky the Bar* notes cite "the gentleman scholars of Heidelberg [lifting] their steins," and calls him "the Poet Laureate of beer drinkers." So . . . thirsty yet?

## O. C. Smith:
## "The Son of Hickory Holler's Tramp" (1968)

More R&B and less C&W than O. B. McClinton, more C&W and less R&B than O. V. Wright, Louisiana-born O. C. Smith is one of scores of black singers to make country music in the past half-century—if that sounds like a contradiction to you, please hunt down Warner Bros.' 1998 *From Where I Stand: The Black Experience in Country Music* box set or Trikont Germany's *Dirty Laundry: The Soul of Black Country* compilations from a few years later, and school thyself. Anyway, Smith's biggest hit was 1968's "Little Green Apples," which went #2 pop and nowhere on the country chart, then somehow won the 1969

Best Country Song Grammy regardless—maybe because it was also covered by Roger Miller, and Glen Campbell dueting with Bobbie Gentry, but it's hard not to suspect segregation at work. It's a lovely tribute to middle-class marital bliss either way, weirded only a little by Smith's anachronistically minstrel-like delivery of one line ("when myself is feelin' low"). Smith did chart a country single earlier in 1968, though—at least if the Canadian country chart, where "The Son of Hickory Holler's Tramp" got to #4, counts. Now, this is dark stuff: Smith recalls growing up with 13 siblings in a destitute cabin; his drunk dad goes deadbeat, so Mom does what she must to keep them fed. Every night, after they're in bed, she turns on the red light.

### John Wesley Ryles:
### "Kay" (1968)

A Nashville cab driver—or at least a Nashville-via-Texas-via-Louisiana singer-songwriter who plays one—spends a night cruising the streets. He misses the lady singer whose New York success he bankrolled, gives a local teen beauty queen a lift to the hospital so she can have her baby, listens to two Fort Campbell soldiers tell him how bad Vietnam's going, hears junkyard dogs and police sirens then learns somebody got stabbed out there. At 3 A.M., a clock strikes, and all the night people look so sad. He doesn't sound rural at all, and neither do his "latest sounds from Music City, U.S.A.," as he puts it: guitar, horns, piano, violins-not-fiddles. But the song went Top 10 country anyway, then charted again a decade later. In 1968, John Wesley Ryles was 18 years old, and though he charted country with 30 songs in the next two decades—hitting the Top 20 as late as 1987—this one was tough to top.

### Tom T. Hall:
### "Homecoming" (1969)

A songwriter with as journalistic an eye and pen as any in the past half-century, Tom T. Hall earned blurbs from Jimmy Carter, Kurt Vonnegut, and bearded academics on the back of his definitive 1988 double-best-of *The Essential Tom T. Hall*. Give or take Creedence Clearwater Revival's 1969 "Lodi"—or Hall's own "Last Hard Town," from five years later—it's hard to think of a more matter-of-fact, less romanticized depiction of a being a journeyman musician than this one-sided, talk-sung conversation from a not-entirely-reliable nar-

Tom T. Hall: *Homecoming* (Mercury, 1970)

rator's compartmentalized life. Basically, a guilt-ridden fellow shows up at his cattleman dad's house after missing Mom's funeral, and as far as we can tell he never gets past the foyer. Almost every line, we learn a new detail, and it just snowballs—he's only fulfilling a routine family obligation, and it's up to us whether his awkward excuses (never even knew Dad had a phone!) makes him a selfish narcissist or just a busy guy. Dad heard one of his songs on the radio—not exactly a hit, but the next one will be. He picked up a cheap and shiny ring in Mexico because "in the business that I'm in, the people call it putting up a front." The road hasn't helped his health—he's lost weight, looks pale like he just left prison—but don't worry, he does his work in "nightclubs," not "beer joints," and you can't get hurt there. Then there's that lady guitarist sleeping in the car, catching a nap after driving from Nashville to San Antone, since she needs to be alert en route to Cartersville tonight. (Women's lib!) And so on—mundane small talk across worlds and generations, and Dad's probably heard most of it before anyway, and real soon it's time to hit the lonely road out of town again: "By the way, if you see Barbara Walker, tell her I said hello."

## Anne Murray:
## "Snowbird" (1970)

Lush, bittersweet, impossibly beautiful music about lost youth and birds mi-
grating south for winter, from a Nova Scotia gym teacher paving the way,
in a way, for fellow Canadian divas Shania Twain and k. d. lang. Basically,
the music *sounds* like birds riding brisk air; Gene MacLellan, who wrote it
and later, in 1995, committed suicide, came from the Maritimes himself. The
beat is a sort of light oompah, the roots of Abba; Murray's vocal influences
were Rosemary Clooney and Brenda Lee, and on the debut U.S. LP this came
from—actually a compilation of her first two Canadian albums—she also
covered James Taylor, the Beatles, Bob Dylan, Canadian Christian liberation
theologian folk singer Bruce Cockburn, and the hippie folk-mass standbys
"Get Together" and "Put Your Hand in the Hand." What all that has to do with
country music is anybody's guess, but who cares? This was a Top 10 country
hit regardless, and Murray wound up scoring in the format well into the '90s,
topping the chart 10 times.

## Barbara Mandrell:
## "The Midnight Oil" (1973)

No two ways around it: this song—a #7 country hit at the time—is filthy.
Barbara is called back into the office late at night to give the boss "a helping
hand," and tomorrow she'll feel "kinda dirty 'cause I'll have that midnight oil
all over me"—yowza! Is her shower broke? And if Peter Garrett knew what
the midnight oil was, would he have named his band that? Regardless, there's
something refreshing about a female singer falling back on the gotta-work-
late-honey lie (see Isley Brothers, "Work to Do"). This is from early in Man-
drell's career, when she was just 24—four years or so before she really took
over the charts, seven before NBC gave her a variety show. Her music wasn't
quite as R&B-infused as it'd be later, though her 1977 Columbia *Best Of* already
had her interpreting songs by Aretha Franklin, Joe Tex, and Texas boogieman Roy Head. Listening now, you can tell why hip people thought of her
covers as squaresville whitewashes; she definitely Pat Boones some of them.
But she could be great, too, and she sure did love those cheating songs: side
one starts with a great doomed end-of-the-affair one called "Scarlet Water,"
where they're gonna "sip the scarlet water one more time." Which water may
well be midnight oil, too.

## Statler Brothers:
## "Whatever Happened to Randolph Scott" (1974)

Every year except one between 1972 and 1980, the Statler Brothers were named the CMA Vocal Group of the Year—not bad for a crew named after a brand of tissues you blow your nose with. They'd come up during the '60s folk revival, but to my ears, their harmonies frequently shook out somewhere between gospel jubilee and barbershop, maybe with occasional hints of doo-wop. They *switched* voices line-by-line/pitch-to-pitch a lot, like doo-woppers (and, later, old-school rappers) did; the bassman voice often hits me as ridiculous, which is either intentional or a generational thing. What's definitely a generational thing is that four out of 11 songs on their 1975 Mercury *Best Of* are list songs, all wondering or bemoaning lost days of yore—early baby-boom/postwar/ mostly-early-'50s pop-culture fads in "Do You Remember These" (not unlike Robert Klein's 1973 comedy LP *Child of the '50s*, especially since there's nothing particularly *rural* about the Statlers' memories); classmates who went on to do all sorts of things (including one who kills himself and one who winds up institutionalized—see also the 1976 book *What Really Happened to the Class of '65?*) in "The Class of '57"; a couple's old photo-album pictures (hence a precursor to Jamey Johnson's 2008 country hit "In Color") in "Pictures." Most interesting, to me, is the lost-Hollywood lament "Whatever Happened to Randolph Scott," not so much for its appropriately nostalgia-kitschy calliope/ukulele-ish arrangement or even its low-register-verse/high-register-chorus schematic as for the fact that I was apparently born too late to recognize almost any of its references beyond, say, Tex Ritter and Gene Autry. But Googling establishes that Johnny Mac Brown, Lash Larue, Smiley Burnette, Allan "Rocky" Lane (who later did Mr. Ed's horse voice!), and Randolph Scott himself were pretty much all mid-20th-century screen cowboys. The Statlers don't stop there, though—they want to be actual film critics, and they are funny about it! They joke about the ratings code, refer like the insiders they are to "the industry," say you've got to take your analyst along to the movies nowadays. Presumably, they didn't much appreciate M*A*S*H or *Midnight Cowboy* or *Five Easy Pieces*: "Everybody's trying to make a comment about our doubts and fears / *True Grit*'s the only movie that I've understood in years." To put this in context: 1974, when this went #22 country, was two years after the Kinks did "Celluloid Heroes," one year after Elton John's "Roy Rogers" and *American Graffiti*, the same year *Happy Days* went on the air, and six years before Ronald Reagan was elected president. Clearly, something was in the air.

## Loretta Lynn:
## "The Pill" (1975)

Link to a clip of this song on Facebook in these war-on-women days of theocrats blocking Planned Parenthood funds, and everybody knows what you're talking about—it's been decades since "The Pill" sounded so *current*. When it came out, it was at least somewhat controversial—sat on the shelf for more than two years after being recorded in late 1972. And enough radio stations laid off that it charted lower than Lynn's previous seven singles—including 1971's epochal "One's on the Way," which its lyrics reference. But "The Pill" still got to #4 when, 37 years of supposed female advancement and empowerment later, it's hard to imagine country radio touching the song. The birth-control pill itself had been approved by the FDA way back in the early '60s and made *Time*'s cover in 1967; among other accomplishments, it led to wider employment for women. But in the song, Loretta's main concerns are tossing out her maternity dress and enjoying sex more without risking a bigger brood—even if Hubbie apparently used to tomcat on the side when she was pregnant. A couple times, she audibly laughs in his face.

## Narvel Felts:
## "I Remember You" (1975)

Narvel Felts, blessed with one of the widest vocal ranges of any country singer ever recorded, is said to have been discovered trying on "Blue Suede Shoes" at his high school talent show in Missouri in 1956; his first chart hit, in 1960, was a Drifters cover. After that, he got no chart action again until well into the '70s, when he was in his mid-30s. Guess you could classify him in the pop-operatically flamboyant fancy-pants falsetto tradition of guys like Roy Orbison, Freddie Fender, and Gene Pitney. Maybe some mimicked Mexican mannerisms, too; and probably also some influence of Charlie Rich—whose singing could also work in flouncy Latinate filigree stuff. Plus, soul music: he hit with Jackie Wilson and Dobie Gray covers. Felts's self-titled album from 1975 had a few hits (I'll take its "Funny How Time Slips Away" over Willie Nelson's), but the most over-the-leftfield-wall vocals on it are in a deep cut called "I Remember You," where his singing shifts smoothly from low-and-manly to almost ridiculously glam-twee: "I remember you-HOO!" Seriously, the high parts could be Russell Mael in Sparks. Can't think of any other country that does that. So: maybe it's a Lou Christie or Frankie Valli thing? If you don't hate it, you'll love it.

## Stoney Edwards:
## "Blackbird (Hold Your Head High)" (1975)

A part–African American, part–Native American, part-Irish hard country honky-tonk singer at a time of soft countrypolitan crossover, Stoney Edwards was an anomaly in more ways than one—according to most sources he was born on Christmas Eve 1929, two months after Wall Street crashed, which puts him in his 40s by the time he made his first records in the early '70s. He might not have even made any at all, if a carbon monoxide–induced coma he'd incurred as a forklift operator hadn't forced him to switch careers. "Blackbird (Hold Your Head High)," a song of fatherly advice about how to turn tables with a positive attitude, was probably his best song and almost definitely his most controversial, for these lines: "Me and you and cousin Jesse gonna ride the train / Just a couple of country niggas, stealin' the rodeo, from Georgia on up to Bangor, Maine." A caveat: Those words were written by a white man, Chip Taylor, of "Wild Thing" and "Angel of the Morning" fame. But Edwards—"arguably the only modern black country artist whose blackness did come through in his music," according to John Morthland's liner notes to the 1998 best-of *Poor Folks Stick Together*—rasps them with untold sadness, then goes on to relate Dad's words about seeing the good in people and not letting the scarecrows stare you down, even if you were born black and hungry on a little Carolina tobacco farm. It got to #41 on the country chart, but he never ascended that high again.

## Stella Parton:
## "Standard Lie Number One" (1977)

Dolly Parton's younger sister Stella was to Dolly as Tommy Cash (big hit: 1969's "Six White Horses," about political assassinations of the '60s) was to Johnny—which is to say, not an icon genius god for the ages worthy of Mount Rushmore, not even close, but in country music of all places perhaps being a regular old human being should count for something sometimes. Stella, who sings like Dolly but less cute, charted country 14 times between 1975 and 1983, but had only four Top 20s (including this one) and one Top 10. Whatever, this is an excellent string-soaked countrypolitan cheated-on single, a species that's either extinct or endangered now, but appears to have been fairly prevalent at the time: Bill Anderson's similarly themed "Liars One, Cheaters Zero," for instance, had just gone Top 10 a few months earlier. But that one was scorekeeping and this one is a countdown (important difference!), and this one is hookier—even if Stella never seems to reveal what standard lies numbers five, six, seven, or nine are.

### The Kendalls:
### "Pittsburgh Stealers" (1978)

On the one-of-a-kind 20-track 1981 Warner Special Products country cheating song compilation *Motels and Memories*, the Kendalls are the only artists to appear twice, a distinguishing trait made even more astounding by the fact that they're a father and daughter singing to each other—both born in St. Louis, respectively in 1935 and 1954. That should probably weird you out, though when I next explain that they sound like George Jones and Dolly Parton with roots in southern gospel, you might get interested anyway. Fairly traditional sounding for the urban cowboy era, actually—not exactly what you'd expect for a duo who first scored with covers of pop hits by Peter Paul & Mary, the Grass Roots, and Bread. "Pittsburgh Stealers," wherein Royce works the steel mill day shift and Jeannie's husband works the night shift, which provides an irresistible opportunity for nature to run its naked course, came right after two big Kendalls country hits with "sin" in their titles. It's also notable for its northern urban industrial setting, always a country plus (see: Bobby Bare's "Detroit City"), and for being one of the few Kendalls songs where Royce sings as much as Jeannie does. So naturally, the Steelers wound up winning Super Bowl XIII. But the pair's inevitable 1982 sequel, "A Dallas Cowboy and a New Orleans Saint," wasn't nearly as good.

### Ronnie Milsap:
### "Get It Up" (1979)

Blind North Carolina adult-contemporary schlock-country piano player Ronnie Milsap has never been especially shy about showing off his roots in soul music—early '80s hits like "Stranger in My House" and "Any Day Now" can sound downright eerie if you're in the right mood, and "Somewhere Dry," off his 2006 album *My Life*, proved he hadn't lost his touch decades after. But he probably never pushed the influence as far as on side two of his 1979 *Images* album, which started and ended with unabashed disco tracks of almost no legit country pedigree, except for the fact that Ronnie was singing them. The side opener was a glitzy cover of Tommy Tucker's 1964 R&B hit "Hi Heel

Sneakers," and the closer was "Get It Up"—basically, a '70s-style full-band party-funk number (think Brass Construction or Con Funk Shun maybe) that got to #43 on the pop chart and country radio avoided like the plague. (Something similar happened again to Milsap a few years later, with his slick Cars-ish MTV new wave move "She Loves My Car," a #84 pop hit in '84.) Anyway, as its title suggests, "Get It Up" isn't just about dancing; it's also about screwing: "You gotta get it up, get down, get it on, get on out / That's the only way to make my baby shout"; he's gonna "drive it home in 4/4 time" and move her "'til it hits the spot." Dropping down low at strategic moments between the horn and string breakdowns, Milsap's singing is rich and lusty enough to convince, too. I'm guessing the song got disco play—wouldn't be shocked if it crossed over some to black radio.

### Eddie Rabbitt:
### "Suspicions" (1979)

When you're a country singer born second-generation Irish in Brooklyn and raised in suburban Jersey, you take what success you can get, even if you're the guy who wrote "Kentucky Rain." But for a while there, Eddie Rabbitt had scads regardless—between "You Don't Love Me Anymore" in 1978 and "You Can't Run from Love" in 1983, 11 of the 13 singles he put out topped the country chart, and almost all pushed the genre's definition in a manner schmaltzy enough to make purists' heads explode. Which means, in his own way, Rabbitt was an innovator, hearing links between the reverb on pop-disco and Sun rockabilly records, and figuring out how to squeeze the Eagles and "Subterranean Homesick Blues" into the recipe to boot. "Suspicions," his most negative-spacious hit, about how when you're in love with a beautiful woman you watch your friends, was also his first to cross to the pop 20, and possibly the most quiet-storming, yacht-rocking country hit ever, from wafting woodwinds to blue-eyed soul falsettos on down. Just gorgeous—no wonder Tim McGraw revived it (gorgeously, too) in 2007.

—*Complex*, 5 June 2012

*All Ears* (Realistic, 1977)

## CB Jeebies

· · · · ·

I somewhat facetiously raised the idea of CB radio songs last year, halfway figuring—without much evidence—that they might've been a brief fad in the
late '70s. ("A short list of Citizen Band radio songs, in case anybody needs
one: C. W. McCall 'Convoy'; Cledus Maggard and the Citizen's Band 'White
Knight'; Rod Hart 'CB Savage'; Gunter Gabriel 'Ich Bin CB-Funker'; MX-80
Sound 'PCB's'; the Fall 'I'm into CB.'") Well, now I have proof—a compilation, released on Realistic Records and sold exclusively through Radio Shack
according to its cover, called *All Ears: 10 New and Original Song Hits with a CB
Theme*; found it for two dollars (a real splurge for me!) at a vintage store in
Austin last week.

No copyright year anywhere on the cover, but I assume not long post-
"Convoy" (which topped the pop chart in early 1976). Best cuts, like that smash,
are basically talking blues: "The Handles Hall of Fame" by Johnny Hemphill
(a list of creative nicknames that makes me think of the one in Kool Moe Dee's
"Wild West West") and "Listenin' CB Blues" by Mac Wiseman (about trying to
get used to all this newfangled technology). "Everybody's Somebody (in Our

CB World)" by Ed Bernet is the most American songpoem-like in its cluelessness, but also the most proto-Internet in concept—namely, the idea that, no matter how you look or whether you're a young girl or an old man, you can create a persona and make friends to talk to via the network. "L.J.'s CB Radio" by Oscar Rey is a cornball *Hee Haw* standup routine; "The Night I Talked to the Lord (. . . on my CB Radio)" has the same concept as Carrie Underwood's "Jesus Take the Wheel," seeing as how God saves the driver from a devastating crash. Other songs—including Shirley & Squirrely's "Hey Shirley (This Is Squirrely)," a Bicentennial Summer Top 50—show an obvious Ray Stevens and David Seville influence. Recurring theme: trying to make sense of all this brand-new slang.

*—I Love Music*, 31 January 2010

## Can't Fool Mother Nature

· · · · ·

Dressed in down vests, flannel shirts, and Earth Shoes, "granolas" are often seen stalking the halls of WBHS with a knapsack on one arm, a pack of Real cigarettes in the other. Their sole purpose in life is to convince people that they are completely unaffected by our technological society. They are generally vegetarians, except for the occasional Big Mac. Everything they eat must be free of those modern demons, BHA and BHT.

Their idea of fun is climbing mountains and catching pneumonia—a rather painful way to prove one's macho. I can't comprehend how someone could enjoy frozen arteries. Everything in their lives is simplistic and unsophisticated, even the 20-speed bicycles they waste their life savings on.

But actually, the backpacking bunch is a valuable resource in these trying times. In a time when everybody wants everything, it's refreshing to know that there are still people around who'll be happy with just a backpack, a pair of Earth Shoes, some hiking boots, a few pairs of flannel socks, some long underwear, a guitar, a cabin up north, a few hundred dollars' worth of cross-country ski apparatus, 12 pairs of Levi's, a couple duck-hunting rifles, some baking soda toothpaste, a three-year subscription to *Field and Stream*, a lifetime supply of granola, a Bill Walton for President poster, a mountain, honorary membership to the Friends of Apple Island, and all of John Denver's albums.

*—Spectrum*, November 1977

## Prog on the Prairie:
## Midwestern Bands Roll Over Beethoven

· · · · ·

On the back of Kansas's self-titled first album, which came roaring out of Topeka in 1974, the band looks like six long-haired farmboys, out standing in their field: blue jeans, Daniel Boone fringe jackets—one big guy even has overalls on. The front cover is a famous portrait of insurrectionary 19th-century Bleeding Kansas abolitionist John Brown; the last track, a eulogy for Mother Nature. Though released on a label run by Don Kirshner, the bizzer who'd masterminded the Monkees, the record never got higher than #174 in *Billboard*. A shame, because "Belexes" had the doom-ridden punch of early British metal, "Bringing It All Back" was a good-timey boogie-woogie about smuggling drugs, and the band had a way of extracting Charlie Daniels–style hillbilly fiddle hoedowns out of demi-classical violin bombast, like they instinctively realized that lots of that high-flown British orchestral foo-foo started off as jiggy dance music to begin with.

Kansas's second and third albums—*Song from America* and *Masque*, which respectively managed to climb chartwise to #57 and #70 in 1975—worked similar pastiches of mean, chunky, even funky redneck rock and 10-minute-plus mini-symphonies overflowing with time changes, crescendos, Moog filigrees, and delusions of grandeur. The heftier harvest mode holds up best: "The Devil Game," "Mysteries and Mayhem," another small-time dope-pusher tale called "Down the Road," and the Nazareth-like vengeance rager "Lonely Street," which may or may not be about hunting down a "black man." (Lyric sheet says "bad man," but your ears might determine otherwise.) But it was the fancy stuff, which lent itself more to ballets than barn dances or bar fights, that most presaged Kansas's lucrative future. In 1976 and 1977, they scored two huge hit singles off of punfully titled Top 10 albums that generally left their crasser hard rock side behind—"Carry On My Wayward Son" from *Leftoverture*, and "Dust in the Wind" from *Point of Know Return*. Complex, windswept, multipart harmonies became a band signature of sorts, but it wasn't long before the group succumbed to the market-researched restraint that turned underground FM radio into AOR in the Lee Abrams–consulted late '70s. Eventually, guitarist Kerry Livgren and bassist Dave Hope were born again, playing music for Christ.

"Q: How do you tell American art-rockers from their European forebears?,"

Bob Christgau asked in 1976. "A: They sound dumber, they don't play as fast, and their fatalism lacks conviction." Not always true. It's impossible to imagine cultured Brit conceptualists like Yes or Genesis dirtying their hands with most of the louder numbers on those first few Kansas LPs, or for that matter the tougher tracks on early platters by the Illinois bands Head East or Styx — the latter of whom, even more than Kansas, stuck it out through several excellent but barely heard albums before breaking through to a big audience with prissier, more pop-oriented material. But prog-rock had initially pranced its way out of England for good reasons, and there's something innately ridiculous, yet fascinating, about hicks from the American heartland picking up on its virtuoso high-brow bombast in the mid-'70s. In the discography at the back of John Rockwell's "The Emergence of Art Rock" chapter in 1980's *Rolling Stone Illustrated History of Rock'n'Roll*, the only Americans listed are expatriates Sparks and avant comedian Frank Zappa, hardly mainstream acts. "In comparison with the British," Rockwell theorizes, "Americans tend to be happy cavepeople. Most American rockers wouldn't know a Beethoven symphony if they were run down by one in the middle of the freeway."

So as often as not, progressive rockers from the midwestern prairie just rolled over Beethoven entirely. In fact, it might be a stretch to call R.E.O. Speedwagon prog at all, if they didn't temper the riverboat-pianoed bonfire-in-the-woods choogle of their first two albums with occasional outrageously ambitious, amp-cranking, Hammond-pumping gloom monsters that, like sundry early Kansas / Head East / Styx tracks, seemed to owe more than a bit to the majestic post-psychedelic organ-metal funerals of the UK's Uriah Heep. The apocalyptic 10-minute epic "Dead at Last" on 1971's *R.E.O. Speedwagon* and the astounding left-leaning dirge-unto-raveup protest "Golden Country" on 1972's *R.E.O. T.W.O.*, especially, will come as shocks to anyone whose familiarity with R.E.O. is limited to their '80s housewife hits. "Five Men Were Killed Today," another menacing debut selection, employs an eerie 1920's electronic instrument known as the ondes Martenot; all the songs about various kinds of ladies ("Gypsy Woman's Passion," "Sophisticated Lady," "Prison Women") have a palpable kick to them as well. On the only slightly less raw second album, five songs out of eight exceed 5:50 in length. Prog enough for you?

Neither record even dented the *Billboard* 200 — an inauspicious beginning for a band that, a few years later, would top that chart for 15 weeks with the savvy popcraft of 1980's *Hi Infidelity*. R.E.O. came from a college town — Champaign, Illinois — and went through three singers on their first three albums: Terry Lutrell, then Kevin Cronin, then Mike Murphy, who somehow managed to stick around for the fourth one. His two 1974 sets, *Ridin' the Storm Out* and *Lost in a Dream*, were more rustic and less heavy than R.E.O.'s first two, but with meaty songs and no lack of tasty Gary Richrath guitar; *Lost in a Dream* even had Sly Stone helping out, and its title track partook in an ornate swing not too far from early Aerosmith. By album five, though, Cronin's high, nasal, not-quite-southern drawl was back. And by 1978's Top 30 *You Can Tune a Piano, But You Can't Tuna Fish*—album eight, if you're still counting—even girls were taking notice. Anyone who doubts just how revered R.E.O. were in flyover country by the late '70s should consult the Facebook page of my 1978 West Bloomfield, Michigan, high school graduating class, where last time I checked, the *only* link was to a 1978 performance of "Roll with the Changes" on NBC's *Midnight Special*.

Original R.E.O. mouth Terry Lutrell, meanwhile, wound up fronting a St. Louis / Champaign sextet known as Starcastle, who barely sounded American at all, opting instead to mimic the convoluted engineering-schematic arrangements and angelic Morse Code harmonies of their heroes Yes. On their own self-titled 1975 debut LP—also their highest-charting, topping off at a mere #95—the guitars remain mostly frictionless and the rhythm section never plows through any cow pies. But the record ends with a wacked-out percussion instrumental called "Nova," and both key lyrics quoted on the vinyl version's inner sleeve notably contain the word "crystal." The LP cover literally depicts a castle in the stars.

By 1978's non-charting *Real to Reel*, Robert Christgau was complaining that "in the great tradition of heartland eclecticism," Starcastle were "adding power-rock and pop-melody moves to the art-rock casserole. With hooks, yet. Lord save us." Sound familiar? Prog in general, on both sides of the Atlantic, was tightening up its fanfare into what the genre's latter-day web-chat aficionados prefer to call "pomp"; by the early '80s, even longtime cult weirdos Genesis would be all over Top 40. So out on the prog prairie, the last great shot was perhaps fired by the Kansas City band Shooting Star, who debuted in 1980 with a refined pop-pomp-powerchord hybrid that used strings and synths for shading, and prettied as often as it stomped; if they'd come instead from England a few years later and named themselves Def Leppard, they'd now be multimillionaires. "Last Chance," the inspirationally cheerleading six-minute climax of their first LP, was some kind of flatland pinnacle, somehow overblown and economical, regal and humble, at the same time. Inside the sleeve of 1982's *III Wishes*, their third and biggest album—peaked at #82, so perhaps it got airplay as far away as Iowa—their violin-cum-fiddle player is shown onstage, and he's posed with his instrument like a rock guitar, as only a midwestern boy unversed in Beethoven would think to do. His name? Charles Waltz. Swear I'm not making that up.

*—Wondering Sound*, 8 July 2010

## Past Expiry Hard Rock Dollar Bin

· · · · ·

**Couchois:**
*Nasty Hardware* (Warner Bros., 1980)

Five Alabama boys who look like Canadian hockey players on the cover, where they're all jovial and partying with, uh, VERY BIG SHEETS OF ALUMINUM FOIL (???) over their heads (and one guy's got a beer and another's spraying aerosol into his hat), not to mention like total douchebags on the back—especially actual Couchois brothers Pat, Michael, and Chris. Tony Jasper and Derek Oliver claim in 1983's *The International Encyclopedia of Hard Rock and Heavy Metal* that "there are enough brothers in this band to start a football team," but I'm pretty sure they miscounted. *Foosball* team, maybe. Anyway, never heard their allegedly ballad-heavy 1979 debut, but this follow-up has a bunch of chunky AOR pop-rockers midway between the Babys and Bad Company (esp. "Trudy You're a Bad Girl," "Pretty Young Girls," "Innocence"), and ends with some awesome Foreigner-going-disco called "Visibility Zero." Plus this thing called "Roll the Dice" later covered by German metallers Rage, Jasper and Oliver say. My copy still has a $0.69 Plastic Fantastic sticker.

**Daddy Dewdrop:**
*Daddy Dewdrop* (Sunflower, 1971)

Some really funky studio musicians here, especially the drummer. Lots of Dr. John in the sound (especially in voodoo hoodoo funker "Abracadabra Alakazam"), and maybe the less rock side of J. Geils (or Peter Wolf in talking mode). The hit, sleazy wet-dream song "Chick-a-Boom (Don't Ya Jes' Love It)," maybe the aesthetic spawn of both War's "Spill the Wine" and the Pipkins' "Gimme Dat Ding" from the year before, went Top 10; album didn't even go

Couchois: *Nasty Hardware* (Warner Bros., 1980)

Top 200. The single kinda creeped me out as a 10-year-old, since it concerned hippie girls with missing bikini tops and bottoms, yet I've always remembered it as Saturday morning cartoon rock—and yep, sure enough (just confirmed this), it was done for a cartoon called *Sabrina and the Groovie Ghoulies*, and Daddy Dewdrop was actually a Cleveland songwriter named Dick Monda. Rest of the album was clearly tossed off overnight, and nobody bought it because 10-year-olds back then only bought 45s, not LPs, but it's pretty wacked out—songs about "fox huntin'" and "diggin' on Mrs. Jones," but the weirdest titles are probably "March of the White Corpuscles" and "Migraine Headaches," the latter of which goes from Huey Smith to "You're Sixteen" to some nutty vaudeville-rock prototype for Disco Tex and his Sex-O-Lettes. Wouldn't be surprised if Frankie Smith, Philly's '80s "Double Dutch Bus" DJ rapper, was also a fan. Most grating is "John Jacob Jingle Heimer Smith," which is the annoying children's ditty and doesn't even get John Jacob's last name right. (Should be Schmidt.) And the single is way beyond grating too, but in some kind of genius way. Totally forgot the part where bikini-hunting Dewdrop opens a door *Let's Make a Deal* style and runs into, uh, Little Richard screaming half-crazy "bomp boom a loo bom a long bam boo." In Africa.

**Diesel:**
*Watts in the Tank* (Regency, 1981)

Oddball Dutch band, had one great U.S. hit with new wave pop disco metal whatever "Sausalito Summernight," which mainly concerned shelling out $80 to fix their Rambler's blown-gasket radiator and peaked at #25 pop anyway. No idea what Dutch guys knew about Sausalito, but it worked. Closest band I could compare them to would be (early '80s) Golden Earring, and not just because they're from Holland. But they also have some Styx / Queen / Foreigner pomp going on, and "Down in the Silvermine" is some total jig-rock (like Horslips maybe? But catchier. Uh . . . Men Without Hats??) about how down in the mine days are long but the work is fine. At least I think they say that. Doubt the work is actually fine, though.

**Good Rats:**
*From Rats to Riches* (Passport, 1978)

Heavier than I would have guessed, and more lyrically and structurally eccentric (almost in a Crack the Sky kind of way) than I figured from supposed barband hacks, with sonic influences running the gamut from doo-wop to prog to maybe even punk. Flo and Eddie produced. Favorite songs: "Taking It to Detroit" (about how they're gonna play Cobo Hall like "Kiss and Seger" and make it huge, which of course never happened—well, they may have played Cobo, I'm not sure, but if so it didn't help much, and I don't know of this actually getting airplay in Detroit, though after Bowie and J. Geils and Kiss had scored there with hard-rocking Detroit songs, you can see why they tried); "Mr. Mechanic" (probably the most high-speed-metallic track, possibly a progenitor of zz Top's "Manic Mechanic"); "Victory in Space" (pomp-rocking plea to the "ladies of the universe"); "Don't Hate the Ones Who Bring You Rock and Roll" (a weird and at least passingly homophobic rocker—starts out "Son of a bitch let me rip his eyes out / Prancing around like a faggot / Painted up ass, like to pull his pants down / Shoot off his works / Then I'd like to bag it—feed it to a maggot," and you're like, what the fuck? But then by the end he's saying "Twisted mothers, twisted brothers, twisted sisters," so I'm wondering whether they were feuding with Dee Snider! Or maybe I'm misreading it and they were on the same side, Twisted Sister being another big Long Island bar band in the '70s); "Local Zero" (blue-collar Catholic song—"Who can quit near our daughters' communion"—that seems both anti-boss and anti-union,

Good Rats: *From Rats to Riches* (Passport, 1978)

like maybe their local was going to go on strike and they were worried about going broke?). Not sure what their day jobs were, but they look like perfectly homely and beefy regular suburban Joe couch potatoes with beards and Jew-fros and sports jerseys, and it's wacky how they're emerging out of dry ice on-stage with that big inflatable football on the back. (Other albums I've heard aren't chopped liver, either. Jasper and Oliver: "The music is a mixture of raw aggressive metal, often tinged with weird jazzy overtones. It is always of high quality, and they are worth their weight in gold." Doubly impressive, because they definitely weren't skinny guys, so that gold would weigh a lot!)

## Madam X:
### *We Reserve the Right* (Jet, 1984)

Hadn't played the world-breakingly remedial-looking Rick Derringer–produced platter by these codpiece-and-bondage-gear-bedecked cucumber-stuffed-down-trousers two-boy/two-girl (including future Vixen drummer hottie Roxy Petrucci and her guitar sister Maxine) huge-hair types for several years, but had fun when I did. (Had assumed I'd mainly just kept it for the cover, which has to be seen to be believed.) Sides both start with Twisted Sister / Quiet Riot–style post-Alice / Slade / Kiss shout-glam stomps for way-

Madam X: *We Reserve the Right* (Jet, 1984)

ward teen dumbasses: "High in High School" (about just what it says); "Reserve the Right to Rock" (which has jokes, sort of, about no shoes no shirt no service); and the Britny Fox–worthy in its doofusitude "Good with Figures," where Bret Kaiser actually brags about being illiterate ("Can't read, can't write, but there's one thing I can do all night"), but nonetheless excelling in math ("I'm good with figures / I like your figure / That figures!"). "Max Volume" is Great Kat–type classical metal showoff wank from Maxine, and both sides close with over-the-top true-metal speed-racers that catch you by surprise. Plus, the bassist calls himself Chris "Godzilla" Doliber!

Nantucket:
*Long Way to the Top* (Epic, 1980)

AC/DC cover (best one ever?) into excellent hard powerpop ("Living with You") into new wave Nazareth partially about law school (??? that's what it sounds like anyway) with a proto-Kix explosion at the end ("Time Bomb") into high-harmony stretched-out multipart road-life hard rock with saxomaphones and squealing synths ("50 More") into a speedy stuttering number about rock celebrities in *Rolling Stone* that again partially recalls Nazareth and has more sax honk ("Media Darlin'") into another bubbly-and-effervescentas-Kix AC/DC rip with boogie-woogie piano ("Rugburn"). Then side two. More new-wave-leaning powerpop AOR ("Too Much Wrong in the Past [for a Future]") into chunky catchy rock with *Who's Next* loopage and singing that could again pass for Nazareth's Dan McCafferty ("Over and Over Again") into a happy finger-snappy one about rock radio that I bet was the AOR airplay track (might even remember hearing it on the air—"Turn the Radio On") into a funky hey-hey-hey frat-party soul-rocker seemingly based either on "Good Lovin'" or "Do You Love Me" or both ("Tell Me [The Rhythm Method]") into some hard-guy macho Bad Co. / Foreigner gutbust with lonely lovelorn yacht-pop harmonies and smooth-jazz sections ("Rescue") into an endearingly dorky kiss-ass early-Loverboy-style powerchord-and-Cars-keyboard semi-ballad just in time to ring in the decade ("Rock of the '80s," where they plead, "Let's have some fun"!). And after that Nantucket stick in a half-minute freebie barbershop-harmonied singalong maybe called "Stella" (but not named on the cover or label) where they rhyme "rock'n'roll" with "doggie bowl." Also, on the back cover, the bassist ("Pee Wee Watson") is crouched down with a silver jacket and a hat with *Highway to Hell* horns (I guess) on it; lead guitarist has a *real* bushy '70s-disc-jockey mustache and chest hair to match and is wearing what looks like a kimono; sax/keyb guy is wearing a Hawaiian shirt; another guy (second guitarist I think) has a button on his shirt that says "FUCK RUS-SIA"; and a skinny scraggly longhaired guy (drummer I think) with a comb (??) sticking out of his back pocket seems to making a mincing stance with his butt sticking out. You can tell which guy is the singer (Larry "L. Factor" Uzzel) just from his pretty-boy hair, Jagger lips, arrogant expression, and the apparent zucchini behind his zipper. (And, oh yeah, almost all their clothes are really bright and colorful, to boot.)

## New England:
### *New England* (Infinity, 1979)

Supermelodic (like, post-Boston at points, also maybe a little post-Queen to go with the inevitable post-Styx etc.) pomp AOR, complete with a super*duper*-melodic hit single "Don't Ever Wanna Lose Ya," which just barely squeezed into the Top 40. But my two favorite cuts are probably the sprint-tempoed "Shoot" and the maybe even more so "P.U.N.K.," which stands for "Puny Undernourished Kid" and I swear revolves around a subliminal (maybe acci-dental? maybe imaginary? you decide) Sex Pistols riff. But of course it's all Billy Joel–style resentment about the stupid younger-brother generation:

"You've got chains for brains / When you eat 714s for supper / Hey kid, you're only 16 / And you've got too many lovers"—714s of course being 'ludes, at least as much a metal as punk drug where I grew up.

### Nutz:
### *Hard Nutz* (A&M, 1977)

Rocks as hard as its name, but it's also proggier than I'd anticipated, given the band's seemingly punkish moniker. Reference points would perhaps include Heep, Nuge, Faces / Humble Pie (in "Pushed Around"), heavy suvvern funk rock (in "Sick and Tired"—of rock'n'roll, it turns out); closer "One More Cup of Coffee" makes White Stripes' version sound like kindergartners in comparison and may well out-heavy any Dylan cover this side of Nazareth's "Ballad of Hollis Brown." But the real shitkicker is side one closer "Wallbanger," which probably has nothing to do with interrogation via the method of swinging torturees by their necks and banging them against walls. But it sort of sounds like it could.

### Skatt Bros:
### *Strange Spirits* (Casablanca, 1979)

Probably either as "rock" a disco album or as "disco" a rock album as ever existed—and yeah, as the muscular male camaraderie on the front and back cover indicate, Leather Nun–level leather-bar gay (seems they were marketed as the "metal" Village People or thereabouts). Best song, "Walk the Night," sounds basically how Wax Trax fascist industrial fetish metal disco (KMFDM or whoever) *should* have sounded, almost a decade early. Most over-the-top hook: "I got a ROD beneath my coat / It's gonna RAM right down your throat / Hooo-ahh!!!" Almost as good: "Life at the Outpost" ("Give your love to a cowboy man / He's gonna love ya hard as he can, can"—plus spaghetti western guitar parts) and "Midnight Companion" (ballad, country in mood if not mode, about disguising one's self as a trucker to meet bikers to prevent lonely nights—best song ever to mention a Rand McNally map). Those three songs are *unbelievably* catchy, though they really don't sound much like each other, even if they all come from the same place—not sure whether this lineup, featuring Richie Fontana (from Billy Squier's '70s pop metal Piper) on drums, ever existed as a live entity, and also unclear the extent to which the lyrics were meant at face value, though supposedly "Walk the Night" did get abundant leather-bar DJ play. "Old Enough," near-six-minute closer about a 12-year-old runaway who winds up living sleazy in the city, is up there too, jump-rope end-chant and all: "Sally, Sally, Sally's in the alley, dancing . . ." Might be a child prostitute, or stripper—same thing Sunset Strip hair-glam bands later sang about—but it's never spelled out. Also possible, given the Skatts' cruiser premise, that she might be a he, and might be doing more than dancing in that alley. But the song's on the side of the kid, whose street smarts get celebrated.

## Slik:
### *Slik* (Arista, 1976)

So, speaking of rock bands like the Tubes (and see also Brownsville Station, *School Punks*, 1974) who did songs about "punks" mere minutes before punks started at least theoretically meaning something else entirely so you couldn't do that anymore (unless you were Van Halen, who waited until 1978 for "Atomic Punk"), turns out the most rocking cut on the apparently only album by Slik is "The Kid's a Punk," which sounds midway between the Bay City Rollers and the Sweet plus a little Elton "Philadelphia Freedom" and speaks of how said punk kid looks like James Dean and you can tell he's a loser because of how he dresses, so watch out. Apparently Slik were another Rollers-style teeny-rock attempt from Scotland (never charted in the U.S.), featuring future Ultravoxer Midge Ure, though I'm not sure which guy he is since none of them look like robots. (Apparently there are also personnel connections with the Skids, and Ure was later in the Rich Kids pre-Ultravox.) They are all wearing unavailable-in-the-UK minor league baseball jerseys on the back, and on the front the guy with the red plaid shirt and a toothpick sticking out his mouth might be trying to look like Bruce Springsteen. All four guys have short, well-groomed hair, too—in 1976! Only song Ure wrote is "Do It Again," which starts like a mix between Motown and Raspberries-style powerpop until some Thin Lizzyfied guitars come in near the end. (A few years later, Ure would collaborate on one of Phil Lynott's solo LPs.) Otherwise, maybe half bleh ballads or fairly softie pop-rock, with a couple exceptions. Side one closer "Requiem" is sort of a Brecht-Weill cabaret merry-go-round swirl bookended by Gregorian Yard-birds gloom, and then there's the last two on side two: "Bom Bom," a cover of a great tropical novelty funk number by Bahaman musician Exuma that Jimmy Castor Bunch had a low-level R&B hit with in 1976; and "Dancerama," partly a crass disco move but opening and closing with ornate demiclassical prancing around, which gives way to some super-funky breaks of the awesome sort that hip-hop guys would later sample off Babe Ruth and Barrabas records.

## Starz:
### *Violation* (Capitol, 1977)

Still not entirely sure I follow the plot of the eternal classic "Rock Six Times" — may or may not be the only song ever written about shoplifting an old vinyl record (which may or may not be called "Walk This Way," which wasn't that old at all, weird) from a thrift store (though Starz call it a "welfare store"); also still fuzzy on why the protagonist of "Subway Terror" is wearing a suit, or when that song came out in relation to the Son of Sam murders and city-wide blackout that sired hip-hop — seems thematically linked, somehow. Also hear a direct rip of Marvin Gaye's (okay, maybe Grand Funk's) "Some Kind of Wonderful" a few cuts in, basically in the melody of Michael Lee Smith singing the line "do it like you need it" in "All Night Long." "Cool One" comes next, Farfisafied bubble-rock about a handjob at a movie: "She reached over and grabbed on my rocks / I lost it all in the popcorn box," ha. And vaguely '50s-ish reissue bonus demo "Rock This Town" makes me wonder whether the Stray Cats (from Long Island, right?) were Starz fans growing up. All in all, a stellar supply of sweathog-rock!

## Styx:
### *II* (Wooden Nickel, 1973)

Not sure if the learned consensus agrees nothing they did ever rocked harder than "Earl of Roseland" and "I'm Gonna Make You Feel It" at the end, but I'm hearing as much Who as Heep in those. And the use of quaint Limey lingo like "yesteryear" and "sport" instead of "sports" as well as the title itself in "Earl of Roseland" are hilarious for a pack of Chicago boys — makes it sort of the '70s pomp-rock answer to "Duke of Earl."

## Thundermug:
### *Strikes* (Epic, 1973)

Picked this up for a buck somewhere along the line because of their name, and because the band members on the back all look like total hangdog hippie slobs, one of them with a neck beard, and the fattest one wearing a ponytail. Turns out they came from London, Ontario. And they really pull off that big-bottom BTO bison-burger-patty hockey-puck funk—in "Jane 'J' James," "Where Am I," the start of "Garden Green" before it goes more hard pop. "Africa," too, though as the title suggests that one adds some nifty fake jungle polyrhythms (and possibly mentions "the colored man"—I'm scared to go back and make sure). Closer "Bad Guy" has the most badassed sound, approaching heavy Nazareth. And they do Beatles and diddybop harmonies elsewhere, when the mood strikes, plus a loud Kinks cover, something called "Mickey Mouse Club" that I gather might be somehow political, and confusedly idiosyncratic hints of prog and glam like they weren't quite sure what those were.

## TKO:
### Let It Roll (Infinity, 1979)

It's not just that Brad Sinsel sings like Roger Daltrey; he also writes kinda like Pete Townshend—has what seems to be a passing literate sociological interest in the lives of teens surviving the urban wilds, most obviously in "Gutter Boy," but also "Ain't No Way to Be," which reads almost like an updated "Summertime Blues" where the kid can't get a job. And the Who-like singing and songwriting really shape these songs. (Honestly, seems weird that band didn't directly influence subsequent hard rock more. I mean, Cheap Trick or whoever, sure, and no doubt Townshend's *guitar playing* inspired plenty— maybe all of it, up to a point. But I still can't think of many bands where you listen and say "These guys are obviously trying to sound like the Who," the way you would with Zeppelin, Stones, Sabbath, etc.) Anyway, TKO's side openers also get at least a bit of Aero-funk going, and the closing track does a kind of Celtic stretch-out that feels like a heavier Big Country crossed with Mellencamp's band, a few years early. So even if these are hired studio hacks as some have suggested, I really don't mind.

## Tubes:
### Young and Rich (A&M, 1976)

(1) Has some of the funniest (not to mention longwinded and multidirectional) liner notes in rock history (see below). (2) It's not so much hard rock as basically an album of genre spoofs—blaxploitation soul, Phil Spector, disco,

rockabilly, jazz, etc. (3) "Pimp" should probably count as one of the world's first gangsta raps—after, say, Lightnin' Rod's *Hustler's Convention* or whatever. The music is *Superfly*-style funk; the rude words (including chorus line one Tube "stole from a ten-year-old black kid he picked up hitchhiking") spoken, and there's a part in the middle where they're actually rhymed rap-style. Though—displaying my utter Zappa ignorance—did Frank also previously have raps like this, maybe even featuring pimps? Or am I all mixed up? (For what it's worth, on their next album *Now* from 1977, the Tubes also anticipated the free-jazzy '80s punk-funk of early Was [Not Was] and James Chance in "Cathy's Clone," not to mention '80s hip-hop turntablists in "God-Bird-Change," a fast sort of fusion collage that goes through all sorts of changes before winding up on an insane extended drum break that sounds like the Incredible Bongo Band before almost turning into "The Mexican.") (4) Wall of Sound homage "Don't Touch Me There" probably influenced Meat Loaf's "Paradise by the Dashboard Light" a year later. Also very Tim Curry in *Rocky Horror Picture Show*, which didn't chart *Billboard*-wise until '78 but actually came out in '75. (5) "Slipped My Disco" ("a chiropractic nightmare in J5 tempo or perhaps in the manner of Crown Heights Affair," say the notes) has to be one of the first disco *parodies* on record. Good one, too. (6) "Proud to Be an American" is obviously their Elvis joke ("solo in tribute to that great American, Scotty Moore"), not to mention "Bicentennial salute" and "slick and commercial, for a necessary dose of rack-job appeal"; also, the words come at you really fast, and I'd like to see them on paper sometime. (7) "Madam I'm Adam," unlike "Bob" by "Weird Al" Yankovic, is not a palindrome. My wife (who mainly knows just the Tubes' early '80s MTV pop hits where it's hard for me to understand how they kept a straight face) says its multiple time switcheroos reminded her of Steely Dan. Which probably isn't far off. Album actually went to #46 in the *Billboard* 200 (way higher than the debut's #113), and "Don't Touch Me There" to #61 as a single (their only pre-1981 Hot 100 hit), so obviously it got some airplay. So who was their audience? Aging glamsters and/or Zappaphiles? Seems they're just too weird and unserious for prog fans, though they probably had the chops for them. (Also, what did early punks think of "White Punks on Dope"? Which was supposedly inspired by Jefferson Airplane, I've read.)

**(Various):**

*WRNO FM 100: The Rock Album Vol. II* (Starstream, 1982)

Bankrolled by Miller High Life Rock to Riches for an AOR station from New Orleans, where all these no-name bands come from. (Now Talk Radio since 2006, Wiki says, after switching to Classic Rock in 1997. Time rolls on.) Most metal-heavy cuts would be Persia's "Don't Let Your Dreams" (NWOBHM-like power drama), Chrome's (not *that* Chrome) Nugenty-riffed "It Was You," and the Rebels' late '60s-style biker acid "Hit the Road." Big-assed butt-rock: Melange's "Lonely Tonight"; Quick Zipper's hefty white funker "Batters Box" (not as full of baseball metaphors as I'd hoped but still maybe the most macho sexist dunderheadedness on an album hilariously loaded with such stuff), and the unbelievable accidental parody WRNO theme (not credited to a specific band, though a good one plays on it) entitled "Rock to the Rock," which (as its title suggests) is a BTO / "Hot Blooded"–weight yellalong with the chorus, duh, "We're gonna ROCK! to the ROCK!," yep. Cover says 20,000 local bands entered the competition (guessing it was maybe a national thing?), and the winner would get $25,000 and a deal with Atlantic, so you could watch "one of your local acts explode and become another Fleetwood Mac or Journey." I wonder who won. Also makes me wonder about the whole concept of independently/regionally released *mainstream* (as opposed to new wave) hard rock in the early '80s, a phenomenon nobody much talks about. There were plenty of bands like that in (probably mostly suburban) Detroit, most of which I ignored and assumed sucked, because I was such a skinny-tie snob at the time. Adrenaline, the Look, Bitter Sweet Alley . . . Who knows if they were any good? Wish I still had the LP by a local Detroit group called the Lordz. And also, were *all* these dorky low-rent early '80s AOR comps of unsigned local bands this good? Seems this one (volume 2 in New Orleans alone) was part of a bigger series; did Miller High Life sponsor these in every major market? Is there anybody who *collects* these things, or has documented them? Has anybody ever tried to compile a mainstream rock equivalent of *Back from the Grave* or *Killed by Death*, from the best tracks? Somebody should! KZOK *Best of the Northwest 1981*, KSJO *Best of the Bay 1982*, and Detroit's possibly legendary circa 1978 *W4 Homegrown* all get the thumbs up, too.

*—I Love Music*, 2008–2011

## Sonic Taxonomy: Fake New Wave

· · · · ·

So, you know how all those left-field indie rock bands got signed to major labels in the '90s alt-goldrush wake of "Smells Like Teen Spirit," and most didn't sell diddlysquat? (*Spin* compiled 40 of them a couple months back.) Well, what nobody remembers is that the same thing had happened just over a decade earlier, after the Knack's "My Sharona" (and to an extent Cars / Cheap Trick / Devo / Blondie, etc.) exploded out of nowhere and convinced big-league bizzers that new wave might mean big bucks. Except new wave's buzz bin wasn't filled so much with avant-weirdos as with the turn-of-the-'80s equivalent of hair-metal bands going grunge: provincial bar-band rockers passing themselves off as powerpop or technopop or punk, via faster tempos, cuter melodies, Carsy keyboards, herky-jerk beats, acting like tough guys from the street, trying on one-noun names or funny haircuts or skinny ties or pink sidewinders and a bright orange pair of pants: if Billy Joel and Linda Ronstadt could make new wave albums, anybody could, right?

Squares trying to play hip, in other words, and almost inevitably being awarded instant cutout status for their trouble. There were scads, a few of whom actually managed to briefly land a tune on the radio between 1979 and 1981: pat your aching back if you recognize the A's, Inmates, Jags, Kingbees, Kings, Rings, Sherbs (supposedly sampled on Daft Punk's new album!), Sports, Headboys, Fabulous Poodles, Flash and the Pan, Sniff 'n' the Tears, Moon Martin, Herman Brood and His Wild Romance. And those were the lucky ones! (At least compared to, say, the Tazmanian Devils.) Fake New Wave dated back to Christ Child's preposterous 1977 Buddah debut *Hard*, but once the Knack hit, the genre really "took off." After sorting through dozens of entries, and deeming candidates such as Doug and the Slugs somehow still not new wave enough to qualify, I've settled on seven Fake New Wave albums that deserve to be remembered, but will continue to keep used-vinyl dollar bins warm 'til they are. Get 'em while they're cheap!

### Hounds:
### *Puttin' on the Dog* (Columbia, 1979)

Chicago's Hounds did not look particularly new wave: too much facial hair, too much chest hair, too much head hair, wrong kind of leather trousers, too comfortable with their bodies in general, they're more like the kind of cock-rock thugs who'd beat new wavers up. First album—*Unleashed*, from '78—had a woman with a dog collar around her neck on the cover, using her chain as a whip on the back. Followup from '79—*Puttin' on the Dog*—had a woman in black underwear talking on her phone, in a lavish hotel room surrounded by shaggy dogs (Afghans and Salukis, probably). But Hounds are nouns, so Columbia naturally stuck the second album's "Do Wah Diddy Diddy" remake on a 7-inch promo EP called, get this, *The Now Wave Sampler*, alongside the Beat, Sinceros, and Jules and the Polar Bears. First album had the Mott the Hooplish "Drugland Weekend" ("Hey city boy, your city looks like someone took a dump"—apparently played for years at 5 P.M. Friday drivetime on Chicago rock radio); "Bad Blood between Us" (starts close to "Blitzkrieg Bop" then gets heftier, and it's about getting into a fight with a "punk," though not a punk-rocker—just a greasy-haired bar creep who won't shut up); and "The Alleys of Love" (teen groupie "doing the pogo" then a recommendation that Jimmy Carter snort cocaine). The "pogo" line suggests Hounds were at least *aware* of punk rock. *Puttin' on the Dog* was, amazingly, even better, despite no less than three '60s British invasion covers—Stones, Kinks, Manfred Mann—a fairly new wave move for '79, suggesting that (perhaps at behest of label A&Rs with Cars in their eyes), Hounds were indeed "Working on My Cool," as side two track one puts it. Yet another song *sounds* like a Brit invasion cover ("Gotta Find a Way to Meet You"), and there's some extremely arch-sounding art-glam called "Spiders" ("can ya do the bug trot or the black widow waltz?") that could pass for 1971 Alice Cooper crossed with 1973 Sparks, plus all these crazy synths that can't decide whether they're new wave or prog or disco. But it's all still superb charging hard rock in the windy Chicago tradition of Styx's heavy early Wooden Nickel albums, peaking back-in-saddle-wise with a bucking disco-metal bronco called "Horses." Robert Christgau ("this is not punk rock") and Dave Marsh ("Woof") *both* hated it! How's that for consensus?

### Yipes!:
### *Yipes!* (Millennium, 1979)

"The members write songs about East Side kids and about girls from Divine Savior–Holy Angels High School," Eddie Finocciaro explained in the *Milwaukee Sentinel* in 1979. "Their writing at times reflects the reckless abandon very evident in '60s rock and now seen in New Wave music." Right on—you can tell Yipes! wanna be new wavers, Wisconsin-style, because despite all their still-blow-dried '70s hair, one of them has oversized glasses frames, a mini-bowtie, and spaghetti suspenders on the LP jacket and inner sleeve, and another one evidently found Dad's old thin necktie. So who cares if Dave Marsh dismissed them as "hard rock tedium, nothing to get excited about": RCA-distributed Millennium Records, also home to fellow also-rans Bruce Cockburn and Chilliwack and Franke & the Knockouts, no doubt had high hopes. Yipes! seem kind of conflicted, though—they do a hilarious ditty called "Me and My Face" about how everybody ("big boys at the rollerdome," "big dudes at the disco," "beach bums in Miami") wants to beat them up, but another where they threaten West Side kids who took their baby away to a rumble on the corner of 42nd and Vine. They also do songs about how both good boys and good girls go bad—like they know from experience! They told Finocciaro they picked the name Yipes! 'cause "we're a cartoon band," and though they're big on class warfare (open the album hoping rich boys turn old and sick and lose their stock-market money), they're also class clowns like the Dictators or Cheap Trick—"Out in California," their surf-garage-with-Sha-Na-Na-harmonies "California Sun" facsimile, criticizes West Coast cars for lacking ceilings, and "Hangin' Around" is about a friend named Jack who buys platform shoes but doesn't fit in at a disco called the Club Detroit, so he gets "unhappy 'cause his parents were white." And then there's the lovelorn border bolero named after Roy Orbison with fake Spanish words ("Ford Grenada, North Korea / Señorita en Córdoba John Travolta"), and this taunting sort of monastery-metal-turned-bouncy-campfire-singalong called "Russian Roll" about how "The Commies are cool, the Commies are square / From Siberia to Leningrad / Their vodka's good but their aim is bad." It's all super-hopped-up technicolor doing-donuts-in-Burger-Chef-parking-lot infectious, too—they don't make 'em like this anymore, and not just because the Cold War ended.

### The Brains:
### *The Brains* (Mercury, 1980)

Atlanta's Brains might be the one band here that critics widely *liked*—"Money Changes Everything," a cynical critique of capitalism corrupting art and romance that Cyndi Lauper later famously covered into a #27-charting 1984 pop hit, has the distinction of being, in 1979, the first independent rock single to finish Top 10 in the *Village Voice* Pazz & Jop poll. It originally came out on a home-grown label called Gray Matter—presumably named for front-brain Tom Gray—and they rerecorded it upon their promotion to the majors, caus-

The Brains: *The Brains* (Mercury, 1980)

ing some to speculate about art corruption for real. So though, say, Robert Christgau awarded the album an A-, he still complained about Steve Lilly-white's heavy production touch and "two atrocious Alfredo Villar songs that would fit fine on a Queen album"—namely, the 5:20 heartbeat-echo-unto-thunder-pomp mood piece "In the Night" and likewise spacious Blue Öyster Cult–riffing martial zoom-crash "Sweethearts." Still, truth is, Lillywhite's metallic edge—applied the same year he produced far better-known albums by Peter Gabriel, U2, and the Psychedelic Furs—gave *The Brains* a power that the band would never match on their (still worthy) 1981 Mercury follow-up LP and 1982 indie bow-out EP, both of which also avoided lickety-split fun-fun-fun technobilly speedboogies like the debut's busy-signal buzzing "Raeline" and breathlessly self-abusing "Girl in a Magazine." "Treason," quite possibly Fake New Wave's greatest instrumental, opens the album conjuring surf-boards, spies, and satellites, and then the noirish intro to "See Me" ensures that nearly four minutes have passed before Gray even opens his mouth. From there, though, he's exasperated all the time, early-Costello-level anxious and nerderrific even when aiming for Springsteen street cool (there's some Warren Zevon in there too), and his electronic keyboard gives the band's rock energy a tangible nervousness to boot, their wires often criss-crossing into perpetual-motion mousetrap machine effects (check out "Scared Kid") like the guys have all been electrocuted by that bolt of light passing through their brains on the album cover. They end with a critique of bohemia called "Gold Dust Kids"—"We like to think of things to say / We like to talk of art"—that may or may not be self-directed. The Brains saw through the bullshit: "If the new way isn't better they say, well at least it's not the same." So were they new wave, or not? They did open for Devo. But then again, Rick Johnson in *Creem* heard them as "a veritable Iron Butterfly for the '80s," and Mercury linked "Money Changes Everything" on a 7-inch promo to songs from Def Leppard and the Scorpions. And guitarist Rick Price wound up playing bass for the Georgia Satellites. You figure it out.

### 4 out of 5 Doctors:
### *4 out of 5 Doctors* (Nemperor, 1980)

Washington, D.C., dudes recording in Miami Beach, all with their shirts unbuttoned an extra button on the album's back cover and ready to board the sailboat or go digging clams, they look really wholesome even if one guy's shoes don't match (and healthier still cooling out in their garage in the inner sleeve photo), but you never can tell. "She's into cold cream, and I'm making bombs in my room / She's like a prom queen, and I'm the prophet of doom / I'm smugglin' firearms, she's readin' *Mademoiselle* / Don't drop the nerve gas, that's not perfume on the shelf"—watch out! That's in the clearly mega-alienated "Not from Her World," the last and admittedly best song on their first album (of two), but there are also forward-looking secret-agent-ring titles on the order of "Modern Man" and "Danger Man" and "Mushroom Boy" that do the Farfisa-of-the-future '70s-prog-nerds-at-the-new-wave-bowling-alley dance like fellow travelers of Rush's and Genesis's keep-up-with-the-Police periods. So that scientist juggling molecules on the front cover totally fits. "Elizabeth" and "Mr. Cool Shoes" dish out some nifty staccato Costello / Joe Jackson angst bop; the segued "Opus 10" (how prog is that title?) / "I Want Her" builds some heavy momentum to end side one. "Waiting for a Change" gets a flute; "Jeff, Jeff" gets a sax. And there's even a number called, get this, "New Wave Girls": "Newspaper panties and pins in their nose," not to mention "knives in their shoes," scary! But just the thing for four strivers capable of having their cake and eating it too, opening for the Clash and Cars on one end of the street and Pat Travers and Hall & Oates on the other. Unfortunately, 4 out of 5 Doctors never managed even the rather fleeting success of their CBS-distributed Nemperor labelmates the Romantics and Steve Forbert. Their ap-

Sue Saad and the Next: *Sue Saad and the Next*
(Planet, 1980)

parent career high point? A bunch of songs performed in a 1983 slasher flick
called *The House on Sorority Row*. Go get 'em, fellas!

## Sue Saad and the Next:
### *Sue Saad and the Next* (Planet, 1980)

Somehow less legit new wave than, say, Pearl Harbor and the Explosions or
Holly and the Italians or Robin Lane and the Chartbusters (all recommended,
by the way), the first and only album by this L.A. five-piece came out on
Richard Perry's Elektra / Asylum subsidiary Planet the same year as the debut
by L.A.'s Cretones, three of whose songs Linda Ronstadt borrowed on her 1980
new wave wannabe classic *Mad Love*. And Ronstadt new wave is kinda what
Saad and the Next (dig that bizzy buzz-bin name!) were aiming for, though the
Pretenders and Pat Benatar (and for that matter the whole '79 Ellen Shipley /
Ellen Foley / Carolyne Mas new-school urban torch-rock thing) also figure in.
Not to mention a little B-52s ("Rock Lobster" riffs in "I Me Me") and Rickie
Lee Jones (seedy back-alley beatnik lamppost lyrics in dark slow one "Cold
Night Rain"). The bassist and one of two guitarists had previously performed
in a "rock musical" but wanted to be in an actual band—L.A. enough? Not

sure if those are the two guys wearing red high-top Chuck Taylors on the cover or not: intriguing contrast to Sue Saad's cowboy boots, either way. Regardless, as tough-gal Faux New Wave corporate hackwork goes, the LP's easily up there with Benatar's first and best two—the rhythm section has oomph galore. On side one, "I Me Me," about how people at parties talk about themselves too much, and the "Walk on the Wild Side" / "People Who Died"–style beautiful-loser roll call "It's Gotcha" pull off sundry tricky changes at nearly punk-overdrive tempos, and "Young Girl" has Saad's mom slapping her face and telling her to avoid boys over AOR ska basslines. Side two opts for Thin Lizzy / Boomtown Rats shamrock-boogie tavern-twang in "Won't Give It Up" and trigger-pulling sex appeal in "Your Lips-Hands-Kiss-Love," then "Danger Zone" closes it all with runaway girls and crosstown boys riding the razor's edge and having heart attacks in the heartland while Saad's singing takes on a bit of Janis growl. Album hit #131 in *Billboard*, and Saad later portrayed a punk-rocker braving a 1996 nuclear war in the 1985 sci-fi thriller *Radioactive Dreams*—just as anybody who had followed her career up that point would've predicted! The movie also apparently featured armed children with weapons, known as the "disco mutants."

### The Fools:
### *Heavy Mental* (EMI America, 1981)

These oft-amusing Boston opportunists actually had a *few* semi-hits, none of them typical of their best stuff: white reggae "It's a Night for Beautiful Girls" got to #67 in 1980; Roy Orbison cover "Running Scared" (at least as good as Nick Cave's version, and a half-decade earlier to boot) hit #50 in 1981; and there was also 1980's poultry-clucking Talking Heads parody "Psycho Chicken," which didn't chart but got its share of *Dr. Demento* airplay. Thing is, none of those really hint at how their initial two probably ironically titled full-lengths, *Sold Out* from 1979 and *Heavy Mental* from 1981, have massively memorable tunes out the wazoo. Best in show on the debut are fraud plan "Mutual of Omaha" (up there with "National Insurance Blacklist" by the Business and "State Farm" by Yazoo as a pinnacle of insurance rock), "Spent the Rent," and "I Won't Grow Up" (titles all clues). Peaks of the aptly weightier-guitared *Heavy Mental* (weightiest in opener "Mind Control" and the sorta psychobilly "Last Cadillac on Earth") are "Around the Block" (one of the '80s' more shattered Stones rips), "Alibi" (guy thinks up lies to tell wife on way home late at night as the band drives fast), and "Dressed in White" (almost–Chuck Berry / Nick

Lowe–level wedding day rock, and also like one of those ubiquitous country hits where somebody's old girlfriend finally marries some other jerk, except funnier and more vicious: "And your dad'll be in a bad mood / And I'll only be there for the food," etc.) The ostensibly in-concert *It's Alive* from 1987, which repeats zero songs from those first two albums and adds three cover versions (Bobby Darin, Simon & Garfunkel, Mar-Keys), is a true *Animal House* toga party a quarter-century after the fact, though less Blues Brotherly when the Fools keep things inauthentic. But their first two—united into a handy CD by EMI reissue imprint American Beat in 2009—are still the real hoot.

### Johnny and the Distractions:
### *Let It Rock* (A&M, 1981)

In their mostly leather-clad little back cover photo, this platoon from Port-landia when Portlandia really mattered (Quarterflash debuted in 1981 too!) just plain look *mean*, and not like they're pretending, either. Johnny and the Distractions is a reasonably new wave name, but their real genre is "badass": like a lager-bottle-smashing gang of pub-rock reprobates from the UK (say the Count Bishops) or Australia (say Rose Tattoo) come back to make blue-collar American powerchord bam-bam that melodically suggests early Bryan Adams or Eddie Money, but bruising with twice as much malevolent punk-or-metal-take-your-pick muscle as those two ever managed—closest cousins might be the Iron City Houserockers, who'd just put out their best album in 1980, but if anything those Pittsburgh lugnuts sound artful in comparison, de-spite a similar bare-fist-with-a-side-of-armpit stench of manual labor: "I ain't got the kind of job to leave a man smellin' clean," Johnny Koonce confesses, wishing he could afford to pay his taxes while braving high Little Richard or Bon Scott squeals. Over a "Boys Are Back in Town" groove in "City Angels," he passes out in his car in Pasadena and tries to figure out how to get back to La Cienega when "all those Spanish boys say no comprende." Gregg Perry's piano boogie-woogies but his organ gets rather fancy, à la the Brains or Pittsburgh's (and A&M's) comparably wave-metal Reds; two guitars race down the main drag playing chicken at sunup. Powerpop never kicked so hard, but new wave-fond A&M probably saw its proliferation as a selling point for this band. Cover just has a sledgehammer slamming down and breaking a safe open, and new wave or not, the Distractions earn it. The fake punks were the real punks now.

—spin.com, 26 April 2013

## Inventing Indie Rock

· · · · ·

Against all odds, 2010 is shaping up to be a real good year for indie-rock albums. Only thing is, the most exciting ones seem to have been recorded 30 years ago.

Matter of fact, I have 10 such platters piled up here, all released in the past eight months, all but a handful of their tracks put to tape between 1977 and 1983, just when technology was making homemade self-releases feasible—as far as "indie" goes, this was the ground floor. All involve artists based in pro-vincial middle-American burgs and 'burbs, away from capitals of entertain-ment and commerce, but only five got entries in 1985's *The New Trouser Press Record Guide*. Most selections have never before appeared in album form: they come from long-gone 45s, EPs, cassette compilations, live tapes lost in the backs of closets for decades, fuzzy mobile-rig-recorded demos. Yet almost without exception, they partake in an energy that puts pretty much any new 2010 indie to shame.

For one thing, most still sound like they're *inventing* something; they're operating in a habitat where "alternative" isn't yet a quarter-century-old marketing concept that's self-defeating by definition. They also represent a moment—a decade or more before grunge broke—when whatever-modern-music-was-called-then neither had been straitjacketed into slamdance nor had ruled out rock-band power, momentum, groove, coherence, and struc-ture as corny and déclassé.

That said, it's notable that a couple acts—two-man art-funksters the Method Actors and one-man art-popster **Kevin Dunn**, both identified with the boho college enclave and proto-indie hotbed of Athens, Georgia—had al-ready abandoned the traditional rock-band format. But while Dunn's *No Great Lost: Songs, 1979–1985* features only one track by his mid-'70s Atlanta band the Fans, it still embraces rock'n'roll enough to include insanely fuzztoned covers of Bo Diddley, Chuck Berry, and "Louie Louie" amid all the herky-jerking Eno loopage. The bands that come off most comfortable in their relationship to pre-punk hard rock seem to be ones who were more or less formed by 1977, the year *Never Mind the Bollocks* came out: suburban Chicago class clowns Tutu and the Pirates; Louisville semi-metal eccentrics the Endtables; Erie, Penn-sylvania's boys'-room smokers Pistol Whip; Akron micro-prog weirdos Tin Huey. Cleveland's even louder Easter Monkeys didn't officially initiate their heavy post-punk psych caterwaul until '81, but guitarist Jim Jones had been perfecting his downer riffs in the Electric Eels and Styrenes almost since the glam days.

The Ohio bands, for what it's worth, had their own boho college enclave and proto-indie hotbed in post-massacre Kent — particularly nutjob virtuosos and longtime one-album wonders **Tin Huey**, whose '78–'79-recorded *Before Obscurity: The Bushflow Tapes* includes a live Stooges cover for Iggy's birthday, yet revels in mixed-and-matched time-changes, sax blats, and raveups owing more to bebop and the Yardbirds (and seemingly Zappa, even if they deny it) than to punk per se. It was compiled by the remarkably reliable little Chicago label Smog Veil, which also put out **Easter Monkeys'** menacing, frequently massive, and (especially when singing about underwear and crucifixion) surprisingly tuneful *Splendor of Sorrow*, along with Ohio-bordering **Pistol Whip's** goofball parking-lot piledriver *Terminal*. For the latter, think pre-punk punks the Dolls, Stranglers, Alice Cooper, Brownsville Station, and especially the Dictators; realize that they have songs called "Six More Inches," "Big Boy," and "Cock Sure," and gauge their usefulness in your life accordingly.

I kinda love them, myself. Same goes for the possibly even more Dictators- (and Zappa- and *Mad*-) damaged **Tutu and the Pirates**, cross-dressing cartoons who crack wise about Son of Sam, Nazis, necrobestiality, zits, janitors, disco, and how Darlene won't give them head on the incidentally hook-laden *Sub-Urban Insult Rock for the Anti/Lectual 1977–1979*. Legend says Tutu's crew introduced punk to Chicago, thus oddly paving the way for their current Factory 25 archive-labelmates **Da–Exclamation Point** (née Da!), whose lunging repertoire on *(Un)Released Recordings 1980–81* is nonetheless considerably less asinine and more angst-ridden, coming as it does from an un-fratty co-ed lineup whose lead yelper, Lorna Donley, sometimes approaches Polly Harvey / Courtney Love territory a decade early.

Donley also, when loosening up a little in Da's kerosene-pyromaniac (see: Big Black) "The Killer" at least, sounds quite a bit like Vanessa Briscoe Hay from Athens's **Pylon**, whose own 1983 sophomore album was recently revived in expanded form as *Chomp More*. Pylon, as all hipster schoolchildren know by now, were all about the rhythm: spare clanking drumbeats, repeated guitar figures, and loud staccato chants that somehow anticipate techno and industrial while referencing funk, surf, and railroad blues. Their indelible 1979 debut single "Cool" / "Dub" was co-produced by the aforementioned Kevin Dunn, who also oversaw the B-52s' "Rock Lobster" and thus helped invent the new wave substyle once known for a couple months as "dance-oriented rock."

Three Endtables, no bed (Photo: Bill Carner)

In that category would also land aforementioned duo the **Method Actors**, whose fractured '80–'81 drum / guitar / vocal workouts on *This Is Still It* come off more severe and mannered than Pylon, but manage to click into volcanic reggae-reverberated harmolodics when allotted sufficient space.

Oddly, it was a less syncopative act from that same Athens scene—R.E.M., featuring Method Actors CD liner-noter Peter Buck—whose murmuring jangle really set indie rock on its ultimate path toward introversion. But it didn't have to turn out that way. In turn-of-the-'80s Kentucky, you might have a band like the **Endtables**, whose superb self-titled collection on Drag City has their gargantuan transvestite frontman Steve Rigot bleating passionately about circumcision, Halloween, and bathtub razor-blade suicides against heroic guitar foil Alex Durig trying to get his Nugent on. Or, in St. Louis, there'd be a band like **Raymilland**, whose *Recordings '79–'81* zip-zaps their science-experiment synth noise and dub-housed axe drones in a manner seemingly trucked down the interstate from the dilapidated North Ohio flats of Pere Ubu and the Bizarros. Pretty impressive that all this stuff was happening around the same time, with barely anybody noticing. Except then, within a few years . . . *pfft.* Whatever you call it, it was on its way out.

—*Village Voice*, 14 July 2010

## Urinals → No Age

.....

In the Grammy-nominated 64-page booklet that housed L.A. noizepop-punkgaze-and-multimedia duo No Age's first-full-album-conceived-as-such *Nouns* in 2008, pages 12 and 13 were devoted to somebody's cassette collection: plenty of metal (Sepultura, Metallica, Iron Maiden, Obituary); rap (Public Enemy, OutKast, Roots, Kool Moe Dee); punk (Dead Kennedys, Black Flag, Subhumans, Germs); alt and indie of sundry other stripes (Fugazi, Ned's Atomic Dustbin, Shudder to Think, several by Public Image Ltd.); a bit of jazz (Miles, Mingus); plus Spank Rock, 2 Live Jews, *The Moishe Dysher Chanuka Party*, *Howard the Duck* soundtrack, etc. Conspicuously absent, given the legacy of subsuming pretty mopey melodies in buzz and blur and fuzz and fur that No Age have inherited: Pavement, Nirvana, Pixies, Dinosaur Jr., Jesus and Mary Chain, Mission of Burma, Hüsker Dü (unless Grant Hart solo counts), or anything on New Zealand's Flying Nun Records. As respective droning in "Defector/ed" and "A Ceiling Dreams of a Floor" on No Age's new *An Object* remind, you could probably trace that lineage back to Joy Division or even the Velvet Underground if so desired. And who knows, given the 1987 all-instrumentals SST compilation that singer/drummer Dean Spunt and guitarist Randy Randall took their project's name from—*No Age* apparently a conflation of "No Wave" with "New Age" in the first place—maybe Paper Bag or Pell Mell or Lawndale, whatever they sounded like, deserve No Age source material points, too.

So: lots of dots to connect, and No Age aren't shy about pointing them out—people call the pair "experimental," but really they're carrying on a tradition that dates back at least to the early '80s they were born in. They've always given as much attention to packaging as music, too; calling their album *An Object* in the age of cloud streams, and designing it to be one, counts as a statement. At any rate, perhaps the band that No Age has worked hardest to identify as forerunners are the Urinals, an obscure (except in circles wherein they're legendary) quintet-turned-trio of nonmusicians initially formed to spoof punk rock at a 1978 talent show in their UCLA dormitory, for which they worked up toy-instrument covers of a Jam song and the theme from the *Jetsons*. No Age covered the Urinals' "Male Masturbation" on a 2008 EP called *Eraser*; a year later, their "sister band" Mika Miko interpreted the Urinals' "Sex" on an EP called *We Be Xuxa* (presumably named for the irresistibly brazen Brazilian bubblesalsa singer and kiddie TV host). Somewhere in there, a revived version of the Urinals wound up occasionally playing—and even collaborating onstage with No Age—at the Smell, the Mexican supermarket turned venue / library / straightedge community center / art-and-vegan-brownie-space in downtown L.A. that incubated both No Age and Mika Miko and that No Age paid tribute to on the cover of 2007's single-and-EP-track collection *Weirdo Rippers*.

Well, "urinals" and "smell" obviously belong together. What makes this confluence intriguing is that the Urinals, at least during their initial incarnation before changing their stinky name to 100 Flowers, released a mere 11 songs—all on 7-inch vinyl. But those tracks, along with a few stray compilation appearances in the next few years, theoretically if inadvertently staked out sonic ground for generations of pop-sweet but abrasively scraping and pogo-worthy bands that materialized in subsequent decades. So it's not hard to trace, say, the staccato scritch of "Lock Box" or spiraling spurt of "Circling with Dizzy" on No Age's new album all the way back to the Urinals' definitive vinyl explosion, 1979's four-song *Another* EP: "Black Hole" (1:18 brain-damaged psych-punk missing link between *Nuggets* and Nirvana: "Fingers clutch my head / Gouge my eyes you want me dead"); "I'm White and Middle Class" (0:54 off-kilter proto-hardcore predating Black Flag's "White Minority" by a year and Minor Threat's "Guilty of Being White" by two while being way less reprehensible than either despite documenting a "pillar of society" who tells you to shove it up your ass while filling out his income tax and also perhaps paying homage to the Urinals' L.A. friends and role models the Middle Class); "I'm a Bug" (1:12 of bongolated drum-intro to Sonics-riffed wise-guy spume as hooky as the Angry Samoans and with entomology about "I've got a stinger / you've got one too baby" to match); "Ack Ack Ack Ack" (1:00-flat intensifying-to-crescendo mantra kicking off with Kraut-motorik noble-savage drum-drum-drum and employing one of history's most walloped hi-hats in service of Johnny's gun shooting you down). The latter, in part thanks to being covered by their early disciples the Minutemen, is probably the Urinals' best-known song.

One could argue that the Urinals' records achieved through expedience, economic necessity, and lack of musical training an underproduced freedom from fidelity that, somewhere along the line—probably as early as Pavement's first few static-saturated EPs, but certainly long before No Age came along—turned into a self-conscious aesthetic objective. In liner notes to the 2005 reissue of *Keats Rides a Harley*, a 1981 compilation on the Urinals' homegrown

Happy Squid Records that set out to document a largely ignored Redondo Beach / Pacific Palisades / UCLA scenelet and wound up roping in rookies the Gun Club and Meat Puppets in the process, producer Vitus Matare remembers recording the band "in garages, bathrooms, or parking structures" on a dirt-cheap 1974 4-track reel-to-reel called the Dokorder 7140, complete with "hokey built-in-reverberation"—a machine that had been banged around for years in car trunks and had parts missing or jerry-rigged and insides sogged to stickiness in spilt beer suds.

To what extent drummer Kevin Barrett, guitarist Kjehl Johansen, and singer John Talley-Jones conceived the Urinals' career as performance art is anybody's guess. Their back-and-forth name changes stem from a logic only they understand, and they tended to obscure band photos "what we do is secret"-style, a negation that lo-fi types like No Age later turned commonplace. But relistening to *Negative Capability... Check It Out!*—a 1997 Amphetamine Reptile retrospective that squeezes 31 archival Urinals performances, including live covers of the 13th Floor Elevators, the Yardbirds, and Soft Machine, into just over 48 minutes—you mostly hear guys trying to rebake rock'n'roll from scratch, which was almost possible back then.

Opener "Dead Flowers," off the Urinals' self-titled 1979 debut EP, suggests they were born as Anglophiles (Talley-Jones has explained that UK stuff was the easiest punk to find in record stores at that point)—sounds like a lost *Pink Flag*–era Wire B-side, and it's even recited in a British accent. The title of "Go Away Girl," a cover of a song by Matare's powerpop band the Last (a group which, in later years, actually included Robbie Rist of late-period *Brady Bunch* Cousin Oliver fame), sounds like Talley-Jones is saying "no wave girl." And though a few stray titles ("You Piss Me Off," "I Hate," "Don't Make Me Kill Again") anticipate slampits to come, the Urinals' berserk forward motion was more twisted than hardcore's ever would be. "Surfin' with the Shah" and "Orange Anal Sin" are razor-wire guitar instrumentals—Link Wray or Ennio Morricone for the New Age of No Wave. There's a lot of surf influence, and even some hillbilly twang—"Sex" and the now-even-timelier-titled "She's a Drone" could almost pass for cowpunk, at least in the very early Mekons or Meat Puppets sense.

No Age, with Jerry Brown the governor of California now just like then, try to turn many of the same tricks beneath their surface noise: surf-punk for sure, being skaters and all, and maybe even some country moves, if their lonely Beckish "truckstop in the middle of nowhere" in *An Object*'s "Running from-a-Go-Go" and the acoustic jangle opening "A Ceiling Dreams of a Floor" count. And good for them—in this world of tribal allegiance, not wanting to be pinned down is a virtue. There's even truth in Robert Christgau's tantalizing 2008 description of their shoegaze side: "Imagine one of Glenn Branca's microtonal symphonies for massed amped-up guitars cut down to two minutes with vocals, chord changes and drums, lots of Spunt's drums." A neat trick—at least 'til you remember that in "Ack Ack Ack," the Urinals performed the same task in *half* that time, with 10 times the humor, three decades before the fact.

—spin.com, 20 August 2013

**2**

·····

**'80s**

**THE TWO SONGS** that most went through my head during weekend Army ROTC field training exercises that seemed to last forever—then during the grueling six-week summer Advanced Camp I almost didn't make it through at Fort Riley, Kansas, in 1981 and the Signal Officer Basic Course at Fort Gordon, Georgia, in late spring 1982—were "Life During Wartime" by Talking Heads ("sound of gunfire, off in the distance, I'm getting used to it now") and "Oliver's Army" by Elvis Costello ("I would rather be anywhere else but here today"). On the other hand, I did eventually figure out that one could lead morning run cadences with verses from Kurtis Blow's "The Breaks." (A skill considered borderline musical in certain circles, by the way. A former servicewoman on one of my ex-units' Facebook page recently remembered that Brian Lange of Charlie Company "called the best cadence. He had a beautiful voice!")

Anyway, once I deployed to Germany and had a job to do, the army somehow really liked me. My September 1983 Officer Evaluation Report (courtesy one LTC James White of the Eighth Signal Battalion): "It has been a rare pleasure having this outstanding young, hard charging officer in my battalion. 2LT Eddy has completely turned around a floundering platoon and made it into a first class outfit. . . . Rarely have I seen a junior officer make such a major contribution to unit readiness in such a short time." That would've been the same month we hit the field for Reforger 83, which culminated in Able Archer, which almost caused a nuclear war; otherwise, army life in Germany was only occasionally similar to Tom T. Hall's "Salute to a Switchblade." Two years later, LTC Smith of 1/59 Air Defense Artillery: "Lieutenant Eddy clearly has the potential to excel in any assigned position. His expertise in Communications-Electronics is unsurpassed. His decision to leave the Army and pursue a civilian profession is a loss to the Armed Forces." After that I spent a few lame-duck months as commo officer in Sixth Cavalry at Fort Knox, Kentucky; got promoted to captain before the door hit me on the way out; then shifted to said "civilian profession," which was . . . what again?

Oh, yeah—writing about music. Some "profession," huh? I sure had Uncle Sam fooled. Actually I'd started moonlighting at it while still a man in uniform; my running joke has always been that everybody in the army figured I was a communist because I wrote for the *Village Voice*, and everybody at the *Voice* figured I was a fascist because I was in the army, though lately I'm wondering whether I just made that up. But facts are stupid things. By the time I got out, Reagan was back for sloppy seconds, a development I'd already lamented in a callow *Voice* piece called "A Soldier's Story" upon his reelection that previous November. So I came home to Morning in America, which mainly meant waking up from the American Dream.

In 1981, Reagan had taken office in January and MTV had gone on the air in August while stagflationary recession kicked in and sax solos filled the air, or at least decorated excellent hits by Quarterflash, Foreigner, and Rick James. In 1982, Musical Youth's surprise reggae crossover "Pass the Dutchie" and Kid Creole and the Coconuts' "No Fish Today" made a party out of hunger (paving the way for Eddy Grant's surprise reggae crossover "Electric Avenue" in 1983 and the Earons' astro-funk "Land Of Hunger" in 1984), and you could hear desperation and doldrums from Grandmaster Flash's "The Message" to

Bruce Springsteen's *Nebraska* to John Cougar's "Jack and Diane" to Hank Williams Jr.'s "A Country Boy Can Survive." The music industry wasn't doing so great, either—Cougar's and Asia's blockbuster albums couldn't sell half of what R.E.O. Speedwagon's blockbuster album had the year before—and the record companies blamed it all on home-taping, with a little help from video games.

MTV, Michael Jackson, and the mostly Brit-synthed silly-haircut stuff labels had begun branding as "new music" spurred a recovery in 1983, though (Robert Christgau wrote a prescient *Voice* essay about it at the time called "Rock'n'Roller Coaster: The Music Biz on a Joyride"), and by 1984 commercial and creative impulses were in confluence like never since. Meanwhile, the industry figured out its best bet was high-end consumers buying high-dollar items—the suits first pushed CDs at audiophile and classical markets, but a million Dire Straits fans were on board by 1985, and the format soon proved a handy way to resell music people already owned: "nostalgia justified by technology," Ken Tucker called it, hitting a bullseye. By 1986, as L.A. duo David & David put it in "Welcome to the Boomtown," all that money was making such a *succulent* sound. Their fellow yuppie one-hit-wonder folk-pop twosome Timbuk 3 caught the zeitgeist, too: "A job waitin', after your graduation—fifty thou a year will buy a lot of beer."

The economy was growing, inflation down, employment up, *Top Gun* in the theaters—Triumphalism all around. "Annual record sales continue to fall," a piece in Detroit's *Free Press* read as 1986 ended, "while CD sales climb faster than the industry expected." The future was so bright that upwardly mobile grown-ups who could afford shiny digital discs had to wear shades, and the music got super-tasteful, usually over the same antiseptic cocained-studio drum pulse, even in Van Hagar's hard rock. "With CD production due to catch up to consumer demand in 1987, and with hardware prices continuing to drop, just about anybody can be a yuppie, at least in terms of sound," Richard Harrington observed in the *Washington Post*. "You've got the brawn, I've got the brains," the Pet Shop Boys chimed in. "Let's make lots of money."

Me, I did a lot of interviews, way more than I've done since. In this section I talk to Leeds, UK, anarcho-post-punk rustics the Mekons, for instance (then get cranky about what they turned into), but the two giants are the Beastie Boys at the moment they broke big and Aerosmith on the eve of their big comeback. They get name-checked in each other's profiles, too, and weirder, they both covered the Beatles' "I'm Down" in '86–'87, though only Aerosmith released theirs. As of this writing, though, the Beasties' rendition, along with two other outtakes my feature names—a "Scenario" that preceded A Tribe Called Quest's and a "Desperado" trailing the Eagles' and Alice Cooper's—can be heard via YouTube. (That site also has actual hotel room break-in footage, if you search "Beastie Boys Prank Home Movie." I can be seen center of screen at 1:19 of Hüsker Dü's "Makes No Sense at All" from the same era as well.)

At story's end, Adam Yauch, who'd only live until 2012, wonders to me if they'll "die doing this." The Aerosmith album wound up titled *Permanent Vacation* of course—maybe I just heard them wrong?—and wound up not only the beginning of their second platinum term but the end of their tenure as one of the planet's great hard rock bands. I lost interest in the Beasties pretty soon after, too—still love "Sabotage" and a few *Paul's Boutique* cuts, but first time they rhymed "commercial" with "commercial" I was pretty much outta there, even if they did become more moral human beings, not to mention introduce my youngest son Sherman to the hip-hop (and, even more so, graffiti) that's obsessed him ever since.

Both features ran in *Creem*, famous for a tradition of rude irreverence that enabled me to cross a line or two in ways that now make me cringe. No excuses, though I was pretty young at the time (I've got *kids* older now), which undoubtedly also explains my astonishment at Aerosmith being ancient relics in their late 30s(!), if not the extent to which I underrated the hair band Cinderella, whose *Long Cold Winter* holds up as well as any rock album of the decade. In fact I probably underrated hair metal in general at first, only to overcompensate later. I also underestimated how much I'd wind up listening to the Pet Shop Boys' *Introspective* over the years (not to mention, apparently, how much Chris Lowe contributed to their sound) in the piece I include about them. And calling hip-hop a thing of the past in 1987 should strike most readers now as nuts; almost three decades later, I still find sustainable quantities of it to enjoy every year. But I still love the early stuff most—see my 2012 "Old Old Old School Rap" Sonic Taxonomy column from *Spin* in a few pages. So okay, I'm the real ancient relic here, obviously.

One very early piece that didn't make the cut (partly because my college newspaper wanted to charge me $50 to include it, and partly because it wasn't all that great) took University of Missouri–Columbia's student radio station KCOU to task in 1981 for ignoring pretty much all black music that wasn't reggae, jazz, a decade old, Joan Armatrading, or the Bus Boys. And KCOU was entirely typical—even when Prince and Michael Jackson and (with Aerosmith's help) Run-D.M.C. eventually broke MTV's color barrier later in the decade, they never really broke AOR's. As for music critics, they'd been favoring Caucasian music in real time for decades—in his 1982 Pazz & Jop essay, Robert Christgau anointed swing-focused '30s *New Republic* pundit Otis Ferguson "the first rock critic," then pointed out that a recent anthology by him gave 13 times as many pages to Bix Beiderbecke as Louis Armstrong, and six times as many to Benny Goodman as Duke Ellington. (Frankly, I hope nobody ever subjects my own books to such math—sometimes the most important artists aren't worth writing about because they've already been written about so much!) On the other hand, Elijah Wald spends a lot of time in his 2009 *How the Beatles Destroyed Rock 'n' Roll: An Alternative History of American Popular Music* spelling out how 20th-century music historians have stayed blind to contributions of Paul Whiteman and Guy Lombardo and Lawrence Welk despite their popularity and influence in their time. But I'm still astounded to come across something like the rock magazine *Fusion*'s 1969 readers' polls for the best '60s records—in the singles tally, no black artists show up until the bottom of the list, where the Four Tops' "Reach Out I'll Be There" and Love's "She Comes in Colors" (if that counts) place #39 and #40—several notches below the Buckinghams' "Don't You Care," which I never realized anybody cared about. Among albums, a Hendrix LP places #5 and Love's *Forever Changes* #31, and that's it. (There were also polls for "Best '60s Drug Song" and, uh, "Best '60s Chick Song," the latter meaning songs *about* women, not by them.)

Those were just readers, again. But maybe some of them turned into writers later—the highest-finishing black album in the *Village Voice*'s 1978 Pazz & Jop poll was Funkadelic's *One Nation under a Groove*, at #27. R&B and hip-hop artists have steadily gained ground in critics' surveys ever since (faster than metal and commercial country artists, not to mention Latin artists, at least)—partly thanks to more black writers, though the '80s certainly opened some ears. But some prejudices stay ingrained. "Black pop is generally a lot less interested in the concept of divinely-inspired individual than the typical white rock critic," Bart Bull suggested in a 1983 Pazz & Jop comment, so "Prince will always have a better shot . . . than the more typical Gap Band / Cameo / Kool & the Klique funk-R&B aggregation." Seven years later, as the '80s ended, Nelson George complained in the same space that "the best R&B classicism (Luther Vandross, Frankie Beverly) and techno-funk (right up through new jack swing) was ignored by most white critics, who either couldn't make qualitative distinctions or deemed these records 'too professional' or 'bourgeois,' disdaining the basic truth that, for those who made the music, bourgeois professionalism was a long-desired goal." Hence, George said, critics also privileged "attitude over form" by opting for "Ice-T and the obnoxious N.W.A" over "radio-friendly entertainers" like Heavy D and the D.O.C. and Regina Belle whose "popularity is based not on what they say, but on how they execute."

Whether I'm guilty of those sins is for somebody else to determine—attitude and form don't always split into such a tidy dichotomy, and I loved Schoolly-D's both. Hip-hop started to lose me late in the '80s partially because it's important for black music to maintain its self-respect and not just clown around for white dorks like me who want to dance, so rappers like Rakim came along and put the emphasis on serious mastery of technique just like Charlie Parker had with jazz decades before. (This happens to white genres, too—think prog rock, or thrash metal—but in African American culture the stakes seem a lot higher.) Here in the 2010s, with N.W.A in the Rock and Roll Hall of Fame and the Spinners and War unlikely to ever join the club, I'd take grown-folks R&B by Kindred the Family Soul or Charlie Wilson or select K. Michelle, Justine Skye, K'Jon, and Jidenna singles (not to mention piles of southern soul ones) over divinely inspired individuals Kanye West and D'Angelo. And I rounded up "Unsung '80s R&B Bands" in a *Spin* column too, and darn right I included Frankie Beverly's Maze. That'll start off this section proper, in just a second.

First, though, a note on what ends the section: namely, an overview of '80s music I published in the Musicland retail chain's now decades-defunct house organ *Request* in January 1990, years before selective nostalgia and long-term collective memory loss reduced the phrase "'80s music" to some barely recognizable caricature of some shrunken fraction of it. (The FX network's *The Americans*, set in the Reagan years and sneaking in stark and shadowy semi-hits from aging '70s classic rockers keeping pace in an era of electronic new wave, does a good job, at least. And Mark Ronson featuring Bruno Mars's massive 2014/'15 hit "Uptown Funk" at least cannibalized reams of that unsung R&B, not to mention George Kranz's "Din Daa Daa" from my German new wave roundup—which article also preceded SundanceTV's Luftballons-inspired *Deutschland '83* by four years.)

Much of the *Request* essay now reads as misguided: When, for instance, *wasn't* capitalism rock's best buddy? Why did I care if country singers wrote their own songs? Why did I think respectability would kill rap and metal? What did I have against Skafish, whose cranky super-schnozzed 1980 new wave weirdo debut LP I still pull out now and then? Which side of Prince's *Dirty Mind* did I think was just okay, again? Also: a flippant dismissal of boho avant-punk that ignores Art Bears, Hi Sheriffs of Blue, Propaganda, Savage Republic, Virgin Prunes, engrossing exceptions galore; not a word on one of my favorite '80s mini-genres, the Caribbean-lilting British low-fat funk of Linx, Imagination, the Quick, Junior, and Chas Jankel. And as an earlier John Anderson piece also hints, blue-eyed-souled '80s country from Razzy Bailey and Earl Thomas Conley did not reveal itself to me until decades later. But at least I sort of predict ambient techno toward essay's end—not to mention "classic rap" radio, which within a quarter-century, according to the *New York Times* Business section and Sunday magazine circa 2014/'15, was one of the nation's hottest new formats. And above all, at least I got my thoughts down, for once—never wrote a decade manifesto like that again. My writing sure was confident back then. Even arrogant. But sometimes I miss having such a know-it-all at my beck and call.

## Sonic Taxonomy: Unsung '80s R&B Bands

· · · · ·

The most radical turn in rhythm & blues history was the shift—in the '80s wake of disco, early rap, Prince, Michael Jackson, and innovations in sampling and studio technology—away from self-contained bands who carried their road sound onto records. This development effectively ended an R&B tradition you could trace back through P-Funk, Sly and the Family Stone, James Brown, Louis Jordan, all the way to Louis Armstrong's Hot Five in the '20s at least. Of course, it's easy to get stupidly nostalgic about the loss of "real musicians playing real instruments"—and it's not like last-band-standing the Roots have made better music than everybody else on the planet in the past quarter-century. Plus, R&B had always had other traditions anyway—label house bands from Motown to Sugarhill, producers shaping dance sounds, singers and vocal groups backed by session hands. Still, it's enlightening to focus on the last decade that actual bands helped rule black popular music. Chic, the Time (whose albums were mostly played by Prince anyway), Cameo, and the Gap Band you should already know about; Washington, D.C., go-go combos like Trouble Funk probably deserve their own separate category. But who knows—even Joe Carducci might approve of the eight '80s albums below. If you can't be rockist about R&B, what can you be rockist about?

**Fatback:**
*Hot Box* (Spring, 1980)

Named by drummer Bill Curtis for a jazz rhythm named after the cut of pig-meat responsible for pork rinds and slab bacon, and with high-cholesterol funk to match, this Brooklyn ensemble put eight albums on the *Billboard* 200 between 1976 and 1982; this, their highest, peaked at just #44, and zero of the 30 or so singles they placed on the R&B chart between 1972 and 1985 crossed over to the pop Hot 100. In the '70s, those included songs about doing the bus stop and doing the Spanish hustle and (four years before Frankie Smith's "Double Dutch Bus") doing the double dutch; in 1979, they got the foresight to put a rapper on their record, and "King Tim III (Personality Jock)" beat "Rapper's Delight" to the racks by several months. Supposedly, Fatback were past their peak by then ("on the downward spiral" and not loved much by MCs up in the Bronx, David Toop reports in his early hip-hop history *Rap Attack*), but you'd never know it from the excellence that is *Hot Box*. The title refers to the big portable radio on the cover (maybe too cheery-looking to blast the ghetto—and the subway graffiti on the wall isn't too convincing either—but they were trying), and also to a certain female body part in the big-bottomed title track. "Love Spell" drips just as much juicy groove, but on side two they move beyond mere funky filler, starting with two Top 10 R&B hits: the partly cartoon-rapped "Gotta Get My Hands on Some (Money)," embracing an old-school early-Reagan recession theme that nobody talks about much any-more—see Prince Charles and the City Beat Band's "Cash (Cash Money)" or Divine Sounds' "What People Do for Money"; then the farty-keyboarded "Backstrokin'," about swimming, tennis, massage, your choice. Then Fatback close with the awesome "Street Band," with lyrics about Harlem kids making summer beats with whatever junk's on hand, chanting that picks up on both naughty playground rhymes ("bang bang spoon spang") and the rope-a-dope Ali/African bent of certain subterranean '70s disco, and horns that feel like a throwback to Mardi Gras parade jazz.

**Maze featuring Frankie Beverly:**
*Joy and Pain* (Capitol, 1980)

Just as joyous as Fatback, but way more spiritual and less grimy, gospel-and-doo-wop-bred Philly transplant Frankie Beverly's Oakland septet Maze were another black band too uncompromising to cross over to white fans: seven of the 10 albums they put on the *Billboard* 200 between 1977 and 1994 wound up in that chart's Top 40, but they never scored a pop hit higher than #67. Every studio album they released landed in the R&B Top 10 and went gold, but none went platinum. Yet like their apparent role models Earth, Wind and Fire, there was something curiously prog about Maze: both in Sam Porter's fancy electric piano and synthesizer doodling in tracks like the instrumental smooth-fusion workout "Roots," and in their album covers, which almost always featured their giant cosmic hand-maze logo and often added mystic topographical vistas—on the back of 1978's *Golden Time of Day*, the band's on a snow-covered mountain plateau; the cover of 1979's *Inspiration* is even more an interplanetary tundra, almost worthy of a Finnish doom-metal gang like Amorphis. As for the musicians, they all look like middle-aged African American dads; on *Joy and Pain*, only guitarist Ron Smith lacks facial hair, and lead tenor Beverly is of course wearing his ubiquitous baseball cap. The seven band members' credits on the cover catalog grown-man values they care about: "love," "strength," "warmth," "fire," "inspiration," "gentleness," "soul." The music? Gorgeous, utopian, a nonstop relaxed groove secure in its manliness, embracing "Family" and "Happiness" (two song titles), assuring a mature audience that they'll survive these "Changing Times" (another one—most uplifting song on a hugely uplifting album), acknowledging that life comes with both "Joy and Pain" (another—sampled eight years later, in the same-named Rob Base and D.J. E-Z Rock hit). In his 1988 book *The Death of Rhythm and Blues*, Nelson George pegs Maze as pioneers of both "quietstorm" and "retronuevo" R&B and praises Beverly's "working class" refraction of Marvin Gaye, particularly on 1981's also superb double-vinyl *Live in New Orleans*: "He sounds like a dedicated husband still madly in love with his wife after all these years." In other words, as reliable as his band.

### Slave:
#### *Showtime* (Cotillion, 1981)

Slave—from Dayton, Ohio, home of the Ohio Players—also had arena-rock in their genes. Their audacious name shoved American history in your face, long before Prince wrote the same word on his; the cover of their 1977 debut album showed a shirtless black man carrying a giant globe on his shoulders. But their first few albums took hard rock guitars into account, in a much more blue-collar, less artsy-fartsy-Zappafied way than, say, Funkadelic did. Robert Christgau, in 1977, even compared Slave to "third-generation" Middle American prog bands like Kansas and Starcastle. And on 1981's *Showtime*, which rightly seems to be the consensus choice as their most solid album, they even put an arena on the album cover: an outer-space one, no less, with the stage under a glass pyramid. But sonically, they'd toned down their rock side through the disco years. Visually, too: on the back of that '77 debut, they look like street toughs and sweathogs, with impressive afros; on *Showtime*, they're upwardly mobile, spiffy in sports jackets that won't upset the doorman. Three members had just left to form the group Aurra; lead vocalist / percussionist Steve Arrington, after this record, would leave to form Steve Arrington's Hall of Fame and find Jesus Christ. *Showtime* is "dedicated to allah for the Concepts of Pure Growth!!," but post-1981, both spinoff bands would make much better albums than Slave would. Here, though, Arrington gives bassist Mark Adams's muscular throb a more consistent sense of melody than it ever found before. From opener "Snap Shot" (about taking a girl's picture—for the cover of *Life*, not porn) to closer "Funken Town" (presumably about Dayton), these are actual tunes, even when they are just chants. And the funk is the no-nonsense kind—even when the chants are nonsense.

### Vaughan Mason and Crew:
### *Bounce, Rock, Skate, Roll* (Brunswick, 1980)

Not all '80s funk bands were '70s holdovers. In February 1981, Michael Freedberg wrote a great essay for a now long-forgotten paper called the *Soho News* about a now long-forgotten urban street genre called "strut": "The strut is as much rhythm from the bottom up as disco was about people of the bottom rising to the top." A few 12-inches mentioned in the piece are early rap; several others might intersect with the kind of post-disco electro-funk that DJs later labeled "boogie." But the primary focus of "Struttin' with Some Belly Laughs" was an Atlantic City DJ named Vaughan Mason, who had gone #5 on the R&B chart in 1980 with "Bounce, Rock, Skate, Roll," an eight-minute disc designed for roller discos ("Rrrrrrrrrock . . . SKATE! Rolllllllllll . . . BOUNCE!"), built on a Chic bassline but booby-trapped with multiple conga/bongo/hi-hat/ Moog-bass breaks where the musicians improvise while skaters can shuffle in line or spin. The song was immediately sampled by rappers Trickeration in "Rap, Bounce, Rockskate" and has been put to use since by everyone from L.L. Cool J to J.J. Fad to Daft Punk. In 2005, the Lil' Bow Wow movie *Roll Bounce* took its name, among other inspiration, from the song. Two other long tracks on Mason's rarely heard LP ("Roller Skate," "We're Gonna Funk You Up") show his band taking similar extended rhythmic feints and dodges, often with whistles, handclaps, wails, and "baby-bubbah" baby-bubbah"s spooned in; sometimes, it sounds like the birth of house music, which later in the '80s Mason would reinvent himself for, under the moniker Raze. "Cravin' Your Body" is more tribal and blurry and ominous, reminiscent of '70s black rock bands like War or the Jimmy Castor Bunch; "Thinking about My Baby" is six minutes of drippy piano mush, about which the less said the better. (Liner note: "This album offers Funk, Ballads and Roller Skating music"—another lost genre!) The four guys on the back cover (out of eight musicians credited in the notes) are a sight: dark-skinned and light-skinned disco dudes trying to look cool; a taller dude with pimp hat actually looking cool; and a very skinny dude with long snaky dreadlocks looking like a serene wise man. According to the Freedberg essay, that one's Mason, and "onstage he wears a boa constrictor and wishes he was Alice Cooper." Freedberg claims the Crew's hit is "the most reggae-influenced funk cut ever to get over," with negative space worthy of dub; he traces strut's self-deprecating aesthetic back to "the cakewalk in early jazz." Nobody else ever picked up on those ideas. But imagine if somebody had?

### Skyy:
### *Skyway* (Salsoul, 1980)

"Nor are the house party revelers of Skyy's 'Skyzoo' or Grandmaster Flash's 'Freedom' ashamed that when they blast from their kazoos it comes out as babies squalling through pacifiers," Freedberg wrote in that same strut piece. Odd pairing, still possible in pre-"Message" days: acclaimed ground-floor hip-hop originator with a co-ed octet from Brooklyn, eventually known mainly for 1981's super-cute Top 30 pop bubble-funk hit "Call Me," where you root for a girl trying to steal her girlfriend's boyfriend even if that makes her a jerk. The earlier and much stranger "Skyzoo" really did have a kazoo hook wafting through (hence its name), not to mention wacky repeated call-and-response ("Whatcha wanna do?" "I wanna play my skyzoo!"), Jimmy Castor–style troglodyte grumbling, and other disco reference points. It showed up on Skyy's second album, the title of which you're forgiven if you confuse with *Skyyport*, *Skyy Line*, *Skyyjammer*, and/or *Skyylight* (their third through sixth). Included among Skyy's eight members were two mustachioed white guys and three singing Dunning sisters (the most zaftig of whom, Bonny, commendably gets the center spot on *Skyway*'s back cover); nonmember Randy Muller, who had '70s bands B. T. Express and Brass Construction on his résumé, did most of the producing/arranging/writing. But really, the group's bass-plucking, string-surging sleekness was a testament to how much Chic had changed black pop. And the first half of *Skyway* is relentless, reveling in low-register fuzz, Captain Kangaroo / Mr. Green Jeans namedrops, and swiped '70s novelty hooks ("Car Wash" / "In the Navy" handclap beats, direct quotes from Castor's "Bertha Butt Boogie" and Daddy Dewdrop's "Chick-a-Boom") over variations on the Chic formula. Side two, in comparison, is a perfunctory but functional coast until the closer, "Music," where cowbells, guitars, and wolf howls conjure the '70s rock definition of "boogie" while one of the Skyy guys fends off a bill collector trying to repossess his Cadillac, blue jeans, and cowboy boots: this ain't no disco. Later ("Miracles," 1982) one of the Skyy gals would learn to do a sweet Michael Jackson; for now, this'll do.

### Kleeer:
### *License to Dream* (Atlantic, 1981)

More post-Chic New Yorkers—nine of 'em, this time, dressed to the nines too, but once again including three lady singers and two white men with mustaches. And like Big Apple Band alumni Nile Rodgers and Bernard Edwards themselves, Kleeer had a '70s past playing (allegedly) hard rock: Pipeline, they were called then. You can totally hear remnants of that in the two side-closers of *License to Dream*, the most middling-successful of the three '80s albums this band charted: "Hypnotized" kicks off with a Grand Funk cowbell, then turns into a kind of Santanafied Latin blues with robotic proto-Italodisco shy-girl backup; "Where Would I Be (without Your Love)" is pop funk verging on yacht rock. But those are nothing compared to the two longest cuts: the 8:17 "Get Tough," where the players stretch out their buttery jam around comic mimicry of the recently buried John Wayne (three years before "Rappin' Duke"), and especially the 7:22 "Running Back to You," where Woody Cunningham's hypermasculine blues/soul/gospel testifying counterpoints wild percussion breakdowns and offhand synth squeals. Cunningham heartily throws down in opening theme track "De Kleeer Ting," as well, and the band pushes hard and fast for this genre—think "Chic Cheer" gone thrash, almost. Except they do soft good, too: the ballad "Sippin' and Kissin'" is way above funk's why'd-they-slow-down norm, and "License to Dream" is a lush ode to positivity that builds like it senses deep house music over the horizon. So no way will you mix up Kleeer with Klique or Klymaxx, right?

## Champaign:
### *Modern Heart* (Columbia, 1983)

Is this even an R&B band? Well, they did have two Top 10 R&B singles, both wedding-ready ballads, both pop crossover hits, both pure swooning, cascading genius—"How 'bout Us" in 1981 (which also went #1 Adult Contemporary), then "Try Again" in 1983 (which is here, and if it won't persuade you to patch up your relationship like nothing since "Reunited" by Peaches & Herb, you were born with no soul). On the other hand, Champaign are such clueless midwesterners they named themselves after their hometown (always a danger sign)—Champaign, Illinois, also home of R.E.O. Speedwagon! European ancestry seems to strongly dominate within the sextet's lineup, and they are extremely fond of lite Caribbean lilts that they seem to have picked up straight from either (1) Culture Club and Haircut 100 videos, or (2) some band that had a residency in the Terre Haute Ramada Inn cocktail lounge, or maybe (3) Lionel Richie (though "All Night Long" was still a few months away, so maybe not). One of their more island-riddimed things is even called "Cool Running," a decade before that movie about the Jamaican bobsled team! And they follow it with this doo-woppish sort of Manhattan Transfer finger-snapper called "Walkin'," which nonetheless manages to build momentum and get taken to church at the end. Side one thus complete, side two then bridges two fluffy ballads with two new wave robo-funk ditties (all the rage in '83—even Shalamar were doing it on *The Look*), the last of which derides "the toys of multinationals." Champaign, Illinois: weirder than you think!

## The Deele:
### *Material Thangz* (Solar, 1985)

But of course the guy who really brought new wave into R&B—and arguably the guy most responsible for the death of R&B bands, given his tendency on record to play most instruments himself—was Prince. The mid-'80s saw zigzaggy ideas that Prince picked up from the Cars or Devo slipping into black pop across the board, and not many did it better than this last-ditch Cincinnati five-piece. They dressed hip, too: skinny ties, Jheri curls, bright collarless shirts. Pencil-mustached guitarist/keyboardist/vocalist Kenny Edmonds, on

The Deele: *Material Thangz* (Solar, 1985)

the cover, could almost pass for Thin Lizzy's Phil Lynott if not for his plaid smoking jacket (nothing underneath, natch) that looks almost the same as the one El DeBarge wore on the cover of *Rhythm of the Night* that year. Edmonds was appropriately in charge of DeBarge-type vulnerable falsetto croon songs; the Deele would get a Top 10 pop hit with their loveliest one, "Two Occasions," three years later, perfecting a changing-seasons motif he instigates on this album's "Sweet November." Slow ones, though, aren't what *Material Thangz* is about, which might partly explain why it was by far the least lucrative of their three albums even though it was probably their best. "Let's Work Tonight," "Stimulate," "Sweet Nothingz," and the title track are irresistibly elastic and boisterous machine-funk, working the kind of rubber-band beats and sarcastic asides that Prince had concocted on *Controversy* but had already mostly shelved by *Purple Rain*; poor-guy/rich-girl rom-com "Material Thangz" itself also seems to nod to Madonna (who'd just scored with "Material Girl" a few months before), and "Suspicious" aims the gothic-horror-sound-effect paranoia that Michael Jackson was ruling the world with at a crafty lady stealing their stuff. Distrustful Deele tracks like that one also feel like blueprints for New Jack Swing and producer-driven pop R&B to come—which seems apt, given that Edmonds would revive his Bootsy-granted nickname Babyface before long, and he and Deele drummer L. A. Reid would soon be creatively charting R&B's future at LaFace Records and beyond. Bobby Brown, Boyz II Men, Paula Abdul, TLC, Mary J. Blige, *The Bodyguard*, Mariah Carey, Pink, Rihanna: on their way. Bands? You had your day.

—spin.com, 6 December 2012

## Country Rap: The '80s

· · · · ·

### Trickeration:
### "Western Gangster Town" (1980)

Evidently named after some Cab Calloway jive, this mysterious B-boy pair made only one 12-inch, short by 1980 rap standards—each side fits both songs. "Rap, Bounce, Rockskate," less than five minutes slung atop Vaughan Mason's almost identically titled roller-disco jam "Bounce, Rock, Skate, Roll," partially concerns a restless country cousin who moves to the city and learns to skate. But "Western Gangster Town," a mere 3:27, is cowboy rap's Rosetta stone, not to mention probably the first "gangster" rap (four years before Schoolly D's "Gangster Boogie"): Disco Rick visits an old-time burg where everybody carries guns; after the clock strikes high noon he smokes cheeba with a fly young lady in a house of ill repute. When her 6′4″ boyfriend walks in upstairs, Rick presses a gun to his head, but the big guy remembers seeing him onstage in Tennessee, "and you're the baddest MC since Deadeye Dick," so everybody gets out alive. Then Basic warns city kids from experience about doing jailtime for ripping off subway passengers. There's way more packed in, and the backing groove feels downright earthy, but the disc does its business quick, and it's as propulsive as old-school—maybe any school—ever got.

### Malcolm McLaren:
### "Buffalo Gals" (1982)

The original "Buffalo Gals" was a blackface number from 1844; Mark Twain called it "rudely comic," it proved geographically flexible (listed as "Charleston Gals" in 1867's abolitionist-assembled but misleadingly named *Slave Songs of the United States*), and it never went away: Homer Simpson even sang it once. Malcolm McLaren, the P. T. Barnum of punk rock, typically passing off hucksterism as anthropology sometime between appropriating mbaqanga and Madam Butterfly, borrowed the ancient minstrel standard's title in 1982 as a frame for conflating World Famous Supreme Team turntablism with square dance calls: go 'round the outside, do-si-do your partners, all that scratchin' makin' you itch. On his 1988 compilation *Buffalo Gals: Back to School*, McLaren says he'd personally discovered hip-hop in 1980 by running into Afrika Bambaataa ("huge black guy — massive man"), who was wearing a Sex Pistols shirt on a Harlem street. Who knows if that's reliable; what's undeniable, though, is that on whosampled.com the list of records since incorporating "Buffalo Gals" contains well over 100 entries: Beastie Boys, Neneh Cherry, Cypress Hill, Eminem, J Dilla, Madlib, Schoolly D, Skee-Lo, Snoop Dogg, Weird Al Yankovic, on and on to the break of dawn and then some.

### The Bellamy Brothers:
### "Country Rap" (1987)

Shamelessly harmonizing Florida Sunbelt-billy siblings Howard and David Bellamy might not have been the only country act to rap in the '80s, or even the first — check out, for instance, most of 1982's *The Bird* by Jerry Reed, though to be fair he was already pretty much rapping before rap existed. Ricky Skaggs's 1985 "Country Boy" video even featured kids breakdancing to bluegrass on a New York subway (not to mention Ed Koch lip-syncing). But the Bellamys were more blatant about it — "Country Rap" wasn't just a #31-country-charting single; it was the title track to their #21-country-charting 1986 album. Hey, why not? They'd already had a hit called "Get into Reggae Cowboy," right? And their rap had a tangible backbeat, albeit not far from the swampy one Jim Stafford had stuck under his huge pop version of David's "Spider and Snakes" in 1973. They rhyme about what they know, or pretend to know: farm animals, soul food, pickup trucks, redneck girls, rowdy bars, cows for sale. "An unlikely hybrid," Walter Carter opined in the notes to the Bellamys' 1989 *Greatest Hits Volume III*, "combining the traditional country concept of 'recitation' (rapping) with a decidedly hip urban form." Well, sort of.

### Sir Mix-A-Lot:
### "Buttermilk Biscuits" / "Square Dance Rap" (1988)

Seattle's big buttman did not come from the South, but he sure sounded like it sometimes. Even beyond their hick shtick, these two tracks from his debut album *Swass* are the kind of late-period cartoon-voiced robo-rap usually associated with Miami. Sir Mix is repeatedly called a "cotton picker" (evoking not just the South, but the plantation), and we are told the following locations "rock": Seattle, L.A., Miami, D.C., Carolina, Houston, London, and Your Mama. Before that, and before a B. B. King sample and some human beatboxing but after complaints about "everybody rappin' 'bout welfare line," a yee-hawing yokel instructs us to grab partners' derrieres where the sun don't shine and do-si-do. The likewise hillbilly-toned "Buttermilk Biscuits" instead recommends grabbing some lovin' while said biscuits are in the oven, eating them with KFC, and, most audaciously, "From L.A. to Carolina / Drop them suckers in Aunt Jemima," thus referencing in one fell swoop both breakfast syrup and one of America's most enduring racially stereotyped figures—a full 99 years after Missouri newspaper editor Chris Rutt heard the probably African American–composed minstrel song "Old Aunt Jemima" performed in red-bandanna drag by a blackface duo, whereupon he trademarked the name for his pancake mix.

—spin.com, 30 April 2013

## Sonic Taxonomy: Old Old Old School Rap Albums

· · · · ·

No one knows when rap started. Maestros like Kool Herc and Grandmaster Flash imported sound system basics to the Bronx from the Caribbean through the '70s, but there were eons of antecedents—reggae toasters, jazz scatters and jivers, radio DJs, comedians reciting dirty poems on party records, drill sergeants shouting out cadences, Muhammad Ali, Bo Diddley, griot vocal traditions that probably arrived via the Middle Passage on slave ships. Routines that sound at least as much like "Rapper's Delight" as "Rapper's Delight" sounds like what we call hip-hop in 2013 were seemingly a staple of black vaudeville and black and white minstrel shows at least back to the early 20th century—Pigmeat Markham, whose late-'60s rhymed funk-talk records "Here Comes the Judge" and "Who Got the Number" are full-on rap in all but name, had begun performing in the 1910s and unveiled his judge shtick onstage way back in 1929; Emmett Miller, who recorded a surreal but unmistakable rap duet called "The Gypsy" in 1936, was as much the end of a line as the beginning—a drastic throwback to a blackface minstrel tradition that had existed, in some form or other, for nearly a century before he first recorded in 1924.

Still, it took until 1979 for rap to be recognized as a recorded music genre. And even then, it was the music of 12-inch singles (and block parties and disco gigs, even more so) for years—or at least that's always been the accepted truism; Wikipedia's list of "Important Rap Albums" starts with Run-D.M.C.'s debut in 1984, pretty much universally accepted as the disc that finally broke the longplayer code. Sure enough, many important early rap artists—Spoonie Gee and Afrika Bambaataa, for starters—didn't release full-lengths until years later. Reissues like Soul Jazz's 2005 *Big Apple Rappin': The Early Days of Hip-Hop Culture in New York City 1979-1982* and Stones Throw's 2004 *The Third Unheard: Connecticut Hip Hop 1979-1983*—not to mention retrospective comps from labels like Enjoy, Sugarhill, and Tommy Boy—are still the easiest places to discover stacks of amazing old-old-old school stuff. That said, several rap albums did in fact come out before 1984: Sugarhill Gang had three; the female trio Sequence had three; Philly double-dutcher Frankie Smith had one; Too Short, way out in Oakland, put out his first cassette in 1983. Here are eight that both beat Run-D.M.C. to the racks and stand the test of time.

### (Various):
### *The Great Rap Hits* (Sugarhill, 1980)

Sugarhill, run out of Englewood, New Jersey, by seductive-soul-novelty veteran Sylvia Robinson of "Love Is Strange" (1957) and "Pillow Talk" (1973) fame, was arguably not the first great rap label—its best early groups started out on Enjoy, then jumped over. But starting with the ad-hoc-concocted Jersey trio Sugarhill Gang's "Rapper's Delight" in 1979, Sugarhill was undeniably the first label to figure out how to turn this urban African American folk idiom into mass culture that might play in Peoria—and the imprint did it by letting golden voices and hearts of steel ride one of the most polyrhythmic house bands ever assembled. Early on, Sugarhill put out two similarly titled six-song compilations of classic singles. *Greatest Rap Hits*, from 1981 (sometimes called *Vol. Two* to distinguish it, though on my German pressing copy those words are nowhere on its cover or label), is maybe less flawed, given three essential Grandmaster Flash tracks, including the unparalleled prototype scratch mix "Adventures on the Wheels of Steel." And Funky Four Plus One's 1981 "That's the Joint"—quite possibly the most exhilarating record in the history of the human race, with five 17-year-olds thrusting the beat by swerving the beat and passing off lines behind backs like Globetrotters while lady plus-one Sha Rock rock-shocks the whole darn place—makes their 1980 "Rapping and Rocking the House" sound in comparison like the merely mind-blowing rough draft it was. Plus, on the 1980 set, the latter is chopped down to 8:30 from its 16-minute Enjoy 12-inch version; "Rapper's Delight" gets abbreviated as well (to 6:30 from the original 15-minute endurance test), though you still get chicken rotting into something that looks like cheese.

Nonetheless, in retrospect, *Great Rap Hits* might be the more fascinating document. Spoonie Gee—a bridge between the hardest blues and hardest gangsta rap—and Sequence—ring-a-ding-ding-ding-donging and yodeling and channeling Millie Jackson and referencing Yogi Bear and Fred Flintstone—did their best stuff early; "Rapper's Delight" might be less legit than Sugarhill Gang's later "Eighth Wonder," but pop culture has never forgotten the former for very good reasons. Most mysterious on *Great Rap Hits*, though, are two artists nobody talks about anymore, both linking directly to a tradition of jive-rhyming radio DJs who laid groundwork for rap. Super Wolf—from Jackson, Tennessee, and it's hard to find anything else about him—howls like the son of Wolfman Jack and awkwardly tries to keep pace with the bass; actual Philly radio jock Lady B, though, sounds incredible, with a ragged, creaky hitch in her rasp, and boasts about rocking the dead with two turntables in her casket and (her man?) busting out sweet young girls. "I'm not Perry Johnson or Butterball," she tells us, naming two classic Philadelphia black radio personalities, the latter of whom put out his own unbelievably prescient rap single, "Butterballs," around 1967. Worth noting, by the way, how many of these early Sugarhill acts were *not* from New York—Sequence, for their part, started out as cheerleaders, then a singing group, in Columbia, South Carolina. One of the three, gospel-trained Angie B, grew up to be better known as neo-soul artist Angie Stone.

## Kurtis Blow:
### *Kurtis Blow* (Mercury, 1980)

If any rap album set the bar Run-D.M.C.'s debut aimed for, it was this one—and not just because they both include versions of a recession rap called "Hard Times" and both have hard rock crossovers with Eddie Martinez taking badass guitar solos (Blow's cover of Bachman-Turner Overdrive's blue-collar bison burger "Taking Care of Business" thereby presaging both "Rock Box" and Run-D.M.C.'s later and bigger Aerosmith cover). Joseph "Run" Simmons had even started out onstage in 1977 as Blow's actual junior sidekick, opening for groups like the Commodores. Blow had put out four albums by 1984, all on the major label Mercury, where he stayed through most of the '80s. His biggest hit, "The Breaks," is basically a comedic catalog of things that go wrong in life (think Alanis Morissette's "Ironic," only way funkier) that also succeeds at applying a more conventional verse-chorus-verse structure to early rap's motormouth sprawl while punning on the title with super-percussive timbale and tom-tom breaks. The party line's always been that the rest of the album is mostly filler, but that's baloney—almost *every* track, even the BTO cover, gives Blow's crack combo time for instrumental breakdowns, and that's not all the songs do. "Rapping Blow (Part 2)" strings together readymade rhymes and even a Village People reference in masterfully random style, and hands it over to extended piano, pinpointing Harlem rap's roots in Harlem jazz; "Way Out West" is a propulsive cowpoke yarn predating both Trickeration's "Western Gangster Town" and Kool Moe Dee's (and, uh, Will Smith's) "Wild Wild West" over spaghetti western guitars clearly indebted to the old-schooler-beloved '70s prog-rock band Babe Ruth; "Throughout Your Years" builds aspirational advice atop barrelhouse salsa-woogie keyboards that sound surprisingly like hip-house eight years early; "Hard Times" moves from proto-"Message" social concern to proto-human-beatbox scatting and bandleading that pays homage to James Brown, whose records Blow had spun as a mobile DJ before rap pioneer DJ Hollywood converted him to hip-hop. There is one mushy ballad attempt—*one*—and it's no mushier than scores of rap ballads since. Respectable batting average, as this genre's albums go.

**(Various):**
*Live Convention '82* (Disc-O-Wax, 1982)

Hip-hop was live music years before anybody vinylized it, but though shows were sometimes taped and passed around in cassette form, recorded evidence of the early club experience has always been preciously scarce to come by. In the early '80s, though, an obscure label called Disc-O-Wax put out two records, subtitled *Bee-Bop's #1 Cut Creators*, that stick you smack-dab in the middle of the action at T Connection in the Bronx. (The collector site Discogs actually lists a few more volumes—allegedly recorded from 1977 to 1980—that appear to have been released in Japan in 2008; whether these are the real deal or not is a subject for future research.) The '82 edition is chaotic, to say the least—no "songs" per se; each side plays continuously from start to end without track breaks. But they also never let up. The headline act is Grand Wizard Theodore—a DJ, not an MC—and the lengthiest rap parts hype him;

MCs come and go haphazardly and usually not audibly announced, though Busy Bee and the Treacherous Three's L.A. Sunshine make appearances, and there's a lengthy roll call of other guys "in the house" (K. K. Rockwell, Master Rob, Starski, Stylee, Ernest D, Shorty Block, Key Jump, Ruppy Rup—or at least that's what it sounds like their names are). Theodore opens with an awards show presentation nominating *Shaft in Africa* (supposedly off a 1973 album by Masterfleet), then slices up disco breaks from Rufus Thomas, New Birth, the Chicago Gangsters ("gangsta boogie, gangsta boogie!"), and who knows where else while voices rap about lemons-to-a-lime and "we got one Puerto Rican and the rest are black" and "I'm DJ Bust-A-Nut, in your face and in your butt" and zodiac signs ("Libra! Sell ya cheeba!") and female audience members of differently colored clothes ("young lady in yellow got a faggot for a fellow"—boycott if necessary). The scene grows wilder and more dangerous, then lightens up toward the end for a bunch of slogans from '70s TV commercials (Sugar Crisp, try it you'll like it, valley of Jolly Green Giant, can't believe I ate the whole thing, Charley loves my Good and Plenty), often recited mock hillbilly style. Finally, there's some turntabled porn moaning. Whole dang thing leaves your head spinning.

**(Various):**
*Wild Style* (Animal, 1983)

Grand Wizard Theodore also spins on this soundtrack to Charlie Ahearn's graffiti-obsessed grassroots cult flick—supposedly the first hip-hop movie ever made. And while neither the film nor the album were technically documentary projects, lo-fi production values and off-the-cuff performances—for instance, a nearly a capella fingersnapped "Stoop Rap" from Double Trouble, a.k.a. Funky Four Plus One alumni Rodney Cee and K. K. Rockwell—sure make the record *feel* like a raw sequel to Smithsonian Folkways' *Street and Gangland Rhythms: Beats and Improvisations by Six Boys in Trouble*. Theodore starts off with his basic-training-shooting-range-inspired "Military Cut—Scratch Mix" ("ready on the right, ready on the left, ready on the firing line"), then there's an MC battle and a crew battle, the latter preceding a basketball game. The Cold Crush Brothers and Double Trouble get live tracks, the latter reprising some lines from "That's the Joint." (The 1994 Cold Crush reissue *Live in '82*, incidentally, is exhausting but educational; Discogs lists a couple Funky Four Plus One CD collections of questionable legality, plus a curious split French album with the Crash Crew, but good luck tracking copies down.)

Later, there's also a galaxy-scratching amphitheatre performance by Rammell-zee and Shock Dell with Grand Mixer D.St., probably recorded before Ram's insanely influential gothic futurist 1983 graf-beatnik rap "Beat Bop." There's violence in a lot of this album's lyrics—N-words, MF-words, talk of sleeping with guns and "walking through the jungle with a stick in my hand" in case you get jumped—that belies misconceptions of early '80s rap as teacher's-pet party pap. And there's noise in the sound, too—a distorted fuzziness loudest in "Fantastic Freaks at the Dixie," muffled background chants intoning "down by law" out of nowhere—that might well be the inspiration for the Beastie Boys' "A Year and a Day." Can't beat that with a stickball bat.

### Grandmaster Flash & the Furious Five:
### *The Message* (Sugarhill, 1982)

With isolated exceptions like "Adventures on the Wheels of Steel" and "Flash to the Beat," Grandmaster Flash mostly didn't appear on his group's own records; in their most famous song, the cautionary street-to-jail-noose opera "The Message" itself, the Furious Five members who aren't Melle Mel barely show up either. Their debut album omits their first several singles, three of which had been collected the year before on *Greatest Rap Hits*, and another two of which—incomparably dexterous and energetic in the way they traded off vocal lines to push the rhythm—were both called "Superrappin'" and both came out on Enjoy. Melle Mel's verse from one of those, in fact, served as the basis for "The Message" itself and did an even more powerful job the first time. Little of which bodes well for this LP, but somehow they got one of rap's first great pop albums out of it regardless. Yep, pop—first song kicks off a sort of Rick James tribute with a Jimmy Castor sample; second one has group members introducing themselves in five distinctly buoyant and often humorous voices ("I'm Cowboy, the real McCoy, chocolate all over like an Almond Joy") and Melle Mel rapping in French over the Tom Tom Club's "Genius of Love" beat. Then they hitch their Vocodered Zapp-rap move to a zodiac sign title from Dennis Coffey and sound both bubbly and avant-garde doing it; then a Spinners update about how kids are the future, which doesn't feel so positive once preachers and teachers start making the future sound horrible since we'll never stop dropping bombs. Then side two: sweet pop-funk dedicated to Stevie Wonder ("Hey Flash, do you think we'll ever meet Stevie?"—album notes by the way give thanks to "the creator God, our parents, Mrs. Robinson, Martin Luther King, Jr., Stevie Wonder, Rick & Tina, Sugar Ray Leonard and

Grandmaster Flash & the Furious Five: *The Message*
(Sugarhill, 1982)

Muhammad Ali," Tina presumably being Teena Marie); some absolutely sincere talked-not-rapped piano gospel for Jesus from Rahiem (in all the ladies' dreams), one of at least two Fivers blessed with surprisingly agile singing voices; then "The Message" itself: "Broken glass everywhere, people pissing on the stairs, you know they just don't care." Synth riff worthy of their R&R Hall of Fame induction on its own. "Subterranean Homesick Blues" cadences. "HUH-huh-huh-HUH-huh-huh." You know the rest—or should.

## Treacherous Three:
### *Whip It* (Sugarhill / Vogue France, 1983)

This album, from one of early rap's supreme groups, barely exists in history books. AllMusic Guide doesn't know about it. It never came out in the States, and I might well be convinced by now that I'd dreamt it if I didn't hang onto the copy I bought in a Frankfurt record store when it briefly appeared in 1983. Still sounds relentless, though, and as good-natured as any rap—almost any *any*—album ever has. The Treacherous Three were Special K, L.A. Sunshine, Kool Moe Dee, and DJ Easy Lee. You might remember Kool Moe Dee for the top-notch albums he made at the end of the '80s, or at least for the report card he put inside one of them where he graded rappers (Beastie Boys 70 C, Run-D.M.C. 82 B-, Kool Moe Dee 95 A+, ha ha). Anyway, for a couple years there, the Treacherous Three could do no wrong; only problem with this album is that it showcases only six of their first eight singles, and 1980's "The New Rap Language" with Spoonie Gee—still one of the fastest raps ever—is missed. Shortest song here lasts 5:36; four check in above 6:58. The opener is 1980's "The Body Rock," and the most important word in its title is "Rock," which means the same thing it would in "Rock Box" a couple years later. "Feel the Heartbeat" and "Whip It" flip their tricks over grooves from Taana Gardner and the Dazz Band, the latter with a soothing guest vocal (rap meets R&B, already!) from the Spinners' Phillipe Wynne. "At the Party" literally sounds like it's at one; "Action" is as wholesome an orgasm metaphor as you'll hear. But the masterpiece is "Yes We Can Can," which takes off from Lee Dorsey via the Pointer Sisters, laments the evils of stagflation and Reaganomics and racial inequality ("eve of destruction, tax deduction, price inflation rocks the nation, unemployment's on the rise, and if it lasts like this for a long enough time won't lead to nothing but a higher level of crime") but gives b-boys some strong, and strong-voiced, big-brother suggestions about how to weather it: even if they want to join the Army to escape the ghetto where hoodlums with knives try to take their lives, see, they'll need that diploma to enlist. Bootstrap rap, so scoff if you feel the need. But can they rock it from the east to the west? Yes yes yes, yes yes yes.

**Jonzun Crew:**
*Lost in Space* (Tommy Boy, 1983)

Given the ubiquity of his Kraftwerk / Yellow Magic Orchestra–inspired arcade-rap spaceship "Planet Rock" in 1982, not to mention his stature as a big-thinking conceptualist in general, it's perplexing that Afrika Bambaataa didn't manage a full album until 1986. Nowadays, that's no problem; Tommy Boy put out a retrospective called *Looking for the Perfect Beat 1980–1985* in 2001 that'll get your Bam party started right. But in 1983, you would've just been happy that the British label 21 included two of his best singles on *The Perfect Beat*, an archetypal electro-hop sampler that also had a few by Planet Patrol and Jonzun Crew. Those two entities' own albums weren't bad, either— Planet Patrol, masterminded by Arthur Baker and John Robie, were an interesting mishmash of Temptations rips, Gary Glitter and Todd Rundgren covers, proto-Latin freestyle beats, and shout-rapping à la Run-D.M.C. (who had put out their own first single, "It's Like That," in early 1983). As for Jonzun Crew, based in Boston and led by future Peter Wolf collaborator Michael Jonzun with major input from future New Edition / NKOTB svengali Maurice Starr, some at this point might dispute their inclusion in a rap survey at all. But in 1983, so-called "electro" had not yet split off from "rap" or "hip-hop"; they were all in the same tent—David Toop included this album (along with *The Perfect Beat* and the Street Sounds UK comp *Electro*) in the short rap-album discography of his indispensable 1984 old-school history *Rap Attack*. He also reveals that the Jonzun Crew's wiggy image was "based on a black composer who gave proto multi-media concerts in Europe in the 18th century." As for the robotics, they're clearly on a continuum leading from "Planet Rock" to Maggotron's early Miami bass. "Space Is the Place" and "Pack Jam" obviously owe debts to Sun Ra (thanked on the LP cover) and, well, Pac Man. But "Electro Boogie Encounter" precedes apparent allusions to David Bowie's "Space Oddity" with astro-beats Newcleus seem to have swiped in "Jam on It" a year later, and the irresistibly goofballish "Space Cowboy" has actual rap bragging (aimed at "all the hip-hoppers") amid its Morricone swipes and yodel-ay-hee-hoos. Hip-hop forgets such fun at its own peril.

### Whodini:
### *Whodini* (Zomba, 1983)

Seems like, by the time Brooklyn duo-plus-DJ Whodini showed up on the scene, hip-hop had pretty much staked its claim as global pop culture. Of course, the tug-of-war between mass commerce and urban authenticity was never fully decided—its tension is part of what's kept the genre vital in decades since—and the dichotomy was too simplistic in the first place. But in the case of Jalil Hutchins, Ecstasy (the cat in the Zorro hat) and Grandmaster Dee, none of that mattered. They made videos (the one for "Magic's Wand" is said to be rap's first ever); they worked with techno-pop dweeb Thomas Dolby (the "Blinded Me with Science" guy); they recorded in London and Cologne; they hit with a Halloween novelty, "Haunted House of Rock," that owed a lot both to oldie-station funnybone favorites like "Monster Mash" and "Dinner with Drac" and to "Thriller." Note the song's title—calling it "Haunted House of Rap" would limit crossover potential, and though its breakdance hooks are synthed, not guitared, Wolfman Jack and the Grateful Dead provide party entertainment. (There's also a crazy chick called Voodoo on a Stick.) "Rap Machine," perhaps inevitable after years of soul-radio sex and love and dancing machines, is partially rapped by an actual mechanical man—amusing in the video—even if humans prove victorious in the long run. And Dolby-produced debut shot "Magic's Wand" itself was made to promote sometime rap-moonlighting WBLS DJ Mr. Magic, who later (in 2009) died of a heart attack even though the song's lyrics take pains to distinguish that ailment from rap attacks and Big Mac attacks. "Rappin's always been around," Whodini tell us, "It's just that it's big time now"—true on both counts. Though who knew then how big it would stay?

—spin.com, 22 February 2013

## Public Enemy Do the Punk Rock

• • • • •

Hip-hop advanced from its unrecorded, urban folk-culture origins into the mass media nearly a decade ago, and it's inevitably begun to take on self-conscious art-world trappings. So we get "significance" flags, "content" flags, "innovation" flags. And as the fight against the powers that be turns more specific, making hip-hop "intellectually okay," it also risks pretension.

Yet so far, as a whole, our boogaloo buckaroos and turntable tacticians just keep getting harder, meaner, funnier, smarter. The top acts rap all the way to the bank as their increasingly race-and-class-aware anger and dread and escape impulses turn supposed commodification on its pointy little head. For a sound constructed on the idea of musical collapse, the street beat has allowed for more expansive disruption than punk ever did; it's impossible to keep up with all the sublime one-upmanship out there. No other pop style has produced even half as many rewarding records in 1988.

One of the best, and in more ways than one the most insurrectionary, is Public Enemy's *It Takes a Nation of Millions to Hold Us Back*, a disc whose building-burning turmoil and eccentricity aspires to an unprecedented depth and scope. To say that rage this pronounced is now rare in black (or any other color) rock is an understatement—Chuck D's Black Power slogans and turntable-terrorist Terminator X's coagulated rhythmic-noise lumps aim to foster outright ghetto hostilities. Public Enemy's intellectual-manqué funk makes for more alarming agitprop than anything the Last Poets or Linton Kwesi Johnson or Gil Scott-Heron or the Minutemen ever managed.

Like the post-apocalyptic *Mondo Manhattan* of their honky NYC homeboys Chain Gang, *Nation of Millions* is a live-and-studio pastiche that mixes all sorts of blare into some bulging basslines and bedspring beats, as well as crowd clatter, chilling caws and cackles, spoken-word snatches, backwards-symphony scratches, and incidental electronic buzzes at migraine frequency. *Nation of Millions* has its duff tracks, tool-and-die time-outs, half-baked experiments. You could end the album midway through side two and lose nothing. Still, compared with the group's loud but lethargic debut, *Yo! Bum Rush the Show* (notable for too much loose talk about firearms), it's a godsend.

Chuck D, a self-proclaimed "rhyme animal" who bellows as if his butt were corked and throws his mouth around like a fist, still tends to sacrifice rhythm for his scrunched-up rhetoric; when he proclaims in "Bring the Noise" that "Beat is for Sonny Bono / Beat is for Yoko Ono," he's wrong. His own outfit needs some too. No surprise that *Nation of Millions'* most mesmerizing cut, "Cold Lampin'," belongs to Flavor Flav, the jabbering speedo-soliloquist who plays Baba Louie to straightman Chuck's Quickdraw McGraw. "Cold Lampin'" is high-stepping and hard-swinging mumbo-jumbo, "live lyrics from the bank of reality," pouring gravy on graveyards and picking teeth with tombstones and blurting Cab Calloway's "Zah Zuh Zah" into the domain of *Trout Mask Replica* and the Hombres' "Let It All Hang Out."

The rest of the LP is more somber. Public Enemy are black-supremacist bohemians dealing the rebellious gesture, middle-class cheerleaders severing their college-man ties by identifying with an underclass that might well not want them around. Their onstage entourage wear Special Forces uniforms and carry Uzis. In interviews, their black-might forebears' paramilitary Semite/homo/female-phobia comes home to roost.

*Nations of Millions'* platform asserts in the same breath that Louis Farrakhan's a prophet, J. Edgar Hoover conspired against civil rights, "false media" (that which Chuck D doesn't agree with) shouldn't exist, black radio's too white, bad reviews are a bummer, and "Who gives a fuck about a god-damn Grammy?" You know Public Enemy are punk-rockers, 'cause they bitch about rock crits and airwaves so much. Chuck D wants to "reach the bourgeois, and rock the boulevard"; that way, you can meet his pit bull.

Amid all their references to Coltrane, Clinton, Scott-Heron, Malcolm X, Martin Luther King, Marcus Garvey, the Temptations' "Cloud Nine," David Bowie's "Fame," and Isaac Hayes's "Shaft," Public Enemy reveal their primary fantasy: they wanna get tossed behind bars, the way they are on the LP cover, because then they can bust out of Cell Block Number Nine. Chuck D repeatedly imagines himself arrested for sedition, plagiarism, draft resistance, you name it. In the righteously long-winded "Black Steel in the Hour of Chaos," he's locked up for refusing involuntary servitude in the army of "a land that never gave a damn about a brother like me."

Sometimes, the politics is so pharisaic it's funny. One of my favorite Public Enemy editorials is "She Watch Channel Zero?!," big-time woman-hating that poses the "leisure culture is the opiate of the masses" fallacy over genocidal Slayer riffage, concluding that the love-in-the-afternoon audience ain't revolutionary enough, especially when it keeps Flavor Flav from seeing the Super Bowl. There's more commitment than analysis here, but superficial or not, the dogma's what keeps it exciting.

—*Boston Phoenix*, 12 August 1988

## Beastie Boys: Lay It Down, Clowns

· · · · ·

At 32 minutes past two on the morning of 16 January 1987, two Beastie Boys broke into my West Hollywood hotel room and dumped a wastebasket of extremely wet water on my head, my bed, the carpeting, and my Converse All-Stars. (I'd stupidly left the chain-lock unsecured, and I suppose they bribed the night clerk into giving them a key.) Earlier that evening, after Pee-Wee Herman had visited their dressing room and before they appeared on Joan Rivers's show, the Beasties were tossing parsley at me, dropping ice cubes in my hair, and "dissin'" (graffiti-artist lingo for "saying bad things about") my brown socks and flannel shirt. I interpreted all of this to mean that they did not like me.

But I don't feel alone. Just days before, they'd been evicted from the Sunset Marquis for throwing chairs out their window into the swimming pool. And that week, they'd also become the first group ever to be censored on *American Bandstand*—Dick Clark, who'd put up with Johnnies Rotten and Lydon in past episodes, apparently decided that Adrock's mid-song crotch-grab was just too much. The Beasties had previously been banned from the Holiday Inn chain after they'd cut a hole in the floor of one suite to serve as a passageway to the one directly below; they'd been banned from CBS Records headquarters after allegedly ripping off a camera at a label party. And MCA brags that he punched a *Bay Area Music* interviewer in the face not too long ago. These guys are total jerks, and they've got the fastest-selling debut album in CBS history.

MCA, real name Adam Yauch, says he's skimmed through *Hammer of the Gods*, a book that depicts Led Zeppelin's early career as one massive, Satanic orgy, complete with fishing for sharks out hotel windows and siccing the prize catches on baked-bean-marinated groupies. "It happens that we are living up to that reputation, but it's not intentional," MCA tells me. "We respect what they did. They were the only band that never buckled under to their label, and they sold more records than anybody." Beastie Mike D, whose stage handle is shortened from Michael Diamond, is wearing a *Houses of the Holy* T-shirt. The first noises you hear on the Boys' *Licensed to Ill* album are John Bonham's drums, lifted from Zep's mega-swing classic "When the Levee Breaks." I ask Mike D what his favorite LP of 1986 was, and he answers *Led Zeppelin IV.*

Upon arriving in Los Angeles to meet the most famous Caucasian rap trio in the history of Western civilization, I found that their record company has sent a limousine to the airport to pick me up. I'm talking one of those huge black ones where the celebrities can look out but the peons can't look in, and of course I've never even *touched* one before, and I thought it was obscene. The driver gave me the scenic route down to Sunset Boulevard, and he pointed out Engelbert Humperdinck's abodes, and we passed UCLA. The driver showed me this monument made of four white columns at the top of a small hill. He said Al Jolson was buried there.

Like Gigolo Al, and like Bob Wills and Elvis Presley and the Rolling Stones and the disco Bee Gees as well, the Beastie Boys are white people making what is supposed to be black music. Like Jerry Leiber and Mike Stoller, who wrote all of the Coasters' hits and whose "Girls, Girls, Girls" MCA claims did not influence the group's very similar "Girls," and like the Dictators, whose *Go Girl Crazy* anticipated punk and whose White Castle infatuation MCA claims had no effect on his crew's own sliders-by-the-bag fetish, the Beasties are young middle-class Jewish males chronicling the dilemma of urban-American teen hooligancy. Or rather, in the Beastie Boys' case, half-Jewish. "Purely coincidentally, we each have one Jewish parent," explains MCA. Adrock and Mike D, now 17 and 19 years old respectively, grew up in Manhattan; MCA, 20, comes from Brooklyn Heights. MCA and Mike D "have been friends forever and were boys together," MCA says; Adrock, a.k.a. Adam Horovitz, met the other two in junior high school. Noted playwright Israel Horovitz, Adrock's dad, left home when the Beastie was a baby. MCA's first criminal act was setting a print shop on fire.

"All the kids from our high school listened to Deep Purple, crap like that," Mike D says. "When you see that shit it doesn't make you want to go out and play it." Yauch, Horovitz, and Diamond opted for the (then) unpopular alternative, dying their hair orange or shaving it off, checking out the Stimulators and Sham 69 at New York clubs, and eventually starting their own hardcore squads.

"Everyone we knew was in a band," Mike D says. "That's what was cool about punk." The original Beastie Boys comprised Yauch, Diamond, and two more; Horovitz's band, the Young & the Useless, would open shows. Eventually, the combos merged. After releasing the 7-inch *Polly Wog Stew* EP on the Rat Cage label in 1982, lured by a Gotham rap subculture that seemed to parallel punk in the do-it-yourself-music department, the Beasties decided to expand their horizons.

"We went into the studio and recorded 10 songs, and we did the song 'Cookie Puss' as a joke," MCA remembers. "We were making fun of Malcolm McLaren, and the whole downtown art scene that was exploiting hip-hop." A poor mix caused eight tunes to be shelved, but "Cookie Puss" came out as a 12-inch single, backed with a rasta-toasting / Musical Youth parody called "Beastie Revolution." The A-side was a seemingly sexist and racist stylus-scratch rendering of a pornographic phone call to an ice cream sandwich store, and it turned out to be 1983's funniest novelty record. Rick Rubin, a club jockey whose band, Hose, did grunge-metal versions of Ohio Players and Rick James numbers, heard the disc and liked it. Beastie gigs gradually evolved from "a lot of new wave Wild-Style Burner Style music with the turntable next to the drum riser" (sez MCA) to all-the-way-live rap, and Rubin produced 1985's awesome "Rock Hard" / "Party's Gettin' Rough" / "Beastie Groove" EP. The record kidnapped sections outright from AC/DC's "Back in Black" and Zep's "Black Dog." The Beasties chanted, "I'm a man who needs no introduction / Got a big tool of reproduction."

Furthering their ironman-funk synthesis on the "Soundtrack from the Video 'She's on It'" single, and helped along by a distribution deal Rubin's Def Jam Records had established with CBS, the trio burst onto MTV in late '85. A year later, after a summer of opening for the suddenly huge Rubin-produced Run-D.M.C., the Beasties were bonafide stars; within six weeks of its release, *Licensed to Ill* had already sold over a million copies and was kicking its way up to the Top 20. If you go to high school or live in a college dorm, you most likely know the thing forwards and backwards by now. *Licensed to Ill* has pushed rap into the whitest corridors of America's heartland, and (along with D.M.C., Metallica, and the Rubin-produced Slayer) has made the future safe for dangerous teenage music, a form that seemed to have died. CBS, concentrating on

Beastie Boys: *Licensed to Ill* inner gatefold (Def Jam, 1986)

Bruce S. and Michael J., has an unexpected blockbuster on its hands. And the Beastie Boys are playing their 15 minutes of fame to the hilt. "Five years from now I might be selling used cars on the lot," MCA says. "I really don't give a fuck, 'cause I'm having so much fun now."

For example: I'm at the hotel, as are members of the Beastie entourage, which consists of Sean, their hepcat British manager; Hurricane, a brawny DJ who carries lots of gold junk around his neck; Cey, who has known the Beasties since childhood and now serves as roadie and astrologer and all-around nice guy; and Eloise, an overweight go-go dancer who's supposed to look "sexy" when she strips down to her black lace, I guess, but mostly just comes off as gruesome. The Beasties aren't there, and the limo driver says it's time to leave for the Rivers show. All of a sudden a luxury machine burns rubber around the corner, just missing the limo, and skids to a halt in front of the hotel gate. MCA jumps out and runs inside, and Adrock takes the wheel even though he's never driven a stick-shift before. MCA's done doing what he was doing, and the treacherous three are ready to go now, but they're not riding in the limo; they've just rented a Town Car after getting bored with a Ferrari and a Rolls, and they don't want their dollars to go to waste. "We ride three in the front, you in the back," Mike D tells me. "That's the rule."

The limousine goes first, and we follow. The auto I'm in is manned by derelicts: MCA's wearing a wrinkled long-sleeve white button-down, a black leather jacket, and a five o'clock (or five-day, maybe) beard-shadow; Adrock has an "Appalachian Basketball Camp" shirt, a red Texaco baseball cap, and a light-blue windbreaker; Mike D, skinnier, and nerdier-looking than his cohorts, has a gold Volkswagen pendant, black horned-rim glasses, and an earring. Their jeans have holes, their Nikes lack laces (some new fad, I think), and I'm no queer but I know that these are not the prettiest men I've ever seen. Anyway, we're chasing the limo, and Metallica's "Battery" is blasting from our tapedeck, and the dudes in front of me are banging their heads toward the windshield as if they constituted one organism. They release their seatbacks so they can ride horizontally, they "accidentally" bump bumpers with the limo a few times, they shout catcalls at the usual feminine suspects. ("Before we were successful we used to stand at the streetcorner and yell at girls," Mike D later informs Joan Rivers. "Now we can sit in a Ferrari and do it, and it's a lot more effective.") And they doo-wop along with the cassette, which plays the Coasters, Elvis, Roxanne Shante, Marvin Gaye, ? and the Mysterians, Stevie Wonder, and—as a tribute to their adolescent homeboys, I gather—Deep Purple.

Afoot in our land is disillusionment like has not been seen since the Watergate years. For the generation weaned on Danny Bonaduce, awakened by Haldeman, Ehrlichman, and Dean, and enlightened by punk and its progeny, this disillusionment casts doubt and cynicism on not only our leaders, but also on the mass media that stimulate our national mood. Be a sourpuss and call it premature nostalgia if you need to, but the current interest in early '70s rock is no retreat; fact is, punk promised more and then failed more miserably than any other rock'n'roll ever has. When Redd Kross covers Kiss, when "Walk This Way" goes Top 10, when the Golden Palominos hire Jack Bruce, it's not retreat—rather, it's a necessary return to unfinished business. If the Sex Pistols never happened, we'd probably be better off than we are now. And if the Beastie Boys don't come right out and say this, their record certainly implies it. To me, the most amazing thing about *Licensed to Ill*'s success is the youth of its audience. That children of the '80s are buying it proves how universal its ideas are. Because to get all of the details, you have to be a child of the '70s.

As I've said, Bonzo slapping his drumkit starts off the thing. But before the vinyl's been exhausted, we've also heard musical or verbal snippets from Black Sabbath's "Sweet Leaf," Zep's "The Ocean," War's "Low Rider," Steve Miller's "Fly Like an Eagle" and "Take the Money and Run" (plus they did a cool a cappella "Joker" during the Joan Rivers rehearsals), Brownsville Station's "Smokin' in the Boys Room," Aerosmith's "No More No More," Creedence's "Down on the Corner," and some Barry White tune whose title eludes me. It's no accident the record starts with a song called "Rhymin' and Stealin'"—the oeuvres of Bill Haley and Bobby Fuller and Kurtis Blow and Schoolly-D are plundered, too. But *Licensed to Ill* isn't just about creative in-joke robbery; if it was, it wouldn't be worth much. All those borrowed bits and pieces are used to make connections, to outline the perimeters of the youth culture on which the Beasties' B-boy-brat stance depends. When I asked MCA about the lyric "sit around the house, get high and watch the tube," he answered, "We're not using it because it's in a Steve Miller song. We're using it because it's a good line."

So in the long run, what makes *Licensed to Ill* a great album—one of the best of the last year, and one of a mere handful of *listenable* recent ones on major labels—is that it's got great songs. First off, they *sound* great; Rubin is one of the few current producers out there who refuse to sell out rhythm to disco-syndrome water-torture monotony, and this album's got his biggest beats ever. With him the Beasties could get by on their cockiness alone. But what I really mean by great songs is great *songwriting*, by which I guess I just mean common sense. Wiffleball bats and swirlies and Phyllis Diller and Kentucky Fried Chicken and Budweiser and Rice-a-Roni and angel dust are things we live with in this world, and sometimes even things we talk about in real life, but I'll be damned if anybody else has ever written songs about them, and even if somebody has, they never wrote a couplet as unpretentiously jocular as "My pistol is loaded, I shot Betty Crocker / Deliver Colonel Sanders down to Davy Jones' locker" or "Went to the prom, bought a fly blue rental / Got six girlies in my Lincoln Continental." It's all about specificity, I reckon. And when the words fall together into a fantastic delinquent anthem like "Fight for Your Right (to Party)" or a fantastic rock star raveup like "No Sleep till Brooklyn" (with glaciated guitar from Slayer's Kerry King) or a fantastic ghetto-gangster boast like "The New Style," I just can't figure why a person would resist. If being "offended" is what bugs you, you don't love rock'n'roll.

There will always be party-poopers whose knees jerk whenever rap is mentioned; it takes no "talent," they say, *anybody* could do it. For all I know they're right, but I don't think it matters—if punk should have taught us anything, it's that rock is the property of ordinary people, not super-geniuses. It's not what somebody "could" do that's important; it's what they *do* do. And though when I listen to *Licensed to Ill* I wonder why, nobody has ever accomplished what the Beasties accomplish here. I'm nevertheless more cynical about hip-hop than they are—to my ears it peaked around 1982, and (save for a couple big acts who transcended the form) it's mainly devolved into cliché-recapitulation, best exemplified by all those "Roxanne, Roxanne" answer-records and television theme mastermixes. According to the Beasties, if I lived in New York—where "you hear it in the clubs and you hear it on the boxes in the streets," Adrock says—I'd think differently. "There's more copycat metal than copycat rap," MCA opines, hitting me in my soft spot. "We hereby challenge Bon Jovi to an MC contest," taunts Mike D.

To be fair to those still skeptical about this stuff, I thought the Beastie Boys were less than brilliant live—reminded me more of a high school talent show than a rock gig, and all the somersaults and funky chickens and spastic ticks didn't conceal the fact that they dance even worse than Madonna, who they toured the country with in '85 and were scheduled to eat dinner with the evening after they doused my bed. Of course, the Rivers show may have been an atypical performance; "they told us if we fuck up one more time on live TV, we're done," Mike D had related earlier. Maybe they were toned down, or maybe they were over-rehearsed, or maybe I just haven't seen enough rap shows to know I'm supposed to watch when all that's onstage is a turntable and three kids with microphones. The interview with Joan was certainly entertaining—MCA sat in her chair, Adrock on her desk, Mike D next to her with his arm around her; they gave her an apple with a bite taken out, and told her they were working on a concerto at Juilliard. When we'd walked into her studio that afternoon, we'd seen a picture of Run-D.M.C. on the wall between Dr. Ruth and Vincent Price, so perhaps Joan digs this boogaloo thang enough to invite the Boys back. Don't know whether she appreciated the *Extended Sexual Orgasm* book they presented to her and her hubbie backstage at the end of the night, though.

Well, you can't claim good fortune has spoiled these guys—from what I hear, they've *always* been like this. But they say they enjoy the fame, even if it means meeting dimwits like Dweezil Zappa, and even if they have to put up with fools who ask them whether they're actually black. "When my mom first heard [the album] she said it sounded like it would be real successful," MCA says, and I expect an A&R department to give her a call any day now.

The Beasties have run into a brick wall or two—Michael Jackson, who owns the Beatles' catalog, refused to grant them permission to include their surf-guitar / doo-wop version of "I'm Down" on the LP; an intended non-LP B-side called "The Scenario," a murder story that the group calls their best song, proved to be too graphic for CBS. The label also advised (but didn't demand) the Beasties not to call their album *Don't Be a Faggot*, which was its working title. But the threesome is mostly satisfied with the freedom they've been granted, and they realize it's a rare thing in the age of Tipper Gore and Muzak Top 40. Says MCA: "The unique thing about the Def Jam deal is that we get the power to do what we want to do."

The group expects to contribute "The Scenario" to a film soundtrack in the near future. Another unreleased cut, "Desperado," will be included in Rubin's *Tougher than Leather* flick, due for release this year. Meanwhile, the Beasties are barnstorming America's auditoriums with funk-wavers Fishbone and laff-core phonies Murphy's Law, spreading their decadent sex-and-drugs gospel to the initiated and uninitiated alike. (David Lee Roth asked them to open his tour's concerts, but they wanted to headline this time.) After that, who knows? "I don't know if we'll die doing this," MCA remarks. "And I don't think we should disappoint our audience by letting them know what we got planned."

*—Creem*, May 1987


## Aerosmith, Endangered No More

· · · · ·

Can't say for sure whether an Aerosmith plate was on the table that first time I courted reefer madness back in Mike Murphy's garage; coulda been Kiss or the Nuge, but as I recall Murph was especially into 'Smith, so it might as well have been them. No doubts whatsoever about that time my older and younger brother had a serious fight about whose copy of *Toys in the Attic* was whose; seems one or the other had been lost in the basement. And I remember that some kid flunked his Oral Communications class record-pantomime for doin' the do to "Big Ten Inch Record," and my wife says Carol Tortorici used to play a tape of *Rocks* in her car on the way to swim practice at seven o'clock every morning, not to mention at lunch and on the way home. Where I come from, Aerosmith was the environment.

And they deserved to be, no matter what all those old-fart flower-power hippie-dippie counterculture critics (who added the blues covers to Steve Tyler's fleshy singing-lips and got a sum that said "Stones ripoff") thought. Heavy as metal even though they only dropped the lead-Godzilla neutron-bomb about once per album ("Round and Round" on '75's *Toys*, "Nobody's Fault" on '76's *Rocks*), Aerosmith was funking out some kinda unique freaky-deke riff-rock, big on the bass and rhythm lines and seasoned with maracas and cowbells, at a time when hard rock was something you were supposed to throw cherry bombs at instead of dance to. They overhauled chestnuts by Bull Moose Jackson, Rufus Thomas, James Brown, the Johnny Burnette Trio, Kokomo Arnold, the Shangri-Las, and the Beatles, but their sleazy/teasy time-changes made them definitively "rock," not "rock'n'roll." They were fast and catchy. And they had words—verbose, detailed, raunchy language that came across like "Too Much Monkey Business," *Naked Lunch*, "The Jumpin' Jive," and *Narrative Poetry from the Black Oral Tradition* tossed together into a classified-documents shredder and then burned in a hashpipe. "Blood stains the ivories on my daddy's baby grand / I ain't seen the daylight since we started this band." "Back when Cain was able / Way before the stable / Lightnin' struck right down from the sky . . . She ate it / Lordy, it was love at first bite" (this last from a tune called "Adam's Apple"). "Schoolgirl Sadie with your classy kinda sassy little skirt climbin' way up your knees / There was three young ladies in the school gym locker when I noticed they was lookin' at me." "Home sweet home, can't catch no dose / From no hot-tail poon-tang sweet-heart sweat / Who could make a silk purse out of J. Paul Get / And his ear." Enough?

I guess you know what happened next. Or maybe not: Drink. Drugs. Debauchery. Rumors, at least, of falling down on, maybe even falling off, stage. Albums that sounded more rococo, more rote, softer and slicker each successive time out. Guitarist Joe Perry went solo and was replaced by Jimmy Crespo. Rick Dufay replaced rhythm guitarist Brad Whitford. The old fans grew up; the young ones bought the Next Big Thing, which, as often as not, sounded even more like watered-down Aerosmith than the new Aerosmith did. By the time Whitford and Perry rejoined the group, Perry and Tyler were using Antabuse and attending rehab programs to curb their alcohol and heroin problems; they even did an anti-DUI public service announcement in their hometown, Boston. An album was due out, but at this point, who cared? We'd written them off.

*Done with Mirrors*, released in late '85, knocked my socks off. This thing was urgent, do-or-die, more like a give-it-all-you-got alley-band (with chops) debut than the cynical crap we usually get from struggling past-their-primes in the Age of the Comeback. It was more basic and straightforward and stripped-down and gutsy than Aerosmith had sounded in a decade—not prissy or glossy or souped-up like the rest of those Kiss/Nuge/Firm/Purple/BÖC me-decade holdovers. And it had words: "East-house pinball-wizard / Full-tilt balls-unpaid / Second-floor-checkin' makin' Wall Street out the door." For radio stations that think "rock" means Simple Minds and Survivor, it rocked *too* hard; save for token stabs at "Let the Music Do the Talking," rerecorded from Perry's solo LP, they didn't play it. It died on the charts, and when Aerosmith toured, fans only yelled for the old stuff.

First thing I heard when I entered the Vancouver sound studio where Aerosmith were finishing work on their new album was a supersonic classical-bombast fanfare-instrumental that I thought sounded like heavy-metal ELP, or maybe Europe with the stupid music but no stupid words. Not exactly the sound of the streets, I thought—a shame, especially when you consider that these guys' most recent claim to fame was last summer's "Walk This Way" remake with Run-D.M.C. Producer Bruce Fairbairn, whose own most recent claim to fame was Bon Jovi's album (ick!), gave me a cassette of the new 'Smith LP (tentatively titled either *Endangered Species* because of all the taped-over animal noises or *Party Vacation* because of whatever), and I listened to it and didn't like it much. I mean, there sure were lots of ideas—everything from mooing killer whales to midtempo radio-metal to back-porch Delta blues to a big ballad to zoot-suit scat-sing to another Beatles cover ("I'm Down," following in the footsteps of "Come Together") to steel-drum calypso (with lines borrowed from "Day-O," "Montego Bay," and "Summertime Blues") to a minstrel gospel howl that was probably the tape's best song. The drum sound was hardier than most I'd heard lately, there was more "blackness" than 'Smith had displayed in ages, there was a compositional complexity that *Done with Mirrors* lacked, and at least they saved the supersonic fanfare for the very end. But it seemed that "craft" and "ideas" (way too many of 'em) were being embraced while immediacy and personality went by the wayside, and I didn't hear balls or brains in either the lyrics or the hooks. This was a calculated "producer's record" in great CD-era fashion, and the damned thing didn't rock.

So guess what I talked to Joe Perry and Steve Tyler about? What bugged me most is that they acted like (hell, they *said*) that the commercial failure of *Done with Mirrors* was their own fault. "It was, like, finding our place again as far as writing and the direction we wanted to take the band," says Joe, dressed in black from his leather-fringed jacket down to his reptilian boots. "*Done with Mirrors* was the best record we could do at the time, but it wasn't the best record we *can* do. We should have had a month with those tracks as they sit on that record, instead of having one week, which is what we had." Joe says that when he listens to the record now, it sounds "half-formed." I asked him if he feels the same way about *Toys in the Attic* and *Rocks*, and he said he does. I think he's been brainwashed by engineers and producers and his own ego and by all the fallacies that equate rock'n'roll with fancy licks, neatfreak-perfection, and an absence of surface noise. And I think he's full of baloney— who rocks harder, Oscar Madison or Felix Unger?

Of course, Aerosmith's odd couple defend their new record. They say Steve's verbiage in "Dude," "Hangman Jury," and "St. John" ranks in weirdness and raunch with any he's ever penned in the notebooks he carries around. And with a few more listens I still might discern some substance under the abundant style myself, though I'll have to wait and see. "Lyrically, I think this is together," Joe says. "There's some great stuff on there." And Steve, seated next to a punching bag and bedecked, very funkily indeed, in a yellow pastel cowboy shirt with geometric designs and sky-blue jeans with flowers stitched into the ass, has this to say: "Why I like this album more than the last one is because I had 10 times more fun doin' it, and also because we let the songs mature. We spent another month on it, and a month is a long time to weed out stuff, play it better, accentuate on it." He says this in the kind of rough, bedraggled voice that you'd have, too, if you'd been screaming "baaaaaaack in the saddle" for 11 years, and I'm sure he's sincere. But again, I think he's wrong: I mean, who the heck wants to hear somebody "accentuate"? These guys had been cooped up in Vancouver since March: I suppose they had cabin fever or something.

Steve's words of wisdom started to make some small sense when I asked him what he'd thought about punk rock when it happened; in retrospect, I told him, *Rocks* and *Toys* seem more genuinely "punky" to me than the Ramones or Sex Pistols. "I thought it was, like, undone," he says, and when I note that what he calls "undone" some people would call "raw," he answers thusly: "Yeah right, raw. But not that it should have been polished; it's just that if you have a song and the beat falls out, when the guitars are out of tune, is that music? It is to some people, but I don't like it like that." (It's not insignificant that Aerosmith paid some of their early dues at legendary new wave emporium Max's Kansas City, in New York.) Likewise, here's how Steve hears the new album by the Cult: "They could have made it sound bigger. And they're not mature — it's like you take the pie out before it's done, and sure, you can lick the berries out of it, but you can't eat the crust. I like the band; I think that guy's voice is a little weird — you don't sing that way over ballsy-ass rock'n'roll." And his snide thoughts on the Beastie Boys: "It's fun to watch a little kid take his first step, and you hope he can make another one." All things considered, he prefers Concrete Blonde. What a sicko!

Which brings us to the part where I marvel about what a huge role Aerosmith has played in shaping the sonic output of bands whose members used to smoke dope to "Sweet Emotion" in high school parking lots. Most impressive are a handful of smart American indie post-boogie outfits who start at the extremes that made 'Smith great, then twist and expand on that extreme 'Smithness in a quadrillion different ways — Wisconsin's Die Kreuzen, Michigan's Necros, Ohio's Royal Crescent Mob, Washington's Green River. These are the good guys; the bad "guys" are soft-metal sissies like Ratt and Poison and

Mötley Crüe and their ilk. "There's probably 300,000 hard-core Aerosmith fans out there, but there's people who've never heard of Aerosmith, who don't know where Cinderella copped their style," Joe Perry tells me. "That pisses me off a lot." These Max-Factored nincompoops set out pretending to be "metal" bands, so they retain none of Aerosmith's rhythm and blues, none of the song-writing cleverness, none of the complicated structures, nothing that delves beneath the surface. "They get Steven's scarves right, though; that's what it's all about, I guess," Joe scoffs. "But as for the soul that we try to put into it, they just don't have roots that go back that far."

If you figure Joe has tons of old blues records, though, you should figure again. "Not tons," he explains. "I have some, but I have a lot more funk records. Meters, Junior Walker, James Brown, stuff like that. Some of that stuff is amazing—Graham Central Station, Sly, know what I mean?" And the guitarist says he gets the same funk feeling from rap music, which is one of the reasons he agreed to collaborate with Run-D.M.C. "It was new and challenging, and we wanted to see what a heavy metal band like Steven and I would do to a rap song. If R.E.M. had called us up and said, 'Listen, you wanna play on [their cover of] "Toys in the Attic"?,' we wouldn't have done it. Rap is young kids doin' street music, and that's what I think about it—it's young and punky," Joe says. "We got a lot of flak from our hardcore fans; we got some phone calls, and we got some bummed-out letters, but that's to be expected—not everyone's as free-thinking as all of us." Weird thing is, anybody who's ever really listened to Aerosmith would realize that they've *always* made booty-shake music, even back in the days when Boston bars like Bunraty's wouldn't hire 'em 'cuz their stuff was too raw to dance to. And then there were those stiff-assed stadium crowds dedicated to the destruction of disco, and they *never* danced. "Well, they kinda danced *in their own way*," Joe laughs.

The biggest strides the guys in Aerosmith have made in the last couple years have involved their personal lives, and it'd be negligent not to take note of these advances; to begin with, they're the main reason the band exists at all right now. "It's a state of mind; for people like me and Steve, who've been drinking and drugging so much for so long, it's just a matter of breaking a psychological habit," Joe says. "We're not into drooling on the floor anymore." Not that they've mellowed or anything, mind you; they're still demolishing the occasional hotel room, and Steven Tyler has one of the most deviously dirty minds of anybody I've ever conversed with. The question remains whether men in their late 30s, men who've been doing this gig as pros for a decade and a half, can make music as honest as they could when they were in their early 20s and not rich and not sober and not jaded. I think perhaps not, but Aerosmith is determined to prove me wrong. Meanwhile, they're sponsoring a Boston Little League team. And, Joe insists, playing their Sweet Sassafrassies off: "The bottom line is sex, drugs and rock'n'roll; no drugs leaves more time for the other two. And that's no bullshit—you *feel* better. All morning, when you suffer from a hangover and try to figure out what you did the night before; you don't have to put up with that. You get up, you're ready to get started again. It's great."

—Creem, 1987

## Metallica: *Kill 'Em All* Turns 30

· · · · ·

In their 1983-copyright *International Encyclopedia of Hard Rock and Heavy Metal*, Tony Jasper and Derek Oliver claim that two different California bands who put out debut albums that year sound like Motörhead. The entry for Bitch (led by "ex-Ska band vocalist Betsy 'more than ample' Weiss") is longer than Metallica's, but they're both pretty short. If anything, Jasper and Oliver seem more excited by Ottawa's "very wild, furious" Exciter, whose thrashing debut *Heavy Metal Maniac* apparently preceded Metallica's freshman album by at least a month: if *Kill 'Em All* was "Rapper's Delight," Exciter's first might be "King Tim III."

*Kill 'Em All*, which came out 30 years ago this week, didn't chart in the U.S. until 1986, in the spring wake of a 250,000-strong first-week sales eruption by Metallica's third album, *Master of Puppets*; even in 1988, when the big guns at Elektra tacked on two covers of songs by New Wave of British Heavy Metal cult acts Blitzkrieg and Diamond Head to *Kill 'Em All*'s original Megaforce Records configuration, it never got higher than 120 in *Billboard*. Critics widely ignored it too, and not just the 99% of metal-oblivious ones—even NWOBHM-loving Brit hard rock mag *Kerrang!* didn't put a Metallica album on its year-end best list until *Puppets*. (1983's #1? *Pyromania* by Def Leppard.)

In 1984—the year *Kerrang!*'s Malcolm Dome is said to have coined the genre name "thrash metal," though (like "grunge," "rap," "punk," etc.) "thrash" itself had been used as a descriptive long before defining a style—I published a metal essay in an anthology in which I lumped Metallica into a "genuine independent-label heavy metal underground . . . from out of nowhere" with not only Slayer (debut album December 1983) and Anthrax (debut album February 1984), but also the more trad Manowar, Armored Saint, and (them again!) Bitch. My primary knowledge of Metallica at the time, as far as I remember, consisted of marveling suspiciously at the hideous orange horned shirtless cheese-demon ogre on the cover of their "Jump into the Fire" 12-inch, which seemed to be constantly eyeing me from Frankfurt record store shelves on days off from my Signal Corps lieutenant duties. (Wonder if anybody's ever written an appreciation of the disco-indebted '80s vinyl glory days of metal "maxi-singles"?)

So anyway, what all of this is leading to: *Kill 'Em All* did not crash the gate and immediately change the game, and didn't necessarily blow many minds beyond the demo-tape-trading fanatics who already worshipped the band. Regardless, it has accumulated cachet over time as one of those music-would-never-be-the-same records, in this case the one that decided once and for all that the powerlifting pomposity of metal could coexist with the amphetamine velocity of punk rock. Metallica, who were all between 19 and 21 when they recorded the album and sure looked it on the zitted-and-peach-fuzzy back cover photo, were praised (by me a couple years later, for one) for presenting themselves not as rock star icons but as regular denim-and-leather dudes just like their fans. Problem with that formulation is, the NWOBHM bands that drummer Lars Ulrich was so obsessed with were already doing it, and not just the ones that only record-collector geeks like him knew. Motörhead most obviously, but even Def Leppard—in the same age range as Metallica circa their 1980 debut—could've been the heshers next door at first.

Metal tempos had been speeding up steadily, too (or speeding *back* up, since lots of early '70s metal was fast in the first place). But *Kill 'Em All* synthesized a bestiary of high-decibel influences—mostly British ones, from Iron Maiden to Saxon to Venom to Discharge—and Americanized them by making them *even* faster, *even* rougher, *even* less polite, thus contrasting with how intentionally less serious party metal from lipstickier Californians like Ratt and Mötley Crüe (both indie label graduates themselves, by the way) was making girls dance. So in other words, Metallica didn't merely recharge metal's battery and open doors for hacks like Anthrax—they also upped the ante, and thereby established "upping the ante" as a thing metal should do. And metal—black, death, grind, nü—has been trying to top itself, raise the bar, get nastier and more truly "metal" (what at least three *Kill 'Em All* songs are *about*) ever since. Which may be a diverting insular parlor game for children, but unfortunately is no guarantee of music actually worth listening to. Which might explain why several smart young metal bands in recent years (Toronto's Cauldron, who sound like early Metallica crossed with early Def Leppard; Virginia's Corsair, who list as one of their influences '80s Metallica *instrumentals*) have decided the genre was more fun before all this "extreme" "brutal" horseshit, which is at least in part Metallica's fault, got so out of hand.

So, okay—now that credit and blame have been assigned, how does the LP formerly known as *Metal Up Your Ass* (at least in its creators' banging heads) actually, you know, hold up? Well, it depends how you look at it. Metallica got both more and less pretentious later (also better, for two or three albums), but especially with James Hetfield still squealing like a teenager, *Kill 'Em All*'s ridiculous war-violence-hell-metal-metal-metal lyrics have a naive charm: the atypically lustful "your bodies waiting for his whips / The taste of leather on your lips" (were they Accept fans?) wins the gold ribbon, though "stabbing the harlot to pay for her sins / leaving the virgin" certainly deserves a mention, given the dearth of female protagonists in Metallica's later oeuvre (at least 'til their Lou Reed collaboration anyway). Jasper and Oliver to the contrary, only the instructively titled "Motorbreath" (still Metallica's shortest original ever at 3:08) *absolutely* "sounds like Motörhead," though others sort of do for a balls-to-the-wall riff or two, and Lemmy must've thought highly about the record, seeing how he repurposed the title of "No Remorse" for a best-of album a year later and eventually covered "Whiplash."

"No Remorse" might also start with ex-Exoduser Kirk Hammett's best guitar solo on the album, but there's lots of competition, including a covert Lynyrd Skynyrd tribute in "The Four Horsemen"—and who cares if the blistering leads were allegedly all swiped from Dave Mustaine, who'd been kicked out just weeks before and co-wrote four songs? Not-dead-yet Cliff Burton is ace as well, and the time-changes already sound plenty prog even if he hasn't quite figured how to get his gothic ice-age drama together like on 1984's *Ride the Lightning*—some people complain that his four-minute-plus bass solo "Anesthesia (Pulling Teeth)" drags on forever and perhaps rips off Manowar's '82 *Loan Ranger* ripoff "William Tales" in the process, but I've always appreciated the onomatopoeic way he yanks those molars at the end. "Hit the Lights" (most raging early '80s metal-punker about conserving electricity this side of the Angry Samoans' "Lights Out"), "Whiplash," and crusty boot-march "Metal Militia" totally burn down the Christmas tree farm, too, and "Seek and Destroy" is a chugging melodic fight song that swings enough to suggest Metallica hadn't quite settled on being rhythm-impaired yet.

They went on to be a lot of other things, too, of course—rock star icons,

Napster haters, group therapy patients, makers of lousy albums, curators of hobby-showcasing music festivals. Whether that's more marks for their plus or minus column is above my pay grade. So instead, how 'bout we do for Metallica what *Kill 'Em All*'s title implies? Let God sort 'em out.

—spin.com, 25 June 2013

## Fates Warning and Possessed
## Open Up and Say . . . Ahh!

· · · · ·

Both of these records have sleeves that depict obese monsters with their mouths wide open, and if that doesn't say something about the oral fixation currently plaguing the thrash-metal counterculture, then this correspondent certainly doesn't know what does. I prefer Fates Warning's creature myself— kind of a big blue toad masquerading as a cave; slimy, sure, but almost jolly-looking, though I suppose that's part of the trap. Possessed's beast (off their "new monster LP," the sticker says, except I first read that as "new *Monster* LP," as if that was the name of the record) is too technological for my tastes— metallic, purple, all that stuff, with door-hinge jaws and a car-grate mouth and ye olde pentagrams on his forehead. One could infer from their respective record covers that Fates Warning (with no apostrophe in the "fates," implying thereby action rather than, er, possession) draw on the past, and that Possessed draw on the future. And one would not be too incredibly off-base.

Except that, in the dynamic world of heavy metal, these time-period distinctions don't mean a whole lot. Fates Warning's press kit talks about 'em "traveling through new hemispheres," but the way they accomplish this is through the mega-futuristic realm of ancient mythology and classical symphonies, tales of Brave Ulysses dancing with banshees through Valhalla and battling Vikings on Mount Olympus, true space-cadet material, in concept album / rock opera form like they're reading a book whose storyline you wouldn't be able to follow if they strapped you to a guillotine. I will note that this has been *done* before, and even before I heard the parts of "Guardian" that could pass for Kansas and all those "na-na-naaaa-na-na-na"s in "Prelude to Ruin" that bring to mind some Journey song, I was telling myself that back in the days before Metallica made classical music cool again, we used to have a word for this trash: pretentious.

That said, I ought to add that I sort of *like* this record. Musically, parts of *Awaken the Guardian* strike me as pretty wonderful—I hear "Children of the Grave" (groovy Black Sabbath song, youngster) in "The Sorcerers," but then I also hear "Children of the Grave" in "Call Me" by Blondie, and many people call me crazee. John Arch, Fates Warning's vocalizer, has a swell aria/aviary post-Plant/Geddy sing-song, and he doesn't screech much, which is considerate of him. (But then, the press kit calls Fates Warning "sensitive to the needs of others," so I guess good manners are just one of their gimmicks.) And Steve Zimmerman's drums crack into one of the most amazing non-Rubin/Laswell-produced sounds this side of Kenny Aronoff, but that doesn't stop the rest of the music from getting real tedious after awhile, and if I had to pay for the album I'm sure I wouldn't say complimentary things about any of it.

Possessed's promo sheet says they've got "a dark, driving sound that's unique in death metal," but that's ridiculous—*all* death metal is dark and driving, guys! And that's the rub: if I'd never heard Slayer or Venom, I'm sure *Beyond the Gates* would blow me away, but I have, and it doesn't. There's the same locomotive aura to the stuff, the same idiot-savant musicianship, the same frilly intros here and there, the same codified solos. I appreciate how "The Beasts of the Apocalypse" and "March to Die" swing to and fro, I welcome the slow sections of "Phantasm," I enjoy the cymbalwork in "No Will to Live," but I've got a feeling those are just the moments when my attention wandered from changing diapers or eating Grape Nut Flakes back to the record. "Restless Dead" even prompts thoughts of Celtic Frost's nuke-rock, but so what? I have very little in common with the people who make this music, and maybe I'm jaded. I just put on Coltrane's *A Love Supreme*, and it jams.

—*Creem Metal*, 1986

## Dead Milkmen vs. Thelonious Monster:
Battle of the Lame

• • • • •

Hey, I've got a *great* sense of humor, really I do. Thing is, I kinda prefer my jokes to be *funny*, know what I mean? Most disgusting fact about all this indie/alternative pap is that so much of it tries to excuse its laziness, its fear of new ideas and passion and true audacity, by hiding behind some tepid trash-aesthetic concept of forced insignificance (what these dinks smugly refer to as "fun"). Since I've been asked to digest two new records that subscribe pretty exactly to this phenomenon, I figured I'd conduct one of those time-honored battles of the bands. The zillion-dollar question: Who's lamer, the Dead Milkmen or Thelonious Monster? Let's find out.

1. WHO'S GOT A MORE RIGID RHYTHM SECTION? The Dead Milkmen try fake reggae, fake funk, fake Eurodisco, and fake cumbia, all of which come out hopelessly stiff. Thelonious Monster at least have some hope, I guess—they get by with this laid-back corporate-boogie rolling motion (it's "ironic," see), and hence don't *need* to swing. WINNER: Dead Milkmen.

2. WHO'S GOT MORE ATROCIOUS MUSICAL INFLUENCES? The Milkmen want to be the Dickies, or maybe Oingo Boingo. Thelonious want to be the Doobie Brothers, or maybe Styx circa *Equinox / Crystal Ball*. WINNER: Dead Milkmen.

3. WHOSE LED ZEPPELIN REFERENCES ARE LESS SUBTLE? The Milkmen sing part of "Dazed and Confused" in "Jellyfish Heaven." Thelonious have numbers called "Swan Song" and "Lookin' to the West," and in the latter they brag that they used to be big Zep and Kiss fans (yeah, sure—I bet they liked Harry Chapin), but music means nothing to them now. WINNER: Thelonious Monster.

4. WHOSE NON-ZEPPELIN REFERENCES ARE LESS SUBTLE? The Milkmen perform an original called "I Am the Walrus," and insert sections of "Gloomy Sunday," "Ballroom Blitz," and "Sweet Jane" into other songs. Thelonious end "Tonite" with a scat from "Roadhouse Blues." WINNER: Dead Milkmen.

5. WHOSE VOCALIST SOUNDS LIKE THE MORE WORTHLESS TV CHARAC-TER? The guy in the Milkmen whistles his *s*'s like the gopher in those Winnie the Pooh cartoon specials; also, he likes to sing in goofy voices, such as through his nose. The guy in Thelonious Monster inhales his vowels like the dad on *Alf*; also, he sounds bored. I hate bored singers. WINNER: Thelonious Monster.

6. WHOSE SENSE OF PARANOIA TOWARD THE REAL WORLD IS MORE TIRED AND HYPOCRITICAL? The Milkmen make fun of health spas, K-Mart, Bruce Springsteen, Casey Kasem, Mormons, Eskimos, hillbillies, and Elvis fans, and in "Theme from Blood Orgy of the Atomic Fern" and "Instant Club Hit (You'll Dance to Anything)" they pretend that "art-fags" are more self-conscious and phony than they are. Thelonious Monster, I'm happy to report, don't give a darn. WINNER: Dead Milkmen, by a long shot.

7. WHOSE SENSE OF TEDIUM IS MORE TEDIOUS? The Milkmen are tedious in an annoying way. Thelonious are tedious in a pleasant way. WINNER: Thelonious Monster.

8. WHICH BAND IS LESS IN TOUCH WITH ITS OWN SUPPOSED MUNDANITY? Thelonious do a dumb song about watching *The Odd Couple*, rooting for Michael Jordan, going fishing, and paying bills. The Milkmen do a dumber one about eating at Tacoland. WINNER: Dead Milkmen.

9. WHOSE ATTEMPT AT A "WILD" FRAT-BLUES TRIBUTE SOUNDS WIMPIER? In Thelonious's "Pop Star," some creep yells "Roll it back!" and "Where's that guitar solo?" In the Milkmen's "Big Time Operator," some creep yells "Kill the motherfuckers!" and "Look out Stevie Ray Vaughan, look out Charlie Sexton!" WINNER: Thelonious Monster.

With all my barf-bags used up, I find that the Dead Milkmen's *Bucky Fellini* is indeed marginally more awful than Thelonious Monster's *Next Saturday Afternoon*. Worse luck next time, Thelonious.

—Spin, September 1987

## Einstürzende Neubauten / Killdozer:
The Graystone, Detroit, 11 June 1986

· · · · ·

You probably won't believe me, but the most amazing thing about the best new wall-of-industrial-noise kitchen-sink-plus-metal-machine-musick combos is that they're so incredibly rhythmic. I don't mean rhythmic in some hi-culture-jazzbo conservatory sense; I mean they got the big beat like Run-D.M.C. or Trouble Funk or somebody. Clamor crews like Chicago's Big Black, Austin's Butthole Surfers, and England's Mark Stewart and Maffia incorporate hip-hop beatboxes and/or multiple drummers, and New York's Sonic Youth fire their exploding load with Madonna's "Into the Groove" pumpin' in the background. Even Gotham axe-meanies the Swans, for years the most stiff-derriered band on the planet, get the funk on their recent "Time Is Money (Bastard)" single. This stuff takes the idea of the disco inferno to its logical conclusion.

And sometimes takes it literally—waiting for West Berlin air-conditioning-duct-beaters Einstürzende Neubauten's show to commence, I heard stories about the band starting onstage fires in New York (not to mention a "riot" in Houston) during previous tour dates. But the only flamethrowing in Detroit was sonic; the fivesome was well-behaved, though lead screamer Blixa Bargeld appeared miffed both about Mother Nature messing up his day (the group's afternoon flight into Motor City was postponed three hours, thanx to a tornado watch) and the club's electronics messing up his dissonance ("We usually plug electricity into our PA," Blix reminded the soundman at one point, though the real problem was that the amplifier for Neubauten's balance-beam-sized three-shock-absorber-spring bass thingamajig kept freaking out.) These nuisances only further committed his bondage-and-battle-dress-attired quintet to rock the place—bad amp or no, they laid down some monster polypercussive grooves with that spring-thing and their huge drum-and-oil-kettle set. They were sliding dildo-vibrators across guitars, hitting microphones with ball-peen hammers, banging chains on drums, and clanging their giant springs with ratchet wrenches and power drills: the 50-ish guy who owns the club told me Einstürzende reminded him of his younger days at the DeSoto plant. With Blixa pacing back and forth like a caged jaguar, diving across the floor, sweating, drooling, and screeching more German than my two high school years could decipher, it was kinda hard to understand the words. But the artsies and baldheads and thrillseekers in the house boogied anyhow, and not without good reason.

Neubauten started out like a Godzilla heavy metal band (Steppenwolf to the fifth power, maybe), turned into some kind of demonic Eurodisco troupe (sort of a sopor-generation Kraftwerk), shifted gears and became a bunch of Krishna-kissin', Arabian-guitar-strummin' hippies, and then let it all hang out with "Yü-Gung," the most transcendent piece of noisy dance rock Deutschemarks can buy in its Adrian Sherwood–produced avant-dub vinyl version, and a mothership-funkin' joy to behold live. Encoring with their rendition of cosmic cowboy Lee Hazelwood's ballad "Sand," the only English-language song these Jägerschnitzels have recorded, Einstürzende Neubauten came across almost human, and Blixa's deep, guttural r- and l-rolling suggested he's a pretty moving singer for a pretentious punk-rock type. When he intoned "I am a stranger in your land / A wanderin' man / Call me sand," he even sounded homesick for the Old Country.

While Neubauten was rushing to catch their next plane to Chicago, Wisconsin college-boy sludge blues-funk trio Killdozer picked up where their "German bloodbrothers whose name we can't pronounce" left off, demonstrating to the few smart stragglers that you don't necessarily need ferocious contraptions to make a horrible noise. Michael Gerald, clad fashionably in paisley sleeveless and armadillo tattoo, growled about wrestling in "Pile Driver," being born with a spatula in his mouth in "Big Song of Love," and how they make things bigger in Texas in "King of Sex." Killdozer's slowed-to-the-max cover of CCR's "Run through the Jungle" seemed half-hearted, but Box Tops / Cocker's

Sharp-dressed Madison men Killdozer (Photo: Touch and Go)

"The Letter," a tough white-blues singer's test which Gerald aced and then some, roared toward oblivion. Closing with their kid's-day-out ditty "Going to the Beach," Killdozer eclipsed noise rock's beauty barrier like few skronk crews I've witnessed. Bill Hobson crammed a needle-nose pliers onto his axe strings, started the sucker wailing on some bizarre tuning, and dropped the instrument to the ground as the threesome exited stage left. It kept playing, and could have gone forever. If bands like this can conquer Father Time that easily, the rest of rock's last outer limits ought to be a cinch.

*—Creem Metal*, 1986

## New Wave über Alles

· · · · ·

Nobody dared call it a German invasion, maybe because it would've been a really weird time for one, as the Cold War whittled down—hundreds of thousands of U.S. troops spread across West Germany (I was one of them, from 1982 to 1985); the Green Party breaking through nationally; the Red Army Faction exploding vehicles and soldiers near Heidelberg and Kaiserslautern and

Frankfurt bases; 600,000 protesters showing up at a 1983 anti-nuke demonstration in West Berlin. But in 1984, a song sung in German, about nuclear annihilation, just happened to hit #2 on the American pop chart. English version on the flipside got airplay too: "This is what we've waited for, this is it boys, this is war. The president is on alert . . . super high-tech jet fighters . . . I'm standing pretty, in this dust that was a city."

The music was deliriously bouncy teenybop new wave; the video showed the singer, an adorably tomboyish Fräulein known as **Nena**, balancing on a log. Nena was her band's name, too (more confusing than Blondie!), and her four West Berlin boy-pals were almost as cute as she was. Their U.S. album, named *99 Luftballons* after their hit but actually a bilingualized hodgepodge of two previous German LPs, mixed synthy beats, spacey ballads, Motownish basslines, and AOR guitars into über-efficient Europop. Second-catchiest cut was "Just a Dream"; weirdest was an ominous, off-kilter, dub-echoed, male-declaimed slab of bubblegum Kraut-rock called "Das Lang der Elefanten." In the States, Nena were barely heard from again; in Central Europe, though, they (and later she, solo) stretched hits, increasingly atmospheric and adult-contemporary, across the next three decades. "Feur und Flame"'s Killing Joke–like 1985 tribal-doomsday stomp is worth checking out; most others, less so.

Thing is, "99 Luftballons" wasn't even the first pop hit from Germany to score in the Western Hemisphere around that time. In 1983, the monotoning Großenknen threesome Trio had reached #33 on the U.S. dance chart — but also #3 pop in Canada — with their minimalist babytalk ditty "Da Da Da"; Falco, a suave sort-of-rapper from Vienna, Austria (but rhyming in German so it's not like most Americans knew the difference), also got club play for his *alles-klar* drug-bust tale "Der Kommissar," though it took a somewhat toned-down English translation by Brit prog-wavers After the Fire to take it Top 5 in America. "Der Kommissar" was also interpreted (as "Deep in the Dark") by Long Island flashdance-rock belter Laura Branigan, who additionally covered West Berlin synth-pop trio **Alphaville**'s #32 1984 U.S. dance-hit-about-bombs-dropping "Forever Young" (which got to #65 pop four years later as it accepted a permanent invitation to American high school graduation ceremonies); another Alphaville hit, the less transcendently translucent "Big in Japan," went #1 dance and #66 pop. And then there was Stuttgart sci-fi songster **Peter Schilling**, whose stratospheric Bowie update "Major Tom (Coming Home)" hit #14 pop in 1983: astronaut loses contact with earth base, but finds his home in space.

For all we know, Major Tom's still up there, drifting weightless. Apparently

Schilling had a thing for nuclear Armageddon tunes, too. And he wasn't the only early '80s German singing about computer malfunctions. The West Berlin outfit **Spliff**—little known in the States, though they were goth diva Nina Hagen's backing band until she got too "bossy," and two of their four members, Reinhold Heil and Manne Praeker, produced *99 Luftballons*—included a hilarious song about microprocessors making them sick called "Computer Sint Doof" (English version: "Computers are stupid! Computers are dumb!") on their excellent 1982 album *85555*. The record also had its own strategic-defense-initiating robot-rock Cold War number, "Kill!," about fingers on triggers pointed at aliens who look like Russians or terrorists.

People already forget how *on the brink* Germany felt back then—Berlin, remember, was literally on the other side of the Iron Curtain; Nina Hagen, for her part, was born beyond the Wall. The day I got to Bad Kreuznach as a second lieutenant in 1982, I was told I was there for one reason: to kill communists. Never happened, *danken sie Gott*, but it could have. And though it was clearly on Spliff's, and Nena's, minds, they managed to have fun anyway. Spliff's sound combined deeper-pocketed-than-the-Police dub reggae (hence their ganjafied name), Teutonic electro-beats, and meaty shocks of metallic guitar; *85555*'s hot hit across the continent, "Carbonara," was a goofball sort of Italo-pop parody where they led cheers with random words like "spaghetti!" and "amaretto!" and "grandioso!" and "Coca-Cola!" But—as sparse ballads like "Huet Nacht" and "Duett Komplett" (English title: "Passion Play," ha ha) on 1996's *85555 / Herzlichen Glückwunsch* twofer and a couple best-of comps still make clear—Spliff also excelled at a lonely sort of one-night-stand loveliness that predates Kraut indie faves the Notwist by a few decades.

Also forlorn about romantic misadventures, and even more understated about it: **Trio**. "Da Da Da I Don't Love You—You Don't Love Me Aha Aha" (that's its full title, though the real consonant-clicking tongue-twisting of course comes in the un-Anglicized "ich lieb dich nicht du liebst mich nicht" section) has always, perhaps fairly, been considered a novelty hit; in fact, it was the song's fahrvergnügable reappearance in a 1997 Volkswagen commercial that prompted the CD release of *Da Da Da*, which is basically an expanded version of 1983's North American *Trio and Error*. (German new wave's biggest Stateside rock critic success, by the way—it miraculously finished 33rd in the *Village Voice*'s '83 Pazz & Jop poll.) But though Trio were always funny, they weren't really a joke band—more like an art band, whose almost absurdly straight-faced voicings, stripped-down structures, Möbius-stripped lyric schemes, and middle-aged mundanity (fixing breakfast then waiting by the phone, looking at unaffordable furniture in store windows) carry Lou Reed's Velvets-era deadpan decadence through the neon-lights desolation of late '70s Kraftwerk. They thanked Can's Holger Czukay and Jaki Liebzeit in their liner notes, which suggests at least some connection to *alte-schule* Krautrock. And they had a punk side—not so much when turning Little Richard's "Tutti Frutti" into a lederhosen oompah (they covered Lee Dorsey and Harry Belafonte and "Tooralooraloo," too) as in the piston-metal thumper "Boom Boom" (naked ladies! radioactive satellites!) and in assorted other tracks less easy to find on this side of the Atlantic: "Achtung Achtung," "Kummer," "Ja Ja Wo Geht's Lank Peter Pank Schönen Dank," whew.

"Da Da Da," again, got its biggest Stateside push in dance bars. A common phenomenon among German crossovers of the time—U.S. DJs had been open to Continental oddities at least since disco days, and maybe there was also a domino effect from venues that military recruits boogied at outside overseas barracks. And "Da Da Da" wasn't even as strange as things got. In 1984, another slice of danceable dada—namely, "Din Daa Daa" (originally titled "Trommeltanz") by ich-bin-ein-Berliner **George Kranz**, topped *Billboard*'s Hot Dance Music / Club Play chart. A funky avalanche of goose-stepping machine rhythms, ritualistic handclaps, machine-gunner-having-seizure nonsense syllables, and loud verbal crashes, it has since been sampled by rappers like the Ying Yang Twins and Flo Rida, but really it was industrial dance music ("EBM," "New Beat," whatever) before the style much existed. So was "Amok!," a #29 U.S. dance hit the same year, from the Hamburg "sex metal" unit **Ledernacken** (that's "Leather Neck" to you): sweaty weight-room grunts and pants, shattering glass, fascist-sounding Schwarzenegger-accent commands to "shake your boo-tee." The fascism might've been on purpose, too, given that the band's website lists Wermacht-veteran Viennese Actionism artist and convicted sex criminal Otto Muehl along with "jungle drums" and "German marchmusic" as primary influences. Single sides collected on 1985's *First Album* (best title: "Ich Will Dich Essen") barrage you with burps, bongos, saxophones, trumpeting elephants, "hoo! hah!" chants, answering machine messages, borderline racist babble, and theoretically African polyrhythms—main guy Folke Jensen was born in Namibia, which his grandpa had once helped the Kaiser occupy.

Given all this, it's almost surprising that the construction-site clang of **Einstürzende Neubauten**'s great 1985 12-inch "Yü Gung"—the most coherently percussive record of said Berlin power-tool-abusers' long and storied career,

Falco: *Einzelhaft* (A&M, 1982)

mixed by British dub architect Adrian Sherwood and still available on numer-
ous industrial samplers—never exploded on U.S. dancefloors. But Neubauten
were already leftovers from the truly avant-garde early years of Germany's
*Neue Deutsche Welle*, a post-punk movement that at the time claimed its own
sections in Frankfurt record stores, but no press of note in the States, despite
many mysterious artists (Der Plan, Pyrolator, Palais Schaumberg, Ja Ja Ja)
whose playful clatter the rest of the world still hasn't caught up with.

By the mid-'80s, just like with new wave everywhere else, things were
trending more pop—but the pop was still crazy eccentric. **Falco**, equally inspired by the late-'70s Berlin albums David Bowie made with Brian Eno and
by the Sugarhill street-rap that Aryan teens were now breakdancing to on
Frankfurt spielplatzes, was a huge deal in Central Europe; even his eerie 1985
ballad "Jeanny," which didn't get much airplay due to its depicting the kid-
napping and murder of a teenage prostitute, went #1 in six countries. In the
States, again, dancers fell for him first; discos are where his original German-
gutteralled "Der Kommissar" hit. And "Rock Me Amadeus"—the Mozart-hop
extravaganza that briefly made him a wunderbar züperztar—didn't reach the
U.S. Top 10 until after serving over half a year in clubs. Eventually, in 1986, it
went #1—the only German-sung song ever to do so—albeit mixed differently
than the version that had scored in Europe (which happened a lot with these

songs, by the way; lyrics morph in translation, as well). "Amadeus" parodies ("Dr. Zaius, Dr. Zaius!") continue to this day.

In case you never noticed, Falco's song depicted Mozart as a hard-drinking and womanizing "punker" overrun by debt; extended dance remixes (for those, try the "25th Anniversary" edition of 1986's *Falco 3*) carry the metal riffs and collage splices and opera arias over the top. Astonishing forever, and certainly a pinnacle of Falco's 40 years (until crashing into a bus in the Dominican Republic in 1998 killed him)—but not the *only* pinnacle. His U.S. Top 20 follow-up, "Vienna Calling," was quite the oi!-shouting, turntable-scratching, long-distance ring-up, and Electric Six fans owe it to themselves to hear 1986's "Macho Macho." Buddha Records' 15-song 1999 *Greatest Hits* has all his most beloved tracks; like every available Falco best-of, it starts with "Amadeus" and "Kommissar," and proceeds from there. But his 1982 debut, *Einzelhaft* (which means "Solitary Confinement"—he's sitting existentially alone in a dark, one-windowed room on the cover), is solid. Along with "Der Kommissar," it's got the meta-metal "Ganz Wien," carried over from the punk band Falco had played bass in; the talkbox-and-wah-wah disco-rocker "Auf der Flucht"; the propulsively hiccup-rapped Euro-hit "Maschine Brent," with its Sprockety vocal backup and drum wallop worthy of early Rick Rubin. Those all show up on *Greatest Hits*, too, but *Einzelhalft*'s otherworldly title track doesn't, even though its foreboding, speed-cyborged sound anticipates weirdness that future trancemeister Sven Väth would commit in his groups the Off and 16 Bit a few years later.

And from there, of course, the techno that Kraftwerk had invented in Dusseldorf back in the '70s would spread around the world and back. And the Berlin Wall would fall, and the Germanies would reunite, and Hanover's heavy metal Scorpions would celebrate the wind changing in a six-million-selling power ballad. American soldiers left for the Middle East, reunification begat recession begat resurgent far-right nationalism and anti-immigrant violence, and there would meanwhile also be a new underground music movement called "Hamburger Schule" (seriously—Google it!), and KMFDM and Rammstein would tour the States together. And so on. But the new wave mid-'80s will still always remain Auf-Deutsch pop's über-alles moment, as surely as Amadeus rocks and luftballons float in the summer sky.

—*Wondering Sound*, 1 June 2011

## Frank Chickens → M.I.A.

· · · · ·

It's easy, maybe even accurate, to think of M.I.A. as the definitive musical artist of our time, in the sense that only the 21st century's confluence of a flattening world and mash-up technology could enable someone who stirs so much multidirectional class struggle and global rhythm into the curry pot to achieve such a high profile, even in the xenophobic West. Dancehall, Bollywood, piracy, terrorism, dub disappearances, bootleg-tape disintegration, baile booty beats, Suicide samples, Dr. Buzzard bites, bhangra, bombs, graffiti, grime, ginger genocide, guerrilla warfare, refugee exile, hardscrabble riots, Nigerian rappers, didgeridoo hip-hop, kuduro, Congo, Castro, the PLO, purple haze, razor blades, fake passports, Elsa the Lioness, Tamil Tigers, Timbaland: a familiar roll call, by now. With *Matangi*, you might even call M.I.A.'s montage downright predictable. But pre-Y2K (or maybe 9/11), nobody could have predicted it.

That isn't to say, though, that there weren't precedents—even before she stumbled upon the genre explorations of the Clash, the abrasive barrage of Public Enemy, and the revolutionary content and/or branding of both. Maya Arulpragasam grew up in northern Sri Lanka and southwest London loving Boney M, globally gigantic (except in the U.S.) West Indian British vocalists co-mingling Eurodisco and reggae and myriad other musics under the tutelage of West German producer Frank Farian, who would later go on to mastermind Milli Vanilli. M.I.A. has said she wants to "write songs about something important and make it sound like nothing," and a lot of the time, that's exactly what Boney M pulled off: tunes like "Belfast," "Ride to Agidir," "El Lute," "Consuela Biaz," and the Jorge Ben cover "Chica da Silva" chronicled strife, exodus, and triumph among the underclasses of Ireland, Morocco, Spain, the Dominican Republic, and Brazil, though beneath the music's breeze and cheese, you might not notice. Perhaps M.I.A. did.

Boney M were influential deep into the Third World in ways that have yet to be charted—before M.I.A., for instance, they clearly inspired Midi, Maxi, and Efti, three teenage-girl refugees from Ethiopia and Eritrea who united in Sweden in 1992 to make a flawless bubble-dance album immersed in ragga and the savanna, with one song imagining a "Sisterhood of Africa" that hid daily from machine-gun bullets; Columbia put the CD out in the U.S., where the single "Bad Bad Boys" snuck into the basement of the Hot 100, but they never made another record. The radical instincts of punk and hip-hop, by that time, had meanwhile been swapping genes in the UK for well over a decade, since at least the Clash's *Sandinista!* in 1981; on 1983's *Duck Rock*, Malcolm McLaren—another acknowledged M.I.A. inspiration—injected square dance and Soweto into the mix. And in 1981, the collective New Age Steppers—featuring even clearer M.I.A. antecedents such as Neneh Cherry, Mark Stewart, and the Slits' Ari Upp—made the first album on UK agit-prop avant-dub collage producer Adrian Sherwood's On-U Sound label.

New Age Steppers' bass player was a bloke named Steve Beresford. In 1984, he joined forces with the British author David Toop, who that same year published *Rap Attack: African Jive to New York Hip-Hop*, the first great history of the genre. (The subtitle of a later expanded edition, 1992's *African Rap to Global Hip-Hop*, acknowledged that the genre had grown into a worldwide phenomenon; in later years, Toop would also curate and chronicle acclaimed compilations of and books about ambient art music, exotica, and proto-quiet-storm makeout R&B.) Beresford and Toop produced an album by Frank Chickens—two Japanese women, Kazuko Hohki and Kazumi Taguchi, who were living in London and who'd met as part of the Japanese-American Toy Theatre, which put on plays featuring robot and Godzilla figures. At least three songs on the album were explicitly indebted to hip-hop, but in the context of a culture-jamming, continent-juxtaposing, multilingually nursery-rhyme-cadenced, and most of all Asian-centric sound crash that uncannily anticipates M.I.A. in several notable ways.

"We Are Frank Chickens," for instance ("about us—Chicken gangsters—living in garbage," the liner notes explain, a couple years before "gangsta rap" existed), features clucking sounds that could be "Bird Flu" two decades before the fact; "We Are Ninja" has Hohki and Taguchi chopping you in two and "hiding in the drains of Yokahama" where they beat up alligators then take a shower, all over a Mouse Trap game of poly-percussion and incidental sounds that culminates in a minefield detonating. But the real mind-blower is album opener "Cheeba Cheeba Chimpira," incorporating hip-hop lingo *way* early (liner note: "slang for contraband") but also, more astoundingly, building at least as dense and sinuous a metal-machine-music sensory overload as M.I.A. did with "Born Free" in 2010: skids, blurts, armor-piercing ammo, and cross-talk deep in the mix before even Public Enemy (or their crush-colliding British wannabe fellow travelers Age of Chance) tried similar experiments. Even in a bring-the-industrial-noize realm, the song's steel-plated shocks to the system seem prescient by standards of 1984, when even Swans and Test Dept. were

Frank Chickens: *We Are Frank Chickens* (Kaz, 1984)

new at it. But the funk maintains, from basslines at the start to huge echoing drums upon oildrums at the end, and Frank Chickens get their rap in: "Come to London / Kickboy Face / sent to exile / lost in space / On the streets / planet partners / shadow hardnuts / jump and cut."

If nothing else on *We Are Frank Chickens* is so loud or disruptive, almost every track is committed to the beat—often multiple beats simultaneously, many of them evoking the earth's more tropical latitudes. And the subject matter is off the wall, but also obliquely feminist, sometimes upending stereotypes of Asian immigrant women in London in ways M.I.A. might well appreciate: "We are ninja, not geisha—that's not what you expect." "Mothra" is a synth-bricolaged torch tribute to the 1961 Japanese female winged-insect movie monster and a girl group called the Peanuts whom she protects; "Madam Fatal" is a proto-trip-hop tale of a lady DJ "on the 14th floor / surrounded by silver machines," using radio waves as her technological tentacles. There's a traditional "enka" ballad, and a cute ditty called "Green Banana" that sounds like Shonen Knife crossed with Kid Creole and the Coconuts, and a missing-woman mystery called "Yellow Detective" explained thus in the (yes, repeatedly quotable) notes: "Life is getting hard for a lot of people. What can you do except laugh if you don't want to suffer."

The album cover shows scores of Asian businessmen on a beach, fleeing either an erupting volcano or Mothra herself while more colorfully dressed men and women continue their oceanside holiday. On a non-album EP track the same year—four years after the well-named half-Filipino San Francisco new wave singer Pearl Harbour revived it—Frank Chickens covered Wanda Jackson's racially insensitive 1957 rockabilly "Fujiyama Mama," either omitting or obliterating the original's line about Hiroshima and Nagasaki ("the same I did to them baby I can do to you"). And *We Are* also has its own ska-oompah atomic bomb number, "Pikadon."

Frank Chickens wound up putting out a few more records, and doing cabaret-style shows with up to 16 members, for years. More famously, maybe, in 1989 Kazuko Hohki hosted a British TV series credited with introducing karaoke to the UK; she's also, according to her website, created three multimedia performances "based on her experience as a Japanese woman in the UK" and is now working on one concerning—no shit—"faecal incontinence." In 2010, the band won something called the Edinburgh Comedy God Award, proclaiming them funnier in the past three decades than competitors such as Eddie Izzard or Flight of the Conchords despite not actually being comedians, after a scathing Stewart Lee *Guardian* column instigated a groundswell of grassroots voting by fans who may never have actually heard them. How many of those casting ballots also cherish the M.I.A. albums they prefigured has yet to be determined.

—spin.com, 18 November 2013

## Owed to the Nightingales

· · · · ·

For the last couple years, while stateside experts were patting themselves on the back and claiming that the Bruce/Lobos/Fogerty "American resurgence" had stemmed the supposed Brit-pap invasion of 1983 once and for all (a dubious distinction, really, kinda like a superpower knocking off Grenada), a new strain of Angry Young Rock has been materializing in England's small-town outposts, ready to mount its own offensive. Rooted in Beefheart and Zeppelin and T. Rex and Hank Williams, drawing cues from the Fall and Wire and Pop Group and Gang of Four, this eccentric, vitriolic three-chord crunch has been ignored almost as completely in the British music press as in its American counterpart. Even now, the tendency is to manufacture "cutting-edge" justi-

The Nightingales: *In the Good Old Country Way*
(Vindaloo, 1986)

fications for one-idea sensationalists like the Jesus and Mary Chain or redundant crybabies like the Smiths. But the Mekons and Three Johns (after eight years of gutsy music by the former and four by the latter) are finally beginning to get their due, and one suspects the Membranes, Janitors, Age of Chance, and the rest might not be far behind.

Among the chief exponents of this expressionist boogie are the Nightingales, who were a jagged but poppish Gang of Four–influenced four-piece (with subtler politics and less distortion than their inspiration) when they released their homonymous debut EP in 1982. *The Nightingales* showcased the wry self-effacing wit of singer-songster Robert Lloyd, who in four singsongy vignettes managed to mourn his dad's death by alcoholism, chide "arrogant fool" motorway hogs, and quote "Rock around the Clock," "It's My Party," and "The Ballad of Mott the Hoople." Over time, the Nightingales gained in clamor and tempo what they gave up in intelligibility; by 1985 only Lloyd remained from the original lineup. Of the band's two songs on the excellent early-'86 *Communicate!!!: Live at Thames Poly* compilation, "Only My Opinion" sounds like a cappella gibberish, and "Crafty Fag" sounds like a feedback fireball.

On their new *In the Good Old Country Way*, the now five-member Nightingales switch directions the way the Mekons did on 1983's *English Dancing Master* EP (though nobody noticed until 1985's *Fear and Whiskey*)—toward a merger of abstract punk with country and folk music. Like the Mekons, the Nightingales now have a female violin player (Maria Smith), and as with the Mekons, you can finally understand some of the words. But the Nightingales are still more sound than song; even when Lloyd's lyrics are decipherable, they're not especially penetrable. He seems to be droning about having migraines, getting old, saving grocery money, despising Americans, being his own God, becoming an enemy of the state—the trials and tribulations of day-to-day-existence-preceding-essence, I suppose you could call it.

*In the Good Old Country Way* comes across like a mutant fiddle hoedown, with Ron Collins's drums and Howard Jenner's bass providing a heavy, funkless-bop fortress for the crisscrossing and seesawing interplay of Smith's violin and Pete Byrchmore's viola. When Lloyd commands, "Shake it on down!" or "Now take it away!," the hoedown turns into an ashcan-amateur avant-orchestral breakdown—you hear free jazz harmonica, whinnying guitar screeches, background doo-wop, the cracking and wheezing and bellowing and gargling of Lloyd's voice. This is anything but roots-rock purism, obviously: the hyperactive western swing of "Square Circle" and the jump-started bluegrass of "I Spit in Your Gravy" seem no more conventional than the Middle Eastern undulation of "Leave It Out" or the sanctified disco of "Coincidence." *In the Good Old Country Way* is where *Pink Flag* meets *Music from Big Pink*.

Punk-rockers that they are, the Nightingales offer no solutions, only reactions. To counter control over their lives, they threaten anarchy ("Mister, if you're gonna treat us like infants / We're probably gonna behave like those nippers"); to counter the decline of human conscience, they threaten, like the Screaming Blue Messiahs in "Wild Blue Yonder," escape from civilization ("I'll travel around / Maybe I'll even drink from a can / And when I take a piss / I might not even wash my hands"). Unlike the Smiths and the Jesus and Mary Chain, who still look at decadence as some kind of fashionable parlor game, the Nightingales and their terminally dislocated kin are staunchly antidecadent. Or rather, they would be, but it's too late. They know we're in a state of anomie *now*, and they know all too well what it's cost us.

—*Boston Phoenix*, 23 September 1988

## Mekons Stumble toward Oblivion

· · · · ·

The Mekons are what happens when country music is left to wander its own lost highway and never manages to get back on the right track: it forgets where its home was; it attempts to find peace among the Mexicans or Cajuns or Creoles or Jamaicans or Texans only to remember it's not one of them at all; it stumbles upon civilization only to find buildings toppling over into rubble and humans free to be beaten and broken, and it wonders what's so civilized about that; it wakes up in hell and doesn't remember having konked out there the night before, even though the place does look somehow familiar. It veers about as close to the spirit of Elvis following his Blue Moon and Chuck searching for his promised land as rock'n'roll can hope to in the latter half of the music's fourth decade, but it loses what little hope it had and misses the mark. Eventually, arms outstretched like a kid pretending he's an airplane, it careens off the edge of the world, stinking, babbling, falling-down drunk, hating itself and hating the planet and the age but loving every minute of it.

When the Mekons first became Mekons, as college students amid the right-wing politics and textile-industry-in-decay of Leeds during the gory post-Pistols glory daze of British punk rock, they didn't know what country music was, and they didn't care. "I thought it was hick-crap music for hillbillies," remembers Jon Langford, the Mekes' hoedown singer and raunch guitarist, a guy weaned on a steady diet of Slade and T. Rex. He says the Mekons originally just wanted to be "a punk band playing slow songs." Which proved to be something other than what the safety-pin-clad audience wanted, so early singles like "Never Been in a Riot" and "Where Were You" came on like a pogo-party despite their fumingly introverted, self-directed rage. The Mekons were rank amateurs who constantly swapped instruments they hadn't had time to learn, changed their membership from gig to gig and record to record, ignored ephemeral Anglopop fashion fads, and sang about problems in their own boring, working-class lives. While engineering their second album, *Devils, Rats and Piggies*, John Gill of the Leadersound folk studio told them they were "like a village English country band—very plain and full of mistakes," rhythm guitar player Kevin Lycett says. The Mekons didn't know what Gill was talking about.

But they learned. Stateside friends mailed them tapes of *Cowboy Joe's Radio Ranch*, they listened in awe to the Charlie Gillett–compiled *Another Satur-*

*day Night* cajun and zydeco anthology, and they became convinced that Sam Phillips's Memphis rockabilly and rhythm'n'blues label Sun Records was "the greatest label there ever was," Langford says. By 1983's poorly distributed *English Dancing Master* EP, the Mekons were uniting folk jigs with the dub-reggae production they'd learned from Lee Perry records. And by last year's *Fear and Whiskey* album they were going whole-hog honky-tonk, thanking Country Joe and wishing Jerry Lee Lewis well on the record sleeve, designing the "Sin" record label as a tribute to Sun, posing for a promotional photo like the Band on the cover of Dylan's *Basement Tapes*, covering a Hank Williams song, howling out sad new originals about darkness and doubt and dislocation and death, and hiring classically trained violinist Susie Honeyman to frame the new music with her fluid fiddlework. The early-'86 John Peel-session *Crime and Punishment* EP sunk them further into the swingin'-door-jukebox-and-barstool abyss, and the new *The Edge of the World* finds them dancing on their own graves to the tune of Rico Bell's sprightly Tex-Mex accordion.

The country-oriented stuff has been publicized and college-radio'd enough to allow the band to tour the United States this year for the first time ever, not counting a slot opening for their more-ideological Leeds neighbors the Gang of Four in New York on New Year's Eve, 1980. (That show turned out to be the Mekons' last live appearance *anywhere* for two and a half years, due to the band's disillusionment with then-prevalent violence in British clubs.) Nowadays, the group actually prefers playing in the States, "where people are nicer, and know our stuff better," Lycett says. Not bad for a nine-year-old band without a single U.S. record release. Vocalist/axeman Tom Greene says the band has discussed the possibility of a debut American LP, probably a "best of" thing, with indie labels such as Homestead, Relativity, and Enigma. But nothing's official so far.

Live, the seven-or-more-(depends on the night)-piece Mekons trip over one another, call each other names, show off the cowboy hats they got on a discount when they told the guy they were a country-and-western band from England, cheer Susie's fiddle and Rico's squeezebox solos, address in their songs the social mobility which they say has become a central fact of Western life since World War II, forget the words to "You've Lost That Loving Feeling," introduce "Help Me Make It through the Night" with Tom Greene holding his nose, tell the audience to vote Communist, and pretend to tell dirty jokes between numbers. "We often enjoy ourselves when we're playing," understates Langford, who also makes noise for the Three Johns, and who claims he's only happy when he's drunk. If the Mekons seem cheerful onstage, it's only because they've marinated themselves to the point of amnesia, and the hangover hasn't arrived yet. As they drift over the edge of the world in "Shanty," off the new album, they half-chide, half-assure us that "we're not in the same boat at all." No, we're each in our own vessel, but we're all headed toward the same oblivion. And with the Mekons as our soundtrack, we've got nothing to lose but our way.

—*Creem*, 1986

## Mekons: *So Good It Hurts*

· · · · ·

Stinks like halitosis how these UK fugitives-from-justice have turned consummate LP-a-year pros: kinda conflicts with the confusion that made 'em so lovable back in the import-only daze. *So Good It Hurts* isn't as complacent as last year's *Honky Tonkin'*, but it's still real self-satisfied, too damn in control of its own destiny. More and more, the Meke muck-wallow gets blamed on some International Capitalist Conspiracy, and the dogma's a copout. Tippin' over the apple-cart ain't no big deal if you're already set on which way the fruit's gonna roll.

Amateurism's what made this merry flock matter, but the new LP douses the two-step/pegleg ruralisms of recent seasons in a refined campfire-calypso lilt, adds studio drums and AOR axe, but no wild dubbish gene-splicing. "Poxy Lips"'s drunken sputter might've fit on '81's *Devils, Rats and Piggies*, and I like the jokes and tunes in the songs about Nottingham Forest and John Glenn's ghost. (The latter's a single. Lucky you.) But unless you've read every Situationist treatise the band has, your mind's bound to wander. "Fantastic Voyage" unfortunately isn't a Lakeside remake, and I should've foreseen all this tired reveling-in-decadence when Jon Langford told me two summers ago how he felt an affinity with Marc Almond. To hear the chubster make a true spectacle of himself, get ahold of the Jelly Bishops' EP instead: Jon and two pals masquerade as a Detroit raw-power trio and cover Lacy J. Dalton. And they spare us the wheel-spinning didacticism.

—*Graffiti*, 1988

## Pet Shop Boys: 18 Shopping Days Left

· · · · ·

The booklet inside the Pet Shop Boys' *Introspective* claims they aimed for "authentic Latin sound" on "Domino Dancing," their current single. (Lewis Martinée nicks some maraca/piano jump from one of his Miami-disco Exposé productions, and midway through it combusts like Mexican Independence Day fireworks; the words could conceivably celebrate revolution in Central America.) That this Anglotwerp duo would want "authentic" anything stumps me—I always figured inauthenticity (i.e., rejection of soul/folk sincerity for show-tune irony) was their *point*.

"Tonight the streets are full of actors," deadpans actor Neil Tennant in one noir-like number, allegedly "about" Paris '68. (Neil's apparently done all the work on the three or four Pet Shop albums; his playmate's named Chris Lowe.) *Introspective*'s got the first two Pet Shop cover versions, both of which apparently make fun of the originals; Tennant recites most of "Always on My Mind" as if Elvis/Willie's longing and regret were impossible, reads Sterling Void's ludicrous acid-protest "It's Alright" almost as blandly. After 15-plus post-Bowie years of music-about-musicmaking, contemptuous theatricality like this ain't so much subversive as just too fucking easy.

But so's this analysis. Unless you're of Exposé's ingenuous ilk, to say in the post-Bruce age that you're posing is only to say you make no conscious stab at the intentional-honesty lie. Soul-sincerity's as phony as phoniness by now, and distance-from-material encompasses all suckup-to-rockcrit crud from Los Lobos to Mudhoney. British whiteboys singing like British whiteboys beat British whiteboys singing like black men; ditto for products admitting they're products.

And nobody knows products like these consumers of oligopological output in the dead-end world where everything's for sale and money talks and streets are gold, these un-Iggy-like pet-shoppers who'd rather buy a dog than be one. We're all prostitutes, shopping for someone to pet, so romance equals commerce: "I love you / You pay my rent," "You always wanted a lover / I only wanted a job." *Introspective* argues we're taught competition as babes, eventually left not to our own devices but choiceless. The denial of self-determination stupidly distorts reality, but then again when I first heard "West End Girls" three years ago I was "sold" right away 'cause (just like "All the Young Dudes") the first two lines suggest young people should blow their brains out. The cashier took my money.

Theoretically, these Boys negate my entire worldview. Not because they're wimps (I *identify* with their wimpdom—they could probably kick my ass, actually), but because their ironic distance adds nothing, ever. Tennant's toasty tongue-texture and minimalist language are fine, but too often he's content to let us know he's performing—he walks too fast and talks too slow, too constricted and stylized and arid, "conversational" only if people who read books while you're talking to 'em over the phone don't make you nervous. He draws up contracts in our mutual interest, then breaks them. "What have I. What have I. What have I," or that overdramatic confession-booth scene in "It's a Sin," or how suddenly on the new LP he's prissily praising Che Guevara and Debussy with his pinky in the air. Next to Exposé's nubiles, he's sickly, burned out. He whines about betrayal, then betrays us.

When the Pet Shop Boys succeed, they succeed despite themselves. Tennant's monotone usually communicates more when it's singing than when it's rapping; in parts of "It's a Sin," "What Have I Done to Deserve This?" (where at first he's as passionate as his duet partner Dusty Springfield), and "Rent," something's at stake. I was raised Catholic, and I'm a househusband and Bee Gees fan, so lines hit me here and there. The masses take "Always on My Mind" and "What Have I" at face value (à la "Born in the U.S.A.," "Sweet Dreams Are Made of This") because face value is the only way these songs could possibly matter.

On the cover of last year's *Actually*, Tennant yawns. He's yawning at his Fashionable Adolescent Gloom mood—the one that hears disco's eternal-good-time tape loop as an icy rut. *Actually*'s wraparound drone is boring, not "bored." As disco, it's limp: not much tension, no release. The tire skids, glass shatters, jungle clatter, and hummable melodies are less staid than Stock/ Aitken/Waterman for sure, but the supposed "desire" never lusts *enough*.

Yet I'm left breathless by the hogstomping baroque disco-grandeur (shades of Alec Costandinos's *Hunchback of Notre Dame*) that opens *Introspective*, a Shopping Channel sellout that's the best Pet Shop album for the same reasons "West End Girls" is their best single: most gleeful hooks, most persistent throb, most flaming maneuvers, most evocatively dopey writing, least cynical bullshit. The groove's more sensuous, finally closer to Exposé than Erasure. These dedicated followers of dancefloor fashion appropriate not just sunny ethnic congas, but bare-boned tempo-twisted acid-stutters and (tip o' the topper to guest host Frankie Knuckles) that juke-joint pine-top Chicago House's

Pet Shop Boys: "Left to My Own Devices" (from
*Introspective*, EMI Manhattan, 1988)

sons of Albert Ammons are so fond of. If the Boys are still more "about disco"
than "disco," well, Poison's more "about rock'n'roll" than "rock'n'roll" ("Your
Mama Don't Dance" might be a joke too, y'know), and *Introspective*'s confusedly jubilant enough to earn the comparison. These sly devils are a (plastic)
pop group, not some late-capitalist zeitgeist. But sometimes they're even funnier than the real thing.

—*Village Voice*, 13 December 1988

## Billy Joel: It's Not His Fault!

· · · · ·

Seeing how I've only been to New York twice in my life, it's kinda perverse for
me to defend one of the town's favorite sons in the town's alternative weekly.
Billy Joel's got that New York state of mind, he's always painting those romantic pictures of 52nd Street and Uptown and the Hudson Line and Mister Cac-
ciatore's down on Sullivan Street, and me, I don't even care who your new
mayor is. Like prototypical Babylonians the Dictators, Billy sleeps with his TV

on; like prototypical Babylonians the Beastie Boys, he steals shit from Charlie Daniels ("Goodnight Saigon"). Among his followers he can count on Debbie Gibson and sundry members of Anthrax. When he mentions the Yankees in "Miami 2017," on 1981's bombastic live sampler *Songs in the Attic*, everybody cheers. "They said that Queens could stay / They blew the Bronx away / They sunk Manhattan out at sea," he croons. The lights go down on Broadway, everybody moves to Florida, the mob takes over Mexico.

Urban ruin or no, the guy just gets no respect. Hard to figure why—he's a brat, a pugilist who's busted his schnozz one time too many, albeit a real dip when he gets "deep." With "Only the Good Die Young," very popular when most of my classmates (though not me yet) were losing their virginity, he invented Vatican Rock, the celebrated '80s genre that encompasses X and Madonna and Queensrÿche and now Bon Jovi (whose sign of the cross in his brazen "Livin' in Sin" video is to "Livin' on a Prayer" what "Like a Prayer" was to "Like a Virgin"). In the insanely tawdry "Captain Jack," an unheralded harbinger of *Over the Edge / River's Edge*–type Affluent Adolescent Anomie, his protagonist gawks at junkies and transvestites in the Village, then goes home and whacks off and shoots up and picks boogers while his sister's on a date, then he commits patricide and heads off to jail. A neocon before *21 Jump Street* and a yup hater before yups had a name, Bill's got a manly purr that rolls down into that knowing smirk and you gotta wonder how come not even a single postpunk smart-ass has thought fit to cover one of his tunes. Could be they hit too close to home, but that never stopped Frank Sinatra or Barry White, did it?

In the '80s, Joel's matured into something of an optimist, even started goofing around some. Which is rare—where Richards/Winwood/Clapton/Nicks videos embalm history in drab earth tones, Billy's vids, especially "Pressure" and "The Longest Time" and the inflammable new "We Didn't Start the Fire," are buoyant and colorful and self-effacing, like he's grown to love the form. Produced by the Mick Jones who didn't used to be in the Clash, *Storm Front*, B.J.'s least ignorable LP since '83's *An Innocent Man*, kicks off with fat Delta harmonica, hardly a healthy omen these days. But the blues boots open a more brutal *Sticky Fingers* rip than you'll find on *Steel Wheels* or *Pump* or *Dr. Feelgood*, after which comes the bongo-and-Linn-boosted single, which ain't so much a rap song as a pig-in-time's-python laundry list (sorta like "It's the End of the World as We Know It" or "Jammin' Me," only faster), which list tallies EVERYTHING IMPORTANT THAT HAPPENED DURING THE COLD WAR and says IT'S NOT OUR FAULT. "We Didn't Start . . ." is *already* the biggest hit ever to mention Liberace, Bernard Goetz, Roy Campanella, the Bay of Pigs, and thalidomide babies!

Joel also sings about Christie Brinkley on *Storm Front*, denies that she screws Lear pilots or gulps down margaritas on Barbara Bush's front lawn, but to tell the truth I'm really not concerned with all his petty squabbles with wives (or ex-managers). Like too many white musicians his age and tax bracket, he's been drowning his sorrows in too much old soul music. "Storm Front" buys *Get Happy* Elvis C. a sinking ship; "Shameless" wastes a great title on a queasy John Hiatt imitation. "When in Rome" laps up the black coffee Squeeze spilled on their sheets back in '82. Dickless drum sounds abound. But the sword-fisherman chantey "The Downeaster 'Alexa'" is the latest in Joel's string of classy physical-displacement ditties ("Say Goodbye to Hollywood," "Movin' Out," "My Life"), and besides enshrining my childhood stomping ground Levittown, the post–Cold War parable "Leningrad" is the latest in his string of swaggering city ditties (Highland Falls, Miami, Allentown). If the alone-at-piano coda "And So It Goes" comes off a little too heart-wrenchingly "sincere," that only puts Bill in a class with Paul Westerberg and Tracy Chapman and Bob Mould, none of whom can boast as commendable a sense of backbeat or as commendable an '89 album.

Of course, heart-wrenching sincerity is what we always hated about this self-proclaimed street-life serenader. And believe me, what with a born-again college roommate whose tastes ran toward "She's Got a Way" / "She's Always a Woman," I hated him lots more than you did. This wasn't just maudlin senti-ment, it was *ponderously anal-retentive* maudlin sentiment, and how the heck could anyone love someone "just the way you are"? I *despised* that garbage. But since hearing 1985's *Greatest Hits*, as worthy a twofer as New Order's *Sub-stance* or Motörhead's *No Remorse*, I've learned to tolerate the smarm, and sometimes to dig it, man—that Sammy Davis Jr. crescendo in "Piano Man" where our lounge-punk's patrons "sit at the bar and put bread in my jar and say 'man, what're you doin' here'" is as slimily absurd as classic Joe Piscopo or Bill Murray. Plus it's got a nifty organ-grinder oompah to it.

Which points out another neat tidbit about Billy: he's not the type of guy to shy away from influences some dork back on the block told him were "non-rock." As a pianist, he's no boogieman, less prone to radiating 88s and 96 tears than Elton John or even Randy Newman. Like Randy, and sometimes more so, Joel obviously sees himself partaking in a pop-composer tradition that predates Fats Domino by a good half-century at least. Sometimes he turns into Keith Emerson, but since his baroque archipelagoes (or whatever they're called) are never his Whole Game, they can tickle your fancy pants if you let 'em. And in "Los Angelenos" and "Big Shot" and "Don't Ask Me Why," he rolls his tongue around a maraca-fied lilt and dances a Frito Bandito flamenco. Latinization is the future, y'know.

Billy's been braying about growing old almost as long as Bob Seger, and he's never cared beans about guitars. But he'd rather laugh with the sinners than die with the saints, and he even rides his motorcycle in the rain, and though he's never displayed Elton's knack for whimsy or wearing shoes, he rocked Elton-doing-Stones-rock harder than Elton did in the late '70s in the same way that Elton rocked Stones-rock harder than the Stones did in the early '70s. Unlike Elton and the Stones, Joel never "went disco," which perhaps indicates a lack of gumption but might just mean he knows his limits. He "went new wave" (with *Glass Houses*) when Linda Ronstadt did, and though it took me a while to admit it since I was still putting on skinny ties and buying Bram Tchaikovsky 45s when "It's Still Rock and Roll to Me" came out, I think Weird Al's off-base when he says it's still Billy Joel to him—though his recent Soviet sojourn might represent a backslide of sorts, Billy's '80s inclination against taking himself too seriously runs counter to his entire generation, former *Saturday Night Live* knuckleheads included.

As his discography's expanded, I've learned grudgingly to respect his tenacity, his never-say-die-ness. Relying less and less on ivory as time progressed, he mined both the '80s nostalgia mills (on the doo-wop-and-Valli-informed *Innocent Man*) and the '80s civic-responsibility mills (on '82's *The Nylon Curtain*) more songfully than the competition, no doubt because opportunism's in his blood. *Glass Houses* and *Innocent Man* strike me as crafty and good-natured but flossily lightweight, *Nylon Curtain* as crafty and well-meaning but bathetic. Yet "Uptown Girl"'s falsettos feel giddily silly and "The Longest Time"'s a cappella feels humble, and I love how "Allentown" and "Pressure" *sound*, with all those stressed-out crushed-by-wheels-of-industry orchestrangulations. Onetime Dictators songwriter Dick Destiny, who lives there, tells me the steel factory ain't even *in* Allentown. And any fool knows that those papers you hang on the wall are called "diplomas," not "graduations." But I don't mind, 'cause when we're led to that "place where the only thing you feel are loaded guns in your face," all I can do is gasp for air. Unlike Randy or Elton or Neil or Lou or Declan or Tom Petty or Paul Simon, I'll take Billy Joel's '80s over his '70s. He's living proof that half-wits can improve with age.

—*Village Voice*, 21 November 1988

# John Hiatt: *Bring the Family*

. . . . .

So you get these guys who've all their lives been rebellious cynical schmucks, and the reason they've never made you gag quite as much as the standard-issue confessional-type soul-searching folkie sweetie is *because* they're rebellious cynical schmucks, and they have some personal crisis in their lives that convinces 'em it's time to hit the detox mountain (howdy, Warren), or they meet some curvy young thing and they can stand to be with her and she can stand to be with them so they visit the preacher and commence to makin' lovey-dovey-lovey-dovey all the time (howdy, Lou), and so all of a sudden they decide that they're *happy*, finally, and they've found peace with the world and settled down and decided it's time to be "mature" and all that, and that's all well and good and you can best believe I'm pleased as a pig for them up to that point, but then they go and put out a *record* because they want to tell the world about their newfound joy, and the record makes 'em sound like just one more standard-issue confessional-type soul-searching folkie sweetie, and their record company sends their record to me and the press release says it's the "most honest" thing they've ever done and it's "less smart-ass and much more positive" than their old stuff, and I'm s'posed to *like* it? Gimme a break.

Don't really wanna sound hateful about all this, though, seeing as how the new LP by John Hiatt (who's from Indiana and used to be billed as the "American Elton Motello" or something back in the gnu-wave daze and who's had songs covered by everybody except the Butthole Surfers) is a right listenable disc with nary a single absolutely yucky tune. Recorded in a lickety-split session with Ry Cooder on axe and Nick Lowe on bass (and supposedly somebody on drums, thought you'd never guess that to hear it). *Bring the Family* doesn't crank its shaft nearly as hard as Hiatt's previous *Warming Up to the Ice Age*, but thanks to rawness and improved epiglottal rasp, it's maybe the more credible album. I'm no apologist for Cooder's kind of chickenskin nostalgia, but I'm all for how he helps Hiatt back his R&B into this rickety Brinsley/Band/barnyard lope; Hiatt croons like a King when he catches a groove as smooth as the chorus of "Thing Called Love." And the twanging "Your Dad Did" (unfortunately, the only storyline here detailed enough to enable all-important empathetic identification/connection) is a skewed depiction of the urban everyday that could pass for Tom T. Hall. So anyhow, I'd really like to like this record. But for way too much of it, I get the idea Hiatt's trying to convince *himself* his recent domestic bliss is the best-of-all-possible-worlds that his lyrics claim it is. That could be because "clever wordplay" (like rhyming "amoeba" with "Queen of Sheba") always gets on my nuts and hits me as stilted (because it is) anymore; could also be that the vocalist's certainly impressive mastery of Curtis Mayfield falsetto and James Brown screech and Dylan sustained nasality and Howlin' Wolf wolf-howl and (all over the place) Van Morrison convulsive stutter suggest that this rock'n'roll adult's still too unsure of himself to find his own voice. Mannerism-flaunting this studied can sure convey an appreciation for soulful music, but that's not exactly the same as singing from the soul, catch my drift?

*—Creem*, 1987

## John Anderson Serves the Doofus Majority

· · · · ·

If the citizenship's ever had a time for defiantly self-preserving apathy, this autumn is it. On *10*, his most confident album in three years, best in five, and bitterest ever, John Anderson sings the war of all against all like he's sorry, but that's the way it is.

The single's title, "If It Ain't Broke Don't Fix It," sums up one not entirely unreasonable reason the middle class is being suckered into voting Bush (you know: better the devil we know than the devil we don't) instead of boycotting the ballot box like they ought to. "Lower on the Hog," a big rockin' nod to Hag's "Workin' Man's Blues," sums up another: "There's people standin' with their hands out formin' a welfare line / Savin' their backs while I'm out breakin' mine / I ain't worried 'bout the federal budget or the L.A. city smog / I'm workin' overtime and eatin' lower on the hog." There's deceit here, I think (never trust recording-royalty whining about taxes), but Anderson's truly pissed—when he snarls "there's a lot less scrap to go out to the dogs," it comes out "less crap." The album's ugliest, most hateful, most honest lines, in a crossover-and-western sorrow-drowner called "I Hope Things Aren't Like This Tomorrow," go: "I don't wanna hear how times are hard / I've gotta pull the weeds from my own backyard." Eight years ago, Anderson opened his debut LP with circular blues chords, a moan, and a miner's lament called "Havin' Hard Times."

Back then, this honky-tonker was young blood. He still is—at 32, he's younger than the GOP veep candidate, *lots* younger than most *Creem* cover-boys—but *10*'s daguerreotyped jacket pic pegs him as an elder statesman. In Nashville, he's out of fashion, almost, outflanked by the rootsy menagerie he paved the way for: handsome All-Americans in sleeveless undershirts, overwrought artsongsters who want boats, gnu-waive ironists with 7-Eleven tobacky in their jowls, Walton's Mountain families who sew and pray together, Baptist bluegrass fat-asses, udder-brained minstrel mandrills, all sorts of marginally oddball fauna from Austin and Bakersfield. Outside of Rosanne Cash and those incredible Bellamy Brothers, though, Anderson's the only '80s country person who's stayed interesting for more than a disc or two.

If you've got his *Greatest Hits*, you can live without half his regular albums (his third, fourth, sixth, eighth, and ninth); these are Opry auditions ("tasteful," "sincere"), not John Anderson records. John Anderson records are the ones where he curls the vowels in doofus patter like "cotton-pickin' rage of the age" or "I hadda chunka *meat* in mah hand" around a broken bottleneck. In "Blue Lights and Bubbles," slurping that he's "havin' one o' my heart attacks from the things you do," he's Fred Sanford about to give Aunt Esther one o' these across her fat mouth. "I'm gonna search and find me a better way to talk," his hickoid baritone drawls on '81's *John Anderson 2* (his super-est set, thanx to three marital-strife sobbers, two funny fast ones, and a creepily anomied proto-pigfuck rape-ballad), and the better way he eventually found was to drawl *more*.

Anderson hasn't told a good joke in years—chicken poop's not messin' up his windshield anymore. A shame. His ravers, no-brakes ones like "Shoot Low Sheriff" and "Swingin'" and "Let Somebody Else Drive," where the singing's like George Jones on Starday (or Ronnie Van Zant) and pianos and saxes kick up dirt, always had a wise-guy edge. But with "Things Ain't Been the Same Around the Farm" he started to rock serious stuff, too. That's on '83's raucous *All the People Are Talkin'*, this teenage-rockband vet's only real hair-up-the-butt rock'n'roll album. '85's *Tokyo, Oklahoma*, modestly craftsmanlike, is as much a Mantovani record as the r'n'r record its Jacuzzi-drummed Womack-via-Stones kickoff-cover helps propagandize it as (the wondrously depressive "Down in Tennessee"'s got string-tapestries out of "Lucy in the Sky with Diamonds," even); *10*'s not so much r'n'r as '70s soft-rock, L.A.-style.

Bernie Taupin helped pen "Ballad of Zero and the Tramp," as catchy a Bonnie-and-Clyde (or Captain Fantastic and the Brown Dirt Cowboy?) tune as "Fast Car." Last chorus-reiteration's soaked orchestrally. Anderson sings "How come it feels like Monday / Seven days a week"—more populism (bet he digs *Scarecrow*), and there's more still in the trash-organ-pushed "Down in the Orange Grove," where the artist's old Florida homestead gets overrun by malls. Just wish he could see how the "progress" he complains about here contributes to the welfare line he complains about elsewhere.

*10*'s surly self-pity is aging-star stuff, and filler fills side two like on *John Anderson* and *Tokyo, Oklahoma*. Hope's found in irritatingly usual spots: a woman, God, kids, warm place in the sun, light at the tunnel's end. "The Will of God" attempts an Aquinan teleological proof (drop becomes ripple, the Lord tames tidal wave—he needs to read some Kant, or anyway some Hurricane Gilbert headlines). But "Just to Hold a Little Hand" doesn't sog out like you'd expect, and not just 'cause I'm a dad. Plus, though none of this optimistic sentiment reaches as far as his saddest binges or his yodelingest Appalachian geography, Anderson's husky Hag-like hardness cuts through the bombast and girly-girls like it hasn't in ages.

Admittedly, I appreciated Anderson more back when he was reveling in chosen poverty, waiting on back steps with his bedroll. When he started getting complacent, pulling panicky patriotic pranks like extolling eagles and reviving "Fightin' Side of Me" mid-Reagantime, he jaded me some, made me wanna go shoot birds. *10*'s most hostile parts at least resurrect a kind of danger.

—*Village Voice*, 8 November 1988

## Country Songs III

· · · · ·

### Don Williams:
### "Good Ole Boys Like Me" (1980)

This single, which just missed the top of *Billboard*'s country chart, might well be the most *literary-minded* country hit ever, since it namedrops not only Uncle Remus, but also both Thomas Wolfe (read in bed as a child while tuning into classic high-wattage AM radio R&B deejays Wolfman Jack and John R) and Tennessee Williams ("those Williams boys they still mean a lot to me—Hank and Tennessee"). There's also gin-breathed Dad kissing the boy goodnight under a picture of Stonewall Jackson, and eventually a kid down the street who succumbs to bourbon and speed, and the protagonist surviving by learning to pronounce his words like a TV newscaster. But you can't take the

South out of the boy. Written by Bob McDill (also author of Alan Jackson's "Gone Country," Mel McDaniel's "Baby Got Her Blue Jeans On," and Sam the Sham & the Pharaohs' "Black Sheep"), the song is as sublime as it is pretentious, and, for Don Williams, entirely atypical. He came up with folkies the Pozo-Seco Singers (six Hot 100 hits, 1966–'67), and his gigantic solo catalog seems long on cycle-of-romance ladies' choices and super-laid-back country-comfort food about satisfaction with one's lot in life—gentlemanly and un-redneck enough (he grew up in Texas, but on the Gulf Coast) to enable a major audience in England and across Europe. Critics in his corner swear he retains an undeniable countryness that middle-of-the-road sapsuckers he's inspired only fake. Not sure I buy that, or would care about him more even if I did, but if the ballads ever finally sink in maybe I will.

### Terri Gibbs:
### "Somebody's Knockin'" (1980)

There may not be a darker, bluesier country hit in the post–Jimmy Carter era than this one—and certainly not one that crossed over to the upper reaches of the pop chart. (Went #13 there; #8 country.) Terri Gibbs was a blind pianist from suburban Augusta, Georgia, who sang huskily enough to pass for a man, or at least for Phoebe Snow; no doubt she'd listened to her share of Ray Charles as well. She started out gospel and eventually wound up back there again— "The wheel of life keeps turning as your carriage turns to rust," as her other great hit, 1982's extremely spare and spooky "Ashes to Ashes," put it. "Somebody's Knockin'" takes its pulse from Donna Summer's proto-techno "I Feel Love," and its haunted temptation from Robert Johnson: the blue-jeaned, blond-haired man at the door, asking Terri her place or his place, is the devil. "He must have known I was spending my nights alone / My body's burning so he oughta feel right at home." Even now, the song inspires quotable YouTube comments: "Those blond cowboys are so hard to resist, even for a Presbyterian." "Great song! Maybe somebody can do a metal or gothic-metal cover."

### Sylvia:
### "The Matador" (1981)

Sylvia of Kokomo, Indiana, had a pile of country hits in the early '80s and is remembered, correctly, as one of country's least-country stars ever. But that doesn't mean she was one of country's worst. Her album covers tended to credit a surplus of keyboard players (synths, pianos, Rhodes), and plenty of tracks showed a pronounced and mechanistic sense of flashdance AOR if not genuine disco (sonic reference points: Olivia Newton-John, Laura Branigan, Sheena Easton, Stevie Nicks, Donna Summer, though a couple of those obviously came later). "Nobody," her big crossover hit from 1982, was her one stroke of absolute pop-country genius. But this bullfight serenade from a year before—supposedly soundtrack of the first conceptual country video shown on CMT, a 13-year presaging of Madonna's "Take a Bow," no doubt— was stranger. The flamenco-fluttering opening fanfare suggests Sylvia and/or her producer/boss (she'd been his secretary) Tom Collins had been feasting on '70s gypsy rock-disco records by Babe Ruth or Santa Esmeralda, and the lyrics open on an ominous note: "Everybody holds their breath / as he passes by the horns of death." One YouTube commenter confesses the song scared her as was a kid—makes sense. Sylvia flattens her vowels like a true midwesterner, but Abba's "Fernando"/"Chiquitita" mode figures prominently, and the big chest-haired backup shouts (there's a "bloodthirsty crowd," this being a bullring) are straight out of a Munich leather bar. It's like Europop's misapprehension of western country was being sent back to us, just to mess with us.

### T. G. Sheppard:
### "War Is Hell (on the Homefront Too)" (1982)

So, which lonely spouse on *Army Wives* would *you* want to be deflowered by, if you were a 16-year-old lad—Claudia Joy, Denise, Pamala, or Roxy? Or Roland, for that matter? Imagine the possibilities! T. G. Sheppard did, and not only was that TV show a quarter-century away, there wasn't even a good war going at the time (the Falklands don't count). So he set the Dear John action in 1944, when a *major* lack of warm male bodies were available back in garrison. As virginity-lost-to-MILFs fantasies goes, it's at least up there with the Four Seasons' "December 1963 (Oh What a Night)" or Garth Brooks's "That Summer," and has a more stompingly martial chorus than either. It went #1 country, of course—one of 14 times T. G. did, most of them forgettable. I bought an album by him once—*I Love 'Em All* from 1981, which I really hoped to be as cheesy and silly as its cover, where studly T. G. is being mobbed by all the fawning lipsticked ladies he's loved before, but sadly it was a snooze. (Amusing Joel Whitburn note: "Initials do not signify 'The German Sheppard' or 'The Good Sheppard,' as commonly thought.")

## Sweethearts of the Rodeo:
## "Midnight Girl / Sunset Town" (1986)

The primary gender conflict in commercial country music over the past three decades is this: the boys stubbornly insist on staying put with their redneck identity politics in the middle of nowhere (see, say, Montgomery Gentry's "She Couldn't Change Me" or Eric Church's "Homeboy"); the gals restlessly yearn to get out. This song defines the latter category: Sweethearts of the Rodeo, named for an archetypally country-rock 1968 Byrds album beloved by alt-country bands, were two 30-ish sisters (from the affluent L.A. beachfront suburb Manhattan Beach, but don't tell anybody), married at some point to guys from the country-rock combos Pure Prairie League (Vince Gill, to be exact) and Blue Steel. But here they're harmonizing, with absolute conviction, about being stuck in a one-stoplight/one-horse hicktown where nobody makes noise and where the sidewalks get rolled up at dusk, when they'd rather be enjoying exciting nightlife somewhere bigger. Their follow-up album two years later even had a sequel of sorts, "If I Never See Midnight Again." The music is pop bluegrass way bubblier than the real thing, and "Midnight Girl"—a #4 country hit—served its own nightlife purpose, judging from its inclusion as a "two-step" on K-Tel's instructive 1995 *Country Kickers* line-dance compilation. Just as important, it served as a kind of blueprint for later woman-country escape-from-boondock classics: Trisha Yearwood's "Walkaway Joe," Faith Hill's "Wild One," Dixie Chicks' "Ready to Run," Taylor Swift's "Mean," Lauren Alaina's "Growing Her Wings," and beyond.

*—Complex, 5 June 2012*

## The '80s: One Step Forward, Two Steps Back

· · · · ·

An interesting footnote to '80s rock'n'roll is that there was no single big event halfway through the decade that cleaned the slate and started the ball rolling again—like Elvis in the '50s, or the Beatles in the '60s, or the Sex Pistols (or disco) in the '70s. And as Bob Geldof and Michael Jackson would happily tell you, it sure wasn't for lack of trying. There were just too many slates to clean. We've got as many kinds of heavy metal now as we had kinds of rock a decade ago. When I talk to friends of mine who are supposedly really into this circus and I mention a great chart topper the radio won't stop playing, I might as well be talking Swahili. We've got bald bullies and fanzine phonies and b-boys and aging insider traders — all who barely acknowledge each others' existence, much less admit that the other guy's soundtrack might have some integrity, too. If *Yo! MTV Raps* signals something of a truce is near, it probably won't last long.

Mostly, what happened in the '80s is that we worked against each other. Big deal, you say, all fragmentation amounts to is admitting that you can't please everybody, right? Well, if you think music's some kinda lone wolf, what about cable narrowcasting or VCRs or Classic Coke or designer drugs? Product identification runs rampant! *Sassy* magazine and the Fox Network and Nintendo games tell us more about the future of Western civilization than Tracy Chapman does, I bet.

The joke, and the paradox, of course, is that all this nuclear fission happened while musicians sweat blood trying to join forces against their lengthy roster of common enemies. By '85, everybody wanted to save the world — via Farm Aid and Live Aid and "We Are the World" and Artists United against Apartheid and Art Meets Labor. Springsteen donated dollars to miners' wives; Madonna marched against nukes.

Shrouded in vague hippielike notions of community, social consciousness took the spotlight away from our ears or worse. I fully expect respectability to exterminate rap and metal. It takes more than coming down on the politically correct side of a controversial issue to make a great record, and it'll be a long time before realism seems relevant or significance seems significant again. Rock's gotten too big for its britches, and the pop world's empty gestures might as well be made by George Bush. Nonetheless, quasi-altruistic '80s activism did help pop regain the countercultural visibility it had lost in the '70s (as did MTV). Your mom might not know Def Leppard or N.W.A, but she knows Bruce and Madonna and Boy George. They even placed among *People*'s 20 people who "defined the decade."

Say what you want about '80s rock, it was always in the news. If nowhere else, it was in the business pages. I'm talking boom years and bust years, doom years and dust years, tie-ins and buyouts and PMRC boycotts, consultancies and consolidations and corporate sponsorships, new music seminars and alternative A&R departments and trusts-never-sleep deregulation. Celluloid sells vinyl as vinyl sells celluloid, and this Madison Avenue madness is considered sacrilege for reasons I've yet to comprehend.

Sony, singled out back in '82 as the slant-eyed devil of home taping, has bought CBS Records, which only proves what goes around comes around. Now a sham called CDs has got bizzers rolling in dough, and capitalism has become rock's best buddy. We're living in a material world, where Billy Bragg just demonstrates his dorkitude when he exaggerates the qualitative effects all this strong-arming has on the songs we hear. Regardless, I'm convinced the long-term legacy of Reaganomics is a surplus of work-ethic / invest-in-the-future professionalism that by now has fouled up everybody from Tiffany to the Flaming Lips. Obviously, it ain't a state of affairs that's conducive to great rock'n'roll.

Still, video killed the radio star, at least to the extent that Metallica and rap can prosper in Boise, so if somebody's gotta be blamed for the '80s, it ain't the industry. Starting around '84, the big labels made like Hollywood by concentrating on blockbusters and sequels. If the sequels were barely bearable, the blockbusters were at least palatable. The decade's most consistently forward-looking confounders of sound and image, by whom I mean Prince and Madonna and Michael Jackson (all of whom made confusion seem smart and sexy, and all of whom also dealt us a lot of crap), were the hottest stars out there.

Save for a few rap 12-inchers from before hip-hop crossed over, my favorite '80s singles were sizable Top 40 hits. It's conceivable that "Death of the European" by the Three Johns or "Ha Ha Ha" by Flipper might've made the list if FM radio had indoctrinated me with them as it did with all that platinum, but I doubt it. Bananarama and Steve Perry and Rick Springfield and the Human League and Billy Joel and DeBarge and the Deele all provided artifacts more durable than "Sun City" or "World Destruction" or anything by Tom Waits; Jello Biafra never came up with a protest half as gutsy or audacious as Genesis's "Land of Confusion" video. On the cusp of the '90s, as often as not, the most rampaging rock is the cynical output of complete money-grubbing hacks. Inasmuch as I feel solidarity with anybody nowadays, it's with the screaming pube masses.

So, like, what the heck happened? Well, for one thing, everybody who ever mattered turned to shit. Your Costellos and Thompsons and Springsteens and Moulds and Fogertys and Reeds read too many fellating reviews calling 'em God and started to believe the hype; your Laurie Andersons and Pogueses and Neil Youngs and Was (Not Was)es wore out their welcome and kept plugging away regardless. In 1989, John Mellencamp turned into Bono Vox, Paul Westerberg into Julian Lennon, Prince into Rick Wakeman, and LL Cool J into

Peter Cetera. Great songwriting's gone the way of great drumming, and everybody holds their throb in check 'cause they're worried about selling out their artistry. Those '80s classics you always hear about were never that classic to begin with: *London Calling* has fewer killer cuts than *Sandinista!* or *Give 'em Enough Rope*; *Dirty Mind* has one great side; *It Takes a Nation of Millions to Hold Us Back* has two great half-sides; *Born in the U.S.A.* is stodgy; *Shoot Out the Lights* drags except when "Walking on a Wire" is scaring you back to Stonehenge.

*Remain in Light* and *Graceland* excite me even less. Both records typify one of '80s rock's most disgusting diseases — call it meta-music. Especially on indie labels, combos strived so hard to be dangerous (Flesheaters, Skinny Puppy, Diamanda Galas) or funny (Cramps, Mojo Nixon, Young Fresh Fellows) or quirky (Skafish, Alex Chilton, Sugarcubes) or sincere (Fugazi, Soul Asylum, Waterboys) or political (the Ex, Midnight Oil, Boogie Down Productions) or naive (Beat Happening, Half Japanese, They Might Be Giants) or eclectic (De La Soul, Arto Lindsay, Poi Dog Pondering) that they wound up affirming nothing but their own deluded smirks.

By patting only its own back and hiding from any sounds that couldn't be filed behind a single adjective, the concept obliterated the music. Posthardcore's semi-ironic '70s revival, which by my count started with Bad Religion's *Into the Unknown* back in '83 and has rolled downhill ever since, will never kick rump the way AOR's real sludge did. Aerosmith and Led Zep (and Sylvester) were funkier than 24-7 Spyz or the Red Hot Chili Peppers (or Talking Heads) will ever be, not least because they never made funkiness their point. It just seeped out, see?

That's why the underground sucked. Parading an eccentricity it never really had and flailing away at pop with semi-pop gimmicks, it replaced the beat with deceit. The most radically entertaining '80s underground white rock, late fallout from British punk, was pretty much gone by '80 or so. Vanguard movements thereafter repeatedly undertook do-or-die quests for roots and values on a displacing and amoral planet via moans from the abyss and a stretching of the air-raid curtain (or something like that), but they increasingly fell prey to their own joyless smugness and self-defeating semi-professionalism. Blame it on a sense of hopelessness or just good sense, but there's not enough hunger for the fruits of capital, only this putrid willingness to settle for mediocrity. No Wave amounted to very little, hardcore to less, speedmetal to less still. If I'm not mistaken, acid house is over already.

Almost as if by design, Minutemen and Mark Stewart and Membranes LPs that shook up my earth just two years ago hold up as crummily as any psyche-delphic '67 mind trips you can name; whatever was once startling about them has already evaporated into the ozone. Steves Albini and Morrissey turned out to be nothing more than middling method actors with good guitar sounds that evoked nothing more than good guitar sounds. Put on *New Day Rising* or *Zen Arcade* now, and you'll wonder why Hüsker Dü's rhythm section is wearing back braces. Local scenes are wonderful, but one thing the '80s proved is that cult audiences can be as passive and slavish as anybody, at least if you flatter them enough. You can innovate and bellyache to your liver's content, but hooks and grooves aren't optional. There's more r'n'r voluptuousness in George Michael's "One More Try" than in the entire Shimmy Disc catalog.

Indie-rock subversion is the mirror image of bucks-rock fossilization, another '80s phenomenon that made thinking beings sick. By mid-decade, in a lot of suckers' minds, anything born in the U.S.A. with a hillbilly twang or bluesy snarl or Spanish surnames or romantic words about trains and/or hard times was good to go. Thirsty for substance, tired of synthetic craftsmanship that supposedly left emotion by the wayside, every rugged retro/jingo opportunist who ever wanted to be a regular guy had a flag to wave and a few taunts to toss at England's haircuts, as if Yankee barbers are innately more honest. In place of Haysi Fantayzee, we got us a heap of new sincerity and cowpunk.

The last-gasp grasp for traditional standards that make no sense in an untraditional world was grounded in the fallacy that, by reviving certain antique images, you can revive the feelings those images gave you when you and they were young. Roots neoclassicism is as close as rock got to Reagan. As with Reagan, you couldn't help but be at least a little bit susceptible. It comforted you, made you feel warm all over. The decade's best country album, 1981's *John Anderson 2*, helped usher in a neo-trad movement that's evolved toward clean-cut creeps who can't even write their own songs; before long, they blended into a sanctimonious swarm of granola-gobbling Joan Baez / Armatrading retreads with serious stuff to say about poor people and war. With Ten City, we've even got retro house music!

This ostrichlike authenticity schtick was, of course, applauded by all those zillions of menopausal has-beens who refused to fade away this decade, even the least senile of whom (Randy Newman, Don Henley) were too bland and out-of-it to matter. With Guns N' Roses ruling the planet, what Keith Richards does with his time is irrelevant, and if Keith can't figure out why everybody doesn't just let him grow old like some poor boring blues guy, I guess Keith never understood what made the Stones so great in the first place. Not that, say, Pere Ubu's or the B-52's' refusal to chuck it is any less reprehensible. The biggest threat to rock'n'roll's future is its past. Period.

The late '80s were an era of classic rock stations, the Rock and Roll Hall of Fame, the reissue boom, greatest-music-in-history-type music. Problem is, all that archival garbage *destroys* rock'n'roll. And don't think for a second that the music didn't know it was dying. After making *The Wall*, *Hi Infidelity*, and *Asia* the blockbusters of '80, '81, and '82, AOR radio was sucked into its own vacuum. The true folk music of 7-Eleven-parked teenage MidAmerica was a squeaky-clean/peachy-keen, CHR/MTV, Springsteen / Van Halen hybrid shouting about losing something that means a lot. In songs like "Livin' on a Prayer," "If I'd Been the One," "Summer of '69," "Boys of Summer," straight white males mourn as youth and prosperity and rock'n'roll slip-slide away. Needless to say, the long-term forecast doesn't sit well with said demographic. Which explains why Andrew Dice Clay, William Bennett, Axl Rose, and Hilton Kramer are running scared.

The '80s really didn't belong to rock at all; the decade belonged to disco and rap, to Latins and blacks and whites who wished they were. With a few brief lapses, like that period in '85 when all the buppie bop wasted itself beige and upwardly mobile with Michael McDonald duets, the ghetto dancefloor's where the life was. That's where you could find successful indies: Tommy Boy, Profile, Prelude, Def Jam, Sleeping Bag. While rock was shellacking its history bronze or trying to reduce it to some camp joke, rap master mixers were courageously plundering the past for sounds, reinventing what those sounds meant, refashioning 'em for present-tense use.

Give or take Def Leppard (who might well be rock's last hope just 'cause they don't know any better), rap and disco are the only musics where anything's allowed to happen just for the hell of it anymore. Disco (you know, house or freestyle or techno) is more viable than rap; rap peaked early on, and it's been hobbling ever since it got wind of its own importance. It'll enter its own retro phase before long, and soon we'll start reading interviews about "the best Public Enemy LP since *Jewblood on the Tracks*," and 20 years from now Tone-Loc's reunion tour will land him on the cover of *Time*.

Or maybe L'Trimm will turn out to be the new Sex Pistols, and old fogies like Chuck D will be relegated to classic rap stations. and nobody'll care. Then UK sampler duos will revive prog-rap, just like the prog-rock revival King's X and Metallica and Midnight Oil are pulling off now, and critics'll hate the stuff, just like they hated Rush and Kansas the first time around. Axl Rose will get butt-raped on the streets of Compton, then he and his pal George Michael will start playing crash-and-burn versions of old Labelle songs. World music will filter into the heartland from Nuevo York, Neneh Cherry will link up with Tito Puente and his Voivod Salsa Orchestra, and finally it'll all start to make sense to everybody, 'cause by then we'll all have had Spanglish lessons seeing as how that's gonna be the new official language. The Japanese and Russians will start throwing polyrhythmic Nerf-metal mudpies in our faces like they invented the stuff, and sooner or later, some smart-ass'll decide that the only credible music works as Muzak (as long as it's got a good beat).

Maybe we'll just keep getting more of the same. Or maybe everything'll just keep getting worse. If that's what's supposed to happen, we'll finally all get the joke and it'll make rock'n'roll fun again. Or maybe when we hit the millennium mark, the sun will explode. Then we won't have to worry about all this junk, will we? We can only hope.

—*Request*, January 1990

**3**

·····

**'90s**

**BETTER GET THIS OFF MY CHEST** right away: I have a serious
'90s problem. Music-wise, at least. My most commented-on Facebook post
ever (10 April 2014): Chuck Eddy "is celebrating the 20th anniversary of how
lousy rock music was in the '90s." (Daniel Brockman's reply: "It was a time
when young people literally dressed up in mailman clothes.") And yeah, I was
born in 1960, hence starting to get old and grumpy by then, but somehow I
got less grumpy later—at least a bit. One's 30s are tough for a man (or at least
a critic). But I still feel the codification of college radio (especially after *CMJ*
started publishing, in 1993 apparently) has a lot to answer for. Though, to be
fair, a lot of stuff got even worse afterward. Grunge sure did, and probably Brit-

pop. (As lame as Oasis were, at least they weren't Coldplay.) Also pop-punk, and seems like rap and Europop lost ground too. (Country actually got *better* later, for a while anyway.) So I can't explain why '90s music strikes me as deserving its own special ring of decade hell—maybe I just wasn't paying as close attention at the time. I *definitely* was ignoring metal through most of the '90s, seeing how I'd just finished writing a metal album guide at the decade's outset and needed a decade-long break. (Can still live without all that Eyehategod and Helmet kinda crud, though.)

Actually, lately, I've been trying to reconnect with what I can—picking up used rock CDs I'm vaguely curious about from dollar bins (Gin Blossoms, Mordred, Big Chief, the Big F—all passable at best), and spending more time with also-rans from my shelf—Adventures of Stevie V and Captain Hollywood Project, Colourhaus and One 2 One, Lionrock and Pimp Daddy Nash, Bloodstar and Skyclad and Anacrusis, Love/Hate and Kik Tracee and Warrant after their hits stopped, Carlinhos Brown, Caroliner Rainbow, New Kingdom, debut albums by Sophie B. Hawkins and Linear and Mark Morrison and Savage Garden, Michelle Shocked's post–Lee Atwater minstrel CD from 1992. Industrial-identified stuff—rocky La Muerte and Tattoo of Pain, dancey Neon Judgement and A Split Second—holds up better for me than any other style widely considered "alternative," though critics rarely acknowledged its existence beyond a token big-selling mediocrity or two. Maybe I'm "prone to finding virtues in things I disliked as soon as they're unfashionable," to swipe an old Tom Carson line.

Haven't heard a Sponge or Alanis Morissette album since the ones I wrote about then, and have no real desire to. But now I'm wondering about Cause & Effect and Pankow again, and I actually kept up with Treponem Pal, whose decades-on *Survival Sounds* was one of my favorites of 2012. (Also still have a sentimental attachment to both Charles & Eddie and Cordelia's Dad, though the latter band may be unaware that my daughter Cordelia now has a higher college degree than me and has been known to teach gender studies to undergrads.)

Still . . . when Nirvana broke in 1991 and alternative a.k.a. complaint rock (which had been there all along) hit the jackpot, it theoretically erased everything else and set the agenda for years—and god, what a drab and dire dogma it spawned. Not a shock, given its primary source: i.e., Nirvana's groundbreaking synthesis of Bob Mould–style vocals with Hüsker Dü–style music, as Frank Kogan astutely put it once. Though admittedly that simple equation leaves out all their *other* hip '80s guitar-band borrowings, from R.E.M.'s marble-mouthed baffling-with-bullshit to the Melvins' Sabbath-dirges-done-even-slower shtick and general lack of physical propulsion.

Most '90s rap makes me shrug, too—fairly certain I'm wrong about that one, since nowadays everybody from Comedy Central's *Broad City* to the movie *Dope* to VH1's early 2016 *The Breaks* swears the stuff was incredible, but beyond a bunch of one-off singles it never quite won me over. And I don't often get the idea people touting '90s hip-hop have "MyBabyDaddy" or "Dazzey Duks" or "Doo Doo Brown" or "C'Mon N' Ride It (The Train)" in mind. Which bugs me some, given the influence of that brand of booty bass on so much crunkology since. Judging from the Kriss Kross / TLC piece that starts this section, I located rap's future in the South pretty early. I love hip-housey pop from 1990 too, and Big Beat at decade's end, but those eras belong to the '80s and '00s in my head. And it's not like all the wacky Loco Mia-to–Los Umbrellos Eurocheese in between or 1997's festive "How Bizarre" / "Tubthumping" / "Barbie Girl" / "To the Moon and Back" Top 40 resuscitation get much respect in retrospect, either. On the other hand, when Dan Weiss asked me recently where I stand on Moby's *Play*, I told him outside a broken phone booth with money in my hand.

Without doing all the math, I'm pretty sure I prefer the '90s' second half to their first. But I'm also pretty sure my favorite year from the first half of the '90s is 1990—an *especially* odd year, not just because it directly preceded "Smells Like Teen Spirit," but because it was the last year revenues for pre-recorded cassette tapes exceeded CD dollars. And since the primary retail format was entirely disposable—people at least *saved* old vinyl; tapes just wound up in landfills—it could go down as a lost window in music history. Nobody might notice, given the planet's ever exponentially expanding music mountain, but sometimes it feels like music that fell through that era's cracks melted into thin air. As with lots of now obsolete pre-Y2K technology—VHS, digital audio tapes, floppy disks, LaserDiscs, pre-Web word processors, dial-up modems, fax machines, answering machines—lost hardware means lost software, too. As late as 1998, Will Smith was rapping about figuring out where to plug in his kid's *101 Dalmations* CD-ROM.

Back in the 1990 I knew, newfangled samplers were destined to knit music into a crazy quilt of all *kinds* of music, S-Express or KLF-style. *Hack*, the pet-shopping, commercially flopping, electro-freestyle-house-hopping sample sale of a second album by Minneapolis Anglotechnophiles Information Society, sounded great then and sounds even better now. Pop, as one overly conceptual Brit bunch of the day put it, was eating itself—which, of course, pop always has, just usually not so self-consciously. Hot sounds came from producer-constructed dance-girl groups like Seduction and house music going Europop (Snap, Leila K, Technotronic, Black Box). And conventional wisdom, as one Nesbitt Bireley predicted in the December 1990 issue of Tower Records' house magazine *Pulse*, was that guitar rock was old hat for old men, so "the next big, self-contained pop music phenomenon—like Elvis, Beatles, etc.—will most likely be a rhythm-pop act."

Well, Nirvana sure shot down that theory quick, didn't they? And to those few of us who'd given up on the wheel-spinning and wall-flailing and incrementally more microscopic and insular formal advancement of indie-label pre-grunge rock's manlier strains several years before, the miracle that kept punk alive was a bit of a letdown. In 1985, *Grunge Music* had already been the title of a children's book about Teddy Ruxpin! I found it really difficult not to cringe at supposedly nostalgia-immune self-proclaimed Generation Xers' sheepish and self-obsessed imitation of the baby boomers they supposedly despised; no other age groups in my lifetime have seemed so full themselves. Way beyond the '90s, just like boomers before, they resisted letting their has-been heroes—Chili Peppers, Foo Fighters, Smashing Pumpkins, Pixies—slip gracefully into the middle-aged irrelevance their music had long earned. Then again, of course generations are a moot-point myth in the first place—not that you'd know it from the barely bearable 2015 movie *While We're Young* (starring Beastie Boy Ad-Rock!), where aging Gen Xers try to keep up with crafty Gen Ys who, hey wait a minute, prefer VHS, vinyl, and Polaroids. Plus in 2006 I personally wound up marrying the Lalena for whom her high school friend, screenwriter Helen Childress, named Winona Ryder's character in Gen X touchstone *Reality Bites*. It's complicated.

Lalena's nowhere else in this section herself, by the way—didn't meet her until 2001—but other real people in my real life are, especially in reviews I've included from Phil Dellio's songs-on-the-radio fanzine *Radio On*. These were largely written when my first marriage was fizzling, and in a few places I may well mansplain with undue presumptuousness and perhaps even unreconstructed sexism that I sincerely hope got reconstructed later. More generally, though, I also write in them about my family—something I tend not to do anymore. In fact, as the world's moved in one direction since—posting children's photos all over social media from the day they're born, status-updating every milestone—I've tended to move in the other, maybe because it's come to strike me as both a cliché and, as my older kids hit adulthood, an invasion of their privacy. As for my youngest daughter, born in 2008, Lalena and I don't even mention her by name or post her face on Facebook; maybe we're paranoid, but it just seems kinda risky.

Still, it's possible this section doesn't get confessional *enough*. I left out probably the two most personal pieces I published all decade: a long essay about class war on the gentrifying streets of the traditionally blue-collar ethnic Catholic Philadelphia neighborhood I lived in then—"Searching for My Main-line: The Social Geography of Manayunk"—from Frank Kogan's zine *Why Music Sucks* and a four-page "review" taking off from Shania Twain's "Any Man of Mine" that appeared in the summer 1995 (Mark Fidrych cover!) issue of *Radio On*. In hindsight, I decided they both maybe revealed too much about a couple of single moms down the block.

Shania or no Shania, though, a few surviving '90s reviews still demonstrate that I'd started paying more attention to country music. Which was a somewhat conflicted world at the time: on one hand, the theory goes, you had boomers who flocked to country because all the dance and rap on pop radio scared them away, so now Randy Travis could go platinum singing about George H. W. Bush's thousand points of light without ever crossing over. And on the opposite extreme, you had so-called house-country remixes of "Boot Scootin' Boogie" and "Chattahoochee" rubbing shoulders with C&C Music Factory ("currently the hottest nightclub format in Dallas," Michael Corcoran reported in *Request*) and gay dance halls like Rawhide in North Hollywood going gaga over burly acts like Confederate Railroad: "If Travis Tritt were to walk in this door right now, we would literally fall down on our knees," an LA club manager told *Billboard* in 1992. "This community literally worships that boy." To what extent that story inspired my silly Travis Tritt marriage equality fantasy is anyone's guess, at this point—just one more thing about the '90s I haven't figured out. Nonetheless, redrawing the map has been fun.


## TLC and Kris Kross: Women and Children First

· · · · ·

Well, as David Lee Roth would say, you might as *well* jump. If all it takes is some ghetto bastards bragging they're down with O.P.P. for rap to figure out that there's nothing wrong with being catchy, maybe everything *is* going to be all right. For the first time in years, groups are remembering how to accumulate momentum by passing the microphone. And am I imagining things, or is hip-hop's solar plexus suddenly slipping below the Mason-Dixon? Every time I switch on Video Jukebox some kid's paid two bucks to drool over dirty Miami punanny, and in Houston the Geto Boys are veering close enough to country-blues that a Garth Brooks duet can't be *that* far behind (they even have the same initials). To top it off, this spring's two BIG pop raps come from Atlanta younguns who know the power of hooks, clothes, and fancy footwork.

Both Kris Kross's *Totally Krossed Out* and TLC's *Oooooooohhh . . . on the TLC Tip* open with spoken intros that tell us how the perpetrators dress (Kris Kross: backwards; TLC: baggy), a feat performed with more color/movement/vim/vigor by the videos for their respective "Jump" and "Ain't 2 Proud 2 Beg." TLC, three 20-ish girls, wear Axl Rose–style catcher's gear or condoms as eye-patches, and point out muscular men's butts. Kris Kross, two boys (age 12 and 13), spin like gyroscopes and, well, pogo.

Kris and Kross, alias Mack Daddy and Daddy Mack (pronounced "Daddy Mackerel" in the hit—anybody know which kid's which?) say they decided to do a song about jumping 'cause anybody can do it, it's not like a dance where you need to learn steps. (So maybe white men can jump after all.) The voices that jump the word "jump" every five seconds belong to background employees Studio 4 Crew, though either Mack's or Daddy's does the song's *best* slam-dunk squeal when he says "High! How high? *So* high!" They elect themselves lovable huggable guys and quote "O.P.P.," and one of 'em breaks once for this ridiculous little woodpecker cackle. Mainly, they never slow down, so they hit #1 faster than any rookies in 15 years.

Kris Kross distinguish themselves from last year's subteen sensations, double-Dutch revivalists Another Bad Creation, by calling R&B-rap "bull crap." But they also thank TLC (who don't return the favor but quote "O.P.P." anyhow) inside their CD sleeve. And TLC *are* R&B-rap (maybe it's okay in their case, being women and all). T-Boz sings the gravelly slinky parts, Chilli sings the bright soulful parts, the irrepressible Left Eye swings the nasal rhythms. Nineteen-year-old Kris Kross producer Jermaine Dupri also oversaw one TLC cut, though not "Ain't 2 Proud 2 Beg." (Which has the same relation to the Temptations that "Jump" has to Van Halen: they're present in spirit.)

"Ain't 2 Proud 2 Beg" talks about sex, baby, just like Salt-n-Pepa say we should. It's about being able to draw the shades anytime you want. But there's such a perky grumbled bagginess to its strut that you wind up making up your own words, kinda like that old Nirvana song. From the vid I picked up that TLC are scared of being called freaks and that we're supposed to board their paddy wagon. Also something "rocks harder when it's draggin'," which worried my inferiority complex. Not till I read the lyrics did I notice the "kiss both sets of lips" line (which I *think* makes it a Top 10 first) and the all-lengths-created-equal egalitarianism (whew!).

*Totally Krossed Out* and *Oooooooohhh . . . on the TLC Tip* are like most other rap albums with an unforgettable single—the Geto Boys' *We Can't Be Stopped* or Young MC's *Stone Cold Rhymin'* or my man Vanilla Ice's *To the Extreme* (or, this year, Das EFX's *Dead Serious* or Brotherhood Creed's *BHC*). That is, not so much bad as beside the point: imitations and diversions. In a right world, both Kris Kross and TLC would wind up one-hit wonders, perfect unblemished pop fetishes. But you know darn well they'll be milked dry, same way as how "Come as You Are" ended up being "Good Girls Don't" to "Smells Like Teen Spirit"'s "My Sharona" (only not as cool). How can we keep our heroes when the multinationals won't leave well enough alone?

Mack and Daddy spend too much time trying to come off tough and petulant, as if tough petulance isn't just as wearying from 13-year-olds as from 23-year-olds. They hit on hotties, give the finger, call themselves bad niggas. And their music's all tough petulance, too—*Totally* is dense but not tense, with piles of heavy bass and blatting technology; yet another one of those hip-hop discs that defines "hardness" as how slow and low you go. (That this is exactly the same fallacy as in current punk sludge could work to somebody's benefit. Wanna stay rich for the next 20 years? Hook these brats up with Wisconsin's Old Skull. I know they're only 11, but *C.I.A. Drug Fest* is already their *second* album.) And why does the party stuff ("The Way of Rhyme," "Warm It Up," "Can't Stop the Bum Rush") have so much more oomph than the ghetto sociology lessons? Maybe because teachers like you to sit still when you're at school.

When suburbanites Mack and Daddy miss the school bus, it's not only more fun, but their voices ("standin' on the corner like a *fool*") sound more *scared* than when they have a nightmare about a buddy getting smoked. I mean, I *guess* I "appreciate" "It's a Shame"—electroparanoia about kids checking over their shoulders for big bad guys in big bad cars and other kids stabbing classmates in the head for their clothes—but it doesn't exactly reach out and *grab* me. ("Mind Playing Tricks on Me" is like the Velvets' "After Hours": amazing record, inadvisable influence.) Kris Kross do okay by Brit and Jamaican patois, but when they say they're gonna rap "old school" they sound more 1987 than 1980—a *real* shame, since in the mock Q&A that begins the CD they call their interviewer "Fatback," and in his 1980 roller-boogie rap "Charley Says," Fatback Band spinoff King Tim III said, "Kris Kross your legs in and out, ya turn around and ya do the bounce." (Or, in other words: "Jump, jump!") *Totally Krossed Out's* funniest moment outside of "Jump" comes from somebody making *fun* of kids putting pants on backwards: "Hey, I used to wear bell-bottoms. At least I didn't have to unzip my *butt* to take a leak."

TLC hold-up slightly better CD-wide mainly due to melodies and wider production variety: space train pulsations sampled from Amerindie legends ESG chugging through, boogie-woogie piano helping the jive roll, noise (buzzes, bangs, honks) that at least jar you a little instead of merely following rules Kris Kross–style. *Ooooooohhh* . . . is mostly pieced-together new-jill swill—TLC don't like being called hoes but they call other women hoes anyway. Still, they toss off a cute disconnected line or two ("L-E-F-T E-Y-E E-I-E-I-O"), and they sling nasty-sweet blues about dealing with men: "What about Your Friends" (backstab-warning à la Jody Watley's "Friends" or Joan Jett's "Fake Friends"), "Bad by Myself" (independent womanhood), "His Story" (Clarence Thomas and William Kennedy Smith must die). Kris Kross sound like they've known more rap records, but TLC sound like they've known more *people*. In their most notable nonhit, "Hat 2 the Back," blotto partiers revel behind them whilst the girls make zany Kleenex-like mouth squeaks and defend themselves for dressing like misfits. Which basically means wearing the krossed-out look—must be one o' them Atlanta things.

—*Village Voice*, 26 May 1992

## Cause & Effect: *Trip*

· · · · ·

Hardly anybody except 14-year-old girls was paying attention, but two of the top '80s British synthesizer bands finally made their best singles ever in 1993: Depeche Mode's "I Feel You" got a Yardbirds-gothic feel out of a macho punk-blues voice and Sonic Youth guitar noise, and Duran Duran's "Come Undone" turned lyrics about shoelaces coming undone into hard, soulful disco.

Okay, I lied about the shoelaces. It was more like that line in "Janie's Got a Gun" by Aerosmith—"Her *whole world*'s come undone." Cause & Effect are three Sacramento guys who play '80s British synth-pop in the '90s the way American garage bands used to mimic the Beatles and Stones, and teenage worlds come undone all through their new *Trip* CD: alone girls talk to walls; cold-hearted "stone girls" run away from confusion; stoned girls invite the singer along for the ride. Between thrilling zigzag electronics and psychedelic guitars in "Crash," the ride crashes.

Cause & Effect's career crashed in 1992, a year after their first album, *Another Minute*, came out, when an asthma attack killed keyboardist Sean Rowley. Keith Milo was hired to take his place, and *Trip* is more varied and coherent than the debut, even though no lyric is quite as intriguing as the boy-scolding-another-boy-because-he-couldn't-name-the-books-his-girlfriend-read stuff in their A Flock of Seagulls–like '92 MTV hit "You Think You Know Her." *Trip* starts with mandolins or dulcimers being fingered, tower bells clang, *Sgt. Pepper*'s strings surge. "Stone Girl" revives the piano-and-rain introduction from the Doors' "Riders on the Storm," just as boring techno hype Moby did somewhere on his *Move* EP last year, but Cause & Effect improve on Moby by turning the intro into a *song*. ("Techno" in general was way more fun back when it used to be called "Eurodisco.")

I like the idea of these out-of-it American boys playing a kind of music that's undeservedly become unfashionable, despite sounding less old-fashioned than almost any grunge or rap lately. They've got gorgeously gloomy melodies, too, and if I'm reading them right, they drink holy water to persuade shy Catholic women to sleep with them, because without Catholic women they'll never have anything to believe in. Their cute synth-blip rhythms are still too slow too often, but if I were a freshman girl coming undone, I'd fall for these deep-thinking sophomores in a second.

*—L.A. Weekly*, 5 August 1994

## The Cure: Spectrum, Philadelphia, 16 May 1992

· · · · ·

So who's cooler: Robert Smith or his fans? Well, it depends. From what I saw, none of his devout cultists (at least male ones) have guts enough to *dress* like him, or wear their hair that way. Smith had on high-top sneakers, flood jeans, and that wacky coiffure, but all the suburban teenage white boys in the audience looked boring and harmless with hair cut neatly above their ears like new lieutenants. I used to *be* a new lieutenant (ROTC commission, 1982), but my hair looked more like Smith's than anybody else's, and that's just because I'm too lazy to get it cut and it gets sloppy sometimes. I was also the only person besides the guitar player who wore argyle socks.

On the other hand, Smith still thinks he sings sad songs, but his audience knows better. They all came with bunches of friends, as if it were a big hockey arena–size party. If they've got friends, why would they need to hear sad songs? All the girl fans kept doing this happy Hare Krishna dance where they pantomimed washing their un-Smith-like hair. When Smith said he was a fly caught in a spiderweb, the girls played itsy-bitsy spider. The one in front of me barfed, cleared two rows of squeamish kids, then came back and boogied drunk after helpful Spectrum personnel mopped up and disinfected the spew. So, when Smith sings "Let's get happy," he no doubt means to be ironic à la R.E.M.'s comparably irritating "Shiny Happy People," but his fans like it because they *like* being happy. (His *human* fans, that is—not the big electric fans onstage blowing dry-ice smoke around and keeping the Cure from sweating too much from all the exertion they put into standing still!)

I've never really comprehended the supposed gloom myself. The Cure pissed me off by not playing enough of the early, fast, catchy songs from *Boys Don't Cry*, which were rickety powerpop just like Buzzcocks, Wire, and the Adverts. The last couple of albums, the ones with the Top 40 hits, have countless meaninglessly angular hooks per minute sunk into pretty and unobtrusively arty clatter (not unlike the new Pavement album, now that you mention it). Since I can't begin to imagine what the words are about, to me this stuff just seems kind of *quaint*. And nice.

I even hear jokes in there sometimes, and frankly, I expected Smith to display some sort of sense of humor in concert. No such luck. The stage is where the gloom comes from. The spotlights shining on the band were a *wee* bit colorful, but they used the dark midnight-blue one more than the lovely spring-green one. The Cure likes to use symbols that suggest misery as an *idea*. The drum and bass were Eurodisco slowed down, with all the push taken out, or to be more accurate, they were Uriah Heep, especially during the wahwah solos, except Uriah Heep had more rhythmic imagination (some Latin parts) and a more interesting singer (those proto-Mariah screeches; where do you think she got her name, anyway?).

But Smith's whine is easily the *most* interesting thing about this band. It's the only place Cure melodies come from. (In the ballads, they don't come from *anywhere*.) I tried real hard to dance to the trance, but my feet wouldn't move.

—*Spin*, August 1992

## SOS from the Metal of Nowhere

· · · · ·

Burnouts aren't the only scared teenagers. That's my main problem with Donna Gaines's book *Teenage Wasteland*, where a Long Island social worker with a doctorate in sociology ventures bravely into New Jersey to unravel the mess that inspired four "upper-poor" turnpike-trash headbangers in Bergenfield to asphyxiate themselves in a wrong-side-of-the-tracks public garage six years ago. Donna is lively, moving, even funny describing what it's like to elude policemen behind 7-Elevens, or to hang out with 14-year-olds just learning mating rituals in a roller rink or with 18-year-olds fucking and fighting and getting wasted in an abandoned *Parents Magazine* warehouse. Boys go watch Slayer while girls stay home picking up occult tips from Stevie Nicks records— this makes for smart, gripping journalism. And Donna doesn't come off like an outsider: more like an older sister who's been there herself.

But Donna also wants to improve the local situation, and when she starts making generalizations (especially musical ones), she falls flat. She thinks society never gives these metalhead brats the benefit of the doubt; I think she *always* does, which seems just as unfair. Teachers and parents identify them as "emotionally disturbed" losers early on and leave them to rot in reform schools; okay, fine, but how does that make the tattooed dirtballs' plight so much worse than any other kids' out there? Donna sees them as futureless nonconformists rebelling against overregulated lives, but to me it sounds like they have a pretty damn free rein in their town. What about kids who don't belong to any cliques at all, who don't *have* buddies to fend off boredom with? All teens are alienated from the adult world; to me it'd be more interesting to hear about kids alienated from *other kids*. Which Bergenfield's bums *are*, to a certain extent—they kinda hate those neighborhood jocks. But sometimes people really do dig their own graves, or at least provide the shovel.

For all that, there's no denying that the best parts of *Teenage Wasteland* make for one swashbuckling TV movie of a tome; with subject matter like this, it's hard to go wrong. But music about the same stuff rocks harder. *Method to the Madness*, the fourth album by Toronto foursome Killer Dwarfs, starts in the same land as Donna, a boomtown gone bust and taking innocent victims down with it: "S.O.S. from here in the lost and found / Slip through the cracks disappear without a sound / Alien in your own hometown / Hard to laugh when you feel that you're just a clown." Stuck on the ladder's bottom rung, you either take the first rail out or die in the middle of nowhere. If you're lucky (in "Driftin' Back" and "Doesn't Matter"), you get advice from your big brother, who used to be crazy and shy just like you.

Out since last summer, *Method to the Madness* slipped through the cracks itself, maybe because its groove throbs with too much melodic warmth and whoa-yeah harmonizing for Bergenfield's cold-blooded Metallica fans. Or maybe the cracks it fell through are the ones in Russ Dwarf's voice—he does a *Wayne's World* version of Steve Tyler or Robert Plant, where hitting high notes feels like hitting puberty, very apt. It's a style previously employed by undervalued tunemeisters like Kix (who are a bit more creative and flamboyant) and Ratt (whose echoey showboat-free bump is echoed in Killer Dwarfs' cheeseburger-riffed grind). Ratt used to sing about being rats in a cage too, but Killer Dwarfs have more heart.

Their early LPs were too loaded with plod-heeled posturing, but Andy Johns (svengali behind Cinderella's epochal *Long Cold Winter*) makes *Method* sound more garage, less heavy. It could still use shorter verses and fewer cornball beercries, though.

Killer Dwarfs claim they're "pissed off for a living," but their name comes from Russ Dwarf being 5-foot-4 like old Royals shortstop Freddie Patek (shades of Ronnie Dio's Elf!), so really they're self-deprecating, and maybe too polite. To ensure the greatness *Method* hints at, I recommend they hire Bushwick Bill of the Geto Boys—a *real* killer dwarf.

—*City Pages*, 16 December 1992

## Motörhead Überkill

• • • • •

"We're still here, because we shoulda died a fucking long time ago, but we *didn't.*" That's Lemmy Kilmister about his band Motörhead, on *No Sleep at All*, a live album recorded in Finland in 1988. Nine years later, Motörhead's *still* alive. At Lemmy's 50th-birthday party at the Whisky last December, Tom Arnold, L.A. Dodger Mike Piazza, and porn star Ron Jeremy (whose "Freak of the Week" rap video Lemmy cameos in) all dropped by, and Metallica dressed up as "the Lemmys" and covered Motörhead songs. "It's a *life*, not a job—not something you do from 9 to 5," Lemmy says. "I'll do it as long as people want me to." Which might be quite a while: some Motörhead Web page was wondering recently who would win in a fight, God or Lemmy. "God, probably," Lemmy concedes. "He's got more people on his side than I do."

Still, he admits, "You can never re-create the blind thrill of being onstage when you were 18." Thirty years ago, Lemmy was getting his blind thrills being onstage with the Rockin' Vicars, "not really a garage band, more a show-biz group in black with collars like vicars." The Vicars' first 45 was a cover of "It's Alright," a sort of larval-stage, Pete Townshend–penned version of the Who's "The Kids Are Alright." From there, Lemmy worked as a roadie for Jimi Hendrix (a job eventually inspiring Motörhead's "We Are the Road Crew," the best song about roadies this side of Jackson Browne). By the early '70s, he was playing bass in the eternally droning British space-rock ensemble Hawkwind: "Underneath all the electric saxophones, they were basically just a three-piece rock band. In concert they'd do songs for 22 minutes. But I'd never laugh at them; it was a great band to begin in."

In 1975, though, Hawkwind sent Lemmy packing, attributing the pink slip to his bust at the U.S./Canada border for possession of cocaine (which Lemmy insists was actually speed). "It just wasn't the *right* drugs," Lemmy tells people perplexed by the idea of one of the planet's oldest acid-rock institutions booting somebody out for indulging in chemicals. "Hawkwind were just on acid all the time." He hasn't ingested said drug since that era, preferring amphetamines and the alcohol he believes has kept him healthy like all those grandpas from Soviet Georgia who live to be 150 by gulping daily fifths of vodka. When your liver has that much booze in it, Lemmy figures, "no diseases can get past it."

Upon leaving Hawkwind, Lemmy formed Motörhead (briefly known as Bastard) with Lucas Fox and Larry Wallis from the weirdo-rock trio Pink Fairies. Covering ZZ Top numbers and produced by rockabilly goat Dave Edmunds, Motörhead began basically as a hard pub-blues garage threesome, not musically far from Chiswick Records labelmates like the 101ers (featuring future Clash hero Joe Strummer) and the Count Bishops. In 1976, with Fast Eddie Clarke replacing Wallis, Motörhead amphetamized their sound and became (in the poetic words of Martin Popoff's metal-album guide *Riff Kills Man*) "the first metal band who weren't trying to look good, play good, or record good."

At their first gigs, Lemmy laughs, "The audiences were *amused*—all these blank people standing with their mouths hanging open, just like when we opened for Ozzy's tour in 1981. Nobody's gonna be eating chicken out of a basket when *we're* up there." Somewhat more receptive were the punk-club audiences of the Damned (with whom they collaborated on a few cuts in 1978) and Adverts (whose members wear Motörhead jacket patches on the jacket of their great 1978 debut album).

"People call us heavy metal because we have long hair," Lemmy scoffs. "If we had short hair, they would've called us punk. They just look at the surface, the clothes; they didn't want to look at what we really *do*. We're a *rock* band. I *am* rock & roll; I've seen the whole thing. I remember Elvis's first record. Heavy metal is people who shriek and plod around. I think we have more in common with the Band—when we first started, we were playing 'Good Morning Little Schoolgirl' and all these Yardbirds-style songs. I wanted to be the MC5. We *bend*, like dance music. Except it's too fast to dance to."

He may have a point there—Lemmy insists Motörhead is a democracy, but since he's the ubiquitous spokesperson, by choice or not, it certainly *seems* like a bass player–led combo, and sounds like one too. Fast Eddie Clarke tended primarily to use his guitar as rhythm—to bolster basslines. Old Motörhead always had a beat that *swings*.

"I never liked *Ace of Spades* much," Lemmy confesses, dismissing the 1980 album generally considered Motörhead's greatest ever. Then he pits it against a collection they put out 11 years later: "*1916* pisses all over *Ace of Spades*. Our new stuff is much more varied, not just 'Let's do it in two weeks and say we're done.'" For instance, the trio's new *Overnight Sensation* has an epic called "I Don't Believe a Word" where Lemmy starts out not bellowing but almost *crooning*, and the final track, "Listen to Your Heart," comes as close to a wimpy power ballad as any Motörhead has ever cut. "It's my Everly Brothers influence," Lemmy says.

Which would all be well and good if my favorite track on *Overnight Sensation* weren't "Murder Show," the one track that seems like it *could* have been on *Ace of Spades*. "Nobody asked why the *Beatles* would come out with a different-sounding record every time," Lemmy points out. Maybe so, but it's still hard to figure exactly what *purpose* Motörhead serves in 1996—after 15 years of thrash and grunge fusing punk and metal till we all throw up, there's no void to fill like there used to be. By now, there's something *conventional* about what Motörhead do, and my theory is that, as their style becomes more commonplace, they want to branch out and be unpredictable. Lemmy doesn't exactly agree: "I like Seattle grunge; to me it just sounds like four geezers rocking out. I liked Nirvana, and Kurt Cobain, though he was obviously a weak man. But I don't think we were the original grunge band—I don't think we were the original *anything*."

Lemmy rightly calls most speedmetal "crap, just clubbing you over the head with it all." Metallica he's got more mixed feelings about: "I don't think they should do those eight-minute-long songs; I think it's a mistake—I never liked it in Hawkwind, either. But I saw them at Lollapalooza, doing their short songs, their new ones, and they were fucking unstoppable." To top it off, Metallica closed Lollapalooza shows covering Motörhead's "Overkill"; meanwhile, Lars Frederiksen sometimes wore a Motörhead T-shirt during Rancid's set. Lemmy found Rancid entertaining, too, "sort of like Jimmy Pursey" (of the late-'70s rah-rah Clash-wannabe tube-station-anthem gang Sham 69).

Well, at least he didn't compare them to Skrewdriver, the prototype skinheads with whom Motörhead also shared Chiswick roster space in the '70s, famous for cheery egalitarian tunes with titles like "White Power." Their singer was a notorious National Front thug, and Lemmy says he "let him sleep on my floor once so I could argue with him about Nazism. He'd say black people and immigrants are taking the jobs, but I didn't see it that way—Pakistanis had just opened a store in Notting Hill Gate and kept it open all night, and I was really *glad* to be able to buy a sandwich in the middle of the night."

The paradox in Lemmy arguing with the great white dope in Skrewdriver is that Lem happens to be a bit of a Nazism fanatic himself—an avid collector of daggers, for one thing. "Part of it is the pageantry of it—they had hundreds of different organizations, all with their own insignias. And they were here and gone in 12 years, and Germany's real small, but they changed the whole fucking world, so it would never be the same. The boundaries of countries are different. Hitler was a magnetic speaker, and he came out of nowhere to take over a country he didn't live in. As a person, though, he was so boring—a vegetarian, no smoking or drinking. And a short haircut.

"Wars are always the most interesting parts of history. Nobody wants to hear about agrarian reforms," Lemmy insists. Which explains why so many Motörhead albums have titles like *Overkill*, *Bomber*, or *March or Die*, and why the group used to use a replica of a World War II jet as a lighting truss. Mr. Kilmister is far from a Nazi himself—"I'm an atheist and an anarchist. I'm anti-communism, fascism, *any* extreme." And though Lemmy admits that fans might not pick up on all the messages, *Overnight Sensation* might contain the band's most politickled statements ever. "We haven't learned anything in the last 2,000 years. Nothing's changed except the technology. People get dressed up as the SAS and get all this equipment just to kill a fucking helpless deer"—this is the topic of "Eat the Gun," the new CD's most crazily caveman-primitive cut. Despite having covered "Cat Scratch Fever" in 1992, Lemmy is not interested in discussing gun control with Ted Nugent: "I don't think running around the woods in a loincloth killing deer with a bow and arrow makes you more of a man."

Three things in the world Lemmy thinks are underrated are Motörhead, chocolate milk, and conservation. But actions speak louder than words, and I know he thinks women playing rock & roll are underrated as well. Over the years, he's helped out Lita Ford, Nina Hagen, Wendy O. Williams, and most notably Girlschool, with whom Motörhead collaborated on a 1981 EP and toured: "I thought they fucking rocked," the man correctly raves. "So we were the first [male] band to take a girl band on the road with us." The one woman he'd most like to work with is Janet Jackson: "I wanted to do a version of 'Black Cat' with her, but Sony wouldn't let me. You could tell from the video that she was having a good time, that this loud rock music is what she really wanted to be doing."

Then again, maybe Lemmy just plain likes *all* women. He swears the chase really *is* better than the catch: "It's like a girlfriend of mine who once fucked Mick Jagger; I asked her what he was like, and she said, 'Well, he was good, but he was no Jagger'!" My friend Anne told me Lemmy has great legs, and wanted to know why he doesn't show more skin in his videos. So Lemmy reminded me of all the grief Thin-Lizzy-alumnus-turned-very-temporary-Motörhead-guitarist Brian Robertson got for his green satin shorts on the band's 1983 tour. "It's considered obscene if a guy shows his legs. At least here in America, people start thinking you're homosexual. In England people don't worry about that. Me, I have no problem unless somebody forces it on me. If I *was* homosexual, I'd be fucking guys in the ass for sure." Spoken like a true outlaw.

—*L.A. Weekly*, 7 March 1997 / *Rip*, January 1997


## Pankow and Treponem Pal Ring in Desert Storm

• • • • •

Like everybody else in this wonderful land of ours, during the week of 13 January I stared at the tube every night until I inevitably dozed off dreaming of doomsday. When I needed music, which wasn't often, the only thing my nerves could bear was war-rock—"Sloth" by Fairport Convention perhaps, but usually just pure-assed NOISE. Smart-bomb technology, Scud-boom sludge, foreign accents conducting pagan-ritual sorties on my tympanics in languages I couldn't make out, as if sung through a gas mask.

Eventually I absorbed the battle as just another okay rerun and my listening habits returned to normal. "Industrial" bands turned back into growling geeks, piecing together an audience from decadent danceclubs and sleazy slampits all over Teenage Subcultureland, awaiting the day they'll follow hip-house and art-metal into the mainstream. At very best, salvaging necessarily impersonal machines by injecting something wacko into 'em.

For instance: Treponem Pal and Pankow, who straddle borders between synthcrash and speed-thrash, treading unholy paths scorched in the late '80s by Ministry, Voivod, skunks of that stripe. If not for Desert Storm, I never would've paid attention, but I'm glad I did—Pankow, especially, are genuine court jesters, with a coagulated riff/grunt/beep/honk dub-roll that never gets serious enough to lose track of its hooks. They've got Italian surnames, yell out phlegmy profanities in inebriated unison, verbalize through vocoders, cover Prince and "Warm Leatherette" and the *Eraserhead* theme, drape their torsos with animal offal. On their nicely loose new live ROIR cassette *Omne Animal Triste Post Coitum* they stick to their three pet themes: alcohol ("Wodka," "Deutsches Bier"), scatology ("Me and My Ding Dong," "Happy as Horses Shite"), and fascist dictators: Saddam himself oughta cover "Let Me Be Stalin." And though Big Black's "Il Duce" beat it to the Benito punch, "Der Mussolini"'s more like if Steve Albini had honored Mayor Daley instead, which is to say it comes from the right place.

Where Treponem Pal come from is France, and they harrumph and grind not unlike their homefrogs the Young Gods, which is to say pretty great, though with less cabaret-funk samples and pulsations, which isn't. *Aggravation*, their second and most beastly plat of splat, boasts a raunchy remake of Kraftwerk's proto-nuke-disco "Radioactivity," plus much absurdist advice to "bruzzers and seesters." Pal oughta speed up sometimes, and they could really use more melánge, or maybe half a wit. Still, when the body count gets me down, they do the job and then some.

—*Creem*, 1991

## How Nirvana Didn't Kill Hair Metal

· · · · ·

The Myth of Nirvana has always demanded that the band be seen as a sea change in popular taste—for instance, there's the completely meaningless but oft-rehashed factoid that *Nevermind* knocked Michael Jackson's *Dangerous* off the top spot on the album chart, as if sales turnover didn't exist until Kurt Cobain came along. But the most enduring fable has always been the one about how Nirvana, and in turn grunge in general, "killed hair metal." Until all those cool Seattle boys changed the world overnight, the story goes, foofy coiffures and pink guitars and power ballads ruled the roost. Problem is, it didn't happen.

Basically, by the time *Nevermind* charted in October 1991, hair metal was already long on the way out. Glam poodles of Poison's ilk had wiped off their mascara and were trying to get serious—Cinderella's 1990 *Heartbreak Station* was a purist blues-rock record; Skid Row's *Slave to the Grind*, out in June 1991, was pop-shunning arena turbulence that went #1 without a hit single. A certain kind of boogie-based, old-school hard rock had also been on the way back ever since Guns N' Roses and the Cult broke through circa '88/'89; Black Crowes' debut album reached #4 in 1990.

Guitar-based "modern rock" from bands like R.E.M., Midnight Oil, Love and Rockets, and the Church was anything but obscure in the late '80s, and by the turn of the decade, even the hot breakthrough metal-leaning acts had a pronounced boho bent: Living Colour, black Manhattanites led by their slumming avant-jazz guitarist; St. Augustine–quoting Houston eggheadbangers King's X, led by their black gay Christian bassist; proggish San Francisco reformed rap-punks Faith No More; art-funking Boston eclectics Extreme. And maybe most significantly, given the emerging Lollapalooza Decade, New Age L.A. sideshow beatniks Jane's Addiction, whose *Ritual de lo Habitual* went Top 20 in 1990. Not a Sunset Strip sleazeball in sight. The year before "Smells Like Teen Spirit," one of the biggest rock hits even came from Seattle—namely, Queensrÿche's "Silent Lucidity," a Pink Floyd pastiche by thinkers-of-big-thoughts more given to high-flown concept albums about technological conspiracy than lowbrow groupie gropes.

So what changed after Nirvana, exactly? Well, the haircuts, maybe. And within a couple more years, radio and MTV were overrun by such exciting and innovative new bands as Collective Soul, Candlebox, Live, and Silverchair. The more things change, the more they don't.

—*Spin*, December 2009

## Sponge: From Grunge to Glam

. . . . .

Being the first Detroit Rock City band to hit the charts in years allows one to make certain claims. For instance. Vinnie Dombroski, the hook-nosed/orange-haired vocalist for bandwagon-grunge (though they prefer the often-more-accurate "hillbilly glam") fivesome Sponge can get away with spieling like a wise guy: "You mean you can't hear the sound of the factories in our tunes? The exhaust of bus fumes, the sweat of unemployment—and the Big Three! I ooze that from my pores." Sitting in a pork restaurant in the boho-boutiquey suburb of Royal Oak, Dombroski drains the last of an O'Doul's and declares: "I could fill this whole glass of pudding with the pain and suffering of the people in this city!" Trust me: this was no small pudding glass.

Dombroski also likes to boast that Sponge never fail to pull in all those drag queens working on the assembly lines—appropriate, since the band's latest, *Wax Ecstatic*, has not one but two ballads with the phrase "drag queen" in the title. The album is a long way from their noisy-riffed debut, *Rotting Piñata*, which held MTV by the throat last summer. It's actually a lot closer to their smash "Molly," an atypically jangled throwback to the *Pretty in Pink* sound-track that didn't earn the combo much respect; Dombroski jokes that he still attends a biweekly support group for second-generation grunge stars in hopes that people will stop yelling "Wannabe!" at him when he's parking his car.

For Dombroski, what separates Sponge from the post-Seattle slew is how the band "never looked at our music as something where we need to define our manhood by being so heavy—in fact, I think we're doing some things to define our *womanhood*." He says that for *Wax Ecstatic* they originally planned an all-drag-queen concept album dedicated to fans in Memphis who made him feel like a transvestite outcast the last time he played there. "I took the stage and I was like, 'Hipsters, flipsters, and finger-poppin' daddies, knock me your lobes.' And they just weren't buying it. They weren't in on that headfirst spin to death and destruction!"

Bantam guitarist Joey Mazzola claims that Sponge's average fan is, in fact, in her mid-teens—not unlike Mazzola's own 13-year-old daughter Rosalyn, who with the help of Sponge (disguised as the nail-polish-color-monikered 27 Mauve) recorded the spunky Rapunzel/Hillary/Charo/Nico-homage single "I'm a Big Girl / Femme Fatale" last year. But Dombroski swears Mazzola's bluffing: "No, man, we play to *factory workers*. First we put a call into the union hall, then flyer all the cars in the neighborhoods." Would you buy a used Ford from this man?

—*Spin*, August 1996

## *Radio On* Reviews I

· · · · ·

### Oasis:
### "Don't Look Back in Anger" (1996)

After liking "Live Forever," I'm starting to get the creeps from these guys. "Champagne Supernova"'s hippie poetry sounds even more idiotic now than it would've 30 years ago. But they do know how to be pretty, and not *all* their words are LSD nonsense: "come outside," it's summertime, "Sally can't wait." Sally's our neighbor, married with a 12-year-old son. She befriends Nancy, a veterinarian who walks her dogs around the block. So Sally gets it in her head to fix up Nancy with Cliff, the piano teacher, seeing how Nancy's told her how she doesn't feel she's attractive to men, but (Sally says) "She sure looks to *me* like she'd be attractive." Problem is, well, let's just say Nancy looks to *me* like she'd own lots of Me'Shell NdégeOcello records, maybe even Holly Near and Meg Christian ones. A *handsome* woman, you could say. And Sally, who generally seems somewhat gray and down-in-the-dumps as if her better days have passed her by, well, her face just *sparkles* when Nancy's around. Sally's got this pet cat named Mickey, and Nancy likes to sit on Sally's porch petting Sally's kitty. And Sally doesn't even realize her kitty's being petted. But she will. (7.0)

## Reel Big Fish:
## "Sell Out" (1997)

By far my favorite recurrent contradictory reaction to *Accidental Evolution* is all the people who first say too many lists bog the book down, and then say I shouldn't have left such-and-such song off the lists! (The *same* people, I mean.) I for sure shouldn't have left Neil Young's "Mr. Soul" or Ricky Nelson's "Garden Party" off the pro-sellout song list, but nobody has complained yet about either of those, strangely. Reel Big Fish, if they'd come out earlier, obviously could've made the sellout chapter too; ditto their fellow fake-ska one-hit-wonders Less Than Jake with "Johnny Qwest Thinks We're Sellouts"; must be a trend. (And now there's a reggae-ish song about selling out on the new Everclear album called "One Hit Wonder"!) Reel Big Fish turn selling out into a celebration—we don't wanna work at McDonald's all our life, so the record company's going to give us lots of money, and we're throwing a party with it, and you're invited. They sound like they feel guilty about it, but not *that* guilty. (7.0)

## Counting Crows:
## "Daylight Fading" (1997)

Is there a precedent for how this has almost the exact same words (about it's getting cold wasting another year in California) as the Crows single that directly preceded it, "A Long December" (8.0—about smelling like hospitals and oysters so please come to Boston so we can drive through the canyon to Hillside Manor and Hotel California where maybe this year will be better than the last)? (7.0)

## Peter Gabriel:
## "Come Talk to Me" (1993)

Supposedly Pete wants his Real World Experience Park in Barcelona to "combine passive experiences—like those available on rides at other theme parks—with interactive ones." What passive experiences is he talking about? Passively waving hands above your head, passively puking up cotton candy, passively screaming "Let me off!!," passively bleeding to death if bolts are loose on the rollercoaster? (2.5)

**Ric Ocasek:**
**"Hang On Tight" (1997)**

A disappointment (not that I expected to be blown away exactly), but what the heck, it finally gives me a chance to pontificate about "nuclear boots and drip-dry gloves." (Martina always thought that line was followed by "and when you bite your lip it's a reaction to your nose," by the way.) Last year Liz Armstrong asked me what nuclear boots were, and I suddenly remembered that I not only knew the answer, but that I've *worn* them—in the army, no less. I was the NBC (nuclear biological and chemical) officer for B Company Eighth Signal Battalion when I was in Germany in the mid-'80s, so I had to run the NBC room where the (*very* uncomfortable) gas masks, far more comfortable (sort of rubber-or-maybe-charcoalish-inside-lined olive-green sweatsuit-like) NBC suits, atropine injectors (an antidote for some poison), and floppily loose-fitting black rubber drip-dry gloves and nuclear boots were stored. We didn't call them that, though. Anyway, said boots were for in case you ever got caught in chemical warfare or whatnot, and we had to train with them sometimes in the field. (The mask came in a case with a belt attached that tied around your waist, and somebody would yell "GAS!!!," and you had eight seconds to yank it out, "don" it, and do something to the cheeks and nose—pinch them somehow whilst taking a deep breath—so you didn't suffocate. Or else you'd die.) Obviously, the big joke was that, in the case of a nuclear war, none of this stuff would've helped worth beans, but the army has to *pretend* it would... Anyway, I doubt any of the Cars were ever in the military, so I don't know if they were talking about the *same* nuclear boots. Knowing slick Ric, he probably meant some attire far more fashionable, sparkly-white and up to the knees. (6.0)

**Beck:**
**"Jack-Ass" (1997)**

I went to see him in Philly this spring, and he totally rocked the Catskills like an etiquette book. He wore a classy suit and whipped the stage with a bullwhip and pulled out binoculars and looked for his "freaks" in the audience and kept saying he wanted to "regulate" and dish out the West Coast jams, East Coast jams, Middle Coast jams. They played Afrika Bambaataa's "Planet Rock" over the PA before his set, and midway through his Hanukkah trip-hop chant "Little Drum Machine Boy" (9.0—his best song ever, I think, which he only played part of actually; it's not from any of his albums but rather from a multiartist Xmas compilation from last year called *Just Say Noel*) he started reciting Bambaataa's old "I want to rock the body party" mantra, which eventually evolved into an "I want to rock the body orgy" mantra. I read some interview where Beck said his audience in his early "anti-folk" days was mainly people in their 40s and 50s, and he was extremely freaked out when his shows started drawing teenagers after "Loser" became a hit; I figured the Philly Spectrum audience would be a lot older, at least mostly college educated, and I was really surprised that it was almost *all* teenagers, and some kids (possibly there to see opening act the Cardigans) looked even younger than Linus (who seems to think of Beck as a rapper or "parents' music" or something). But it was still really hilarious and inspiring to see this skinny white geeky guy up there being so alive and dancing so much and taking command of such a huge crowd (his biggest ever as a headliner, he said). He even did this straight R. Kelly–style falsetto soul ballad ("I Wanna Get Witchoo"), which was a complete surprise because he does nothing of the sort on any of his albums (Martina claimed it had jokey words about "I want to buy you a good meal," but I mostly just remember stuff about taking a girl for a car ride), and dedicated it to some woman he'd been "getting Loc-ed with in the LBC." And then he starts crying at the end of the song and goes around and hugs all his bandmates! I still doubt he has much of a singing voice—his falsetto worked okay in his high lonesome acoustic blues stuff, and the soul ballad was more convincing than I would've predicted, but I doubt if I heard it on the radio and didn't know it was Beck it would especially stand out. Maybe he should take voice lessons, just because everybody would expect him *not* to. I think he's trying to challenge his audience, see how much freedom they'll give him, like when Dylan went electric. And I wonder what he's got up his sleeve next; maybe he'll cross over to the soul charts, like David Bowie used to. He's in a weird position, in that when he does anything gaudy or over-the-top or big-pop-concert-like, his more indie fans just assume he's *making fun* of pop music, when really I get the idea he might *love* it. He insisted he wasn't being condescending when he praised Color Me Badd, and I'm almost surprised he didn't do the Macarena up there. I can't remember if he did "Jack-Ass," and as I've written before I never noticed the song much on *Odelay* either. But now that I've heard its desolate desert-highway sound late at night on the car radio alone in the middle of nowhere a few times, I'm starting to dig what people dig about it (give or take its gratuitously noisy ending, just like "Devil's Haircut." Those braying burros are cute though; I hereby name them Brooklyn and South Bronx). (8.0)

## House of Pain:
## "Put On Your Shit Kickers" (1993)

Flashing straight razors and slugging like their man Wade Boggs and putting on their shitkickers and kicking some shit (in a catchy way) is what I want these stickball veterans to do, but the only times they pull it off are "Jump Around" (9.0 by now) and this song here. Their album has a couple other okay cuts (or cuts with okay blues riffs), but mostly it's way too slow and verbally obtuse. I want House of Pain to be *punks*, like Cypress Hill or Skid Row (first albums only), or like the gentrification-hating young white males of Manayunk (where I live) who congregate on each other's porches wearing brushcuts and plain T-shirts and backwards baseball caps and shorts past their knees and probably kick the shit out of Spin Doctors and Radiohead fans at their high school every chance they get. Said Phillybilly bastards' favorite Phillie is probably Lenny Dykstra since he chews the most snuff (and takes the fewest baths, with the obvious exception of John "Grog" Kruk, who isn't as dumb as he looks, but then again neither are most two-toed sloths; I kept expecting the Phillies to fall into a big slump so Jim Fregosi could make them all go on diets and get haircuts). And Manayunk's favorite redneck band to blast out car windows is indeed House of Pain, followed by Cypress Hill and Onyx (though occasionally I also hear Digable Planets, which makes about as much sense as Arrested Development on the cover of *Circus*—July issue, I think). (8.0)

## Onyx:
## "Slam" (1993)

Linus saw them on TV and asked how come they're called "Oink." They look like a whole backfield of Otis Sistrunks and shriek like speedmetal lugnuts doing a Das EFX imitation, all oogly-boogly nursery-rhymey frantic and impossible to listen to. But unbeknownst to all the tykes buying "Slam," these baldies (if indeed they were bald then—"Let the bald be bald!!") actually put out a great flop single called "Ah and We Do It Like This" in 1990, a rap record that reminded me of Delta blues more than a year before "Mind Playing Tricks on Me" did, not so much because of the riffs as because of the drunken mumbled collard-green accents and the out-of-the-blue paranoia and violence in the middle verses (a big surprise since they're surrounded by jolly pals-on-the-mike party stuff about people "jammin' around to our country sound that makes you get down"): "What's a man to do if you're livin' in fear / Reach for a gun and 20 years of his life / So he can't see his wife," a pay-for-dumb-mistakes kind of theme like "Bohemian Rhapsody" or "18 and Life" or "Folsom Prison Blues" or "Charles Giteau" (by Kelly Harrell, 1927) or "The Ballad of Those Two Guys Who Killed Michael Jordan's Dad." Finally it ends with lots of Frito Bandito blllllleeee-haa!-type frijole-yodeling and put-on-your-dance-shoes check-it-out check-it-out. (5.5)

### Meredith Brooks:
### "Bitch" (1997)

I keep expecting Meredith to start saying "I'm your mama, I'm your daddy, I'm that nigga in the alley, I'm the doctor when you need, have some coke, have some weed." Some kid in my seventh grade class back at Our Lady of Refuge used to walk around the playground reciting those lines, and it totally used to creep me out, never having heard the Curtis Mayfield song at the time. Around the same time, I also got scared when I read in a newspaper that Peter Tork was arrested for marijuana possession. A few years earlier the scariest playground chant came from Chuck Berry, I think—something about "get myself a good lookin', get married start a-hookin', settle down and write a book, uh huh." I think "hookin'" meant "sex," or at least that's how I translated it at the time. Can't remember what song it's from—"Too Much Monkey Business," maybe. (7.0)

### Patti Rothberg:
### "Inside" (1996)

She sounds pretentious in a young field-hockey way, like Janis Ian or Suzanne Vega, which makes her infinitely more effective than if she sounded pretentious in an old fishwife way, like Sinead O'Connor or the Cranberries. Plus, somebody told me her clothes are as far out in left field as that crazy chick in 4 Non Blondes! (7.5)

### Indigo Girls:
### "Shame on You" (1997)

"Girls will be boys and boys will be girls it's a mixed-up world" department: in the year of Jane-Dark-is-a-man-and-Hanson's-singer-is-a-boy-and-White-

Town-could-never-be-your-woman-either, it's somehow appropriate that I would hear an upbeat and high-voiced and possibly border-rhythmed pine-cone rock track called "Shame on You" on an adult alternative station back in March that reminded me of "Mr. Jones" by Counting Crows because of its sha-la-la-las and lines about beautiful barrio women, so I asked everybody if they knew the name of the guy who sings it, only to learn five months later that the guy who sings it is the Indigo Girls. (8.0)

—*Radio On*, 1993–1997

## Travis Marries a Man!

· · · · ·

My favorite Travis Tritt video is the one where he leaves the hospital where he used to be a wheelchair basketballing Jon-Voight-in-*Coming-Home* Vietnam vet (he got his appendages blown off à la Metallica's "One") and he and his pregnant wife go for a long walk on a short, slippery pier and she falls off and conks her head on a rock and dies, but gives birth to a beautiful baby anyway, thus making Travis a single dad with a lucrative life-insurance income until he marries his gay black best friend from the veteran's hospital.

OK, maybe the weird camera angles confused me and I got a few specifics wrong. I'm pretty sure the song was "Tell Me I Was Dreaming," which sounds almost the same as "Anymore" and "Foolish Pride" (i.e., *dirgy*), but it's still the best cut on Travis's *Greatest Hits* since it comes closest to capturing Lynyrd Skynyrd's wind-tunnel guitar ache from "Tuesday's Gone."

Travis has actually had a couple of Country Music Television hits that might be equally as good, but for some reason are left *off* his best-of—namely, his stuttering talking blues "Bible Belt" and his Jimmie Rodgers / Great Depression tribute "Lord Have Mercy on the Working Man." At least half of *Greatest Hits'* tracks I've never even heard on CMT.

Travis's cover of the Platters' "Only You" isn't as moving as Garth Brooks's cover of the Fleetwoods' "Mr. Blue," but for the most part Tritt's better off crying in his beer than trying to act drunk—"Here's a Quarter (Call Someone Who Cares)" takes a wittily mean-spirited dump on some chick who dumped him, but "The Whiskey Ain't Workin'" merely proves that Travis's frequent duet partner, glambilly phony Marty Stuart, has one of the blandest voices in country. "Put Some Drive in Your Country" and "Country Club" are just your usual kiss-up-to-Waylon-and-Duane-Allman-and-people-who-drink-from-paper-cups-and-drive-pickups.

"T-R-O-U-B-L-E" and "Ten Feet Tall and Bulletproof" boogie a bit harder, I suppose, but Travis never once convinces me he's a true death-row rowdy on the order of, say, David Allen Coe — sensitive love-mushers like "Can I Trust You with My Heart" and "Drift Off to Dream" seem bigger clues to his unfashionably hatless grooming habits. To quote the Barbarians: hey Travis, are you a boy or are you a girl? With your long brown hair, you look like a girl.

*—Eye Weekly, 11 January 1996*

## John Mellencamp: *Dance Naked*

. . . . .

Old hacks Alabama have a country hit now called "The Cheap Seats," which is both the best minor-league-baseball song I've ever heard and the best John Cougar record since "Some Girls Do" by Sawyer Brown two years ago, which was the best John Cougar record since *The Lonesome Jubilee* in 1987.

John's own current single "Wild Night" is a too-slow cover of a catchy Van Morrison song my baseball-fan college colleague Chris Dupree taped for me once when he was working at a newspaper in Wisconsin. John's version has some tambourine and squeaky percussion and a guest spot by bald black woman Me'Shell NdegéOcello, whose music I couldn't care less about, but whose name is a masterpiece of creative-apostrophe-use rock, up there with A'Me Lorain, Kassav', the Chantay's, Izzy Stradlin', and Joe LeSte' of Bang Tango.

John Cougar did 10 of the 18 best punk songs to come out of southern Indiana between 1979 and 1982. "Jack and Diane," "Thundering Hearts," "Hurts So Good," "Cheap Shot," "Hand to Hold Onto," "Welcome to Chinatown" (a.k.a. "Every Picture Tells a Story That I Wanna Be Your Dog" because of its Rod Stoogert hybrid, à la "Let It Go" by Rose Tattoo), "Pray for Me," "I Need a Lover," "Small Paradise," and "Untitled Ditty about a Girl Sitting on John's Lap and Playing with His Tool and Nuts" (not really as good as "Miami" or "Taxi Dancer," but big deal). That's more than the Gizmos (five), Panics (two), and Jetsons (one) combined!

My Alabama buddy Don Allred pointed out once that John had a Nixon-like genius for stealing other people's ideas and was therefore a perfect bard

John Mellencamp keeps shirt on,
thinks about too much. (Photo:
Mercury Records)

for the swap-meet and secondhand-shop boondocks. Used to be no matter how hard he tried otherwise, some bratty insolence with a good beat would leak out. *Uh-Huh* livened up '70s Stones murk with calypso lilts, glam drums, and AC/DC chords; "I Need a Lover" stretched into a six-minute disco-thick trance. But ever since he changed his name (to "John Cougar Buttmunch"), Cougar's career has been a depressing descent into respectable maturity, from "all the women around the world want a phony rock star" to "I don't wanna be a pop star." That was six years ago, and he's still sinking.

*Dance Naked* has some words on it (at least in "Brothers," about still hating a sibling who used to let you get beat up). But the music's all mumbly and stunted and tuneless and endless and beginningless: "jams" instead of songs. The only minor exceptions are "L.U.V." (an overpolitical rap that sounds like "1969" by the Stooges), "Another Sunny Day 12/25" (a gloomy Woody Guthrie imitation), and "Too Much to Think About" (a gloomy Kurt Cobain imitation). "Wild Night" isn't horrible either, I suppose. But all the stonies won't dance to it on the radio.

*—Eye Weekly*, 23 June 1994

## Sawyer Brown: *Café on the Corner*

· · · · ·

John Deere cap, work boots, flannel shirt with the sleeves torn off. That's what Sawyer Brown's singer, Mark Miller, wears on the front of *Café on the Corner*. He dresses exactly like this goober across the street from me who stenciled "One Bad Junkman" on the rear window of his pickup-truck cab. In their #1 country hit "Some Girls Do" last year, Miller claimed he's neither high-class nor white trash, but every movement he made in its hilarious video looked pretty white trash to me.

He bounded off the back of his pickup and danced on the stairs and drawled about "doing James Dean," like John Cougar before he wimped out by adding Mellencamp to his name. And in their "The Race Is On" vid from 1989 or thereabouts, Sawyer Brown pissed off George Jones purists by sliding around the stage as if they really wished they were Poison singing "I Want Action," albeit without the pink guitars.

The clip for *Cafe on the Corner*'s big hit, "All These Years," is a big switch. Mark Miller's alone in some empty old house, dressed middle-class and middle-aged and capless so you can see his receding hairline, and all these rusty leaves are blowing in, and the wallpaper is a hazy shade of winter. It's a prayerful dirge related by a guy who didn't realize his marriage was over until he caught his spouse with another man. He blames himself for being such a workaholic deadbeat. And the weirdest thing is the guitar, which goes Garth Brooks's well-publicized Kansas fandom one better by actually strumming those doomed notes from "Dust in the Wind" all the way through. My wife says Mark Miller's deep croon reminds her of Gordon Lightfoot. Which makes "All These Years" like an old-time movie about a ghost from a wishing well, in a castle dark or a fortress strong, with chains upon his feet.

*Cafe on the Corner* also has some catchy-fast, jig-rhythmed dance reels, and Miller sings "Sister's Got a New Tattoo," about a girl who joins the army and winds up in the Persian Gulf 'cause her grades aren't up to snuff, like he's got a pinch of snuff between his cheek and gums (which is how he sang "Some Girls Do," too).

I can only barely tolerate the sub-Cougar all-the-farms-are-dying seriousness of the title track, and the Motown-as-minstrel-music "I Kept My Motor Running" gets on my nerves. Still, I like Sawyer Brown a lot—Miller's an ex-jock, and bassist Jim Scholten used to play in the disco-country group Star-buck (of "Moonlight Feels Right" fame). Southern frat boys love them, and they got their big break on Ed McMahon's *Star Search*. A band to watch? You are correct, sir. They may already be a winner.

—*Eye Weekly*, 19 March 1993

## Patricia Conroy: *A Bad Day for Trains*

· · · · ·

My latest dumb theory is that country rhythms nowadays might be around the same step on the evolutionary ladder that soul rhythms were in 1972 or so, a couple years before disco happened. I wouldn't be completely shocked if the most interesting dance music (at least in places where people speak English) in the '90s takes off from, say, the mariachi lilts in Brooks and Dunn's "Lost and Found" or the "country lambada" steps boot-scooters do to Lorrie Morgan's "Watch Me." Country grows more sonically open-minded every day, and its audience is getting weird. Last fall, *Billboard* even had a front-page story head-lined "Country Music Striking a Chord with the Gay Community," with Nash-ville biz honchos making the disco analogy from an economic perspective.

What makes my theory a pipe dream is that country still doesn't have a production prophet of Barry White's standing, much less an Isaac Hayes or a James Brown. But I can still imagine in my head a glitzy and obsessive popu-lar music that expands on current country dance-club rhythms the way disco did with R&B, as a natural extension rather than a "fusion," resulting in far-ranging cultural impact—the potential is there.

If I played a synthesizer, one song I'd be paying attention to now is "Bad Day for Trains" by Vancouver's Patricia Conroy. I saw its video on Coun-try Music Television in the States, all midnight-express blue and sexy and doomed, with lots of packed-together shifting gears to make it feel "industrial" in ways Nine Inch Nails wouldn't dare. Its sound builds on the locomotive syncopation that's been C&W currency for some 65 years, ever since Jimmie Rodgers, yet it somehow feels very hard and modern. Conroy piles on the ten-sion by telling us to "Stand back!" and "Watch out!" before she speeds up be-cause she's scared and her soul is screaming. Then we're racing out of town as "Sparks are flying from the friction of the steel / My dreams are dying as the engine turns the wheel," like she heard Hank Williams's lonesome whistle, only to find out it was Tammy Wynette heading into Mu-Mu Land on KLF's last train to Transcentral.

The rest of *Bad Day for Trains* is more reserved, but still kinda nice. "My Baby Loves Me" pounds like "Born in the U.S.A.," while "What Do You Care" is a bitter depiction of a just-divorced working woman's mundane day, sort of Abba's "The Day Before You Came" backwards. But her Rosanne-cum-k.d.-style ingenue classiness is way too reined-in, so I hope that on Conroy's next album she concentrates on the friction of steel. I want more flying sparks.

*—Eye Weekly*, 11 February 1993

## Grupo Exterminador: *Dedicado a Mis Novias*

· · · · ·

How to dance to "El Venao": stiffen legs like Frankenstein's monster, open eyes wide, spread fingers above forehead like antlers, stomp around to loco tropical rhythms. (First couple times I saw it, I didn't realize the words were about a deer, so the hand part frightened me a little.) Punctuated by monster-clearing-its-throat gurgles and originated by Dominican Republic merenguers Los Cantantes, "El Venao" is the latest '90s smash (after "Macarena" and "Vuela Vuela") that combos all over the Latin map compete over.

Grupo Exterminador, four Mexican cowhands from the Rio Grande whose name kills bugs deader than Black Flag and who wear clothes seemingly designed from fancy window curtains, do the catchiest "El Venao" I've heard. They also do a nearly identical song called "El Tiburón," which my *diccionario* translates as "The Shark," leading me to wonder how the shark dance goes. Their record label told me Exterminador are a banda group, maybe because they wiggle their polka oom-pahs with plenty of accordion sustain and do lots of cover remakes. But Exterminador's more Tex-Mexy border stuff, including half of this album, is too slow for banda—it'd be fairly orthodox conjunto or corrido if not for how the songs all start with sounds like clanking cantina glasses, horses' hooves, cocks fighting, and guns executing banditos.

Exterminador's real category, I think, is "novelty act." The most energetic tracks on *Dedicado* are also the silliest—the deer and shark ones, and their cover of 2 in a Room's 1990 hip-house hit "Wiggle It." Exterminador play the song even faster and looser, with voice-chanted drum rolls, "Hasta la vista, bay-bee" endings, squeezeboxes honking "shave and a haircut, two bits," kids calling-and-responding louder than the singer. Grown men chirp like little girls chirping like birds, and Juan Corona shouts out questions and leads cheers so his band can set up vamps within vamps, expanding polka beats into genuine Caribbean funk. In 1996, this might be the most brand-new bag papa's got.

—*Spin*, August 1996

## When FSK Play, Schnitzel Happens

. . . . .

Frank Kogan, in his latest issue of *Why Music Sucks*, says, "Basically, a polka is something that has a lot of features in common with other things that are called polkas; and if a polka band plays a waltz or schottische, etc., then those are polkas too."

On *The Sound of Music*, FSK bassist Michaela Melian reads her letter to BBC DJ John Peel: "A zweifacher is an Eastern Bavarian dance that alternates between waltz and polka time. Here is our 'Hobo Zweifacher,' about incest and trains." FSK are folk Munichians (as in "praise the Lord and pass the damn Munichians") who play old-timey or Old World two-step clippity-clop dances as rock, with trumpets, cornets, fiddles, cowboy yodels, and bierhall stein-hoisting countering the oompah-pahs with sprightly secondary syncopation. The guitars slowly volksmarch uphill into doomy raveups and fun-filled feedback. "Jazz im Dritten Reich" double-times from waltz-wobbling into a fast square dance without missing a beat; "Shiner Song" improves on Adolph Hofner's 1948 Tex-Czech western swing version by sticking a Marshall Tucker rockjam in the middle. FSK's "Diesel Oktoberfest," a washboard jig with funky drums and über-rubber quacks, is just plain *jolly*.

David Lowery, singer for Camper Van Beethoven before wisely selling out to hard rock with Cracker, helps out on *The Sound of Music*. He claims FSK are more like Camper Van than Camper Van were, and I see his point—Camper's catchy world-beat instrumentals like "Border Ska" were always funnier than their dumb bowling-skinhead jokes (which had too much Too Much Joy in them). FSK turn Cracker-like when they slow down and let Lowery croon about lady spies and lady doctors with hairy backs, but their sweetest ballad is "Lonely River Rhine," sung in a lederhosen accent by Wilfried Pitzi, who imagines he's a Yankee soldier overseas drowning his Fräulein when she finds out he's got a wife back home. FSK are obsessed with Americans in Germany and Germans in America.

While I can't pretend to love FSK's "Die Original Trapp Familie (John Coltrane)" as much as "The Lonely Goatherd" or "Sixteen Going on Seventeen" on the old Americans-in-Austria concept album also called *The Sound of Music*, I'll definitely take it over "Climb Ev'ry Mountain."

—*L.A. Weekly*, 22 September 1995

## *Radio On* Reviews II

. . . . .

Technohead:
"I Wanna Be a Hippy" (1995)

Post-Rednex square dance bubbletechno with cartoon characters coughing and yodeling and cackling and honking horns and making crazy Spike Jones sounds and chanting "mari-marijuana" and "I want to get high, I want to get high, I want to get high but I never knew why" in sugar-high chipmunk (or Cornholio, says Sara Sherr) voices, this is as giddy as music ever gets, so it'd drive any genuine self-respecting hippie either out of the room or out of his mind. According to my older brother Louie, back when I was 9 or 10 I myself always used to say that I wanted to grow up to be a "fat hippie." Which later in my adolescence I repeatedly denied, claiming that I'd probably said I wanted to grow up to be a "fat hippo" instead (hippos *were* my favorite animals as a kid, and they *are* fat, so it's not that farfetched), but Louie was probably right in this case, how embarrassing. So anyway, following my appearance on a panel at a "Music and Myth" conference put on by the DIA Arts Center in New York early this year, somebody wrote a conference article in the *New York Press* containing a glowing and flattering review of my presentation, but it called me a "recalcitrant poindexter" who's "emaciated" and "shaggy but balding" with oversized glasses—Sara Sherr told me only Run-D.M.C. could get away with frames like that, and Laura Morgan (whose leopard-skin coat I borrowed for the presentation so I could match what the two main women running the conference were wearing) called them *Star Wars* glasses, so eventually I replaced them with skinnier wire-rims. But Martina insisted that though my hairline might be *slightly* receding on bad hair days, I'm hardly "balding," and not only am I not "emaciated," but I could afford to lose a couple pounds. I don't have anything remotely resembling a gut, though (in fact, in my past few months as a bike Nazi I *have* lost weight, so now I'm maybe 5′6″, 140), so I really don't think I've quite achieved my fat hippie goal yet. But I still plan to work on it one of these days. (8.5)

## Chemical Brothers:
## "Setting Sun" (1997)

In Jason Fine's Chemical Brothers cover story in *Option*, he called "Setting Sun" (which barely even creased the charts) one of the biggest-selling electronic singles of all time, somehow ignoring "Popcorn," "Fly Robin Fly," "I Feel Love," "Star Wars Theme / Cantina Band," "Pop Muzik," "Funkytown," "Chariots of Fire," "Don't You Want Me," "Owner of a Lonely Heart," "Planet Rock," "Axel F," "Rock Me Amadeus," "West End Girls," "Into the Groove," "Let the Music Play," "Fascinated," "Rocket," "Pump Up the Volume," "3 A.M. Eternal," "Gonna Make You Sweat (Everybody Dance Now)," "Unbelievable," and thousands of other electronic singles. Other critics have compared the Chemical Brothers to Public Enemy's Bomb Squad, but I doubt "Setting Sun" (which actually reminds me more of Depeche Mode, no pop-chart slouches themselves) would quite be considered a smash by P.E. standards, either. (7.0)

## Robert Miles:
## "Children" (1995)

"The tune of the summer," *Details* says, pulling our leg I hope. "A glorious, weepy Euro-techno groover with not the slightest hint of cheese." Well, personally, I think somebody better tell Mr. Miles to *stop* cutting all the cheese. He's stinking up the place. (0.5)

## Butthole Surfers:
## "Pepper" (1996)

Obviously peppier than anything I expected to hear from them again in my lifetime, and probably peppier than anything I heard from them *before* in my lifetime; only competition is "Hey," from way back on their first EP a century ago, back when you couldn't write the word "Butthole" in a newspaper, much less say it on the radio. The mere fact that these performance-art mutants have a pop hit is so mind-boggling that, well, it boggles the mind. The chorus (the quasi-Arabic twang of which makes me think "Yardbirds") is lovely—my only question is how come Gibby smells me in his clothes instead of his nose (which is where *I* always smell me when I sing along). Some 16-year-old girl filled out the "physical description" block on her subscriber profile in our local Internet service's online registry by writing in "YoU nEveR kNoW jUsT hOw YoU lOoK tHrOuGh OtHeR pEoPlE's EyEs" (that's how she typed it!), and I wished I'd thought of it first. The rap verses (which make me think "88 Lines about 44 Women" by the Nails more than "People Who Died" by Jim Carroll more than "Walk on the Wild Side" by Lou Reed) are sensationalist horseshit, recited too monotonally. But that's what initially bugged me about "Loser" by Beck, too, and it still kinda does, though more when I'm thinking about it than when I'm hearing it. So maybe it's just nitpicking. (8.5)

**Insane Clown Posse:**
**"Chicken Huntin'" (1994)**

The Box Network has a menu listing all the videos you can pay to see, and this one kept scrolling up onto the screen late last year, and I had no idea what it was, but the title and band name seemed so ridiculous that I was tempted to dial it in for two dollars anyway just to find out. I never did, but I wound up hearing it a few months later—turns out it's white rap guys from Detroit (where no hip-hop I'm aware of has ever come from, bizarrely enough, despite the something-like-85%-black population and the eternal legacies of George Clinton and Electrifying Mojo). And it also turns out the guys dress up in clown costumes and rock their frat-rap close enough to Cypress Hill to get by. Their lyrics may or may not deal with murdering hillbillies. (7.0)

**Jodeci:**
**"Stay" (1992)**

When we first got cable, these guys (doing this song, maybe) were all over Video Jukebox *all the time*. I figured they were the kid brothers of somebody at the station, and they just used them to fill dead time when nobody was calling in. (1.5)

**Raven-Symoné:**
**"That's What Little Girls Are Made Of" (1993)**

An editor who wanted me to review Raven's album told me she was "trying to be like Mary J. Blige," which is kinda funny because the only thing I remember about Mary J. Blige is that on *Saturday Night Live* she wore a big floppy hat pulled down over her face in a way that reminded me of Dumb Donald on the *old* Bill Cosby show. If you ask me, Raven's more like Stacy Lattisaw. (7.5)

**SWV:**
**"Right Here (Human Nature)" (1993)**

"Weak" was completely boring, so this is a nice surprise. Linus says one of these women looks like his math teacher. No, let me correct that—he says one of them *is* his math teacher. He's always saying things like that. If we went to Peru, he'd see classmates plowing the beanfields. (Are there beanfields in Peru? Maybe I mean fishfields.) (6.5)

**Salt-n-Pepa featuring En Vogue:**
**"Whatta Man" (1994)**

Music dream of the year: I'm with Coco, in the front yard of a house whose floor plan matches my childhood Michigan one (the only house I ever dream about). A limousine drives by, and I notice Salt-n-Pepa in there wearing the yellow-and-red track suits they used to wear when they were good, so I wave my hands and yell "Salt-n-Pepa! Salt-n-Pepa!" until they turn around and get out of the car. I ask Coco if she knows who one of the two is, and she cheerfully exclaims "Salt!," strange because even *I* don't know which one is which, and I write about music for a living. (I doubt Coco's ever heard of them in real life.) I go get some "fresh and fly" hip-hop pants I supposedly just bought (even though I'd never buy or wear any such things while awake) to show Salt, but when I come back both she and Coco are gone, so maybe Salt kidnapped her! I return to the yard, and Coco's out there on her tricycle, but the rappers and their limousine are long gone . . . What makes the dream so odd is that, when I'm not dreaming, Salt-n-Pepa really irritate me nowadays, maybe because of how they're always trying to cram so much sex junk down my throat instead of just making it playful like in "Push It." I don't like how they're always trying to cram good-for-me old R&B spinach down my throat, either. Their clothes *and* voices were brighter back in "Push It" days, and judging from the singles, every subsequent album they've put out has sounded more reserved and less catchy than the one before it, like the Clash or somebody. (And even "Push It" was a step down from "Simon Says" by Sequence from 1980, where girl rappers *first* compared themselves to "salt 'n pepa, pepa 'n salt.") (5.5)

## Paula Cole:
## "Where Have All the Cowboys Gone?" (1997)

Big riddle is whether she's being ironic or not. I think both—she lusts over macho men, wonders where's her "Johnny Wayne" (sounds like), but she's not *really* yearning to wash dishes while he drinks his bee-urr, is she? (Courtney Love, "Plump," 1994: "I don't do dishes, I throw them in the crib." Marilyn French, *The Women's Room*, 1977: "'I hate discussions of feminism that end up with who does the dishes,' she said. So do I. But at the end, there are always the damned dishes.") Paula clearly wants to have her cake and eat it too. I know women like this; dreaming of some huge dominant but sensitive brute who'll ravish her against her apartment building's outside wall on the second date without any prior hints on her part, then take command in bed but take orders everywhere else, a guy who'll fix appliances blindfolded then always notice her new dress. Most such women seem to fret a lot about always being alone on Saturday nights; gee, I wonder why. Anyway, Paula comes up with a decent rhythm, not unlike Sheryl Crow's last few singles, and I like the yippie-tie-yi-yos. Maybe she can even yodel and vogue at the same time. But she oughta whisper less, and skip that showing of *Bridges of Madison County* next time it's in town. (7.5)

—*Radio On*, 1993–1997

## Alanis Morissette: Addicted to Love

. . . . .

Alanis Morissette sold her first 16 million records by being an intense, spazzy live wire who makes you want to run away from her but also makes you want to run away *with* her. She's got a ditziness that makes being pissed-off seem really comforting; it's endearing how her big, brazen mouth growls its *r*'s, how it stretches and compresses words. She's Snarly Spice, she's the wicked chipmunk of the West. But like anything else you might say about her, that's not all she is.

Her mode of singing changes every couple lines—maybe there really *are* four Alanises, just like in that "Ironic" video in the car. She's got her teeter-totter voice, her arfing-hound voice, her angel-baby voice, her gargle-with-salt-water-to-cure-your-sore-throat voice ("sandpaper on spinach," Frank Kogan calls that last one). She sort of did for nag-folk sob-sisters what Axl Rose did for macho rockers a few years earlier: invested a moribund genre with rhythm, melody, urgency, schizophrenia, and wacky extraneous asides ("I certainly do," "yeah I really do think"). All of which added up to *Jagged Little Pill* working the way music almost never does anymore—its vocabulary became part of everyday conversation, so the unforgettable lines about char-donnay and fellatio now belong to the world.

Now that we've got an older version of her, is she just as perverted? *Supposed Former Infatuation Junkie*, Alanis calls her new album; what an amaz-ingly ambiguous Sex and Love Addicts Anonymous title! (Like, does "sup-posed" modify "former" or "junkie"?) Sounds like maybe she flunked the 12-step program: she yearns to be stuck on a deserted island with some boy along with her three favorite CDs; asks another if he's still mad 'cause she kept sleeping with him after they split up, plus she compared him to all her 40-year-old friends. The album opens with "Front Row," as in "with the pop-corn"; pretty funny considering what she was swallowing in theaters on her last album.

She likens herself to a four-year-old in two different songs, but sadly, she's wrong. Too many of her new songs show her devolving into mundane matu-rity, bypassing the bratty vernacular viciousness that served her so well in favor of impenetrable complexity and attempts at social consciousness. In the eternal tradition of Elvis Costello, John Cougar, Liz Phair, and the Beastie Boys, she's feeling pressure to pass herself off as respectable, but sacrificing energy in the process. Last time out, her sneering proto-feminist rebellion in-spired sheltered Middle American girls in sneakers and cutoffs just like hers to stand up for themselves and grow their hair weird. But I don't think she's identifying with her hard-won late-teen/early-20s female demographic (not even Monica Lewinsky!) anymore.

Then again, she never claimed to be a punk, did she? (Having the same dreadlocks as the singer for the Offspring doesn't quite count.) Back in '96, indie zealots acted like Alanis was compromising some imaginary ideal of angry-young-woman purity, when really if she compromised anything (like

Jane Child and Alannah Myles and Celine Dion before her), it was the eccentric French Canadian post-disco subculture of Martine St. Clair and Mitsou she had actually emerged from. A few cuts on her new album have industrial klanking or African drums underneath (always popular in Montreal clubs), and "Front Row" and the Madonna soundalike "So Pure" rank with her more successful new tracks simply by virtue of their fluid dance rhythms. A little bit ironic (don't you think?) seeing how so many kneejerk skeptics have given her guff for starting out as a teenage dance-pop artist.

Too often, though, *Infatuation Junkie*'s music is muddled and leaden in ways even non-hit *Jagged* filler such as "Perfect" and "Forgiven" wasn't. Heavy-hearted dirges such as "The Couch" (about therapy, natch) show her biting off more than she can chew, forgetting all the bubblegummish little hooks, lines, and sinkers—giving us 10,000 spoons when all we need is a knife. Her psycho-bitch voice is not always her best voice—she's often most palatable (in "U.R." and "Unsent," for instance) sounding merely vulnerably pretty. But in the two near–a cappella lullabies that close the album, both swamped in Glen Ballard strings, her singing unfortunately just hovers Tori Amos–style up there above the clouds, never touching down or connecting.

Ballard's Sahara-combing guitar bridges hint that the Puff Daddy–esque "Kashmir" section in her *City of Angels* hit "Uninvited" started something new, though. Now and then, those guitars combine with Alanis's high wordless hic-cup mantras to attain transcendence. "Baba," based around an "In-A-Gadda-Da-Vida" riff and ending with "Ave Maria" chants, is a cynically Arabian-undulating answer to the guru meditations on *Ray of Light* by Madonna, who founded Alanis's record label. My other favorite cut, "Unsent," consists of letters to seven former infatuations whose names almost all deviate from the names on the lyric sheet the label provided at the pre-release hearing, suggesting somebody changed them to avoid lawsuits. But otherwise, I can imagine being on the receiving end of most of the harangues on this record and wondering exactly what bush Alanis was trying to beat around. I miss her *directness*. What it all comes down to is she still hasn't got it all figured out just yet.

—*Spin*, December 1998

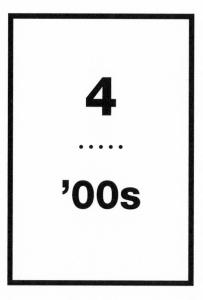

**4**

· · · · ·

**'00s**

**AS I TENDED TO DO** on Mondays at the time, I stayed at Arlene's
Grocery on the Lower East Side way past midnight into the wee hours of 11
September 2001, singing (or, maybe more accurately, tunelessly rapping) Billy
Squier's "The Stroke," backed by Rob Kemp's real live Heavy Metal Karaoke
band. A few hours later the world would change, and my life would, too—my
future second wife Lalena, known to do a version of Rush's "Limelight" that
made nerdboys at Arlene's heads explode (a *girl* who knows Rush lyrics—is
this a dream or what??), stayed over that night for only the second time.

Everything else unraveled from there, of course, though really it was already unraveling: the poor and working class, minorities and rural whites,

were dropping off the radar and being demoted to nonpersons, thanks to the digital divide and disintegration of manufacturing jobs and dismantling of the social safety net and regression of taxation and privatization of everything privatable, with poor folks' own supposed laziness and stupid life decisions and inability or refusal to participate in undemocratically implanted George W. Bush's "ownership society" the scapegoat. Household incomes shrank as immigrants moved next door to freaked-out suburbanites (see: Clint Eastwood's *Gran Torino*, 2008) while money mostly stayed in the cities. In parts of Europe, immigrants pretty much *took over* the suburbs, inspiring xenophobic nationalist recoil that's snowballed ever since and I sincerely hope didn't spur any of my favorite Continental tradition-and-technology-loving folk-goth-industrial-metal bands toward the extreme right. But with that stuff, dystopian albeit triumphalist and fixated on ancient ancestors digging the nature scene as it is, you never quite know.

Mainstream Western guitar rock was meanwhile settling on being pep talks, sob stories, and therapy sessions for the rest of its life—either that, or a dreary kind of whining-bully revenge porn for a generation pathetically grossed out by female body hair. For many Americans in uniform, the decade's most important rock song—maybe also the worst, though that's more subjective—was probably the Dallas band Drowning Pool's #6 "mainstream" / #12 "alt" Clear Channel radio hit from 2001 "Bodies" (as in "let the bodies hit the floor"), which soldiers, contractors, and/or their surrogates apparently found quite useful to blast repeatedly at high volume at terrorism-accused, stress-positioned prisoners sequestered in extraordinary rendition sites set to extreme temperatures. Yet war crimes or no, the 'oos were supposedly the decade when hip-hop displaced guitar rock as the premier popular music in the land—though actually, that may not be the case if you consider rock changing its name to "country" (or, at least, country subsuming lots of sounds that had long been considered "rock"), or you consider figures suggesting catalog and live ticket sales kept rock in the lead well into the 2010s, or you simply just remember Nickelback. Or maybe the real fallacy is pretending rock ever dominated in the first place: i.e., conjuring a consensus when none ever existed.

At some point, commercial country also became the music that most dominated my own 'oos listening, more than it ever had. Weird, given that I spent most of the decade in New York City, even if (as I explain in one piece) the genre dealt more directly with wartime America than any other music did. I wasn't alone in crossing over, either: pandering authoritarian Ted Cruz, who says he grew up on classic rock, claims he has listened only to country music since 9/11. On *Billboard*'s list of the top 20 ticket-selling concert acts of the decade, the closest ones to new artists were Toby Keith, Kenny Chesney, and Tim McGraw. And of the top six SoundScanning album artists in the '00s overall—Eminem, the Beatles, McGraw, Keith, Britney Spears, Chesney—half were country. The genre didn't turn out how it was supposed to, either: in mid-2001, Brian Mansfield posited in *USA Today* that *O Brother, Where Art Thou?*, Brad Paisley, Nickel Creek, and Patty Loveless were helping return country to its Appalachian bluegrass roots, partly in reaction to Britney, Backstreet, and their ilk. But the towers falling a couple months hence brought on a more belligerent backlash instead. It got louder, too, thus turning Maya Angelou and me into Montgomery Gentry and Toby Keith fans. Further down the line, Eric Church put out his worst album in 2014 and best album in 2015, Ty Herndon came out of the closet, and Occupy anarchists fell for Keith Urban's "Cop Car."

In my 3,000-worder about country in Mexico, though, I probably should've spent some time on narcocorridos. Latin music was the decade's fastest-growing radio format, with shifting demographics particularly accelerating the importance of regional Mexican no matter how little rock critics like me paid attention. Yet in the decade's second half, Latin retail sales plummeted even more severely than everybody else's, owing both to immigration crackdowns and shuttering of mom-and-pop stores where the audience was still accustomed to buying physical product in an increasingly downloadable age.

The decade's biggest story, in my mind, was how new technology allowed bands who play, say, strip malls in suburban Ohio, to bypass labels, promote and distribute their music internationally, and market it through social networks—albeit frequently with a diminished sound quality that more and more listeners didn't mind. One figure cited at a late-decade Future of Music Summit estimated that, out of 5 million artists on MySpace, nearly 106,000 put out albums in 2008 alone—the most ever, apparently, but it still might not be far-fetched to suggest that almost a *million* albums came out in the decade. Add in songs that weren't on albums at all, and there's no way to keep up with a fraction. I tried my best—though through most of the decade I still remained woefully oblivious to the drill-sergeant-shouty proletarian post-rave Hamburg "jumpstyle hardcore" stadium Eurotechnocheese goofball trio Scooter, who in retrospect may well have made the era's most irresistibly high-energy music while shifting some 25 million units across Europe.

On the other hand, while editing at the *Village Voice* through April 2006—New York presented to me on a platter and venues within walking distance in every direction—I saw more live music in the '00s than in any other decade. (Distant second: the '80s.) My favorite show occurred 23 June 2004 at a still-alive CBGB, and featured the famous punk-rock combo Big & Rich, transforming country into a circus and making it bounce with B-52's and Donna Summer basslines. The two worst concerts I saw were both by Cat Power, at Bowery Ballroom and Knitting Factory, at least one of which had Chan Marshall melting down halfway through; somehow, the 2000 Roseland one where Fiona Apple did the same thing was funnier. For a while, I spent every Saturday from midnight to 4 A.M. dancing and drinking while Gogol Bordello's handlebar-mustachioed and inevitably ultimately sloshed and shirtless shaman Eugene Hutz deejayed an impossible mix of Mano Negra, Rachid Taha, Teutonic disco, Captain Beefheart, Devo, and Slavic wedding music to a young Eurotrash / Latin American / Middle Eastern crowd on the second floor of an Eastern European restaurant at Broadway and Canal, alternately called 416 BC or Mehanata or the Bulgarian Bar. Then I'd head back home to South Park Slope, Brooklyn, still affordable rentwise at the time—or "Greenwood Heights," as some maps called it, after the cemetery. Though I preferred "EHoDe": East of the Home Depot.

I did get around, though! Ten most memorable abandoned spots I trespassed: (1) High Line railroad before it was a park; (2) St. Augustine Monastery, Grymes Hill, Staten Island; (3) Renwick Smallpox Hospital, Roosevelt Island's south end; (4) Hudson and Manhattan Railroad Powerhouse, Jersey City; (5) Red Hook's nine-story grain elevator; (6) World's Fair site, Flushing Meadows, Queens; (7) Staten Island ship graveyard; (8) McCarren Park pool before it was a venue; (9) Octagon Tower of New York City Asylum for the Insane, Roosevelt Island's north end; (10) Widow's Mansion, Bushwick.

To cope with stress of the city that never sleeps, I soaked in CDs of experimental minimal composition that came in the mail—Mark Applebaum's *The Bible without God*, Warren Burt's *Harmonic Colour Fields*, Tom Hamilton's *London Fix: Music Changing with the Price of Gold*. Won't pretend I understand their math, but I still put those on. One thing I didn't do as much of in the '00s, though, was *write*—or rather, I wrote all the time, just rarely in a format worth preserving. At the *Voice*, and later more stodgily at *Billboard* for a year or two, that meant thousands of fleeting headlines, kickers, captions, show previews, and rewrites of other writers' work, almost none of it with my name on it.

After I left the *Voice* in 2006 I didn't even write up curmudgeony end-of-year Pazz & Jop critics poll comments anymore. (Maybe just figured I had nothing left to prove.) But when I returned to the hardscrabble scratch-and-claw freelance world by decade's end, I started piling up bylines again, often in quasi-blog form—for instance, the biweekly "Next Little Things" column I did for the website Idolator, excerpted at this section's end, wherein I crack ridiculous about as-yet-unknown-to-me artists who'd just debuted on usually inconsequential *Billboard* charts. For what it's worth, I later wound up appreciating Lady Gaga at least somewhat more than I initially assumed I would. As did the world. MySpace's days of relevance, by comparison, were severely numbered.

## Singles Again: Backstabs in the Material World

· · · · ·

This time: hits, many about the drama of romance and finance.

### Daft Punk:
### "One More Time"

The James Brown trick: say "one more time" 100 times; see what happens. Hence, a repetitious disco song *about* repetition, like "Running in Circles" by Gino Soccio or "Here Comes That Sound Again" by Love Deluxe. On record, it's too much house-diva "Music Goes Better with You," not enough punk-daft "Da Funk." But crossing its ticktocking Bee Gees chirp over to Top 40, it's pop muzik, and all the funnier for it.

### Pink:
### "You Make Me Sick"

Funny how she looks so much like Karenna Gore, funny how she makes the title a compliment, and funny how this sounds exactly like her previous two hits: mini–operatic breakdowns and the hardest teenpopgirl vocalizing anybody's yet sassed over post-Timbaland beat-science. Redundancy you can dance to, one more time! Pink's pinnacle, though, is still "Most Girls," the one about not needing a man with the mean green ching-ching bling-bling, and the one whose egalitarian economic policy thus ended the "No Scrubs" era and paved the way for double-Dutch treats like "Independent Women" and

"Love Don't Cost a Thing." Young MC's old got-no-money-got-no-car-got-no-woman-and-there-you-are algorithm no longer holds!

## Profyle:
## "Liar"

No attorney fees, but easily the *Here, My Dear* of the year, with a funky space reincarnation of electric Teddy Riley rhythms underneath to boot. Dense, gurgling, male-harmony blues: very adult. At first I assumed it was a solo singer (R. Kelly, to be precise) working some 1973 proto-disco deep-soul thing; now I notice the oily harmonies behind him, plus tattoos and torsos inspired by D'Angelo. Starts and ends with a conversation between a couple guys, sort of like in "What's Going On" or "The Message." The main guy goes to buy himself some shoes, and when he gets home catches Wifey "screaming ooh ahh" with another man. He's awful polite about it until you hear gunshots, though the chorus preceding them is intense: "You're a liar, a cheater, deceiver, heartbreaker . . . I'm taking the house, the car, the kids, the dog." Come to think of it, his last words to his friend at the beginning were "I'll call you, Dog." Makes you go hmmm . . .

## Shaggy featuring Ricardo "Rikrok" Ducent:
## "It Wasn't Me"

Finally, the male-bonding equivalent to every girltalk classic since the Shangri-Las—a flat-out boy-boy relationship-advice record. Dig if you will a picture: buck-naked on the bathroom floor with the babe next door, and your fiancée with that extra key catches it all on camera. The message, as Britgrrrls Fluffy put it a couple years ago, is "Deny everything." By now you've memorized the plot even if the goofy kinetic energy of Shaggy's ragamuffing will take your ears years to translate, but to whom do you compare the marginally West Indian early-'80s tinge of Rikrok's gentle soul tenor? Junior? The guy from Linx? Dancehall toasting, like metal, gets respect mainly when it's harsh and self-important. So Shaggy's considered a sellout, a shame since he's the one going against the grain, and his two huge hits right now have more "Earth Angel" in them than any reggae crossover since Chaka Demus & Pliers did "Murder She Wrote."

## Backstreet Boys:
## "The Call"

Her telephone rings, and he's got a napkin over his mouth. He's in a noisy club, her voice is fading because his cellular batteries are running out (he tells her repeatedly); he's blurting "say again" as if communicating by walkie-talkie from the jungle. He says he's gotta go 'cause his boys are heading somewhere, so don't wait up for him. But a few of his buddies they sure look shady, and when one backstreet backstabber clues his girl in to the truth, it's too late. Max Martin's music rocks harder than even in "Everybody (Backstreet's Back)" or "Larger Than Life," opening with flamenco strums then raising the Latin-rhythmed garage-band-stomp ante of 'N Sync's "Bye Bye Bye" via Destiny's Child tempo changes and Bee Gees somebody-help-me-I'm-going-nowhere night moves toward a tragic-tryst darkness somewhere in the vicinity of the Jacksons' *Triumph*. Compute in the unjustly maligned *Black and Blue*'s only slightly less brutal "Get Another Boyfriend" and "Not for Me," and it's clear Backstreet are carrying on rock's great double-standard tradition of wanderers who won't stand for Runaround Sue.

## Outsiderz 4 Life:
## "College Degree"

White boy band on Blackground Entertainment, five voices as usual, *all* bad boys who look like dangerous thugs (though one kid's cheekbones also link him to Hampton the Hampster)—what a smart concept. Potential audiences: (1) white girls who'll soon outgrow 'N Sync; (2) white boys; (3) black people. Timbaland carries their first single over the top with crooked plinks and plonks and open spaces and drunken classical strumming and sour New Orleans funeral-wake tubas or foghorns or whatever; the rap part has a low sluggish flow that's a ringer for Biggie's, and the mournful blues guitars on the album hint at Afghan Whigs. These guys sound *loose*, and the lyrics' lesson— basically, drop out of school!—is not to be taken at face value; money doesn't *really* fall from trees onto scrubs bragging about leeching off Mom and Dad with their GEDs, after all. So make sense of "They say that drugs kill / I'm still standing stable."

**Dream:**
**"He Loves You Not"**

Riding David "Don't Disturb This Groove" Frank's blatant drum'n'bass ripples as they dodge cute piano arpeggios and funk-rock guitar raveups, plucking petals from daisies their rival has picked to help her cherry lips and batting eyes steal the Boy; Caucasian chicks financed by Puffy (and photographed by *Billboard* in New York Dolls and T. Rex T-shirts) make like Destiny's grandchildren. They're not sending anybody to fist city. But the Boy is theirs anyway.

**Janet Jackson:**
**"Doesn't Really Matter"**

Janet was always just a "normal" substitute for people who never understood how Michael's strangeness was intrinsic to his genius; big sis Rebbie's vocals in "Centipede" had way more personality. But this is Janet's best since (Lemmy from Motörhead's favorite) "Black Cat" in 1990. Somehow the melody's subliminal Asianness makes the nothingness of her piddly voice pretty—fragile like rice paper. Or like Kyu Sakamoto's "Sukiyaki," the 1963 chart-topper that set the table for Masanori Murakami breaking Major League Baseball's Japan barrier a year later.

**SheDaisy:**
**"Lucky 4 You (Tonight I'm Just Me)"**

When we last noticed them, they were kissing off a beau by confiscating his Dodgers cap and Buddha statue and TV and leaving behind the VCR. Their new one is *Three Faces of Eve* country: "Number Five just cries a river a minute / Seven wants to tie you up and drown you in it / 14 just wants to say so long, bygones / 32 wants to do things to you that'll make you blush / 10 would key the El Camino that you love so much / And there ain't nobody wants to mess with 23." If the Dixie Chicks are *Let It Bleed*, SheDaisy are *Exile on Main Street*, or at least their muffled sound is. So the first time I heard all those numbers on the radio, I assumed they were *ages*. Schizophrenia is taking them home. And it's gutsy how the personality who ties the guy up isn't even the one doing blushworthy things.

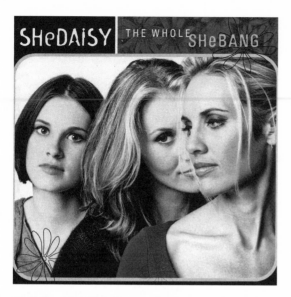

SheDaisy: *The Whole SheBang* (Lyric Street, 1999)

## Jo Dee Messina:
## "That's the Way"

From an album that may well have received the intelligentsia support it deserves had it been marketed as adult-alternative instead of as Nashville, by a woman who consistently matches the heat if not the eccentricity of her transplanted-northern-urbanite predecessor K. T. Oslin, more Shelby-style post–Sheryl Crow country, all the way down to the life-as-winding-road metaphors: bend when the wind blows, roll with the punches (to get to what's real?), you live you learn, you crash and burn. Jo Dee's follow-up single, also about burning, seems to be sung in the voice of the devil, exchanging job opportunities for souls. And on both hits, Tim McGraw's production crashes and burns just enough: in the '70s and '80s, that sneaky little disco-ish keyboard lilt halfway through would've pegged "That's the Way" as pop or rock, not country. But these days, if you're a white woman over 25 with powerful pipes, Nashville's your refuge. Even if you're Italian, and from Boston.

Five-headed monstrosity Matchbox 20 (Photo: Andrew Macpherson)

## Matchbox 20:
## "If You're Gone"

Dudes still have rock stations. And once in a blue moon, might still hitch their forced soul to some horns and miraculously find a way to help pristine powerballad-vulnerability schlock build and chime. "If You're Gone"'s tune and tics borrow from John Waite, Lou Gramm, Kevin Cronin, somebody; it's a huge improvement over the hookless-with-guitar-solo Pearl Jam imitation "Bent," Matchbox 20's most forgettable (was it ever actually on the radio?) single ever. I love the conditional of the title: He doesn't *know* if she's gone? And if she's *not* gone, maybe it's *not* time to come home? And who's coming home, anyway? Her? Him? His dog?? He spends the whole song practicing what he should say to her, overanalyzing a cloud from both sides now, then finding five or six more sides. Tells us he thinks too much: no shit. Not so much a breakup song as a maybe-we're-gonna-break-up-soon song. And the more room Rob Thomas gets, the less he can move. How smooth.

—*Village Voice*, 13 March 2001

## Bruce Springsteen: *Working on a Dream*

• • • • •

Two listens in (which is all I'm gonna attempt), by far the funniest thing about the new Springsteen album is how the background "doo-doo-doo"s in the opening track "Outlaw Pete" sound *exactly* like "I Was Made for Loving You" by Kiss, their late '70s disco move which has since been covered by countless gay Euro Hi-NRG acts.

And I guess it says something for the album that I was actually able to make it through twice without pushing reject, but not that much. I think Bruce's voice is just really shot and coagulated and sodden these days—but then, I've thought that for almost two decades now, and if the songs actually had some energy to them, I might not mind so much. What I *really really really* hate is Brendan O'Brien's totally vacant and antiseptic New Age bachelor-pad Muzak schmaltz production touches, which I gather are supposed to give the music space and drama, but to me just drain it of any life.

Not that it would have that much to begin with, but at least, sometimes, in the first half of the album, some semblance of Springsteen's old knack for *melodies* seems to be there, albeit submerged somewhere under O'Brien's bloat—like, in "My Lucky Day" (didn't he already have a boring album with a name like that?), you can sort of hear the amusement park sound of *Born to Run*, but it's way out there in the distance, like you're listening across a couple bodies of water and all this wind, which just dampens the effect and makes it all moot.

I like the straightforward lyrics of "Queen of the Supermarket" okay (he's got a crush on the cashier who bags his groceries, like Jonathan Richman at the bank), but then I think of how catchy, say, Kenny Chesney could make it (hasn't he had grocery cashier as heroine songs in the past couple years already?). And another thing that kind of amused me is how, in "Tomorrow Never Knows," Springsteen's voice sounds so much like tired late-period *Mellencamp*, who back in the '80s everybody thought of as a Bruce ripoff to begin with. And then toward album's end there's this song called "The Last Carnival" that comes off like a much lamer version of "County Fair," which was probably the most tolerable song from Mellencamp's mostly lame '08 album; I guess circus-as-aging metaphors are a new trend. (Is that a Tom Waits thing?) Then, next and last song ("The Wrestler," alleged "bonus track"), Springsteen mentions a scarecrow! And oh yeah, not that it necessarily would have salvaged the thing, but I really expected Bruce to be an opportunist and somehow tackle the economy—layoffs, foreclosures, plants closing, etc. Isn't that part of why he *exists*? And if not now, when? He practically *owned* the Reagan era recession. But nope, there's none of that at all.

—*I Love Music*, 29 January 2009

## Frat Daze, Clambake, Anyways,
## It's Still Country Soul to Kenny Chesney

· · · · ·

More Billy Joel fans in more harbor bars will hear Kenny Chesney's album (which has better singing and drumming) than the Hold Steady's (which has more words) this summer, so it's appropriate that Kenny, too, deals with both topics on *When the Sun Goes Down*: the former in a song where "Only the Good Die Young" and "Jack and Diane" remind him of dead buddies and 50-yard lines; the latter in a lovely end-of-August '70s-Springsteen facsimile where "Cleveland" rhymes with "In the mornin' I'm leavin'." There's also a staggeringly blurry-eyed hangover waltz; a restless marriage song recited like Tom Petty's "Here Comes My Girl"; the best hit since Bob Seger about a woman hitting the road with a man's American Express; and a wonderfully sympathetic ballad about a ladder-climbing mom who's a "gopher and a chauffeur and a company chairman."

But most of the record pretty much *is* a harbor bar: old James Taylor words about Mexico (over riddims from Trinidad, like in all male country lately); suntanned Myrtle Beach clambake soul with hair-metal Mellencamp chords and Uncle Kracker playing Dobie Gray and Lambda Chi Alphas hitting on Kappa Deltas and catfish jumpin' and cotton high and A1A cruises and pinball and skeeball and bare feet in the sand and kegs in the closet and pizza on the floor and dogs named Bocephus in the front yard. Alcohol figures prominently, as do pianos. The perfect nostalgia party for a disappearing epoch of entitlement and invincibility: "Spring breaks down in Panama / For a while we had it all / We never dreamed it wouldn't last." Swing-voter music that swings.

—*Village Voice*, 13 April 2004

## Country Music Goes to Mexico

· · · · ·

When Jimmy Buffett released the Parrothead national anthem in 1977, his lyrics didn't place Margaritaville on a map. They did, though, offer a clue about the utopia's location, even if Jimmy hadn't a clue how the clue—his brand-new tattoo of that Mexican cutie—got there. In the decades since, a deluge of modern-day male country singers — beginning with Brooks & Dunn's "Mexican Minutes" in 1993 and Tim McGraw's "Refried Dreams" in 1994 — have taken that tattoo to heart, turning it into a mini-genre of its own. When they want to flee the fast-paced life above the border (where "every minute has a heart attack in it," as Brooks & Dunn put it), and waste away a weekend or a season blowing their paychecks on exotic tropical drinks and exotic Latin beauties, country singers tell us, they visit Mexico. Like Jimmy Buffett postulated in the single that followed his most famous song: "Changes in latitudes, changes in attitudes."

But Jimmy Buffett's tattoo didn't invent Mexico, of course. Nor did James Taylor's 1975 "Mexico," which talks about sleepy señoritas with fiery eyes, and how life is so mellow down there that "you need a reason to move" — and which song Brooks & Dunn quote by name in "Mexican Minutes." Nope — in country music, the template goes back all the way to at least Gene Autry in 1939, telling Mexicali Rose to dry her big brown eyes because he'd be back some sunny day, or to Bob Wills with his Texas Playboys in "New Spanish Two-Step" in 1946, leaving the señorita who held his hand — the one whose "eyes told me more than words could say" — down near old Rio Grande. You could draw a line from Wills's song all the way to Gary Allan's easily swinging 2001 country-jazz waltz "Adobe Walls" — where Gary doesn't understand a word, he confesses, but "your brown eyes tell me all I need to know."

Country music's fascination with North America's southern frontier has picked up steam at a time when Hispanics are the fastest growing ethnic group in the U.S. — and, not coincidentally, a demographic that Nashville's music industry has been slowly reaching out to of late. And what makes Music Row's most recent obsession with Mexico even more intriguing is that it's also coincided with a renewed nationalist hysteria about immigration: increased border security and vigilante patrols, congressional calls for barricades, conservative radio talk shows brimming with racist commentary. So perhaps it's no surprise that, in country lyrics, Mexico is a place you can't really trust — a nation where innocence gets corrupted.

The narrator of hard-boiled duo Montgomery Gentry's expansive, ominous 2004 "All I Know about Mexico," for instance, loses his girl to a biker "all hopped up on that marijuana," and now she's sunning with him on a blanket in the Mexican sand while the singer's back home trying not to think about Cinco de Mayo, habaneros, and scary Tijuana jails. "There's things down here the devil himself wouldn't do," Toby Keith tells us atop a clave rhythm in 2004's "Stays in Mexico," wherein insurance salesman Steve from Sioux Falls and grade school teacher Gina from Phoenix hook up over tequila at Sammy Hagar's Cabo Wabo Cantina. They feel guilty about it, but not guilty enough to keep from repeating their indiscretions before Steve returns to his wife and kids.

The Latin counter-rhythms in "Stays in Mexico"—and the ones in Toby's "Good to Go Mexico" from two years before, where a less deceitful couple escape the cold November wind but want to avoid establishments "overrun with the gringos and touristas" other than themselves—are bolder than in most of Nashville's recent Mexico moves; whatever you can say about Toby's foreign affairs policy (and you can say plenty), there is nothing timid about the guy. Great singer, too. But even if few of them match Toby's, Mexico songs tend to rank among the liveliest tracks on male country singers' albums, across the board. Invariably, they're sexier and dancier than the Nashville norm. And why not: American musicians of European descent allowing their beats to move with more energy when they're condescending to darker-skinned ethnic groups, and opening up to an erotic physicality they've attached to stereotypes of those cultures, is a phenomenon dating back at least as far as minstrel shows.

At the turn of the '60s, especially—the era of banana-boat calypso and bachelor-pad luaus and girls from Ipanema—American popular music's fetishization of exotic foreigners hit full force. Pat Boone probably never rocked or rolled like he did in his Top 10 1962 novelty hit "Speedy Gonzales," featuring the peerless voice actor Mel Blanc as a sex-addicted, alcoholic Mexican cartoon mouse with more cucarachas than enchiladas beneath his leaky adobe. Irreverent Latin acts like Charo and the Mexican TV clown Cepellin covered the song in the '70s, and by 1967 Blanc was offering up similarly questionable stereotypes in TV commercials as the Frito Bandito. Presumably reaching a more collegiate crowd of Anglos, folk revivalists the Kingston Trio made jokes in both Mexican and Japanese accents in their 1958 version of "Coplas" and presciently shuffled Gulf geography in a calypso called "Bay of Mexico" the same year. The liner notes to *Watch Out!* (1966), the highest-charting album from ethnic instrumental explorers the Baja Marimba Band (led by a sideman from Herb Alpert's immensely popular Tijuana Brass), raved about their "lazy Latin sound" and "horsehair moustaches, fuming cigars, and ill-fitting haberdashery [reminiscent of Wallace Beery as Pancho Villa]." The current stereotypists of country music tend more toward political correctness, though the Kentucky Headhunters' rambunctiously ay-yi-yi-ing 1991 "Big Mexican Dinner" (which should have been spelled "beeeg Mexican deeenner") was certainly a throwback.

But ethnic stereotypes can come from all directions. In 1965, a Mexican American navy vet from Dallas named Domingo Samudio hit #2 in the U.S. with "Wooly Bully," one of rock'n'roll's woolliest and bulliest moments; it started off "Uno! Dos! Tres! Quatro!," and Domingo's band, Sam the Sham and the Pharaohs, offered a singular gimmick: dressing up in turbans, as Arabs. "Juímonos (Let's Went)," a whooping areeeba-rock instrumental on their *Wooly Bully* LP, featured the following enticing bit of border-crossing dialogue: "You like to travel?" "Sí!" "Where you like to go? "Juímonos, Baja California!"

Crazy stuff; you can bet longtime Texas Mexicanophiles ZZ Top (who have albums entitled *Rio Grande Mud*, *Tres Hombres*, *Tejas*, *El Loco*, and *Mescalero*) were paying attention. Though in ZZ's 1975 "Heard It on the X," Billy Gibbons says he learned to play guitar so raunchy while listening to "country Jesus hillbilly blues" on Mexican outlaw border radio "back in 1966." The theme was updated in L.A. singer-songwriter Warren Zevon's 1976 "Carmelita" ("mariachi static on my radio"), L.A. rockabilly band the Blasters' 1981 "Border Radio" ("50,000 watts out of Mexico"), and L.A. new wave weirdos Wall of Voodoo's 1983 "Mexican Radio" ("no comprende, it's a riddle"). Later in 1983, the Butthole Surfers took Sam the Sham's and ZZ's insanity a step further into the asylum with "Mexican Caravan," a seriously stoned garage rocker in which front-nut Gibby Haynes squeals like a javelina in heat about heading down to Miguel to score brown heroin. That's territory that Nashville wouldn't dare tread—though Nashville's weirdest, funniest, most creative 'oos act, Big & Rich, just might try someday. Their 2005 track "Jalapeno" opens echoing Sam the Sham's Spanish countoff from "Wooly Bully"; turns into shouted, intermittently disco-percussioned boogie about a spicy two-stepping señorita named Maria; then segues into a wacky number—part Tex-Mex polka, part hoedown, part jugband swing—called "20 Margaritas," about a chef named José who cooks up some mean guacamole and tamales. Modern Nashville has rarely sounded so unhinged.

Still, Big & Rich—and Toby Keith, too—are far from alone in their race to be Nashville's leading current chroniclers of stereotyped Latin culture. Tim McGraw has "Refried Dreams" and, from 1999, "Señorita Margarita," the former skirting the issue of Montezuma's revenge and the latter featuring a mariachi break and both of them quite cleverly punned and catchy. Teen phenom Blaine Larsen put "I've Been to Mexico," a good-natured tune with the same moral as Brooks & Dunn's "Mexican Minutes"—namely, that people in the U.S. need to learn to slow down like their southern neighbors—on his

2004 debut album; on his 2006 sophomore set, his mock mariachi "I Don't Know What She Said" took the gringo-mistranslating-Spanish concept to a ludicrous extreme: he follows a brown-eyed girl down the hall and she tells him "muy guapo and something about hohos." Garth Brooks "set sail with Captain Morgan" (and made his big calypsofied Buffett move, though he left Mexico out of it) in 1997's "Two Piña Coladas" and was faced with a difficult choice in 2002's rowdy "Rodeo or Mexico," eventually letting yet another pair of dark brown eyes help his decision along—at least until her knife-wielding husband walks in. Best joke: "Does anybody know the Spanish word for wife?"

In the age of Martina McBride and Sara Evans and Faith Hill and Carrie Underwood and the Dixie Chicks (all of whom, by the way, have recorded excellent songs about hitting the highway in search of a more exciting life), it's worth noting that Nashville seems to present its Mexico myths as an exclusively *male* fantasy. Unless you count the three albums of traditional Mexican and Spanish songs that Linda Ronstadt recorded between 1987 and 1992, you'd have to bend the perimeters beyond their breaking point—maybe to Nicolette Larsen's bittersweet 1978 country-rock version of the Drifters' "Mexican Divorce," or urban-sophisticate country chart alumnus K. T. Oslin's doubly horny 2001 girls-night-out ditty "Mexico Road" (which probably isn't about the nation at all), or New Orleans teen fiddle prodigy Amanda Shaw's sweet 2008 "Chirmolito," an ode to the Chicano construction workers who rebuilt her home post-Katrina—to find a song by a woman that ventures anywhere near Garth and Toby and Tim's travel brochures.

But maybe that's got something to do with how women fit into the myth—which, again, is a very old story. If you don't mind stretching a bit geographically and genre-wise—and meanwhile maybe speculating why so many country songs about visiting Mexico sound more faux-calypso than faux-norteño—you could do worse than revisit "Rum and Coca Cola," where the Andrews Sisters got all triumphant about colonialism (after all, it was 1944 and they were winning the war), discoursing on two generations of Trinidadian women "working for the Yankee dollar" and making "every day like New Year's Eve."

If the Andrews Sisters never explicitly spelled out what that "working" may have entailed, they at least acknowledged an economic transaction was taking place. Perhaps the tasks were related to the mysterious "dance I never saw before" that rock'n'roll jokesters the Coasters watched a fishnetted castanet player perform in "Down in Mexico" a dozen years later, in a hep jazz bar run by a cat who "wears a purple sash and a black mustache." In 1973, in ZZ Top's comparably comical and typically rampaging "Mexican Blackbird," Billy Gibbons advised in a mock hillbilly accent that when one drives one's Chrysler below the border, one's money is best spent on a certain cantina employee known profanely as "Puta," since "dancin' and lovin' is her trade." Another decade down the line, a long-haired señorita made her intentions perfectly clear when she led neo-trad country drawler John Anderson by the hand then up a tavern's stairs in his flamenco-embellished "Old Mexico." John's impressed by the exchange rate: in Mexico, he notes, "Your American dollar buys so much more." But next thing he knows, his money's all gone.

Those jezebels can be treacherous, see. In Merle Haggard's 1974 "The Seashores of Old Mexico," revived into a country hit for George Strait in 2006, a young cowpoke runs from the law in Tucson and eventually gets a lift from farmworkers after losing his bankroll in Juarez when "one bad señorita makes use of one innocent lad." Years before, in their #3 1964 U.S. hit "Come a Little Bit Closer," New York pop band Jay and the Americans put Latin rhythms swiped from the Drifters and Richie Valens beneath a temptress in a border café who makes Jay's mouth water with her beckoning eyes. But then, you guessed it, her boyfriend José shows up, and the guitar player tells Jay to vamoose. Events of a similar nature no doubt happened in too many old Westerns to name. But I'll make room for Marty Robbins's kindred 1959 U.S. chart-topper "El Paso"—like a Western movie in four minutes which, as its title suggests, does not take place in Mexico per se, but does involve the obligatory date at Rose's Cantina with a Mexican siren who casts evil spells with eyes blacker than night until a cowhand with no manners cuts in on the dancefloor. At which point Marty steals a horse and hightails it to the badlands of New Mexico, where he is eventually shot to death in the chest.

"El Paso" came from an album called *Gunslinger Ballads and Trail Songs*, which probably wasn't so outlandish a title back when country was more Western, and less set in the suburbs, than it is now. Or even back in 1983, when Willie Nelson and Merle Haggard topped the country chart with Townes Van Zandt's Western mini-movie "Pancho and Lefty," about a gunslinger who grows old and cold in a cheap Ohio hotel after murdering a bandit in the Mexican desert: the Federales let him slip away. But give or take Strait's cover of Haggard's vintage seashore ode, most of country's recent Mexican sojourns revolve around being an affluent gentleman of leisure, not a desperate fugitive from justice. Surprising, given the debt that recent country owes to old-school album-oriented rock, and given that '70s and '80s rock radio had its own outlaws running for the border—in ubiquitous hits like Eddie

Freddie Fender: *The Best Of* (ABC Dot, 1977)

Money's 1978 "Gimme Some Water" and Christopher Cross's 1980 "Ride Like the Wind," to name two.

Hip-hop has thrived on similar felonious themes for years as well, of course, but even hard rock (Sammy Hagar's drunken 1999 toga party "Mas Tequila") squeezes its lemons in Cabo San Lucas these days. Recording for a microscopic indie label in 2004, veteran hard country journeyman Billy Don Burns rip-roared through a song called "Running Drugs out of Mexico"—one notable line had AK-47s filling bastards full of holes—but Music Row seems terrified of such stuff. We're a long way from "Wanted Man," Johnny Cash's geographical catalog of all the towns (and women) trailing him. On his *At San Quentin* album, which spent four weeks atop the U.S. charts in 1969, the line that draws by far the loudest applause from prisoners is the one where Johnny gets sidetracked while map-shopping in El Paso then goes "the wrong way into Juarez with Juanita on my lap."

Back in Marty Robbins's "El Paso," the way Robbins's voice keens up on the high notes—sounding "wild as the West Texas wind," like his cowboy nemesis in the song—owes something to the fancy, super-emotional filigrees of boleros. It's a technique that has weaved in and out of country music over the years; Roy Orbison was famous for it. But the country crooner who really made Latin music's rococo vocal embellishments work was Mexican American. Raised in a family of migrant farm laborers, the man born Baldemar Huerta in Texas picked up his stage moniker Freddie Fender in the late '50s, he says in the liner notes to his 1975 album *Before the Next Teardrop Falls*, as a way to sell his music to gringos, "but now I like the name." And the title of his ornately quivering 1975 hit "Wasted Days and Wasted Nights" (first recorded as rockabilly in 1959) sums up the theme of the '90s-to-'00s country-goes-to-Mexico wave as perfectly as "Margaritaville" does. Wasting days and wasting nights is the expressed mission of songs like "Beer in Mexico" by Kenny Chesney (who's been known to jam in Cabo with Hagar, and who is such a latter-day Parrothead that he called his summer 2007 concert trek the "Flip-Flop Tour," presumably in homage to Jimmy Buffett rather than John Kerry).

Freddie Fender is not the only Mexican American ever to hit country radio. In 1973, Johnny Rodriguez hitch-hiked to the top of the U.S. country chart with "Ridin' My Thumb to Mexico"; he had plenty of other, less memorable hits along the way, and even did jail time once for stealing a goat. Conjunto legend Flaco Jiménez has lent his accordion to lovely border polkas by clear-singing country hipsters the Mavericks and Dwight Yoakam; in the mid-'90s, Tejano singers Rick Trevino and Emilio made successful crossover moves; more recently, blues-based bar-band brother trio and Willie Nelson cronies Los Lonely Boys climbed to #46 country with "Heaven." And when it comes to country interacting with the styles now lumped together as "Regional Mexican"—which, after all, is a music where bands dress up like cowboys and often sing about them—that's only the tip of the iceberg. In the 19th century, immigrants from Germany and Czechoslovakia brought their accordions to Texas, and within decades their waltzes and schottisches were cross-breeding with Mexico's boleros and rancheras. As recently as 1985 you could find a tuba oompah combo of central European descent, like Leroy Rybak's Swinging Orchestra in Halletsville, Texas, covering the Mexican traditional "El Rancho Grande."

But there's more than one way to cross over. In 1980, Freddy Fender recorded a number called "Across the Borderline"—written by Jim Dickinson, John Hiatt, and Ry Cooder—for the Jack Nicholson movie *The Border*; the lyrics talked about believing the streets on the other side are paved with gold, but once you get there your dreams are shattered. Domingo Samudio, the former Sam the Sham, contributed to the soundtrack as well. In 1985, comedy duo Cheech & Chong reached #48 on the U.S. pop chart with "Born in East L.A.," a Bruce Springsteen parody about a U.S.A.-born Chicano carted off to Tijuana by a redneck immigration agent; in 2007, cowboy-hatted Houston

Chicano comedy rapper Chingo Bling, who sometimes spoofs hillbilly music in songs such as "Pop Tailgate . . . Wooooooo!!!," charted with an album called *They Can't Deport Us All.*

Toby Keith, for his part, has toured the U.S. with Ted Nugent—a vocal advocate of stepped-up border security who's been known to spout "If you can't speak English, get the fuck out of America" from the stage. And in the comments section beneath Keith's "Stays in Mexico" video on YouTube, a spelling-impaired Internet ignoramus calling himself troak12 babbles, "To bad Mexicans don't stay in Mexico. Instead they come to America cause they are to fucking lazy to fight for freedom in there own country."

Country songs themselves, however, willfully circumvent the controversy, though at least one—Chris Young's 2006 "I'm Headed Your Way, Jose," where the rookie singer good-naturedly decides to trade places with a Mexican immigrant, slapping him five at the border and telling him he better pack a poncho because northern weather's so bad "you'll freeze your ass off"—takes current events into account. And then there's Texas songster Robert Earl Keen's eggnog-spiked "Merry Christmas from the Family," covered by Montgomery Gentry in 2007, where little sister brings home a new Mexican boyfriend, and the relatives get suspicious until he sings "Feliz Navidad." Country music is frequently years behind the curve when it comes to commenting on front-page news, but don't be shocked if, at some point, lyrics about immigration become commonplace. Eventually, that may be inevitable. For now, though, Nashville's stars are still mostly content to lounge lazily with their margaritas in a mysterious land they envision as one big siesta—searching for that lost shaker of salt.

—*Time Out: 1000 Songs to Change Your Life,* 2008

## September 11: Country Music's Response

· · · · ·

September 11 gave Nashville something with gravity to hang its cowboy hat on, a flag of substance to rally around. In retrospect, it might ultimately be the catalyst for country music suddenly sounding as relevant and surprisingly powerful as it often has for the past decade.

It's easy to forget that, in the '90s, country radio didn't rely nearly so much on building every-man-for-himself fortresses against scary outsiders. Garth

Brooks and Shania Twain, who exploded genre sales records throughout that decade, always came off as relatively cosmopolitan, probably no more right-wing than Bill Clinton. But 9/11 brought reactionary cranks out of the woodwork. Within weeks, Hank Williams Jr. was back with "America Will Survive" (his highest-charting country single since 1991), as was Charlie Daniels with "This Ain't No Rag, It's a Flag" (his highest since 1989). And for other artists, it was a game-changer: Toby Keith, until the planes hit, was known primarily for domestic relationship songs.

Keith's saber-rattling "Courtesy of the Red, White, and Blue (The Angry American)" (which ultimately begat *Shock N' Y'all* and "American Soldier" and "American Ride" and "Made in America") is one of two country songs that inevitably come to mind when conversations turn to 9/11. The other, Alan Jackson's "Where Were You (When the World Stopped Turning)," came half a year earlier and was a much bigger hit; beginning in the last week of 2001, it topped the country chart for five weeks, where Keith's anthem didn't get its single week at the top until the following July. (Though interestingly, the week after 9/11, Keith was #1 anyway—with his one-night-stand number "I'm Just Talkin' about Tonight," of all things.) Jackson's song, though, was also something of an anomaly—geographically clueless ("I watch CNN, but I'm not sure I can tell you the difference in Iraq and Iran") but ultimately nonviolent in its intentions.

The United States invaded Iraq in late March 2003. That week, the Dixie Chicks' heart-rending "Travelin' Soldier"—about Vietnam, but undoubtedly identified in many military family minds with the present—went #1 country; just days earlier, Natalie Maines had introduced the song in England by voicing her opposition to the war and to George W. Bush, which instigated a famous backlash. Then in April, Daryl Worley's "Have You Forgotten," which explicitly and unscrupulously linked Bin Laden with Iraq and used that as a justification for preemptive attack, took over the country chart's top spot for seven weeks.

Worley, thankfully, is a bit of a blip. He's had just one country #1 since, and has barely creased the Top 10. But country's newfound openness to fightin' words gave boosts through the decade to a certain muscle-bound breed of male country star—for instance Trace Adkins, who has belted out a few war-themed songs in his big baritone, at least one of which ("Welcome to Hell") damned al-Qaeda terrorists to eternal flames. Even more significantly there's the reliable duo Montgomery Gentry, whose entire career was seemingly built on a kind of defensive anti-urban paranoia about "the world going down the drain" that tied into Tea Party values before the Tea Party even existed. Lately, in Nashville, that sort of stance has been slipping out of fashion—probably one reason, weirdly, that country radio is duller now than it was just a few years ago; there's simply less at stake. But for a while there, it was inescapable.

In early 2002, as the music editor of the *Village Voice*, I put together a 9/11 benefit compilation CD called *Love Songs for New York (Wish You Were Here)*. Though their love for NYC is doubtful, Montgomery Gentry's label asked that "Tattoos & Scars," the battle-veteran-inspired title track from the pair's 1999 debut album, be included; I lobbied for it, but was voted down. It's possible I should have lobbied harder. Not a single Nashville selection made the cut, which seems odd now, given that country—for all its egregious political faults—was the only genre that regularly continued to acknowledge that the U.S. was engaged in multiple wars in the decade following 9/11. Given wars about which Americans were free to wear blinders, that's important. In no other genre could an actual Baghdad vet like Luke Stricklin score with a morose song about his overseas experience ("American by God's Amazing Grace," 2005); in no other genre could the eventually gay-married Chely Wright have a hit defending her petroleum-guzzler's U.S. Marines sticker against bird-flipping private-school elitists ("The Bumper of My S.U.V.," 2004.) So, in both the short and the long run, it's hard to think of any other musical genre affected so thoroughly by 9/11. As Toby Keith would say, that day put a boot in country's ass. It's the American way.

*—MTV Hive*, 9 September 2011

## Battle of the Country Hunks

• • • • •

Country-Rock Hunk No. 1, Rodney Atkins, wants y'all ladies to know these are a few of his favorite things: bird dogs, honky tonks, blackjack, pickup trucks, spark plugs, beer pong, throwin' darts, and extra innings. Hunk No. 2, Eric Church, digs smallmouth bass, Faulkner, NASCAR, Red Man (tobacky not rapper), mustard on fries, sleeping in on Saturdays, not acting his age (which is 32), and hell yes his truck. And Hunk No. 3 Pat Green goes for pawn-shop guitars, crackers in his chili, trustworthy mechanics, inner-city teachers, laid-off Detroit factory workers, boxers past their prime, and giving ex-cons a second chance. Green's thoughtful list, "What I'm For," reads like a cross between Alabama's "40 Hour Week" and Roxy Music's "Manifesto," and his motto—that if you know what he's for, you don't need to ask what he's against—may well be a sign of the times as Nashville awkwardly adapts to a more liberal era. But Atkins and Church know who butters their bread: in "Best Things" and "Love Your Love the Most," they respectively concede that, as cool as all this stuff might be, it still can't compare to a good woman.

All three songs appear on new country albums that came out in recent weeks. As did new albums by **Keith Urban**, Jason Aldean, and Dierks Bentley—none of whom explicitly tally what they like, though none of them seem to mind small towns much. Or arena rock riffs. Or women who can turn them into better men. Urban's been doing the "laid-back unshaven Down Under himbo who just stepped off his surfboard with his greasy hair" thing for a decade now, and *Defying Gravity* is wall-to-wall lovey-dovey fare, primarily about kissing. I keep hoping he'll make a hotshit guitar record someday—maybe even a live album—but he just keeps getting ladies'-choicier. Nonetheless, he reliably still sounds more like John Waite (productionwise) and Don Henley (vocalwise) and Lindsey Buckingham (guitarwise) than like George Strait or Randy Travis. And he's still most fun when he makes lazy haziness his point (surrounded by audible waves and Ferris wheels in "Til Summer Comes Around") or powers his jangle-pop like Bryan Adams crushing on Tom Petty ("Standing Right in Front of You"). He's least fun when he ends his album apologizing through a dark night of the soul, seemingly praising wifey Nicole Kidman for saving him from all that coke—even calling himself "born again," despite being Catholic.

**Pat Green** ends *What I'm For* uncharacteristically gloomy and sober, too— "In the Middle of the Night" of a cold lonely overwrought Boston winter, contemplating "shooting my soul right through the ceiling." The longtime DIY guy has been gravitating toward heartland rock since he sold his San Antonio soul to Music City early this decade, and the only time the word "country" shows up on his current publicity one-sheet is in the title to his paradoxically Mellencampish current single "Country Star." His previous hit, "Let Me," swiped its guitar hook straight from Seals and Crofts' "Summer Breeze." (See also: Urban's "Only You Can Love Me This Way" = America's "Ventura Highway"; Bentley's "Better Believer" = Ringo Starr's "Photograph.") More Green lights: a gorgeously fuguey ode to hard-luck siblings, a hangover number that chimes like "(What's So Funny 'bout) Peace Love and Understanding," and some perfectly humid swamp-soul about how we are all prostitutes.

Like Green's "Lucky," **Rodney Atkins**'s "Got It Good" spells out how rich people have it great but regular folks oughta be thankful for blessings too. Corny, but so what: Rodney's band rips the Stones like Mellencamp's in 1982. Next comes "Friends with Tractors," fast-rolling pro-farmer boogie climaxing with a hoedowned shoutout to Larry the Cable Guy. *It's America*'s hit title track idiotically implies that only in the U.S. do neighbors help out when there's a natural disaster, but Atkins was born with a baritone sturdy enough to put over his prole-romanticizing platitudes, and he's developing a wit to match— when this good ol' boy gives up smokin' and drinkin' and women, it's the worst 15 minutes of his life; when he wakes up at 4 A.M. at album's end, it's not to confess sins but to go fishing. His 2006 *If You're Going through Hell* had four country chart-toppers on it, most notably "Cleaning This Gun (Come on in Boy)," the funniest song ever written about being the dad of a daughter who just started dating; his new set's exuberant pinnacle, "Chasing Girls," winds up in similar if less threatening paternal territory after opening with a reminiscence of flirty tweens pursuing each other around bungalowed cul-de-sacs with squirt guns and water balloons. It's also the best song to mention EPTs since Eric Church's "Two Pink Lines" two years ago. A pink stuffed animal goes to whoever can figure out which forgotten early-'80s Nerf-metal classic its suburb-in-summer guitar riffs come from.

The riff in **Jason Aldean**'s latest smash "She's Country," as far as I can tell, comes from AC/DC; he's easily got the hackiest cowboy hat here, but what sets him apart are frequent hooks that don't just feel hard—they feel heavy. First time I heard his 2005 debut hit "Hicktown," I thought of Black Sabbath. And his follow-up "Johnny Cash," amusingly enough, largely recalled midcareer Bad Company. The Georgia metalbilly's new *Wide Open* features nary a single self-penned lyric, but the title opener about an underemployed gal "slingin' eggs and bacon with a college education" holds its own regardless.

Right now, though, the most interesting thing about Aldean is that **Eric Church** has it in for him. "Ya sing about Johnny Cash / The Man in Black woulda whipped your ass," Church scolds, in a song castigating "one hit wonders." Plus your usual feisty clichés about how Waylon wouldn't've done it that way. That's "Lotta Boot Left to Fill," one of several slide-strewn chip-on-shoulder shitkickers on *Carolina*'s first half; halfway through the album, in "Smoke a Little Smoke," the singer pulls out his stash, the guitars do a hefty back-porch vamp, and you wonder why this usually apolitical rebel thinks we need "a little more right and a little less left." Album opens loud, with Church imbibing and overtiming himself to death; he hangs onto 16 as long as he can in "Young and Wild"; and in "Where She Told Me to Go," hell is a bachelor's

apartment with faulty plumbing and lousy TV reception. On the record's sub-
par second half, he mooshes out—a dame inevitably saves his hard head from
hitting rock bottom, but not from falling short of his '06 debut. There's still a
jaunty "Twist and Shout" swipe, though. And a lush and elongated guitar solo
at the end.

Dierks Bentley's "Little Heartwrecker" is more or less the same song as
Church's "Hell on the Heart": she's a hottie, so prepare to get burned. And
ramblin' Arizonan Lollapaloozer Dierks—by consensus the hunkiest of these
hunks give or take Aussie Urban, and the only other one not born in Dixie—
is going through motions of his own on *Feel the Fire*. As with Urban, slacker
nonchalance is part of what makes him sexy. But four albums in, his rockgrass
roadster is stuck in the muck. There's one great track ("I Can't Forget Her,"
made spacious with spooky spaghetti western guitars and Del Rio desert sand
blowing around), a couple good ones at the beginning (some fugitive funk
with motorcycle sounds and "space bass," some blatant pro–Velvet Rope line-
dance fodder), and lots of indistinctive competence. Which might be enough:
if you need a little help, Babe, Dierks tells you, there ain't a button he can't
reach. Maybe even the ones in your sewing kit, on that really high shelf! But
can he bring home the bacon and fry it up in a pan?

—Village Voice, 8 April 2009

## Country Songs IV

· · · · ·

### Trace Adkins:
### "I'm Tryin'" (2001)

Trace Adkins had not yet settled on his ass-whooping, honkytonk-
badonkadonking muscle-car butt-country persona when he delivered this
throat-lumpingly sparse divorced-dad sigh in 2001; his baritone was already
booming, but not yet bellicose. And unlike most country songs about alimony
and child support, Jerry Reed's hilarious "She Got the Goldmine (I Got the
Shaft)" for instance, there's neither bitterness nor self-deprecating comedy at
work here, just hurt: "Two years since we finalized, still not used to putting 'ex'
in front of 'wife.'" All she has to say to him anymore is send more money and
don't be late, but the bum economy's hanging over his head—"This gettin' up

early workin' double shifts / Gonna make an old man of me long before I ever get rich." He tries to follow his own old man's advice—"Go easy on the bottle, be hard on yourself"—but he feels like Sisyphus. And when violins and cellos of Dan Huff's production chime in, this mountain Trace must climb feels like a world upon his shoulders.

## Ty Herndon:
## "Heather's Wall" (2001)

The most twilight-zoned country hit so far this millennium—and probably the only one sung from the point of view of a dying man just shot by a bank robber—"Heather's Wall" is also something of a phantom record. Originally slated to be included on an album called *This Is Ty Herndon*, it stalled at #37 on the country chart, which caused Herndon's label to lose confidence in his future prospects. The album never reached the stores, and the song was left off the *Greatest Hits* album that came out instead. So it effectively ended his six-year career as a Nashville hitmaker—a career that, way back in Herndon's rookie year 1995 when fans still confused him with fellow rookie Ty England, had already managed to survive an incident in which he was apprehended for meth possession and exposing himself to a male police officer in a park. Charges were reduced, Herndon had hits, but by the early '00s he was weathering other personal travails. As happens in modern America, he'd later resurface as a Contemporary Christian singer, returning to church music he was reared on. But "Heather's Wall" was his last real shot at glory, and God, what a stark last shot—he feels the gun exploding, senses things moving in slow motion, remembers New England in the fall of '99, wonders how he can be dying while walking up stairs. He will never be set free, as long as he's a ghost that we can't see.

## LeAnn Rimes:
## "Life Goes On" (2002)

Some of the best C&W of '00s was actually R&B, and vice versa. Faith Hill's "One" was one sterling example; this was another, and it ticked people off. People, see, had in their minds that LeAnn Rimes was supposed to be some kind of pure country singer, thanks to songs she had once been given that had helped her go quadruple platinum as a 14-year-old. By her next two regular albums, though, she was already covering Debby Boone and Prince, and pretty much her whole career from that point on was a back-and-forth tug-of-war between her alleged old-school country roots and the poppier proclivities she clearly saw as asserting independence. Which they were—when good-taste know-it-alls with sticks up their keisters want to limit you, misbehavior in the opposite direction counts as an act of courage. With 2000's much-remixed "Can't Fight the Moonlight" from the *Coyote Ugly* soundtrack (think *Urban Cowboy* two decades on), Rimes crossed over bigtime to both pop (#11 hit, #61 country) and dancefloors. And in 2002's somewhat less lucrative "Life Goes On" (#110 pop hit, #60 country)—off an album called *Twisted Angel* which was produced by old metal-disco hand Desmond Child and on which Rimes wore several varieties of wanton lingerie in the CD booklet—she stomped under mirrorballs like Laura Branigan or Taylor Dayne while asserting independence from a cad who believes he's the "Daddy Mac." Thing is, nobody else in pop or R&B was mirrorball-stomping that hard anymore in 2002. If it takes a country diva to do it, so be it.

### Rebecca Lynn Howard:
### "I Need a Vacation" (2003)

Kentucky cutiepie Rebecca Lynn Howard debuted at 21, peaked commercially by 23, and by 29 was putting out a country-soul album on an indie label, singing Temptations, Aretha, and Al Jarreau numbers. During her brief big-league career at MCA, she was best playing a bobo in paradise. There was "Pink Flamingo Kind of Love," the most irresistible track on 2002's *Forgive*—tiki torches, one-legged lawn-ornament birds, iced tea, you and me, garden-hose sprinklers aimed at the patio. And then this sweet-toothed staycation single a year later, which never even wound up on an album—this time, the patio has a swing you can fall asleep in; there's a sly hint of threesome kink ("Me and my husband we need a wife / Someone whose sole ambition is a laundry"); the asides are somehow more endearing for being more sitcom-middlebrow than they think ("yeah, I invented shabby chic," "if it blooms, it's not a weed"); and we don't "even have to leave 2523 General George Patton Drive." Pop-country about suburbia: underrated again, especially with big Tom Petty jangles and Drifters castanets and Latin percussion touches leading the way. Now, if only Rebecca Lynn Howard would revive Dionne Warwick's "Hasbrook Heights" someday.

## Gene Watson:
## "Flowers" (2003)

The past couple decades have seen a spate of alcohol-recovery songs from aging country men—T. Graham Brown, Gene Watson's labelmate for a time on indie-label-for-supposed-has-beens Intersound, did some real good ones for instance. But it's doubtful many were as effective as "Flowers," sung the year Watson turned 60. He addresses it to his wife, who—we learn as the song progresses—turns out to have died a year before, in a car that the narrator was driving, after she had begged him on her knees not to. He swears he's been sober since, and of course it's totally maudlin, but Watson's delivery is gorgeously understated, and he nails it: at one point, to illustrate how much he's changed since that tragic day, he mentions a new suit for Sunday he just bought. And how his relaxed tenor rejoices in that high exultant note on "I'm in *church* now" gives you shivers and breaks your heart—it's hard not to believe that, beyond the plot's hyperbole, Watson hears something of his own life in this story. The song appeared on a CD called . . . *Sings*—one of 11 consecutive albums on six different labels (1992 to 2009) listed on Watson's Wiki discography that did not chart at all. Between 1975 and 1997, though, he had charted over 75 songs—including six #1s. Subtle ballads, mostly—some of which may, or may not, be as mind-blowing as this one.

## Jace Everett:
## "Bad Things" (2005)

When Epic first put this single out in 2005, as a follow-up to a #51-country-charting Everett song called "That's the Kind of Love I'm In," nobody much noticed. So I was taken by surprise four years later, when somebody on an Internet message board claimed it had one of the decade's best guitar solos. Then mere days later I went to a Halloween party, and the aging Austin psychobillies who lived in the old-monster-movie-decorated house had instruments set up in the living room and played stuff like "Whole Lot of Shakin' Going On," Link Wray's "Rumble," Sam the Sham's "Little Red Riding Hood," assorted Wanda Jacksony and Crampsy and Etta Jamesy things I couldn't place, and, uh . . . "Bad Things." Which on one hand fit right in thanks to its dirty twang, but on the other hand felt out of place, because since when do crusty old psychobillies pay attention to current Nashville country? Of course, this was all before I learned that, in 2008, "Bad Things" had wound up the theme song to HBO's vampire-oriented *True Blood*, then wound up a small pop hit in England and a bigger one in Scandinavia. Everett's mostly garage-punkish *Red Revelations* next wound up one of the best albums of either 2009 or 2010 (it's complicated), and that had "Bad Things" on it, too. Before you knew it, Everett's Amazon page was promoting him as a "swamp-blues rocker." Which makes it all the odder that the slimy moodiness, king snake crawling, werewolf-rockabilly hiccupping, and playfully threatening eroticism of "Bad Things" (which, by the way, is what the mysterious loner in the song promises to do to you before the night is through) were ever pitched to straitlaced country stations in the first place. But they were.

### Sarah Buxton:
### "Space" (2008)

The title is a pun, an onomatopoeia—space is what Sarah's selfish boyfriend in the song wants, and space is what the music's arrangement leaves plenty of. This is one of the clearest examples of mainstream country's 21st-century trend toward confessional singer-songwriting by young women: Taylor Swift, obviously, and Michelle Branch's country side project the Wreckers, but also Miranda Lambert, Sunny Sweeney, and so on. Bitter about her guy complaining they're moving too fast and going too far, the woman in the song is entirely contemporary. Seemingly single and in her 20s, she could be from anywhere— big city, suburbia, small town, doesn't matter. Though the frustrated sophistication in Buxton's tone certainly does not feel sheltered or provincial—"You need your own room, well how 'bout an island / I bet you can find one, on the dark side of the moon." Imagine a more vocally full-bodied, halfway-to-Stevie-Nicks version of early Liz Phair—with that sexy Peppermint Patty burr at the edge of her voice intact—and you wouldn't be far off. "How does it feel not to need anyone," Buxton taunts, channeling "Like a Rolling Stone." Yet this was a #38 country hit, from a woman who Nashville sadly seems to find more marketable as a songwriter for male singers like Keith Urban, or a featured voice on tracks by male singers like David Nail.

—*Complex*, 5 June 2012

# The Ladies of Triple A

. . . . .

Carlene Carter is 52, Sheryl Crow 46, Shelby Lynne 39, Allison Moorer 35, Tift Merritt 32, Kathleen Edwards 28—quite a span, so don't call them a generation. Only Lynne and Moorer are actual siblings, much less survivors of parental murder-suicide whose new records consist primarily of cover versions. Only Moorer and Crow have dueted on the same Kid Rock song; only Lynne and Carter have ever had more than momentary success on the country singles chart, and it's been a while. Crow and Lynne have by far the thickest press packets this time out, but where Lynne (who has one Grammy) got a six-page *Times* Sunday magazine feature, Crow (who has nine Grammys) had to settle for a Deborah Solomon Q&A. Crow's previous album, 2005's uncharacteristically introverted *Wildflowers*, was her career's floppingest flop at 948,000 copies, a figure any of the other five would be happy to halve anytime; not surprisingly, she switches labels less often, and still records for a major. She's also recovered from breast cancer. Edwards, who comes from Canada, and Merritt, who recorded in France, are both on their third albums. Carter used to be married to Nick Lowe and is now married to soap opera star Joseph Breen; Moorer is married to Steve Earle, who has been known to appear on *The Wire*.

Still. They're all Adult Alternative by this point, right? Not crass enough for country radio even in the critically sanctioned age of Miranda Lambert, but tastefully at home in the middlebrow Starbucks/*Paste*/NPR milieu. And in a dismal first quarter where Kimya and Alicia and Keyshia and Hannah and Sara (that'd be Bareilles—look it up) are suggesting female artists (presumably selling to more than a few female fans) might be the biz's last best hope, these Triple A all-stars are all back in the racks—with albums less exciting than the new one by 62-year-old Dolly Parton, no less. So forgive my lumping them together.

**Shelby Lynne** first; she just opened with her best sales week ever, and she's got the most Pazz & Jop potential. What you might have read about *Just a Little Lovin'*: nine Dusty Springfield covers, one original, all Barry Manilow's idea. What you might not have read: tempos sluggish enough to keep Robitussin in business. That said, the two Bacharach-David songs benefit from Lynne's light touch; the two songs about morning sex benefit from Phil Ramone's almost dub-like open space and alarm-clock ticktock percussion; and the two songs about neighbors residing in run-down 'hoods benefit from an ominous-enough swamp-soul groove. (And right, Shelby wisely avoids Dusty's biggest hit—you know, the one with the Pet Shop Boys!) But her attempts at jazzy phrasing came off less ridiculous back in her pre-critic-sanctioned western-swung Nashville days, and her Dusty album is already swinging her pendulum back toward "overrated" like nothing since her 2000 culturati breakthrough.

Shelby's younger sis **Allison Moorer** likewise seems to be banking on coffee-shopping boomers overhearing her interpretations of the more famil-iar oldies on *Mockingbird*. Her marketing concept, though, casts a wider net: woman songwriters who aren't Lil Mama! The Julie Miller, Gillian Welch, and especially Patti Smith songs, where producer Buddy Miller erects a sturdy if stodgy statue of folk-blues drone, at least set up some semblance of mood. And crooning that bawdy old Nina Simone number about her bowl needing sugar was probably fun. But mostly Moorer's dishing out wallflower wallpaper and schoolmarm folk. And her rote revival of "Both Sides Now" is almost pointless enough to make Herbie Hancock seem courageous in comparison.

On paper, covering "Ring of Fire" seems just as dead-end. But how Moorer slows it down is surprisingly tolerable, and may well help people remember that June Carter Cash wrote it. June died in 2003, four months before Johnny; their respective daughter and stepdaughter **Carlene Carter**'s new *Stronger* is being billed as a "recovery" record (hey, it worked for Rosanne Cash), but it sounds less heavy-handed than that suggests. Also more pure-pop than the lounge kitsch Carter's ex-hubbie Lowe has been selling lately, with some rec-ognizable rockabilly clippity-clop, some fake Fleetwood Mac harmonies al-most worthy of Little Big Town, and a "Jesus Is Just Alright" melody in "On to You" in case you forget producer John McFee used to be a Doobie Brother. But the only time Carlene really cranks up her singing is in "I'm So Cool"—a proto–Gretchen Wilson tomboy shitkicker she first recorded on *Musical Shapes* in 1980.

**Tift Merritt** doesn't kick much shit, but Alison Moorer might agree with her claim that "all girls go through a Joni Mitchell phase," and the well-regarded alumnus of North Carolina's alt-country sphere definitely spends *Another Country* exploring hers. The other country is France; she's a free man in Paris; she closes with a oui-oui slice of café chanson and murmurs through most of the rest of the album as if she's still groggy in her garret. Things pick up slightly in the middle: melody swiped from the Traveling Wilburys in track 7;

some jaunty horns in track 8; and most alert of all in "My Heart Is Free," where thick guitar fuzz supports an apparent tale of a soldier shooting his sergeant to escape the war. Then it's back to the Land of Nod.

**Sheryl Crow**'s thinking about the war, too. Maybe too much. Her muddled protests on the wordy and unwieldy *Detours* map out some absurd amalgamation of Prince, Dylan, Marley, and Madonna (the falafel-joint worldbeat mantra "Peace Be upon Us" is straight *Ray of Light*). She means well, though; even "God Bless This Mess" makes for a bearable refrigerator magnet until the towers come down. She also sounds reasonably bright-eyed and bushy-tailed through, oh, track 11 out of 14—God-reggae fixation or no, Bill Bottrell, who produced Crow's debut 15 years ago, gives her a decent bubblegummy bounce to chew on. But her most coherent politics shows up in breakup songs. And sorry, if you're concerned about petroleum consumption, you might think twice before writing an Armageddon fantasy about how, after the riots of 2017, "gasoline will be free, yeah yeah yeah." (Also inadvisable: hiring jam-folk bore Ben Harper to stodge up the ending.)

Ottawa-born **Kathleen Edwards**'s "Oil Man's War" on her proudly Canada-centric *Asking for Flowers* is more down to earth: basically, to dodge the draft, a horny boy and girl escape to the Great White North, where they'll have a baby and open a store downstairs. Edwards is not averse to creative-writing notebook singsong; there's something affected about the way she's always stretching out vowels. But studio aces (notably keyboard Heartbreaker and former Carelene Carter collaborator Benmont Tench) help a lot. And more than all these other sob-sisters, she just might convince you she's living in the material world. Three of her set's better songs talk about performing onstage, and the metaphor-packed "I Make the Dough, You Get the Glory," which seems to concern a sisterly crush on a bandmate, is a Canuck tour de force, from its Gretzky-and-McSorley hockey references to its hopes for "heavy rotation on the CBC." But the real State of the Provinces address is the one that takes its name from the national anthem: "Oh Canada," pushing its Crazy Horse buildup skyward as it tackles a country's see-no-evil denial of racism and violence. By album's end, Edwards earns the six-minute smooth-jazz string-and-sax stretchout "Goodnight, California"; you get the idea that she deserves the rest. And also that, like Joni, she might still have a little money riding on the Maple Leafs.

*—Village Voice*, 5 March 2008

# Anvil Won't Go Away

. . . . .

Rock'n'roll history is written by the winners. Which stinks, because the losers have always played a big role in keeping rock interesting. Sacha Gervasi's *Anvil! The Story of Anvil* takes that as a given, and has a hilarious, heartbreaking time proving the point.

Still, when I first heard of the movie, I was skeptical. In some sense, small-time documentaries about mentally unstable cult musicians—Roky Erickson, Jandek, Daniel Johnston, Wesley Willis—have became a major cliché. Also, who the heck are Anvil? I've written a metric ton about heavy metal since 1984, but to me, they were just another name I'd half-noticed in record stores over the decades, easy enough to confuse with Alcatrazz or Axe except that all their LPs had, uh, anvils on the cover. Turns out, though, that Anvil were the talk of the then-easy-to-miss metal world for a few months in 1982, when the British rock-zine *Sounds* pegged the crazed speed-scorch on their *Metal on Metal* album as the genre's future. Which, judging from talking-head testimonials in the movie from Motörhead / Metallica / Slayer / Anthrax / Guns N' Roses guys, it was— only that highly lucrative future happened to everybody else, not to Anvil themselves. The Canadians charted only once in the U.S., peaking at #191 with 1987's *Steel on Steel*. Twenty-two years years later, *The Story of Anvil* shows, core members guitarist/singer Steve "Lips" Kudlow and drummer Robb Reiner—now in their 50s, but joined at the metal hip since they were 14—respectively earn their keep as a driver for a children's catering company and as a sometime construction contractor, in hardscrabble neighborhoods on the outskirts of Toronto. One of metal's attractions has always been as a voice of the white working class, and no movie has ever made that identification so explicit. But honestly, you haven't lived until you've seen Kudlow trying to balance a cart loaded with three large vats of shepherd's pie through the snow on the way to his van.

By now, he's a frumpy neurotic Jewish dad, usually seen with an Alpine knit hat flopped over his scraggly thinning hair. But thanks to the wonder of archival footage from Canadian public access TV and obscure Japanese picture discs, the movie starts in a forgotten pre–Spinal Tap era of codpieces, bondage harnesses, zebra-striped unitards, dog collars, Flying V's strummed with dildos—accouterments the serious young thrash bands that Anvil inspired soon set aside, which might mean Anvil laid the groundwork for their own demise. Gervasi, whose previous screenwriting credits include *The Big Tease* and *The*

*Terminal*, had befriended the band as a headbanging London teenager, then roadied for them. But by the time he decided to track them down, he'd left his metal life far behind.

What he found could not have been scripted. Rubber-faced never-say-die fans chugging beer through their noses at Kudlow's dive-bar birthday party, a disastrous tour across the European interior, half-remembered Yiddish ditties about sons schtupping shiksas, the drummer's paintings of lonely East German street scenes and a toilet-floating turd. In Prague, Anvil get lost on the streets on the way to the club, and the promoter tries to pay them in goulash, and when a lawyer fan from the audience asks why the band isn't playing stadiums, Reiner says, "I can answer that in one word, two words, three words—we haven't got good management." A trapezoidal-headed fan named Cut Loose gets Kudlow a telemarketing job selling sunglasses, and he can't do it because "I've been trained all my life to be polite"—this from a guy who made his name writing porn-metal songs called "Toe Jam."

But halfway through, the movie switches gears, and we learn how supportive Anvil's families are—wives, siblings, kids, parents, all the way back to Reiner's Hungarian Jewish jeweler dad, who survived Auschwitz and made him a gold drumstick necklace he still never takes off. Kudlow and Reiner repeatedly fight and make up, like an old married couple but way more likeable than Metallica's Lars Ulrich and James Hetfield in *Some Kind of Monster*. (Actually, Ulrich himself comes off as more likeable in this movie.) And Kudlow proves some kind of zen Pangloss, threatening to jump off a cliff at one point (Reiner promises to stop him) but somehow using circular logic to locate life's bright spot no matter how shitty it gets. At least things could never get worse than they already are, he says, but "on the other hand, if it did get worse, at least this time after all has been said and done I can say all *has* been said and done."

Gervasi finds gorgeous settings for the band, too, amid Japanese temples and the cliffs of Dover. And toward film's end, Kudlow delivers a hyperemotional soliloquy about his artistic dream that suggests he might have achieved more lasting fame as an actor—in fact, a couple times, he lets on that the potty-mouthed, vibrator-wielding "Lips" was just a character he created. Really, he never stopped being a nice Jewish boy. "99.9 percent of bands never get paid," he insists at one point. With any luck, three decades into their hard-luck career, their name now more visible than ever thanks to Gervasi, Anvil might yet wind up part of that other 0.1 percent.

—*Film Comment*, November 2009

# Excellent Boring Metal from Germany

. . . . .

One thing they (whoever "they" are) don't tell you about heavy metal is how boring so much of it is. As often as not, even the interesting stuff these days is boring—music to be half-listened to in the background while skimming the newspaper on a hungover Sunday morning. Invest much more energy than that, and you're sunk. But low-maintenance music has its uses, and so far in 2008, when it comes to bleakness you can lay back and relax to, the Prophecy label from Germany seems to be winning.

Not that Prophecy's quite batting 1.000; for instance, *Throne of the Depths* from northern Germany's Drautran just gives me a headache. And *IIII*, by fellow Krauts **Farsot**, doesn't really grab me until "Thematik: Trauer," the uplifting 20-minute-plus semi-pianofied monster dirge it ends on. (Farsot do have crazy names, though: 10.XIXt does vocals, v.03/170 keyboards, 3818.w and Pi: 1T 5r guitars, R215k drums.)

Those albums are both on Prophecy's black-metal subsidiary Lupus Lounge, as is **Helrunar**'s unpronounceably titled *Baldr ok Ìss*, which probably doesn't literally translate as "having no hair is alright" but which I've actually been liking anyway, especially the solid pagan-chanted drone "Hunta and Boga" and the way the appropriately shivery "Winter" builds up from a gorgeous intro reminiscent of Metallica's suicidal-teen classic "Fade to Black." Helrunar also speed-race over the top in "Loka Lögsaga," break the levee rhythmwise in "Til Jarðar," and mask backwardsly in the concluding scary black mass "Baldrs Draumar." Three more Germans (Skald Draugir, Dionysos, and Alsvartr—do metal dudes have excellent monikers or what?) who say they recorded their new album "within five days, using many first takes," they are said to refer to ice fairly often in their lyrics.

But the new Prophecy album I'm even more addicted to is *The Minstrel's Curse*, from Deutschland duo **Noekk** (featuring Funghus Baldachin and F.F. Yugoth!). Only four "songs," but they add up to 34:25 of music thanks to the 14:26 closer "The Rumour and the Giantess," which climaxes with a mournfully recited and presumably Aryan accented monologue about the end of the world or something. How sad! I also admire how "Song of Durin" builds its manly voiced doom-sludge operetta to a sky-raising group chorus, and how "How Long Is Ever" gets whittled down to extremely slow, super-spaced-out keyboard notes for a couple minutes. Not bad for a band named after an

No Noekk photo this far was making its point as boldly. (Photo: Prophecy Productions)

imaginary sea creature, huh? "No Noekk album this far was making its point as boldly," their English-as-second-language press release boasts, and I'm certainly not going to argue with that.

—rhapsody.com, 31 March 2008

## The Many Ideas of Oneida

· · · · ·

A few Fridays ago, Fat Bobby woke up at 6 A.M. in Boston's "vortex of white suburbia," where he teaches seventh-grade American history and eighth-grade English while also coaching hockey ("We were undefeated for a game — we wound up 1-6-1") at Dedham Country Day School, where his dad's the headmaster. The day before, Bobby'd played the tricky baroque piano interlude from the Beatles' "In My Life" at graduation ceremonies. But now he had to finish up the semester with some meetings, then head down to Brooklyn to link up with his power trio. The most reliably inventive and prolific rock outfit in NYC for nearly a decade now, Oneida—whose ninth-or-so album, *Happy New Year*, came out this week—were scheduled to play the Syrup Room, in a somewhat ghost-town-like East Williamsburg Industrial Park neighborhood, at half past midnight.

The show ran late, but that's OK; Fat Bobby wants Oneida to feel like a dream onstage anyway. The Syrup Room, which formerly specialized in pancake toppings, felt like a barn: a big, claustrophobic space in the middle of nowhere off the Morgan stop of the L train (or "Hell Train," as Oneida's album-length 2000 *Steel Rod* EP put it), with makeshift bar and toilet stalls, a sizable hole in the ceiling, and a refrigerator keeping beer cold. After a set by Home (jammy indie rockers now recording for the Oneida-run Brah label), Fat Bobby's keyboards commenced to blur into Hanoi Jane's bass and Kid Millions' drums as they plunked what sounded like the same note over and over again, for 10 minutes or more. If you listened close, you noticed incremental shifts, but much of the crowd looked confused. Yet by the time the band's set wound down to the new album's key track, "Up with People," which Kid and Bobby say was inspired by stern old Chicago house trax by the likes of Fingers Inc., people were kinda sorta dancing.

Turns out the drone they'd opened with was the intro of the title cut of 2002's double disc *Each One Teach One*, slowed down and stretched toward eternity; in the past, Oneida have kicked off many a concert with that same album's landmark "Sheets of Easter," which goes, "You've got to look into the light light light light light light . . ." ad infinitum for 14 minutes. Starting shows in a trancelike state "is a little bit of a hippie thing, a way to settle in," Bobby theorizes, wearing red-tinted sunglasses and a T-shirt for stoner-boogie bunch Parchman Farm while sipping a Dos Equis and talking a mile a minute on the back patio of a little Mexican restaurant in Brooklyn's Clinton Hill, the neighborhood Oneida call home. "We're not trying to unsettle people." And though Kid says they've given the vocals more production emphasis on their last couple albums (the new one even comes with a lyric sheet), Bobby admits they still purposely sink the singing into the mix during live shows. "For me," he says, "the sound works best when you can't tell what's coming from where."

*Happy New Year* ends, as do many Oneida albums, with an extended epic—this time, the seven-minute "Thank Your Parents," originally planned as the title track of a triple album, a project the band promises it hasn't shelved, just postponed. *Secret Wars*, from 2004, ended with another extended monstrosity, "Changes in the City," which changed almost imperceptibly, just like the city does. Since that time, of course, Brooklyn rents have climbed, and Oneida have watched contemporaries become famous. "More power to them," Bobby says, paying respect to the Yeah Yeah Yeahs and Animal Collective. "But no major labels have come to knock on our door. And I attribute that to their good business sense."

He remains proud of the borough, though. "There's still this acceptance and understanding in Brooklyn: 'Do whatever you do with passion, and I'll give you a chance,'" he says. "I feel like the coolest thing we've accomplished as a band is to help build this community of people—not just music, but art, film, everything."

A few Sundays earlier, in fact, Kid Millions was fixing up Oneida's new recording studio, downstairs from a loading dock in an austere industrial building they now share with the Mighty Robot art gallery at the west end of Metropolitan Street, where Williamsburg abuts the East River. Oneida's old studio, right next door, had been displaced for condominiums. Kid's gym bag revealed CDs by Scott Walker, RZA, Fela, Marshall Jefferson, and Black Sabbath. Hanoi Jane, who has somewhat less hair than his drummer, drove us to a Williamsburg burger joint where they both drank Trappist beers—one red, one blue—from Belgium's Chimay monastery.

Once upon a time, Oneida were a four-piece; now that Fucking Champs / Trans Am guitarist Phil Manley has his own Oneida pseudonym (Double Rainbow—the other guys, when asked their real names, play the hip-hop card), they're looking like a four-piece again. ("We're in the process of figuring it out as we go," Kid explains.) Years ago, though, they were a duo: just Kid and Papa Crazee, now of the art-country act Oakley Hall. "When Crazee left," Jane says, "we were surprised by how much space that left in the sound." And since then, they've explored that space, recording a reggae dancehall track for release later this year and incorporating dainty instrumentation (zither, harpsichord, mandolin, sitar) on last year's uncharacteristically pastoral *The Wedding*. "We've done songs that are freak folk, and they're really well played and intricate," Kid says. "But we don't run around in peasant skirts."

*Happy New Year* begins with a dead ringer for "Scarborough Fair," though Bobby insists Simon and Garfunkel were ripping off an Elizabethan folk melody, while Oneida are stealing a traditional southern funeral song he found in a book of old musical transcriptions in a thrift store. "We're thieves," Bobby admits. Which makes sense, seeing how he first played with Kid in a Grateful Dead cover band, when they were juniors at St. Paul's School in New Hampshire, half as old as they are now.

All four Oneidas are in their early thirties. "It's hard to market us," Jane says. "Maybe we're too old." Two of them are married, and Bobby's got a baby due in November. College towns Middlebury, Vermont, and Oberlin, Ohio, also figure in the band's prehistory; that's where they got into the habit of playing house parties, prepping the group for the ad hoc venues they still frequently frequent. When Oneida first formed, obscure little holes in the wall were the only places they could get gigs, give or take an occasional night at the Knitting Factory, which Kid was helping book at the time.

Now Kid provides computer tech assistance for a living; Jane just got his master's in social work at NYU. "We're not music as a business," he says. "This isn't what we use to pay bills." But Oneida's still an obsession, one the guys plan to keep at forever, even if Jane has to remind his parents that music's more than just a hobby. His mom, after witnessing some rare blue material at one gig a few years back, said Oneida reminded her of Redd Foxx, who she's not much a fan of anymore. In contrast, Bobby's mom—a Congregationalist minister who, until lately, pastored her own church in Dublin, New Hampshire—has compared the trio's music to Philip Glass. Only louder.

Their first show ever was upstate, in Rochester. Two hours east of there, not far off I-90, sits Oneida, New York, where John Humphrey Noyes founded the utopian free-love Oneida Community, for whom Oneida were named, and which eventually evolved into a company that now includes an Oneida stainless-flatware division. "The founder was named *noise!*" laughs Bobby. "I love it." What's more, a multi-great-granddaughter of Noyes is a fan and has invited the band up to visit the community's site sometime. They were also awarded commemorative grapefruit spoons.

But the Oneida Community isn't on the curriculum for Bobby's American-history students, whom he only carries through the Revolution. Bobby admits "the seventh-grade boys are super-obsessed" with the fact that he's in a band. "I don't think I could do it if part of me wasn't still a seventh- or eighth-grade boy," he says of teaching. "I didn't fail anyone, but I don't give out very many A's, either."

Still, he's happy to get a break. For one thing, it'll give Oneida a chance to tour North America. Furthermore, Fat Bobby says, "This is my first summer vacation in years. So I plan to log some time in the hammock."

—*Village Voice*, 12 June 2006

## Next Little Things

· · · · ·

### The Cruxshadows

One fan of this veteran and sometimes rather comely Massachusetts "dark-wave" and/or "electronic body music" act—whose "Immortal" somehow enters the physical-retail-only Hot Singles Sales chart at #16 this week—has this to say: "I've always thought that the most extraordinary special effect you could do is to buy a child at the moment of its birth, sit it on a little chair and say, 'You'll have three score years and ten,' and take a photograph every minute. 'And we'll watch you and photograph you for ten years after you die, then we'll run the film.' Wouldn't that be extraordinary? We'd watch this thing get bigger and bigger, and flower to become extraordinary and beautiful, then watch it crumble, decay, and rot." Mr. Grim N Evil, he calls himself, and you'd call yourself that too if you had such brilliant ideas!

### Rush of Fools

Was hoping this outfit would live up to their name by sounding like Rush except dumber, and I'm pretty sure I got half my wish. No By-Tor and the Snow Dog here, catch my drift? *Wonder of the World* is now at #15 in its second week on the Christian Albums chart. The band comprises five clean-cut young folks from Alabama playing extremely wimpy acoustic scripture-rock, with lyrics directed at the son of God himself. "Label me a prodigal," one song goes. "Bring me back to the place of forgiveness and grace." Most intriguing venue names on their fall tour: Evangelical Free Church of Naperville; The Church in Peaster; The Church at Quail Creek; KLOVE Friends & Family Music Cruise; Godfrey Parks and Recreation; Anchorage Baptist Temple. "Sounds like: A pastor, an auto mechanic, and three guys whose names begin with a 'J' playing on some instruments," we're told. A note from Stef: "Thanks for being awesome guys! Keep up the rockin for JESUS!"

### Big Daddy Weave

Sadly not a fake-hair-obsessed rapper heavily influenced by Bobby Jimmy and the Critters, but rather a totally mushy soft-rock band from Nashville that showed up on the Christian Albums chart at #15 last week with their sixth studio album, *What Life Would Be Like*. Songs on MySpace appear to be about . . . Jesus! Who is their MySpace friend! Or at least some guy who calls himself "Yeshua Hamashia (Jesus Christ)" is! Here's what said Messiah has to say: "Shalom be with you! Thank you for adding me as a friend! I love your page and I'm honored to have you as a friend! May HaShem bless you and your entire family with happiness and health in the powerful name of Rabbi Yeshua Hamashia!" At least two other MySpace chums quote the Book of Philippians, which sure beats the hell out of Leviticus, if you know what I mean. And I think you do.

### Ten Feet

Laid-back fake-reggae folk-rock swill from Hawaii, even more so (more fake and folk I mean) than Rebel Souljahz, who were written about in this space a few months ago; both bands are getting ready to take part in the KWXX Ho'olaule'a on 27 September in Downtown Hilo. (Free admission! Live music! Great food & crafts! Sponsored by Kama'aina Motors and Kama'aina Nissan!) So is this a genre now, or what? Do Jack Johnson and Jason Mraz have something to do with it, somehow? Their photos are both among Ten Feet's best MySpace friends, so I'm blaming them. Ten Feet feature five people (do the math!), and their *Everyday* entered Top World Albums at #13 last week. But Hawaii isn't in the rest of the "world"; it's part of the United States, right? Even ask Barack Obama! What's next, Alaska?

### Haystak

So apparently, Haystak's still around! And I do mean round. The heavyweight hillbilly hip-hopper from Blastville, Tennessee, has a new album called *Hard 2 Love*, and it hits the Heatseekers chart at #13 this week. His MySpace page indicates that he wears glasses now and has seemingly had some sort of stresses in his personal life which he raps about with utmost sincerity in his new album's title track. Then in the slow-riding driveby "B.O.S.S.," he asserts, "I'm a businessman, get out my business van, and we gon' turn your neighborhood into Pakistan." Also, you can order several different T-shirts from him, preferably of the XXXL persuasion. Haystak's MySpace pal Adam sure plans to, so why not you? Here's what Adam writes: "Hey big Homie we got problems. Your shit is too hot. I was late for work because you had me stuck in front of the stereo mesmerized by the lyrics. Now you need to calm down because if I get fired I can't get one of them shirts. Be good bro."

## Big Kuntry King

Given that Big Kuntry King's album, which just finished a solitary week at #98 on the Billboard 200, is entitled *My Turn to Eat*, one might well wonder what sort of food the Atlanta rapper plans to have for lunch. Well, if you visit his My-Space page, you'll see a picture where he is about to bite into a quarter-pound sesame seed bun full of . . . dollar bills! And you know what that means—no Atkins diet for this guy! Another clue, among the many videos embedded on the page, is one for a song called "Goin' Ham," though Big Kuntry doesn't explain whether he prefers the honey or smoked variety. However, he does ask, "Why you haters hate, like a poor sport?," which is very good question. I've always wondered myself why haters have such bad manners. As for his connection to the bagpipe-happy early-'80s Scottish Irish-Spring-commercial-influenced rock band with whom he shares part of his name, your guess is as good as mine: is he not expecting to grow flowers in the desert, but he can live and breathe and see the sun in wintertime?

## Juney Boomdata & Marc Decoca

Atlantans Juney and Marc, who are apparently acquaintances of both Soulja Boy (whose 18th birthday party Juney attended) and Cookie Monster (who hangs out with Juney on his MySpace page), infiltrate the Hot R&B / Hip-Hop Songs Chart at 99 this week with "Wassup wit da Cookies." They do not enter with "Wassup wit da Pussy," which sounds similar but revolves around a different noun. Both compositions seem to mention freaky-deaking and partying like rock stars. The cookie one has been known to inspire fast dancing by young ladies wearing Mall of America shorts. Juney's MySpace also features a ridiculous rap called "Brains of a Bird," not to mention a survey on which he reveals that he is a fan of the letter *a* and Ben Franklin ("thats the man on a hundred dolla bill"), that his biggest plan this summer was to "make sure my AC works," that he will date a girl with kids but "will never play step daddy," that his favorite color is baby blue but his least favorite is "clear," that his best friend is "Sox" but his worst enemy is "anybody who don't like Sox," and that his favorite books are *I Wish I Was Sick Too* and *Supa Head*. Marc has a My-Space page, as well, but it isn't anywhere near as much fun.

## Brianna Taylor

Brianna's self-titled "debut EP available on iTunes" entered Heatseekers at #46 last week, which kind of seems like cheating, seeing how it's digital-only and not a whole album, but hey, I don't make the rules. Seems her key to the kingdom was "appearing on *The Real World (Hollywood)*, on which she is a sought-after housemate"—honest, that's the most interesting thing her MySpace bio could come up with, even though it also insists that "controversy seems to follow the 20-year-old Philadelphia native around wherever she goes." Uh, maybe everybody just wants a controversial housemate?

## Lady Gaga

Lady Gaga's album *The Fame* entered the Canadian album chart at #8 last week and this week hangs on just inside our northern neighbors' Top 10. Meanwhile, her song "Just Dance" with Colby O'Donis (and occasionally Akon), which has spent the past few weeks at the peak of the Canadian Hot 100 mountain, is at #79 on the Hot 100 and #8 on the Hot Dance Airplay chart in the U.S., despite being (not unlike the one other song on her MySpace page) Medium-NRG dancefloor fluff of no notable distinction beyond her relatively tuneless voice. Lady Gaga's bio on MySpace reveals that she grew up on Manhattan's Upper West Side but later experienced a period of "self-discovery" on the Lower East Side which consisted of "dabbling in drugs and the party scene," yikes! She includes "drag queens in general" among her influences, and appropriately lists her "male equivalents" as "Elton John, Freddie Mercury, Boy George, and John Lennon in wig and fishnets at Studio 54." And indeed, all indications are that Ms. Gaga—actually named for the 1984 Queen hit "Radio Ga-Ga," so there goes the joke I was gonna make—dresses like a woman, just like some of those men did! In fact, she insists Peggy Bundy is one of her fashion icons. The video to "Just Dance," sadly, looks more glam-rock than the song sounds. But Gaga is still probably no worse than thousands of other privileged ladies of questionable talent turned quasi-decadent divas before her.

## 3OH!3

Two "Rock/Electronica/Thrash" dimwits already bundled up for a Boulder, Colorado, winter, somehow popular enough (apparently thanks to Warped Touring) to leapfrog the entire Heatseekers chart and enter the *Billboard* 200 at #89 last week with their album *Want*. "Lil Jon Beatz and Dylan Rapz," they self-describe elsewhere. "We call it Lil Dylan." So how come they sound more like Fred Durst with a synth player? Lyrics focus on girls with trust funds back east, and tongues between girls' teeth, and "nice legs, daisy Dukes," "low cut, see through," "tight jeans, double Ds," etc. "Tell your boyfriend if he says he's got beef that I'm a vegetarian and I ain't fuckin' scared of him." Gawd. Fans on MySpace rave about "bomb as fuck dance moves you do on stage." Non-fans on YouTube claim "these dudes suck sooo bad is this for real i wanna beat the shit out of these dudes wtf." Take your pick. Jess on MySpace asks: "Wassup with the Mason symbol tho?"

## Deadmau5

"In this world of ever evolving genres, sounds and trends, the word *phenomenon* is rarely if ever used," Deadmau5's bio unreliably asserts. Except in the case of, uh, this clearly phenomenal fellow, whose new album on Ultra, randomly titled *Random Album Title*, entered the Heatseekers chart at #65 this week. Very informative explanation of his music, from his Wiki page: "Deadmau5 (pronounced 'Dead mouse,' birth name Joel Zimmerman) is a Progressive house and Electro house musician and DJ from Toronto, Canada. His extensive discography includes tracks such as 'Arguru' and 'Not Exactly.'" Got that? You may call him Mau5y, you may call him Zimmy, but you're gonna have to serve somebody. And he's recorded tons of music, including two songs you never heard of before. Cool! Also, he has a record label called Mau5trap. His symbol, or logo, or whatever, is indeed a mou5e, midway between Mickey Mou5e and a computer mou5e, yet seemingly not dead. (Or Mode5t, for that matter. Or On Mar5. Or, um . . . Dangerou5.) Seems like he must be a big deal in the world of electronifica, seeing how he's worked with both Sasha *and* Digweed—not to mention Tiesto, Carl Cox, Laurent Garnier, and other notable techno people whose names sound halfway familiar. And you'd be a big deal, too, if your on-stage props included a "tailor made giant Mau5head complete with powerful strobe lighting eyes that get (your) fans in a frenzy during (your) spellbinding sets." Said head is clearly visible in the live video for "Ghosts N Stuff (Hard Intro Version)" (which one comment-writer insists is actually called "The Reward Is Cheese" instead). Well, actually, the video has *two* mau5 heads, oddly enough, neither particularly "giant," and the mi5e wearing them engage in a wrestling match. Then Deadmau5 works in frightening music such as Vincent Price's evil laughs from "Thriller" and Chopin's "Pray for the Dead and the Dead Will Pray for You." Very goth, not that you'd know that from the frenzied fans. Me, I kinda dig the psychedelic organ stuff that happens between the four- and five-minute mark. But 9:53 is really long.

—*Idolator*, 2008

# 5
. . . . .
## '10s

**A BRIEF LIST** of meaningless things I don't care about: the Rock and Roll Hall of Fame, Grammy Awards, Video Music Awards (which seemed bogus from the get-go), Record Store Day with its prefab overpriced sucker-bait "rarities" killing fun just like what happened to baseball cards decades before, boxed sets padded full of outtakes that were outtakes for a reason, the Song Of The Summer (as if there was ever only *one* song—well, except "Afternoon Delight" and "My Sharona" I guess, but those were a long time ago), anniversaries of pretty much anything (though I wrote about a Metallica one a few chapters back), Twitter feuds, Instagram feeds, the "festival circuit," "updating" whichever version of an album I've got, albums released as surprise publicity stunts at midnight as if that's somehow interesting, 99% of remixes since 1985 or so (totally stodgy of me, but keeping up with regular versions is hard enough!), new U2 albums since 1983 or so (*Under a Blood Red Sky*, man— how many bands ever peaked with a live EP??) embedded within Apple gadgets or not, gadgets in general (Apple or not).

Then again—admittedly—I'm extremely spoiled. I've been getting free albums in the mail (first vinyl, eventually CDs, now both . . . though the quantity's slowed to a trickle lately) for approximately three decades. I get free downloads emailed to me, too, all the time, often months before albums come out, but never click on them unless I have to write about them and have no choice, since they're frequently loaded with frustrating glitches and whatever else record labels Trojan-horse into them, and they come so fast I forget they're even there. I have a free Rhapsody subscription since I'm one of their regular contributors, so I can stream most albums nobody sends me. And when I somehow finally got sent a Hall of Fame ballot in 2015, I couldn't resist voting Cars/Cheap Trick/Chic/Spinners/Yes despite myself. On top of all that, I'm a white heterosexual cis-male of a certain age who grew up comfortably enough in the suburbs (despite occasional familial setbacks), which means I've benefited over the years from all the built-in perks *that* implies. I don't remember ever not living within driving distance of a couple good record stores, and my son William who sells Vitamix blenders even gave me one so I don't have to buy daily vegetable smoothies; I can just make them myself. So I probably shouldn't complain about anything. Ever. I know this.

But. Though certain arrogant (and, let's face it, privileged in their own way) Panglosses and Pollyannas would no doubt consider this the music-world equivalent of denying global warming, I'm still one of those despicably hypocritical old coots who can't shake the ingrained belief that music is somehow less taken for granted when you have to work a little to find it. I'll always be addicted to dollar vinyl bins, where so-called music discovery can still happen in random and untargeted ways inconceivable online. Heck, I even miss mail-order catalogs. And no matter how much music is now available to mere mortals at a flick of the wrist, no way is the omnipresent "cloud" the best of all possible worlds. There was real pleasure, once, in knowing esoteric stuff nobody else knew—or, better yet, trying to figure it out from mysterious clues on album covers, and if you wrote about them, imagining the rest from scratch, since it was still fine *not* to know. Both that secret knowledge and non-knowledge seem barely possible anymore.

I'm not even sure the Internet's to blame. Expert liner notes may have started to kill off ancient mysteries circa the initial vinyl reissue boom of the mid-'80s (or even earlier—*Nuggets* was 1972); I'm no film buff, but I get the idea that's also the era when legendarily horrible monster movies that people had previously only half-remembered from stoned late-Saturday-night viewing of fuzzy local UHF stations started sneaking out on VHS and presumably Betamax. Of course, there are still admittedly plenty of amazing early Bob Seger songs, among other lost 20th-century treasures, you'll never find on streaming services. And Netflix, if it lasts, may well never offer the turn-of-the-'90s NBC-to-Lifetime divorceé-in-New-York dramedy *The Days and Nights of Molly Dodd* or TLC's 2011 reality series *All-American Muslim* set in Dearborn, Michigan. But even those seem easy enough to track down on YouTube.

Generational kvetching like this naturally exasperates those who believe technology only helps the world evolve, never makes it worse—or maybe folks like that are just straw folks anyway. Obviously I'm fighting a long-lost cause here, tilting at windmills. It's probably only fair that suggesting consumption of popular culture was in some ways more fun ages ago would mark one as a reactionary, or that preferring music on vinyl (or even, these days, CDs) to whatever fills your hard drive or bounces off satellites would be dismissed as a fetish. But to keep up with the latest gizmos is fetishism, too—frequently of a way more expensive kind.

Economic class figures here in all sorts of directions. One argument for free downloading was always that it's the only access to music some people could afford, which I'll concede without accepting for a second that's why *most* downloaders ever did it. Either way, digital music's increasing hegemony never helped those who, for financial or geographical reasons, lack access to high-speed Internet or mobile phones in the first place—including, in broadband's case according to the Census Bureau and FCC, most households with annual incomes under $25,000. Adoption rates of new technology tend to be exaggerated by those projecting their own personal practices, and brick-and-mortar store closures may have further marginalized regional styles indigenous to isolated areas that lack infrastructure to provide connection—Tejano and trail-ride zydeco come to mind. And even when smartphones are affordable, data plans may not be.

There's also something to be said for not always giving in to the brave new privacy-stripping, agitation-exacerbating utopia sold by overlords at Apple, Google, Facebook, Yahoo, and their fellow global behemoths trying to anesthetize the way that you feel. And in terms of permanence, an evanescent

Internet really can't match the trustiness of physical objects. Web platforms are business experiments, with finite lifespans. In putting together this book, my hardest pieces to track down weren't ones I'd published in magazines that folded in pre-Internet days (I kept those, after all), but ones I wrote for once allegedly visionary venture-capitalized web startups that long since went the way of Muxtape, Friendster, and the dodo. Europe and Argentina have meanwhile begun experimenting with an ostensibly privacy-promoting "right to be forgotten." Music will begin to disappear, too, if it hasn't already. "The labels are adjusting to an environment where stars will be as ephemeral as a text message," Berklee College of Music Institute for Creative Entrepreneurship director Panos Panay told the *New York Times* in 2015, on the occasion of a chart-topping album by Toronto teenager Shawn Mendes, who got famous singing six-second covers of other artists' hits on the mobile app Vine. For people born in the 21st century, tossed-off amateur YouTube videos count as popular entertainment; by now, that's the way of the world.

A lot of music these days—maybe even most of it—is ephemeral *by design*. Not that there's any reason music needs to last forever: like my friend Scott Seward wisely posited once, the fact that you'll probably never again hear those particular birds that were warbling outside your window this morning doesn't make their song any less pretty. And as I already suggested, sometimes culture being quickly forgotten makes it *more* interesting. Two long-running playlist series that, despite my grumpy digital objections, I had a blast putting together for Rhapsody in recent years (neither excerpted in this book, since they don't make much sense unless you've got the actual playlist in front of you, but searchable online at least for now) have been "Hits You Never Heard Of" and "Obscure Olde Metal," both of which sent me paging alphabetically through record guides—Joel Whitburn's *Billboard* Hot 100–tabulating *Top Pop Singles 1955–1999* and a few yellowing hard rock / metal references, respectively—for intriguing music that's been abandoned beneath the couch pillows of history. But whether you're talking late hip-hop's downloaded stopgap "mixtapes" superseding officially sanctioned albums or indie's unfinished witch-house-to-chillwave-to-whatever bedroom-electro-piddle MP3 and hundred-copies-for-friends cassette culture (from whence sprung the duo Merchandise, who I get snarky about somewhere in this section), music that's here-then-gone increasingly seems its own point.

Evaporating in front of your ears, usually without touching down to give you coherent verses or half a hook to grab onto, is something an awful lot of 21st-century music takes pride in—from future R&R Hall of Fame shoo-ins

Radiohead to Muzak-metal sludgegazers like Deafheaven all the way through narcoleptic FKA Twigs–type pseudo-R&B swindles to D'Angelo's repurposed *There's a Riot Goin' On* / early Funkadelic wooziness minus the sense of menace or thrill of the new. More background space than foreground song, the ultimate great-grandspawn of Brian Eno, Pink Floyd, Kraut rock, dub reggae, and Windham Hill, such amorphousness may have served a quarter-century ago, in germinal stages of "post-rock," "shoegaze," and/or "trip-hop," as a reaction against the indistinguishably jangling jingles of countless college radio bands. I didn't get it much even then, despite occasional practical uses as an anxiety reliever or backdrop for reading—and at some point, it erupted into an epidemic. Judging from the now-venerable indie-crit site's annual best-of lists, it's a bedrock principle of the Pitchfork aesthetic. Which, in turn, seems traceable back to what appears to have been the ambient post-prog leanings of the Internet's earliest musical tastemakers—the kind of proud geeks who, while saner backs were turned, somehow surreptitiously promoted proto-Radiohead art-pop Brits Talk Talk from pleasant early-MTV one-hit wonders into prophets of pure sound.

What helped me piece this puzzle together was a question I Facebooked on a whim on a Saturday morning early in 2015, wondering how and when music commentary had first emerged on the Internet and whether anybody since had historically documented it somewhere, and figuring I was just too much a technophobe to be privy to whatever answer everybody else knew. But it wasn't so simple: what came back was a deluge of responses, easily 100 by nightfall. A few acquaintances whose cyberspace experience long predated mine cited tech-savvy, tape-trading mid-'80s Deadheads inhabiting something called the WELL—Whole Earth 'Lectronic Link, apparently—as a sort of Big Bang; there was also a 20-subscriber "electronic fanzine" that Italian artificial intelligence specialist Piero Scaruffi initiated in 1985. But from there spilled an alphabet soup of nebulously recalled tech outlets, almost all Greek to me: CompuServe forums and Listserv systems and Lotus Notes, Usenet and Telnet and Sonic .net and FidoNet BBS, rec.music.reviews and GeoCities neighborhoods. Amazon before it was a CD store and alt.country before it was a genre. AOL message boards and alt.music newsgroups where college radio DJs and devoted Yes fans and Morrissey-loving teen-girl diarists congregated, The War Against Silence and Addicted to Noise, on and on. A day later, by coincidence, the *New York Times* Sunday magazine ran a short piece about nostalgia for GeoCities and what some subhead writer dubbed the "old, weird Internet." So clearly, secret knowledge and history thrive after all.

Fascinating, right? Yet still, somewhere along the line, the Internet is supposed to have invalidated music criticism itself. Since everybody can listen to new music whenever they want, the platitude goes, everyone is a critic, and since rock crit was mainly just a buying guide or gatekeeper in the first place (hint: it wasn't), the form is now moot. (Not a new misconception, by the way. "Knowing that my reader is able to stop after any word I write and listen to all of 'Light My Fire' before reading the next word, I should feel pretty foolish offering him a textual description": that's Paul Williams. In *Crawdaddy*, in 1967.) Thing is, if computers didn't kill off music criticism, they did *change* it, in all sorts of ways—even beyond obvious surface stuff like shrunken profit margins shrinking freelance budgets, and clickbait listicles penned for peanuts thanks to parasitic post-consolidation grasp-for-straws business plans, and arbitrary limitations imposed by metrics-hoodwinked tech department flunkies justifying their own soulless vocation as sure as the standardized school testing industry. I'll only mention a couple.

Owing in part to the constantly shifting big-story-of-the-day bandwagon media cycle, there's the little-noted but perhaps inevitable return of Ethics Criticism—which in the old days meant boycotting artists who played Sun City, but now might mean sanctimonious nitpicking about whatever identity politics an artist is perceived to have microaggressioned and/or appropriated, usually commencing like clockwork mere minutes after some why-bother awards show and frequently involving cutesie-pie public relations–approved pop-star nicknames that make the writer sound like a fan-club president. Some of the outrage is no doubt deserved—I have no patience for bigots myself, and better Social Justice Warriors than GamerGaters scared of vaginas or psychopaths voicing vendettas against wives on *The Sopranos* and *Breaking Bad*. As a presumed lifetime beneficiary of demographic headstarts, I'm often implicated by definition myself, a situation I can live with. But I rarely entertain an urge to either pile on or argue back.

And then there's the Poptimism Debate That Just Won't Die, wherein self-proclaimed converts to said denomination pat themselves on the back for belatedly opening their ears to music that most critics worth paying attention to had already acknowledged as valid, and were often dismissed as perverse for doing so, well over a quarter-century before. Usually this staking of high ground follows fast on the heels of an inescapably viral-shared weekend essay by some serious striver defending bands-with-real-musicians turf while pretending drab-as-dirt National-style indie-rock middlebrows' hard-earned domination of year-end critics' polls is somehow in jeopardy from Katy Perry, which it never is—by now, such tall tales count as rock-writing's answer to the War on Christmas. As somebody who may well rank among the field's most rockist poptimists and/or most poptimist rockists ever (if either category existed), not to mention somebody who considered all this stuff settled science decades ago, I usually just stay out of it.

All in all, it's even arguable that in recent years the Internet has fostered a new Golden Era of Pop Music Think Pieces—which, hey, at least beats journalism, you know? Not that I've done that much of either lately. Matter of fact, after I got together the pieces I wanted to include in this book, I made a point of not writing anything too *good* for a while, because then I'd want to include that, too, which means I'd have to bump something else, and why complicate things? Actually, what might surprise people is how much work I do these days—and really, have for years—that's not writing at all. It's the modern age—you gotta diversify! Plus, ever since my army days, I've always derived an OCD satisfaction out of performing clerical tasks; I could have been a great secretary. My filing system at the *Village Voice* was without peer! I first programmed a web radio station there too, and I've done several since, for Clear Channel a while back and now Rhapsody, where I also do all sorts of glorified data entry, collaborating with algorithmic robots and warm-blooded humans to facilitate, well, so-called music discovery. One morning every week, I program the digital version of a metal store's new release bin. I enjoy doing it, too—DJing is fun, and I always wanted to work in a record shop.

I also still do editing work now and then—got a mild kick out of overseeing an equipment-company-sponsored series on rollingstone.com in 2014 called Young Guns, where I assigned writers to interview 30 hotshot up-and-coming guitar phenoms, almost none of whom I've actually heard since I've never cared all that much about guitar phenoms. And while it's conceivable I might appreciate Steve Gunn or Mark McGuire if I gave them a shot, you can only keep up with so much. I feel way more guilty about not investigating more mahraganat music from Cairo, enticingly described by Ben Hubbard in the *Times* in 2013 as a "youth-driven, socially conscious . . . rowdy blend of traditional Egyptian wedding music, American hip-hop and whatever else its creators can download for free online." I feel woefully ignorant of 21st-century smooth jazz, largely abandoned by radio just before the 2010s apparently, though tasty Andre Ward and Bob Baldwin stuff I've heard makes me wonder what I've missed. I'm years behind on German party-schlager designed for soccer matches, kids' TV shows, and Mallorca beach bars. And when it comes to Korean pop, Francophone rock, Jamaican dancehall, Mexican regional genres like banda, even the southern soul and gospel I devote longish roundups to, I can't front that I'm more than a dabbler at best.

I say that, though, as somebody who neurotically continues to listen to both as much music and as wide a variety as anybody who still has this gig; it's a rare year when I don't hear a couple hundred albums or standalone singles I legitimately enjoy (even if I never listen to most of them again afterward—the digital era drastically magnifies the "out of sight, out of mind" rule). My year-end singles playlists (i.e., not just random "tracks"—way too many of those; my head would explode) typically sample every musical style I just confessed I merely dabble in, plus plenty of metal and country and select hip-hop and urban adult contemporary and teen dance pop and electronic whatchama-callit I stumble across over the 12 months in question, and maybe a grime, soca, or Afrobeats song or two—even indie rock, if I could stand any. And I don't get stuck in too many old-man ruts. According to *Village Voice* Pazz & Jop critics' poll statistics guru Glenn McDonald, for the eight years starting in 2008—the year I turned 48—I ranked no. 2 out of 1,297 voters in the variable he calls "breadth": i.e., "how close a voter came to picking a different artist for every album/song in every voting year."

Partly that's just because I get impatient quick. If I'm a fan of a band but then they start to disappoint or annoy me or their wheels spin too long, that doesn't necessarily mean I'll never listen to them again, especially if an editor assigns them (see Redd Kross). But I also can't promise I'll stick around to find out where the plot goes. I've made long lists in my time of artists I decided grew worse with every subsequent album (starting with their debut—in lots of cases, even debut EP!), at least until I stopped bothering to check. Which might seem heartless, and probably means I've missed a decent late-career comeback or two. But by that point, new acts have inevitably come around who seem way more promising—time is precious, and life is short. On the other hand, in 2015, I got super-excited about new music by middle-aged foot-notes Feedtime, Maggotron, the Membranes, and Nena, just as I was starting to give up already on Jamey Johnson, Ashley Monroe, and Kacey Musgraves. And the best and most promising single I heard all year, Haley Georgia's hilarious debut "Ridiculous," sounded like Ke$ha gone even more country than she sometimes already was. Goes to show you never can tell.

Meanwhile, it's harder and harder lately to focus on more than just a few select patches of land. But though theoretically the music world is more frag-mented than ever (even though it's *always* been fragmented, and the myth of a bygone "monoculture" inevitably overstates alleged days of consensus), sometimes it can seem just the opposite—oppressively so, since the follow-the-leader publicity-department protocol of social networks so often urges everyone to focus on the exact same release at the exact same time, or the same television episode years after TiVo and Netflix turned simultaneous viewing quaint. Despite all that, even with top-tier pop, I feel out of it as often as not. In any given week, I'm lucky if I recognize the titles of even three of the 10 most downloaded songs in the country—even though I still anachronistically tune into terrestrial radio (12 presets in my Honda Accord, including three Spanish-language ones as we speak, despite that I don't speak Spanish), even though I have a daughter born in 2008 to remind me "Dynamite" and "Let It Go" exist and to make sure I don't cringe too much at "Happy" and "Uptown Funk," even though I'm supposedly one of rock-crit's prototype "poptimists." (In fact, in a 2015 Grantland podcast, Alex Pappademas blamed me for flat-out founding the fad, while editing at the *Voice*.) I didn't realize I like Avicii's Top-10-for-21-weeks 2013 electro-hoedown "Wake Me Up" until two years after the fact. Then again, longtime prog partisan Jon Pareles, who has way more use for stylish new indie poses than I do, has denounced in the *Times* the commercial "dominance of three-minute, two-idea tracks—of the pop song as little more than a sound effect and a sound bite," and while philosophically I've always deplored that attitude in principle, in practice lately I relate to it more than I'd care to admit.

So I'm conflicted. Which might partially explain why I've developed a get-a-late-pass fondness instead for a certain grandeur-deluded breed of male metal melodrama that I'd gagged at ever since Iron Maiden popularized it in the early '80s—as practiced variously this decade by Defyance, Edguy, Grand Magus, Mausoleum Gate, Metal Church, Satan, Steel Prophet, Thunder Tribe, and the like, a few of whom were Maiden's contemporaries to begin with. But aversion to present-day popcraft sure doesn't explain why my favorite musical artist of the '10s so far (give or take, well, Taylor Swift) nonetheless may well be the stark-but-giddy Portuguese-Mexican-American post-Latin-freestyle-style clubblegum talk-chirper Dev, best known for her dizzying cameo in Far East Movement's pop-chart-topping 2010 hit "Like a G6," but who since then made several more modestly charting albums and singles I've fallen in love with, most visibly her full-length *The Night the Sun Came Up*. Might somebody cross Dev's dance-pop trash with overinflated power metal trash, before it's too late? (Babymetal don't count.) Stay tuned!

## *Singles Jukebox* Reviews

· · · · ·

### Martina McBride:
### "Teenage Daughters"

Top 10 things I like a lot about this record, more in order of occurrence than preference: (1) I was the father of a teenage daughter for a while (she's post-teen now) and will be one again in just over one decade, so I totally know where Martina's coming from. (2) The structure opens up as very early '70s AM radio pop—might even remind me of a specific K-Tel classic or two, though I haven't figured out which yet. (3) She needs a drink. Twice. (4) It's in the tradition of runs-in-the-family songs by the Roches and Supremes and ladies like that. (5) More in the tradition of "This One's for the Girls" (generational contrast) than "In My Daughter's Eyes" (mush). (6) Doo-dah-doo-doo doo-dah-doo-doo what're we gonna do. (7) Hard-hitting drum sound, starting a minute in, getting increasingly propulsive as it goes. (8) Being cool mainly means fooling people into thinking you are, and breaking rules is something worth nostalgia for. (9) "Carrrrr" pronounced not the southern but the midwestern way, Martina being from Kansas. (10) Guitars that build with the drums—yet another perfectly jangling Tom Petty pop-rock record, in country disguise—climaxing in hard rock solo, at 2:45. (9)

### Lucinda Williams:
### "Convince Me"

God, she sounds half asleep. For almost six fucking minutes. You know, I do still have my CD copy of *Car Wheels on a Gravel Road*—seems like something I *should* keep for "reference," just like the old Nirvana and Sleater-Kinney and Kanye West CDs on my shelf that I know damn well I'll never play again. But I don't know what it's gonna take to, uh, convince me Lucinda was really ever very good in the first place. Her vocal murmur was always kind of ridiculous, somehow. And now she's mumbling like she's in dire need of codeine rehab. How the mildly diverting but hugely overrated have fallen. (2)

Gang Gang Dance:
"Mindkilla"

The indie world as usual is too ridiculously behind the curve on its own damn music to ever realize it, but this band peaked way back in 2004 (on *Revival of the Shittest* and their self-titled album, to be exact), back when they sounded— at their very intermittent best—like some oil-barrel-banged poly-percussive cross between Chrome, the Pop Group, and Einstürzende Neubauten fronted by a young Yoko Ono. Near as my ears can tell, they're now more some sterile art-collage dance outfit with a performance-art Björk imitator attempting to sound cutesy and/or pornographic on top. Okay, maybe that's not all that remarkable a change, given they've had seven years to devolve. This mess isn't entirely without energy. But it doesn't exactly feel like an exciting portent of music's future, either. (5)

Tech N9ne featuring Yelawolf, Busta Rhymes, Twista, Ceza, JI of B.Hood, U$O, D-Loc & Twisted Insane:
"Worldwide Choppers"

Everybody faster than everybody else. One of whom sounds like Eminem, one like Coolio, and one like Yelawolf. I can guess who the last one is, but as for sorting out the other guys, life is too short. And this is too long. Honestly, I have trouble thinking of cuts like this even as "music"—more like a gymnastics competition, maybe. I'd get bored at those, too. (3)

Big Boi featuring Janelle Monáe:
"Be Still"

I hate the punchline-less teabag/teatime joke-or-whatever at the start, have no real use for the crack-bust skit at the end. And I pretty much can't stand Janelle's show-tune / supper-club / Judy Garland side, which zeroed out the intermittent funky band parts when I saw her live during SXSW; that she's got basically just an average voice, and that there's nothing especially interesting about her conceptualizing besides being, you know, conceptual, didn't help. Anyway, that last complaint admittedly has nothing to do with this song. I have nothing to say about what Big Boi does—he does what he does, and it sounds okay, usually. But he's spinning his wheels. (5)

## Mike Posner:
## "Bow Chicka Wow Wow"

At least when Trace Adkins did this stupid joke last year, he called it "Brown Chicken Brown Cow." And stupid me, I figured it was actually a song about a brown chicken and brown cow, until I read something explaining otherwise! Question: Was that "bow chicka wow wow" sound actually literally *used* in old porn flicks, or is it just a dorky meme that some frat boy started decades after the fact? I never even heard of it until the past few years, I don't think. Shows up in *Veronica Mars* a couple times, but I watched that show years late. Anyway. Posner also comes off illiterate when saying "I can make it sound like" then never completes the thought; actual R&B losers have done that recently too, right? After a few listens I finally deduced that the music itself finishes the sentence, à la "Her Name Is . . ." by George Jones, but whatever. And amazingly, there's still a prettiness to this that grabs me, just a little. I apologize. (3)

## Snoop Dogg:
## "Wet"

Potentially (though not necessarily) interesting spare music (from the Cataracs, I guess? heard their name dropped once, but I'm in no mood to check), made useless by some of the most stomach-turningly clinical porn babble ever. Not that I'm opposed to any songwriting mention of bodily moisture, of course (Olivia Newton-John's "He ran by me, got my suit damp" from "Summer Nights" being one of the sexiest lines in human history), but Snoop's feels entirely devoid of recognizable human interaction. Reminds me of those dead-in-the-water whisper-fuck songs that basically made me stop caring about rappers-I-liked-a-lot Ying Yang Twins and David Banner a few years ago. Except I never cared all that much about Snoop in the first place. He's had a great moment or two, now and then, but mostly I'm convinced people cut his usual mediocrity slack because of his naughty-boy celebrity (kinda like, say, Mötley Crüe—their old best-of CD is all I'll ever need, too). And here he's just, well, a drip: Cheech & Chong's "drip, drip, drip of gonorrhea," to be precise. That he addresses his soggy sentiments to "Mommy" ("Mami," whatever, sounds the same to me) makes them even more gross. (1)

## R. Kelly:
## "Love Letter"

I have a quandary with *Love Letter* the album in that I definitely love at least its *concept*, but (with a couple exceptions, like "Taxi Cab" and maybe the Christmas song), the songwriting generally strikes me as perfunctory-to-nonexistent. This song is fairly typical; the words are, as far as I can tell, mostly a list of non sequiturs that have little or nothing to do with anything that anyone would say in an actual love letter (though admittedly they made *slightly* more sense when I read the lyric sheet and learned that "wedding bells, baby showers, vacation, cellphones" actually ended with the word "sailboats" instead), so the music never really connects emotionally like this kind of mush is meant to. The thin, rather rinky-dink sound falls short on sonic terms as well; there's a tasty hint of yacht-samba in the groove here, but something's *missing*; compared to a crooner even as forgotten and inconsequential as, say, Glenn Jones, I'm not quite convinced R.'s voice would have been full enough to cut it in the '70s or '80s, at least given a production as lacking in lushness as this ("When a Woman's Fed Up" got it right, somehow). Still, both song and album as a whole are likable genre exercises regardless. And seeing how this guy's personality can be so unattractive (and not goofy-clever on an Oran "Juice" Jones / Richard "Dimples" Fields / Ray Parker Jr. level either), I'm not sure I'd like it all more if the songs *did* convey more personality. So I'm giving this the benefit of the doubt, with major reservations. (8)

## Beyoncé:
## "1 + 1"

She don't know much about Sam Cooke, either, I bet. And her yelped "youuu-uuu"s and "tooooooo"s are as painful, pretentious, and preposterous as anything on the radio this year. Her life-during-wartime pandering has nothing to say about said war, but it's the closest thing to a saving grace this record has— well, that and the hack power-ballad guitar solo. So: 1 + 1 = (2)

## Adele:
## "Set Fire to the Rain"

Given that Adele's got the Year's Biggest Album, I naively assumed that, when I finally heard a song from it (this is the first—yes, I do in fact live in a cave), it'd *somehow* feel like a major leap—concept-wise, hook-wise, middlebrow-turned-upper-middlebrow-wise, whatever—from what she was doing last time out. Didn't expect to like it, but expected *something*. But this is just . . . wow. I basically hate Amy Winehouse, and I get how reimagining Amy's constipated faux soul revival minus her unhealthy aspects might add up to a salable commodity. But next to this nonentity, Amy is Aretha. (3)

### Dirtbombs:
### "Sharevari"

Perennially also-ran (i.e., less compelling than Gore Gore Girls, White Stripes, Electric Six, Clone Defects, Detroit Cobras, and probably Von Bondies) Motor City garage-revival outfit with nonetheless notably African American front-man (whose theroretically R&B-derived vocalizing has almost always come off mediocre in either soul or rock terms) resurrects archetypal 1981 Motor City proto-techno classic (theoretically inspired by Kano's 1980 Italo-disco-metal "Holly Dolly," though I've always heard Telex's 1979 Belgian robo-electro "Moskow Diskow" at least as much) on Genuine Rock Instruments (usually a corny move at least in theory), makes a sonic rendezvous with Motor City muscle-car guitar-rock while retaining zee deceptive fake Continental Euro-accent that the previously nameless (until WGPR "Midnight Funk Association" DJ Electrifying Mojo named them) A Number of Names had always preposterously used to chronicle their zeegarrrette-smoking and carrrcassette-blasting disco lounge-lizard cruising with his hot playmate in his Porsche 928 (significantly *not* a Detroit-made car) in the first place. Result: both the Sprocketiest U.S. quasi-Kraut-rock droned in decades, and a record that ties together seemingly unrelated cross-racial streams from America's most musical city in ways even I had never imagined possible. (9)

*—Singles Jukebox*, 2011

## The Dirtbombs: *Ooey Gooey Chewy Ka-Blooey!*

• • • • •

First, two belated observations about metropolitan Detroit's resilient so-called "garage rock" scene, from whence sprung such world-beaters as the White Stripes: (1) It started out super-kitschy and cheesy, so much so that,

Snake-Out: *Gollywobblers from Hell!* (Wanghead, 1985)

when I lived there in the mid-'80s, I remember exactly zero members of bands I spent time with (Necros, Laughing Hyenas, etc.) taking bone-necklaced Hawaiian-shirt nyuk-nyuk googoomuck like Ferndale trio Snake-Out's 1985 *Gollywobblers from Hell!* remotely seriously; and (2) Give or take the theoretically game-changing Gories, stirred into action circa 1986 by the scum-slopped gopher-gut greaser-bands-that-went-nowhere bootleg compilation series *Back from the Grave* but soon imbibing sin-alley R&B howls, it's questionable to what extent toga-party punk of the *Nuggets*-documented era was even the later Detroit stuff's primary inspiration. Or at least, hardly anybody was a purist jerk about it.

Case in point: the Dirtbombs, who ex-Gorie Mick Collins put together on a lark in 1995—the year he turned 30—initially intending to limit the project to occasional 7-inch singles, but who've somehow managed to put out at least six (or more, depending how you slice 'em) albums since. Their two best to date have been covers collections: 2001's soul-and-R&B *Ultraglide in Black* (Parliaments, O'Jays, Barry White, Marvin Gaye's "Got to Give It Up" long before Robin Thicke, Phil Lynott's "Ode to a Black Man" partly because Collins is one like Thin Lizzy's singer was) and 2011's Detroit techno (!) *Party Store* (Cybotron, Derrick May, Underground Resistance, DJ Assault, Inner City, a killer Kraut-motorik take on the faux-Eurotrash classic "Sharevari"). Over the years, the Dirtbombs have also recorded remakes of material by Suicide, ESG, the Romantics, Soft Cell, Sparks, Flipper, and more. Their originals have referenced the Jackson Five, the Allman Brothers, and Peter Schilling's "Major Tom (Coming Home)"; they work in oi! shout and art drone and drag-race rap as much as Dick Dale surf tones.

And now they have a bubblegum album, in a class with the soul and techno ones—hey, Wilson Pickett covered "Sugar Sugar" once, so why not? It has been a long time coming: teased and/or postponed by the band, and awaited and/or dreaded by fans, for a decade. The first 200 LP copies even come out on Fleer-pink vinyl (just like Ruth Ruth's 1996 "Brainiac" 45 and, uh, probably other things), but contrary to long-running rumors *Ooey Gooey Chewy Kablooey!* is actually not a covers record this time—just an amazing simulation, mostly of teenybop smashes by sundry Kasenetz-Katz-produced studio concoctions, followed by the Archies, from between 1967 and 1970. Rock bands have celebrated those happy sounds before (think the Ramones, Redd Kross, Joan Jett, early Poison, Shonen Knife), but maybe not recently, probably not so blatantly, and almost definitely not so rhythmically: always blessed with two drummers and two bassists (though specific names have changed over time), the Dirtbombs really pull off that "jughead beat"—i.e., the chintzy, clattery, probably Caribbean or beach-soul-inspired and disco-inspiring junior-high-dance groove from, say, 1910 Fruitgum Company's "Indian Giver" or the Archies' "Jingle Jangle" or Tommy Roe's "Dizzy." The Dirtbombs' "Jump and Shout," for instance, has two propulsive gratuitous no-fuss extended cowbell sections stuck inside, and the percussion in "Sugar on Top" and "Hey! Cookie" is even funkier—if hip-hop wasn't invented 'til next year, it might wanna swipe some of these beats. The old bubblegum Svengalis employed steel drums and roller-rink organs; the Dirtbombs probably don't, but you never know. They know how to clap their hands in the air and do it doubletime just like Simple Simon said, and while they apparently didn't go full-on bubble-authentic by replacing themselves with anonymous studio pros, their publicity one-sheet does mention "a list of guest musicians so long there wasn't time to credit them on the album cover."

True to the pre–Lancelot Link era it's aping, *Ooey Gooey* bounces through 10 songs in less than half an hour. And where the Dirtbombs' Detroit techno tribute had three songs about cars, this time there are three about sunny days and three about eating sweet things. And in fact, the sweet thing who gets eaten in the sleazily low-registered "Hey! Cookie" ("Ooh, such a groovy scene / Gonna make sure I lick the plate clean") is smackdab in the tradition of the Ohio Express's oral sex obsession. That group's immortal "Yummy Yummy Yummy" also gets directly nicked in "Hot Sour Salty Sweet," where Collins sings "Ooh I wanna see you / Ooh I wanna meet you" to the exact same notes Joey Levine once sang "Ooh love to hold ya / Ooh love to kiss ya." Collins, now in his late 40s, admittedly sounds too grown-up for such cuteness a lot of the time; he's not equipped with Levine's supremely snotty high nasal whine. And his band, whose lineup seems to be increasingly solidifying as time goes on but who've frequently been a bit too hardcore for their own good, needlessly rushes the tempo at times, and the production could usually afford to be shinier. But from the nursery-rhymey first verse—"Ice cream sundae, big banana split / You and me baby now don't forget / One scoop two scoop, never gonna stop / You got the love with the sugar on top"—they do b-gum's assembly-line innocence proper.

The guitars get fuzzy, of course, though not that much more than in the Sweet's early '70s bazooka rock, and not so much to obscure the hooks. And there are plenty of changeups, too. "It's Gonna Be Alright" (with a reassuring "it only gets better" chorus that may well owe Dan Savage) and even more so "The Girl on the Carousel" are late-summer-afternoon-at-Cedar-Point green-tambourine sublimeness in the lineage of the Archies' "Bicycles, Rollerskates and You" or even 1910 Fruitgum's 1910-sounding 1968 "The Year 2001" (distant *future* then—confusing, huh?), relaxed enough to risk being twee if the Dirtbombs weren't so committed to the bottom end. "Jump and Shout" opens with the same bass throb that INXS's "Need You Tonight" (which the Dirtbombs have covered) took from either the Grateful Dead's "Shakedown Street" or Warren Zevon's "Nighttime in the Switching Yard." "Sunshine Girl" explodes out of nowhere à la Plastic Bertrand's Belgian bubblepunk "Ça Plane Pour Moi" (aka Elton Motello's oral-sexed "Jet Boy Jet Girl"), then turns into some cardboard cartoon record from the back of an early '70s cereal box, then finally starts electronically spiraling toward the ceiling at the end.

Said spiraling continues into "No More Rainy Days / Sun Sound Interlude," the sort of rubber-band-plucking cloudscape dorks like the Flaming Lips fill entire albums with, but as a switcheroo here it kinda works, eventually evolving into jerry-rigged whirligig thingamajig techno-whatsis perhaps related to the Japanese-character-titled mechanical Yellow Magic Orchestra homage or whatever it was that that closed *Party Store* last time. Then *Ooey Gooey* itself ends with the double-entendred extravaganza "We Come in the Sunshine," over-the-top with overdubs and multitracked marching band horns and/or whatnot, explicitly ripping "Good Vibrations" and Brian Wilson's Phil Spector period and naive ornate ambitions gone by in general, Collins's hazy lead vocal intentionally warping from the heat.

Uh . . . If I was just reading that part instead of writing it, I might've scared myself away by now, so let me reiterate that, most of the time, *Ooey* Keeps It Simple Stupid. As in "One kiss, two kiss, never gonna stop / Gimme more lovin' with the sugar on top"—you get the idea. "Hot sour salty sweet / Girl your love is such a treat / Apples peaches pears and plums / Can't wait 'til the evenin' comes." That one could've used an umami pun maybe, but it's timely how the song's "eenie meenie miney mo" playground chant links it to one of the best *real* (whatever that means) bubblegum singles of 2013, Tiny-G's K-pop hit "Minimanimo." Like Jim Bickhart wrote in the liner notes to Warner Special Products' 1977 TV-mail-order triple-LP compilation *Super Bubble*: "This is music that sticks to the bottom of your shoes and the roof of your mouth. This is what the high-brows of rock have been running from for years . . . If you don't like it, chew it." The Dirtbombs are five bananas playing in the bright warm sun.

—spin.com, 13 September 2013

## Redd Kross: *Researching the Blues*

· · · · ·

Lovedolls, Tater Totz, Tatum O'Tot and the Fried Vegetables, Sgt. Shonen's Exploding Plastic Eastman Band, Anarchy 6, Carrie Nations, Brady Kids—the Redd Kross guys (and, pre-lawsuit-threat, Red Cross guys) have always been big on your fake bands: covering them, singing about them, being them. They've got a few things in common with Nik Worth in Dana Spiotta's 2011 rock-and-memory novel *Stone Arabia*, who spends decades meticulously auto-chronicling a career of side-projects that exist mainly in his imagination, starting with a powerpop combo called, naturally, the Fakes, who actually played gigs (in the book anyway) but despite Nik's documentation didn't actually become superstars. Like *Stone Arabia*'s protagonists, Redd Kross learned their sensibility from the Rodney's English Disco glam-fakery era of pre-punk '70s LA: hot children in the city loving Bolan and Bowie, running wild and looking pretty under their parents' powdered suburban noses, or at least staying home rooting for the Runaways on ABC's *Rock N Roll Sports Classic* once the Partridge Family were extinct. Awesome Redd Kross title, mysteriously added years later to 1982's Linda Blair–loving, Charles Manson–covering slopbucket of a punk album *Born Innocent*: "St. Lita Ford's Blues."

*Researching the Blues*, their first album in a decade and a half, has blues in its name too, you'll notice; the opening title track is a moderately punchy if not very locomotive train song. Later, probably the album's pinnacle, there's "Winter Blues," a possibly pro-global-warming argument for remaining in sunshine-pop SoCal in order to avoid seasonal affective disorder. That's right: *two* "blues" songs from a band that, despite once-discernible Blue Cheer and Zep-riff swipeage, has never exactly been prone to boogie ("I'm Alright" on *Born Innocent* maybe came closest, if proto–Black Lips counts), much less honor authentic musical roots. Yet despite uncharacteristically funky drums before the hang-10 surf harmonies of the distrusting "One of the Good Ones," these 10 three-minute-ish toons aren't blues-based hard rock, except maybe in the "pretty good Enuff Z'Nuff record" sense. Or, if that's too obscure, think of stuff that Stone Temple Pilots maybe learned from Urge Overkill maybe learned from Redd Kross (who sometimes dress like Urge Overkill now).

In other words: powerpop. Which, though they dissed the Knack (who, sorry, were better at it) on their hilarious first EP (and, sorry again, best record ever) in 1980, has basically been Redd Kross's genre of choice at least since 1987's *Neurotica*, which featured the same three-McDonalds-and-a-Hecker lineup as their new one. Thing is, back then, metal was part of their equation, too (they'd remade Kiss's "Deuce" on the covers EP *Teen Babes from Monsanto* in 1984, same year the Replacements did "Black Diamond"). Which positioned them oddly, given all the then-MTV-ruling hair bands who also dressed like and sang about foxy fallen-angel Sunset Strip runaways while referencing '70s glam, only in a slightly different way. Perhaps Redd Kross's psychological proximity to hair metal scared them a little: "No metal sluts or punk-rock ruts for me, oh noooo," they hiccuped on *Neurotica*, and by 1990's *Third Eye* (your favorite Redd Kross album if you're, like, a Jellyfish fan) they were excising the crunch while emphasizing the fussy and fey. It was okay, in retrospect: "Annie's Gone" was a catchy-enough Modern Rock hit (their biggest ever), tributes to Kasenetz-Katz and Shonen Knife and Zira from *Planet of the Apes* were kinda cute, and chucka-chucka-beat "1976" holds up almost as well as Alan Jackson's song of the same bicentennial name. But the crazy energy of the band's '80s records was gone, and two '90s CDs that followed were just more college rock.

So now it's 2012. Steven and Jeff McDonald, three and seven years old respectively when *Josie and the Pussycats* first aired and super-precocious teens when Red Cross first waxed, are now 45 and 49. They've produced the Donnas (which makes perfect sense) and mashed-up White Stripes, and Steven now moonlights in the not particularly distinctive hardcore-nostalgia supergroup Off!—sort of Anarchy 6 without punchlines. And *Researching the Blues* doesn't have many, either. Also no traces of Eve Plumb, Susan Dey, Kristy McNichol, Squeaky Fromme, Rex Smith, or H. R. Pufnstuf. Uniformly medium tempos, but plenty of somersaulting nasal harmonies—"Stay Away from Downtown" has quite the memorable chorus. Every sha-la-la-la, every wo-o-wo-o, still shines, as the Brothers McDonald once crooned in a Carpenters cover (#45 hit in England!); well, sort of—cleaner production might've buried the vocals less. And sure, sounding cruddy was always part of the point ("We are not stupid boys but we want to do it wrong," they philosophized on *Neurotica*, which Robert Christgau classified as "ill-made" in his 1987 Pazz & Jop essay). But once upon a time, back when they were reminding us how funny and phony the '70s were, the crud was a means to an end.

—spin.com, 8 August 2012

## Mayer Hawthorne ← Robert Palmer

• • • • •

Mayer Hawthorne grew up Andrew Cohen in Ann Arbor, not Detroit (his stage surname came from the street he was raised on), and he lives in L.A. now, but chances are that only makes him more determined to prove he's carrying on a certain Motor City legacy: paying tribute to Henry Ford and Berry Gordy in "A Long Time" on 2011's *How Do You Do*, for instance, or referencing Highland Park and the long-gone Chrysler LeBaron on his new *Where Does This Door Go*. Of course, his main strategy along these lines has been trying to sing like he's on Motown, which on his first two albums his decent falsetto and midregister let him do better than most. As a white person, this initially seemed to link him to a tradition you could trace through any number of soul-history-conscious Detroit garage-rock revivalists all the way back to Mitch Ryder— even if Hawthorne was more likely to cite J. Dilla and Juan Atkins as inspirations; even if the door he came in through was the soul-history-conscious indie hip-hop label Stones Throw; and even if he's generally opted for ladies'-man smooth over wild-man sweat.

On his new album, Hawthorne slicks up even further. His road band the County barely shows up; songs are shaped by a half-dozen up-to-the-minute R&B/hip-hop/British-pop producers; and when the sound isn't aiming to scale charts Timberlake/Thicke-style, its "vintage" seems more '80s than anything: Prince, quiet storm, the post-disco electro-funk retroactively called "boogie," and—in tracks like "Allie Jones," "The Stars Are Ours," and sympathetic first single "Her Favorite Song"—a kind of vaguely West Indian, lightly funked semi-disco intermittently echoing Eddy Grant, '80s Brit-soul group Linx, and Stevie Wonder's "Master Blaster (Jammin')." Which is to say, in two years, Hawthorne's nostalgia has shot ahead 10. Meanwhile, he's establishing a rep as quite the snappy dresser. His suits and ties apparently read "nerd" to some (my friend Jill proclaimed him "the new Weezer," which wouldn't have occurred to me), but what I see, again, is a Romeo thing, from a guy whose first vinyl single looked like a red heart. Add the often conventionally model-like beauties who inevitably tend to wind up as eye candy in his videos, and seems to me Hawthorne's true well-tailored, reggae-flirting, chameleon-like blue-eyed-soul precedent is one Robert Palmer—another dapper dan who managed to maintain just enough cool distance from his material to mask the surmountable limitations of his singing.

On *Where Does This Door Go*, Hawthorne ups the product-placement quotient, and one line Palmer might appreciate—given the apparently recently removed female undergarments strewn about on the covers of both 1976's *Some People Can Do What They Like* and 1978's *Double Fun*—is the advert for Agent Provocateur "accentuating your voluptuous curves." That comes from Hawthorne's Fatback-interpolating "Robot Love," where he also asks not to be treated like a sex machine. He's been known to cover Chromeo like Palmer was known to cover Chromeo role models the System, and on 1980's eccentric *Clues* album Palmer fully embraced newfangled technology, to the extent of interpreting some synthy Gary Numan future shock about being the "last electrician alive" and collaborating with Numan on another track. Palmer explained back then that he heard Numan's "Cars" as "a soul song": interestingly, the same thing that Detroit techno innovators like Juan Atkins thought at the time.

And the Numan tracks were not even the most forward-looking blues clues on *Clues*. The two weirdest and hookiest were both singles, not to mention spare, anxious, herky-jerk new wave moves promoted by outlandishly choreographed art videos for the new MTV crowd: the feather-falsettoed, xylophone-tricked, bouncing and clanging "Looking for Clues," which opens the album worrying that whenever a phone rings horrible news will be on the other end; the ominously drifting, lower-registered, minor-keyed, hum-blurred "Johnny and Mary," in which a depressingly aging couple tire easily and lack a sense of proportion and need the whole world to confirm they're not lonely. Both songs charted in the UK, where Palmer was born and started his career playing northern soul clubs, though he'd grown up the son of a boilermaker turned navy intelligence officer in Malta, later settled in the Bahamas (where *Clues* and other LPs were recorded), then Switzerland, and in 2006 died of a heart attack in France. But where "Johnny and Mary" hit biggest was neurotic, robotic Germany, where post-Kraut-rockers the Notwist would ominously cover it in 1994, when they were still too art-metal for indie fans.

Talking Heads' Chris Frantz helps out bassdrum-wise in "Looking for Clues," a month or so before Palmer helped out percussion-wise on *Remain in Light*, and "What Do You Care" on *Clues* has some frantic David Byrne nerves in its electro-funk, presaging blockbuster beats Palmer later took to the bank in "Addicted to Love" and the Power Station. It's worth noting that Palmer's interest in African music may have predated Byrne's—he showed it off as early as "Off the Bone" in 1976, and it's no doubt where *Clues*'s "Woke Up Laughing" gets its off-kilter vocal cadence and wood-blockish rhythm. Heard now, the track also scans not far from experiments Arthur Russell was trying back then. Add two numbers featuring Free alumnus / "All Right Now" co-writer Andy Fraser on bass—beefy butt-rocker "Sulky Girl" and whipcracking Beatles remake "Not a Second Time"—and its clear Palmer was dabbling all over a map found in nobody else's glove compartment.

So in some ways, of course, he and Mayer Hawthorne aren't totally alike. They were born three decades and a couple weeks apart, but where Hawthorne is now 34 and only on his third album, in 1980 Palmer was just 30 but already on his sixth, after four LPs fronting bands. His solo sets weren't quite as retro as Hawthorne's first two, either—the Meters and Little Feat's Lowell George backed him on early ones, and some optimistic funkers could almost pass for the band War, but though curiously for a late '70s blue-eyed soulster he never really went disco, he wasn't more than a couple years behind on Caribbean sounds: titled *Pressure Drop* after its Toots and the Maytals cover in 1975, for example. Hawthorne's sounding less backdated lately, though, so the gap is closing—especially as his proclivities turn more Anglophile with a Jessie Ware duet, and more global with Steve Mostyn's Turkish saz opening a song where Kendrick Lamar big-ups Bob Marley. Still, what Palmer and Hawthorne most clearly share, on the surface, is a certain sense of style and fine taste in wine-glass women and upscale apartment shots and rare soul grooves. Palmer's hair might've been more perfect. But Hawthorne's could get there.

—spin.com, 31 July 2013

## Kanye West: VEVO Power Station, Austin, 20 March 2011

• • • • •

So hey, here's something that might deflate Kanye West's ego just a little bit: of the main rap artists billed on his overblown and in many ways contemptuous-of-audience South by Southwest–ending GOOD Music extravaganza at Austin's ad hoc VEVO Power Station venue very early in the morning of 20 March, Mos Def proved the most rhythmically dexterous, Pusha T of the Clipse had the richest voice, and Jay-Z the hardest stomp, which partly explains why he got the crowd the most pumped up. Which left Kanye merely the artiest and most conceptual.

But first, everybody had to get in. Or at least the so-called "lucky 2,000" that actually got badges or VIP passes did; the lower-caste horde left pushing outside—which around half past midnight felt like it was about to turn into a 1979 Who audience in Cincinnati—will have to watch a filmed version later. This writer actually had to be personally pulled up through the middle of the crowd by a helpful security agent and to jump over a barrier fence in the process, after circling his badge high in the air to signal his location, and he apparently wasn't alone. And days before that, it was necessary to repeatedly text a cryptic phrase to a secret number, and repeatedly receive texted rejections in return stating capacity had already been reached, then eventually get an email indicating otherwise and from there pick up a secret badge in the bar lobby of a secret hotel—hence hyping up an oddly elitist sense of exclusivity and scarcity that naïfs might foolishlessly think is the antithesis of a festival once meant to democratically showcase not-yet-rock-star talent. And once one got in and the show finally started, one found some of the most impossible sight lines of one's concert-going career, and sonics not a whole lot more useful. That there was considerably more compelling music scheduled not far down the street in Austin at the time (Pentagram! Katey Red! '70s Detroit funk-metal guitar god Dennis Coffey for God's sake! Doctor Krápula of Bogotá, Colombia, for all you know!) only added to the excitement.

That said, it should be noted that the *venue* was really cool — if not so much as a venue, per se, then at least as a wonder of urban architecture. To get to the decades-dormant Seaholm Power Plant, you had to stroll into this no-man's-land where 3rd Street disappears, and walk across an old train bridge onto a large open field. Four giant smokestacks (on this night lighted with the word "VEVO") beckon you in; you follow retired railroad tracks into the building. Once inside, the factory atmosphere of the place is fairly magnificent: gray metal pipes and staircases along the walls climbing up and down into presumed super-ceilings and sub-basements and other possible hidden compartments and hiding spaces. Those, sadly, were off limits to concertgoers. Though dancing girls did shimmy on the stairs themselves, at least when they thought somebody might be watching.

Anyway, the show itself. Around 1 A.M., a big sign proclaiming "GOOD" — probably not the most boring record label name ever, but possibly in the running — lighted up onstage. About 15 minutes later, Mos Def emerged to old-school 1981 Grandmaster Flash beats, rapped about being a Boogie Man, and interpolated the Beatles' "Getting Better." Pusha T came next, sounding gruffer (his voice) and fuzzier (the acoustics). Mr. Hudson covered Alphaville's high school commencement ceremony classic "Forever Young," and Kid Cudi freed his lonely-stoner mind at night. Interesting people walked around with Devo T-shirts or Expos caps or dressed up as cowboys and Indians (one of each); somebody held up an iPad above his head to photograph famous people, which probably annoyed whoever was standing behind.

Around 2:25 or so (much earlier than widely rumored), Kanye came out and for the most part offered an abridged version of last year's *My Beautiful Dark Twisted Fantasy* — a.k.a. the *Sgt. Pepper* of prog-emo rap, with all the overpraise that implies — plus occasional side dishes, complete with guest spots from rappers like Cyhi Da Prince and singers like John Legend (who also did a piano croon about taking it slow) and Bon Iver indie-folk dweeb Justin Vernon. During "Power," the sample machine seemed to mess up; Kanye also still has apparently yet to figure out that it would be more innovative to borrow King Crimson's guitar riffs than just their title phrase. He did do something passing for minimal avant-garde plinks on what appeared to be a synthesized keyboard for a minute or two at one point, though. He brought out a great big marching band for "All of the Lights," and after a while you could even hear the horns a little. And then at around half past three, we got Jay-Z, for a half-dozen or so songs with and without Kanye, including "H.A.M.," "Monster," and a triumphant "Big Pimpin'"—not exactly a surprise, since pretty much everybody expected he would show up, but probably more of him than most would have predicted. Then a couple more group pieces; then just after 4 A.M., after hours of proving "bigger is better" a fallacy once again, they let us go home. It was great!

—rollingstone.com, 20 March 2011

## Taylor Swift and Ke$ha: Not So Different

· · · · ·

The two best new albums I heard in 2010 came from young women born in 1987 and 1989. They both debuted at #1 in *Billboard*, though the one that came out in January sold just 152,000 copies in its first week (but has racked up a couple million since). The one that came out in October finished its first week around the 1,047,000 mark. Each singer put more or less five singles in the Top 10 of the pop chart this year, but only the less respectable singer topped that chart for 10 weeks. The artist considered "country" grew up as part of a nuclear family in the southeastern Pennsylvania exurbs with a grandma who sang opera, and almost every soccer mom across the land thinks she's a perfect role model for kids. The artist not considered country moved from L.A. to Nashville when she was four and grew up fatherless there with a mother who wrote country songs, and almost every soccer mom across the land hopes her kids never meet anybody like her. So, on the surface, Taylor Swift and Ke$ha are exact opposites, right? Wrong. To me, they're two sides of the same coin, with a whole lot in common. Such as:

— They both do vicious revenge songs, aimed at people of both genders. But Taylor does more. On *Speak Now*, I count the title track (the most compelling parts of which are directed at a bride's "snotty little family," not the groom Taylor's trying to steal away), "Dear John," "Mean," and (most explicitly, since it's where she claims retaliation is her specialty) "Better than Revenge." On Ke$ha's *Animal*, there's "Kiss N Tell" ("I hope you cry!") and "Backstabber," though maybe you could also count the swipes she takes elsewhere at dirty old men and rich people and guys' ugly girlfriends. Not to mention maybe at least three songs on her late-year 10-song add-on mini-album *Cannibal* (title cut, "Grow a Pear," Fannypack tribute "C U Next Tuesday"), where she chews up and spits out clingy males who outwear their welcome. (Taylor dumps a guy in "Back to December," too, but regrets it.)

—Taylor's "Dear John" ("Don't you think 19's too young to be played by your dark twisted games," allegedly about John Mayer, which is irrelevant) and Ke$ha's "D.I.N.O.S.A.U.R." ("You should be prowlin' around the old folks' home") both deal with the same topic. However, where Ke$ha slays dinosaurs, Taylor prefers slaying dragons. (See: "Long Live." Maybe even a D&D reference; what a nerd!)

—They both giggle in the middle of songs: Ke$ha all the time, and Taylor at least in "Speak Now," probably her most Lily Allen–like track. Ke$ha's most Lily Allen–like track is "Stephen." Taylor did her own "Hey Stephen" on *Fearless*, two years ago. Both "Stephen" songs are about pining over boys. The opening harmonies of Ke$ha's version sound fairly country, as does her Bubba Sparxxx–reminiscent hick-hop drawling through "We R Who We R," which she has described as an anthem for picked-on teenage outcasts, which is pretty much also what Taylor's Miranda Lambert–reminiscent "Mean," easily the most country song on *Speak Now*, is. Admittedly, Taylor makes the being-bullied aspects far more blatant, and limits her community-solidarity use of "we" to the "band of thieves in ripped-up jeans" that confound her small town's cynics in "Long Live."

—Speaking of small minds in small towns: "Mean" is meanwhile also a rejoinder to an increasingly "pathetic," "alone in life" (Taylor hopes!) jerk-wad who's forever "grumbling on about how *I can't sing*," stuck drunk back in the boondocks when Taylor has graduated to the city. Which points to yet another major thing she and Ke$ha share. Namely: the hall monitors of propriety and would-be *American Idol* judges have a habit of wringing their hands about how evil technology (e.g., hilariously disruptive Auto-Tune in Ke$ha's case) makes it impossible to tell whether either artist can "really" sing as if singing means anything more than performing lyrics with emotion, conviction, energy, and humor, and knowing how to switch phrasing for emphasis or entertainment value. These two both did that just as well as any other vocalist who recorded this year, though it helped that nobody else came equipped with half as many great hooks. I mean, *maybe* Ke$ha personally relates to the line in "Mean" about "your voice like nails on a chalkboard." But if so, it's probably on purpose—goes well with the year's craziest synth solos (seriously, check "Boots & Boys"), not to mention those noisy Euro-voodoo drums and monster roars in "Cannibal."

—They also both do what sound like Kate Bush imitations, toward the ends of their proper albums (14 songs each, incidentally): Taylor's "Haunted" and Ke$ha's "Animal." And they're probably both influenced by Eminem, as well. Taylor's been known to cover "Lose Yourself" onstage, and in "Cannibal" Ke$ha compares herself to Jeffrey Dahmer, a very Eminem thing to do. Though *Animal + Cannibal* is more *Licensed to Ill* than *Marshall Mathers* LP, overall. But forget white rap entirely, if you want: what Taylor and Ke$ha have both said they do when writing a song is start with stuff that's happened to them and people they've known in real life, then craft imaginative scenes loosely rooted in the narrative tradition of country music. Then it gets more complex, because (not unlike, say, Eminem) the voice or perspective you hear might change a couple times through any given song, while offhand asides get tossed in to throw you off. They're both proud of not knowing when to shut up. Taylor: "I always get the last word" ("Better than Revenge"). Ke$ha: "Got here by running my mouth" ("Crazy Beautiful Life").

—Class war! There, I said it. On *Animal*, a "young and broke" Ke$ha attends a "Party at a Rich Dude's House" (supposedly Paris Hilton's—doesn't matter), where she pisses in the Dom Pérignon and pukes in the closet. Take that, millionaire tax-cut-extension proponents! But her real statement of resentment is "Sleazy" on *Cannibal*, where she starts out "I don't need your brand-new Benz or your bourgie friends," then winds up dissing the dork's man-servant and mansion and bottle service in general, saying she'd rather drink in her own basement than "places where all my ladies can't get in." Yes! Taylor never quite goes that far, but does fire "Better than Revenge" at a vintage-dress-clad prep-school hussy who doesn't realize "sophistication isn't what you wear or who you know." Then again, unlike Ke$ha, Taylor apparently wasn't raised partially on food stamps and welfare checks.

—Taylor's better at tragedy than comedy; Ke$ha's the other way around. But both can do both. Taylor's more like Veronica Mars; Ke$ha's more like Amanda on *Ugly Betty*. In more reflective moments, Taylor often retreats to memory: "Mine," "Back to December," "The Story of Us," "Long Live," and especially "Never Grow Up," which is *Speak Now*'s most heart-wrenching song (not to mention an obvious sequel to the

Ke$ha: *Animal* (RCA, 2010)

equally weep-inducing "The Best Day," on *Fearless*). When Ke$ha feels
mellow, she turns vulnerable: "Stephen," "Hungover," "Blind," "Dancing with Tears in My Eyes," "The Harold Song." To be honest, most of
those rank among her weaker moments, musically speaking, but their
hurt still adds something. (Taylor's weak links, for what it's worth:
"Sparks Fly," "Last Kiss," maybe the quaint and courtly "Enchanted.")
Ke$ha fights 'til sunlight for her right to party (in fact, the word "fight"
shows up fairly often in her songs). She brushes her teeth with a bottle
of Jack, heads out with all her fellow animals and cannibals hiding a
water bottle full of whiskey in her handbag (smart way to save money!),
lets the night come to life, tells boys "turn around bitch I got a use for
you" (okay, that was Axl Rose, but Ke$ha makes almost exactly the
same demand in "Blah Blah Blah"), tosses them out like used Kleenex,
wakes up the next day broken like bottles on the floor. If life's a party,
it can crash at any minute. When the hangover strikes, there's a good
chance, just like Taylor, she'll be obsessing over some dumb guy she
met there.

— rhapsody.com, 15 December 2010

# Ke$ha: *Warrior*

. . . . .

Forget the Mayan calendar: Ke$ha Rose Sebert more likely picked up her last-days fetish while growing up on her songwriter mom's food stamps among dispensationalist millenarian suburban classmates who hated her purple hair back in the turn-of-millennium Bible Belt. But wherever it came from, she's made doomsday preppin' her dancefloor mission like nobody since Prince partied like 1999 in 1982—she co-wrote "Till the World Ends" for Britney; cruised up Mulholland to the Hollywood sign just to drunkenly watch the world explode into oblivion in mid-2011's outtake leak "Shots on the Hood of My Car." And now on her new album (her second or third or even fourth, depending whether nine-song "EP"s or questionably legit self-titled rarity-samplers count) she's celebrating the window between Hurricane Sandy and the fiscal cliff by making the most of the night and the magic in your pants before she dies young (and stays pretty, per Blondie) in a too-Katy-Perry-drag-queeny hit single and running out of antifreeze in the way more apocalyptically stark Deluxe Edition bonus cut "Out Alive."

As in "No one gets . . . ," that is—shades of a famous Jim Morrison biography. Which is to say: $he's not alone! Whoopee, we're *all* gonna die! For all her nihilism, Ke$ha comes off quite the team player—works well in groups, or at least wants to foster a disco-to-Gaga sense of Island of Misfits Toys community. "We R Who We R," her chart-topping backlash-at-bullies statement proclaimed two years ago, and on *Warrior* (as in letting-your-inner-one-out, same self-actualization advice as *Animal* and *Cannibal* before), she's editorial-"we"-ing all over the place: "We are the bad kids . . . We were born to break the doors down" in the Benatar-esque title cheer; "We are the crazy people" in the whistly-shiny "Crazy Kids"; "We were the wild ones" in the persuasively sad "Wonderland" (see: Alice), which remembers old living-off-nickels-and-dimes partners-in-crime turned Valley moms and waitresses, quite throat-lumpingly thanks to southern power-ballad guitars and Ke$ha yearning to do a drive-by but being unable to locate the road.

Thing is, we're-all-in-this-together is not a particularly punk-rock concept, at least in the world's-forgotten-boy sense originally conceived by Iggy Pop, who in 1986 made a blah album called *Blah-Blah-Blah* (see: *Animal*'s jarring and lucrative 3OH!3 collaboration), and who calls Ms. Sebert a "wild child" (a few cuts after she calls herself the same) in *Warrior*'s "Dirty Love"—which is, well, even more diverting than her adequately new-wavish duet on an Alice Cooper album last year. Obvious blueprint would be Iggy's only actual Top 40 single, the 1990 duet "Candy" with Kate Pierson of the B-52's, except this time he's got a verse updating Cole Porter's "Let's Do It" to accommodate cockroaches, Afghanistan rug merchants, and Rick Santorum, and Ke$ha's moving from husky frat-soul growl to hillbilly drawl above a jock-glam bleacher beat.

Much has been made of *Warrior*'s allegedly more "rock" and "experimental" bent and replacement of Auto-Tune and Eurobeats with no-artificial-additive singing and guitaring, but stirrings in that direction are fairly negligible (and, according to a Simon Reynolds *New York Times* feature late last month, were apparently reconsidered along the way). The momentarily biting you're-gonna-hear-me-on-your-radio (see: Toby Keith, Joe Jackson, etc.) breakup-revenge threat "Thinking of You" opens with a smidgen of downer-metal sludge that's gone long before Ke$ha introduces a "gold Trans-Am," which, ten songs later on the Deluxe Edition, also provides the title for *Warrior*'s most raucous number, wherein she joneses for a fu manchu ride from a mulleted dude in a Skynyrd shirt over "Back in Black" riffs and "We Will Rock You" stomping—neither of which, incidentally, would be unheard-of on CMT lately, though the wham-bam-thank-you-ma'am here is more reminiscent of mid-'90s bazooka-rappers Shampoo or Gillette.

"Gold Trans Am" is also easily Ke$ha's *funniest* new song (not to mention sexier than the ones where first kisses make her body electric or the snoozy one supposedly about seduction by ghosts): "Burnin' rubber on the southern highway / Gonna take you on a freedom ride," plus sleazy stuff about her Daisy Dukes and his wunderpants. But in general, compared to *Animal*, *Warrior* is curiously deficient in punchlines. The lollipopping second single "C'Mon," for instance, cutely rhymes "saber-tooth tiger," "keepin' it kosher," and "warm Budweiser" (one of many alcoholic references on an album that also drinks in warm wine coolers, whiskey, red wine outside the 7-Eleven, and champagne that tastes like piss), but Ke$ha somehow manages to pack her toothbrush (necessary since she's pulling an all-nighter) without explaining which beverage she plans to brush with! After her Jack Daniels dental care in "Tik Tok," that's quite the missed opportunity. She's not putting out cigars in caviar or urinating in the Dom Pérignon or telling dirty old dinosaurs they need CAT scans anymore. Not to mention puking in rich guys' closets, or dissing their brand-new Benzes and bourgie friends—*Warrior* could use more class warrior.

Then again, being a brat who searches and destroys admittedly isn't the wisest long-term creative strategy. Ke$ha's role models the Beastie Boys had given up brass-monkeyed mutiny on the bounty (and AC/DC riffs) by the time their very arty second album rolled around, but they never again came up with personas as entertaining as the ones they started with. Turn-of-the-'70s Detroit vandals Alice and Iggy were hacks with decent golf handicaps by the early '80s. White punks on Hollywood dope the Tubes stayed weird even after selling out, and teengenerates the Dictators—who got even more mileage out of throwing up on their debut LP in 1975 than Ke$ha would on hers—stayed class clowns even as they mastered heavier chords, but who noticed?

Still, with help from sundry song-doctors, Ke$ha does what she can—stretches "warrior" to 13 syllables; makes like a yodel robot just to get on your nerves again; mixes a few buzzy dubstep breaks and sizzurped crunk cadences into the strobelight bosh; slips in subliminal echoes of '80s MTV classics by Cyndi Lauper and/or Eddy Grant and/or Dexy's Midnight Runners and/or Taco; ends the album proper with an unbearably sincere Pink-style noseholder where she brags about swearing and drinking in the dullest way possible before recommending we all get over ourselves; ends the Deluxe Edition with an enigmatic item about surviving the Ice Age and building pyramids while Wayne Coyne mumbles in the background; voice-cracklingly covers a 1980 Dolly Parton hit her mom wrote on a fan-club-only all-acoustic companion EP called *Deconstructed*, apparently just to prove to stupid scolds that she can "really sing." Too much too little too late: *Warrior* is likeable enough, but not only can't it match its predecessor(s), it's also not nearly as exhilarating or disruptive as what fellow slizzered California trashdancer Dev or assorted K-poppers have done in the past two years with basically the same raw materials. So, kinda disappointing, sure—but hardly the end of the world.

—spin.com, 3 December 2012

## Strange Brew: Metal's New Blare Witch Project

· · · · ·

The last thing metal needs is another witch hunt. But there's no doubt cult and occult values from the era of brown-acid rock are back: Death Valley '69 reborn for the age of Christine O'Donnell. Bands like Toronto flute-doom heathens Blood Ceremony have released the medicine woman from her dark corner in the woods. Holland's nightmare-inducing Devil's Blood even claim to channel their liturgy directly from Lucifer. Secretive Swedish Beelzebub bishops Ghost and venerable Brit bad-trippers Electric Wizard also put out black-mass albums last year; England's Witchsorrow, featuring bassist Emily Witch, pose with rams' skulls; another excellent Swedish band, Witchcraft, has been alchemizing sylvan séance-stoner magick for a decade now.

As metal developments go, it's an unusually listenable one. By uncovering texts lost to history when metal got single-mindedly focused on its metalness — turn-of-the-'70s dark-arts ritualists Black Widow and Coven; mud-booted biker-festival boogie; sinister folk songs from the *Wicker Man* soundtrack; even pre-metal-Grammy Jethro Tull — bands like these are charting forest paths more musical than the muscle-headed sonic ugliness that's possessed the genre for its past black-to-death-to-grindcore-to-powerviolence quarter-century. But the fad's also ridiculous by definition, not to mention media-magnet sensationalist. Good rock bands rightly worry about getting absorbed into the hype maelstrom, then forgotten once the wind changes and ding-dong the witch thing's dead.

For instance: Royal Thunder, from Atlanta; Witch Mountain, from Portland, Oregon; and Christian Mistress, from Olympia, Washington, who have all put out exceptional new albums in 2012. Like Blood Ceremony and Devil's Blood, they're all fronted by women who sing more than scream — in absolutely full-bodied voices, atop heavy churning that frequently partakes in blues in ways most metal has suppressed since thrash took over.

In all three cases, a pair of guitarists concocts riffs first, and the singers carve tormented songs out of the jam. Mlny Parsonz, who became Royal Thunder's belter and bassist by subconsciously conjuring lyrics in another room while killing time during rehearsals by her guitarist husband Josh Weaver's then-instrumental trio, heard a "darkness and a heaviness that came from blues" prior to even joining; Uta Plotkin, similarly, says "a bluesy swagger and swing had been in their sound" before Witch Mountain made her their frontwoman. And Christine Davis says Christian Mistress guitarist Ryan McClain "is real into Mississippi Delta blues" — hence the graceful slide guitar and acoustics opening "The Way Beyond," from their recent *Possession.*

As much as their sounds, these bands' audiences increasingly defy easy metal limitations. For an indie/alternative crowd currently getting reacquainted with rhythm chops and rootsy vocals via, say, Alabama Shakes or Heartless Bastards, maybe this metal isn't so drastic a leap. Or maybe, as the bands themselves all suggest, the metal audience itself is diversifying: letting in more women, for one thing.

Nate Carson, who drums for Witch Mountain and runs the one-man-for-

20-bands booking agency Nanotear, started detecting a change at a 2009 Portland gig opening for Virginia doom fossils Pentagram—the same show, as it happens, that he brought then-Nanotear intern Plotkin out to sing "A Power Greater." On Witch Mountain's 2001 pre-hiatus debut album, they'd handed that song to Erica Stoltz, from Lost Goat—a two-thirds female San Fran trio who always reminded Carson of "Tina Turner fronting Neurosis." He found that hybrid inspiring, and in front of 450 people, Plotkin nailed it. Portland fans responded accordingly: before that gig, there was "the sense of, if I go to a metal show, it's going to be a sausage fest," Carson says. "Now couples go, and they're holding hands."

Others noticed, as well. "When we started out in 2007, there were not a lot of chicks," observes Royal Thunder's Parsonz. "That's changed in the past year, year-and-a-half—a lot of them are young, and they bring their lady friends, and they're digging it." With hair metal now ancient history, Carson theorizes, younger fans don't share older indie siblings' antipathy toward heavy rock. "We've gone through another generational cycle," he says. "Specific styles of underground metal that I like have become respected by the press and popular with kids."

Metal fans themselves, of course, disagree as much as they agree. Christian Mistress and Royal Thunder both record now—happily, they swear—for Pennsylvania-based Relapse Records, which bills itself online as "death metal, grindcore, extreme metal," though these bands are none of those things. "Christian Mistress doesn't fit in with what some people want," Davis admits—occasionally, for instance on a recent European tour with labelmates Red Fang and Black Tusk, a crowd "come there just to see brutal rock" doesn't get it.

**Christian Mistress** get compared a lot to the denim-clad, low-rent early '80s New Wave of British Heavy Metal, partly because their 2010 debut cost only $500 to make, partly maybe because McClain wears an Angel Witch tanktop and the guys look like total hicktown heshers. But Davis chafes at the NWOBHM-throwback pigeonhole: *Possession*'s title track revives a 1986 B-side by obscure Swedish doomsters Faith; bassist Jonny Wulf's CD-booklet tank top advertises Guns N' Roses. And some of Davis's own favorite singers—Diamanda Galas, ZZ Top's Billy Gibbons, the Swans' Michael Gira, Shocking Blue's Mariska Veres, 13th Floor Elevator Roky Erickson (also cited by Devil's Blood, Witchcraft, and Angie Mead of dusky co-ed Chicago duo Redgrave)—aren't metal at all.

"We identify ourselves as a heavy metal band, but our songs are more rock," Davis says. Her vocals have way more rasp than retch, and the guitarists know how to play clean. Front four long-haired employees of Olympia's Oldschool Pizzeria with an Evergreen State grad who spends her summers off-grid in remote California mountains, mapping out plants as a biological technician, and here's what you get: lots of terrain features, but also mysticism to chug cheap beer to.

Davis had the opportunity, at one point, to sing for **Witch Mountain**, and the bands toured together some last year. But Carson says Witch Mountain identifies more with the Ouija-board doom of Blood Ceremony, and with London's Wounded Kings and Wisconsin's very Wiccan-seeming Jex Thoth. Their name harks back to the old orphans-with-ESP sci-fi tale *Escape to Witch Mountain* (1968 novel, 1975 Disney movie), Carson reveals, but also "the tradition of 'Witch' bands such as Witchfinder General and Angel Witch, as well as Leslie West's Mountain." Solo-prone guitarist Rob Wrong is unmistakably "a Hendrix acolyte," as Carson puts it, and the band's tastes are steeped in the '60s: "We love the Beatles, Pink Floyd, Pretty Things, Amon Düül." But also Judas Priest's *Sad Wings of Destiny*. And lots and lots of Sabbath.

So though they have no problem plodding, sometimes for 12 minutes at a time, the plod has groove. Witch Mountain's new *Cauldron of the Wild*, their first album on which Plotkin composed her own lyrics, shows dynamics and nuance not quite there yet on last year's *South of Salem*, mostly written before she joined. She's pushing herself more, too, "trying to optimize the whole range of my vocals," she says: more pyrotechnics, melody, growling, but opener "The Ballad of Lanky Rae" and closer "Never Know," especially, are as comprehensible as metal songs get anymore. The former concerns a woman who grows to seven feet—a "swaggering badass gunslinger lady," Plotkin laughs—who reunites with her netherworld dad; the latter is a dirge with a graphic overdose scene.

Witch Mountain took 15 years to get this far: originally formed in 1997, temporarily shelved half a decade later so two members could raise kids, then sporadically reformed ("like going fishing with my buddies," Carson says) until going full-time when Plotkin signed on. Her story's equally convoluted: piano from age 6, switched to viola at 10, synagogue singing, *Annie*, classical vocal lessons, "hippie psych" and "dream-pop" projects, then the tribal/fiddle/Balkan/punk/doom/art combo Aranya, which still exists. When not on tour, she drives a Portland taxi. Her influences run from Billie Holiday to Cibo Matto, Dio to "Tina Turner and those kinda badass woman singers." She'll "sing along when Sam Cooke comes on the radio," but never imagined singing

Royal Thunder cast bunny-ear spells. (Photo: Kevin Griggs)

that way in a metal band. Ever since *Wayne's World*, she says, "I always loved the concept and image of a wailing woman."

**Royal Thunder**'s Parsonz has likewise journeyed from inconclusive childhood piano classes—in Jersey's southern suburbs, in her case—to soul-metal wailing. Tina Turner figures into her equation as well: her Spain-born mom learned English off records like that back in the '80s. (Parsonz has reams of tattoos—as does her spouse of 11 years Weaver, who initially started Royal Thunder with a brother and best friend who were tattoo artists—but she's especially fond of a recent addition depicting a carnation, Spain's national flower.) "My first experience in singing," she says, "I played piano to a lot of Whitney Houston hits. I had her piano book, and her vocal style was real ingrained."

But it was Nirvana that got her rocking—and Weaver, too. Parsonz eventually reached metal via loud alt bands like Jane's Addiction, Dinosaur Jr., and Sonic Youth (whose "Expressway to Yr Skull" is subliminally echoed to kick off "Black Water Vision," the last song on Royal Thunder's new *CVI*); Weaver reached metal through goth bands like the Cure and Sisters of Mercy. He's also played crust punk, black metal, and tech metal. But he says Royal Thunder—named, erroneously, after Bob Dylan's Rolling Thunder Revue—were first conceived "to find out what we could do besides heavy music." Lee Smith, Parsonz says, "is a way better drummer than we let him be"—despite some nine-minute numbers, there's a conscious attempt to keep things unfancy.

On *CVI*, their vibe often brings to mind a rare species of heavy psyche-delic boogie that appeared in the early '70s wake of Big Brother and the Holding Company—the all-woman foursome Birtha, for instance, or Rama-tam, fronted by guitar heroine April Lawton. Shorter tracks have an almost funky swing; in longer ones, drum rolls, wind-chiming percussion, medieval backup chanting, and strange swirls from organs or delay and phaser pedals keep things levitated. "I really wanted to explore and mess around with guitar effects," says self-admitted gearhead Weaver. Above it all, there's Parsonz—shaking rafters, casting spells. Toward the end of "Drown"—sung "in a real weird position," she recalls, with lights turned down—her cackle turns down-right spooky.

Which brings us, inevitably, back to the supernatural. *CVI* opens with a song about a Parsonz family curse, and has a numerological title—the number 106, Parsonz explains, keeps randomly recurring in band members' lives. She also tells of bandmates finding a half-off taxidermied antelope while thrift-shopping for candles and wine glasses for their stage show, then surrounding it with bones to create atmosphere, just like the frankincense and myrrh they burn when local fire regulations allow it. The one song that shows up on both Royal Thunder albums is called "Sleeping Witch."

But as a concept? "I don't personally know how real the witch thing is for a lot of these bands," Parsonz shrugs. "If it's real, go for it; if it's not, and it's just a performance thing, that's awesome too." But where Royal Thunder are con-cerned, "some of us are on a spiritual path, some of us are not," and they're no witch band. "I don't want to be lumped into that category," says Weaver, add-ing that they've decided the antelope doesn't represent them anymore. "That stuff can become kinda campy."

Witch Mountain, meanwhile, have Witch in their very name—and Salem and cauldrons in their album titles. *South of Salem*, though, was an inside joke. Carson and Plotkin both grew up, ten years apart, in Corvallis, Oregon—south of Salem, Oregon—and that record's artwork mapped out the north-western state thar-be-dragons style, complete with a haggard green crone and goats representing Carson's childhood goat farm. Yet despite feeling an affinity with Blood Ceremony, Carson says labels have passed Witch Mountain over "because we don't have enough occult elements." Except natural ones: "Uta has witchiness in her voice," in other words, "but if you wear a robe or funny hats, you're gonna sell ten times as many records."

The catchiest hook on Christian Mistress's *Possession*, finally, is about a crystal ball. The video Davis directed for their new record's "Pentagram and

Crucifix" has upside-down crosses. "I am death, you are the vulture / Sinew, flesh, and bone at my altar," she recites in "Haunted, Hunted"—stir in eyeball of newt, and you've got a brew recipe. "A manifestation of some deep mental recesses that need to be exorcised," she calls the incantation. "I was raised in a sheltered, closed environment where I couldn't listen to heavy music, and I had to hide everything"; not anymore. But she's no sorceress, either. "We get asked, 'Are you a cult band?,'" she scoffs. "We're not a Christian band, we're not a Satanic band." In fact, one of *Possession*'s best songs, "There Is Nowhere," denies the existence of heaven and hell, both.

"Now that pagan metal is a 'thing,' I don't want to be that," Davis says, apparently speaking for all the metal (not metal) witch (not witch)es here. "Besides, I never knew that metal *wasn't* pagan."

—*Spin*, September 2012

## Metal's Severed Extremities

· · · · ·

Given that the band Extreme were one of the last gasps of one major strain what most people used to call metal until the '90s really kicked in (i.e., very late hair band, vaguely arty/funky/conceptual though nobody remembers them that way, huge singer-songwriter-strummy power ballad hit, singer who later wound up pinch-hitting in Van Halen when nobody cared, guitarist who halfway made Janet Jackson rock once), it's kind of weird that the adjective "extreme" very soon after became the variable by which metalheads with no use for Gary Cherone and Nuno Bettencourt wound up judging their metal. It was a transparent suckerbait concept from the getgo—right up there with "extreme sports." Energy drink music, oh boy! But somehow, it stuck, which I guess from a marketing perspective means it "worked."

So there I was last month, in Austin where I live, watching a sxsw panel called "None More Black: How Extreme Can Metal Go?," whereon five headbang-bizlet movers and shakers (MetalSucks.net editor-in-chief Ben Umanov, HD2 Metal channel radio dude Chuck Loesch, Century Media A&R guy Steven Joh, Relapse promotions director Bob Lugowe, and Mike Schleibaum, guitarist from the D.C. melodic death metal band Darkest Hour) discussed, well, here's the panel description: "Metal music and culture has, from the beginning, intended to push the boundaries of socio-political-religious discourse and sound ever-darker and ever more extreme. But where has that put the genre, and where does it go from here? At what point do we hit the sonic extremes/limits and devolve into chaos? Is that okay? Is that the point? What does the future hold for extreme music?"

Let's just say they were a whole lot less cynical about these questions than I would have been. But they did start out from a truism that I always deemed self-evident back when such demographics seemed worth making a case for: namely, that metal is a music of rebellion in the sense that it represents defiance of dumb authority by teenagers (traditionally white working-class ones, and once upon a time mostly males, but now seemingly whoever wants in) looking for something to grasp on to in a wicked messed-up world, while seemingly reflecting that world. "A place for the rejected," as Shleibaum put it. Or, per Loesch, "finally a group that you feel like you can belong to because your parents are divorced or there's a bully at school that might beat you up." And (this is me talking now) probably part of metal's power is that, at some point, the tormented gets to act like the tormentor—hence the songs of Axl Rose, or Korn, or five million interchangeable bull-in-china-shop hardcore/crossover/metalcore/whatever brats and counting over the past three decades who curiously think they're being insurrectionist by sounding exactly like each other. And hence a lifestyle clique that those bands' record labels can easily target with rote rituals, just like all the other revolting genres out there that all overlap by now anyway.

Further diversion: a couple hours before the panel, I watched a long line of ill-advisedly body-pierced yet absolutely harmless-looking adolescents with dermatological issues coiling around the block on Red River, many of them wearing T-shirts by bands hardly anybody over the age of 25 (20? who knows) can tell apart without a scoresheet: Asking Alexandria, Devil Wears Prada (both of whom had Top 10 albums in *Billboard* last year), Forever the Sickest Kids (who I guess are more pop-punk), Chelsea Grin. Apparently a free show was about to happen at Red 7, but I was just tickled to confirm that *there are apparently human beings out there who actually like these artists!*

Not to blow my own horn, but here's a thought I published in a metal book called *Stairway to Hell* 22 years ago (= 1990, the year of Extreme!): "What the starched shirts in the record industry's penthouses learned quickly, and it is a lesson they take heed of to this very day, is that once one headbang generation has had its fill, another generation is just sitting down to the table . . . Because the cycle is eternal, marketing strategists can revitalize and/or redundify the headbang appetite (preferably in watered-down form) almost annually merely by stamping labels like 'New!' and 'Improved!' on the cereal box." Still true! Like my *Boston Phoenix* pal Dan Brockman, who I watched the panel with, pointed out, metal has always been a traditional and conservative music at heart: even the fonts remain the same. And if you think the genre's outlook has evolved much over time, consider these attributes that Lester Bangs ascribed to it, in his late-'70s metal essay in *The Rolling Stone Illustrated History of Rock & Roll*: "violence," "aggression," "rapine," "carnage," "technological nihilism," "nothing more than a bunch of noise."

Which brings us back to extremeness, right? Those SXSW panelists seemed pretty much in agreement (with each other, if not me) that metal—not just the undergroundy death/black/grind/noise stuff (pig's blood beloved by Austria's Belphegor and goat's heads abused by Sweden's Watain and maggots appropriated by Denver's Cephalic Carnage were cited) but contemporary commercial fare too—seems inexorably to be headed (if not beheaded) in an ever-increasingly "extreme" direction. Schleibaum—who admitted that, growing up, he latched on to lefty vegan Syracuse metalpunks Earth Crisis more than devil-worship bands as a means of pissing off his ex-nun mom—was fairly on-point here. Since the desire to "be outlandish in any way to get attention" is intrinsic in metal culture, he theorized, "when the extreme is pushed, it becomes the *norm*."

When Shleibaum first heard Meshuggah, for instance, "I was like, there's not a chord change in the first three minutes, how will anybody like that?" But Meshuggah's palm-muted high-math-score sonics were eventually adopted by metalcore lunkheads galore. (Or, okay, "djent" lunkheads—I just learned that one a few months ago; Google it.) One kid, the panelists said, might yearn for something more extreme than Metallica and hence stumble upon Cradle of Filth, but another who's only heard Disturbed might think they're as extreme as you can get. "The mainstream learns from the underground," Lugowe offered. "Look at Slayer, they're totally mainstream now. Or Slipknot. Or Pantera." Schleibaum suggested that, give or take Dimebag Darrell's guitar wizardry, "if Pantera came out now, they wouldn't be extreme." Loesch said that, a decade ago, he never would have expected to hear a band as extreme as the Las Vegas outfit Five-Finger Death Punch on the radio.

If you're getting confused long about now, don't feel alone. I personally never cared about Pantera in the first place, and I *really* don't get the amazement at Five-Finger Death Punch—who've had two Top 10 albums, and who basically sound like an even hackier corporate approximation of rap-metal-era Anthrax crossed with frequent 'oos chart-toppers System of a Down—

myself. But then I've long figured the preoccupation with extremeness turned most metal into an unlistenable novelty shtick decades ago, so what the hell do I know? Century Media's Joh talked on the panel about being a teenage Def Leppard / Quiet Riot fan who knew his life was changed forever the first time he saw the cover art of Slayer's *Hell Awaits* in a magazine. And honestly, the fact that he hadn't even heard Slayer's music at that point says a lot—it's directly connected to Relapse's Lugowe stressing the profit potential of gross-out band merch, and Schleibaum (who said the real metal-musician bucks are overseas, or in instrument endorsements) wondering out loud what all these extreme trappings have to do with, you know, the music.

But okay, they all talked about the music too—that bands like Agoraphobic Nosebleed might be pushing it faster than ever, and some other band has a drum kit "as big as this table," and "Every Last Drop" by Chicago's Nachtmystium (Joh said) is extreme without being heavy at all, and you really can't deny Burzum's influence but what Umanov called Varg's "extreme racism and bigotry" sure does complicate things, and maybe Satanic-sounding Christian metal bands like Iowa's For Today are scarier than alleged real Satanic ones because when they beseech kids to "get on your knees before the king of kings" kids actually might obey them. And besides, a few panelists predicted, it looks like dubstep might just out-metal metal anyway, since it's polarizing and kids making it don't have to haul so much equipment around and kids listening to it prefer partying to standing in the corner. Or something like that. Whatever happens, sooner or later, the tables are destined to turn: "We're gonna be on the side of the fence saying those kids are crazy," Schleibaum predicted. "Get ready, because you're gonna blog about it, you're gonna hate it, but everybody's gonna love it." No matter how extreme you think you are, somebody younger, someday, will turn you into the new Extreme.

—rhapsody.com, 26 April 2012

## Walking Dead: The Divided States of Metal

· · · · ·

Heavy metal is suddenly my favorite music (again), and this was not supposed to happen. I don't know how many times I've given up on the genre over the years (maybe as many times as written "state of metal" essays, which is a lot!), and I'm not alone. Metal was supposed to have dug its grave a long, long time ago. Here's Lester Bangs, over three decades back: "As the seventies drew to a close, it appeared heavy metal had had it." The music industry had castrated metal into faceless corporate rock, the story goes, and punk had stolen everything that seemed good about it in the first place. *Creem* magazine, too, declared metal dead in 1979. But by 1980, *Creem* was already saying it was back—there was a New Wave of Heavy Metal over in England, apparently (more about which later). And if you read the funny papers, metal has supposedly managed to revive itself every few years since.

What happened to the genre in the rest of the '80s, of course, was that it got glammified for MTV viewers and thrashified for people who took life more seriously, and these two factions split it in two, and eventually (come the '90s and/or later), historical revisionists decided the former was never even metal in the first place. Which it sort of wasn't ('80s hair bands took their riffs and makeup tips more from '70s glam bands than from Black Sabbath), except when it was. In the '90s and '00s, metal got uglier and more beautiful and artsier and rappier and rapier and grungier (except it usually wasn't considered metal when it did that) and more industrially electronic (ditto, sometimes) and more "brutal" / "troo" / "kvlt" (get a life) and more gothic and more celibate (in thrashier ciricles, lyrics about consensually getting laid turned taboo all of a sudden, even if once upon a time they were what frustrated teenage boys mainly wanted to hear), almost always with really awful vocals and almost never with a rhythm that rolled. Some of it opted to try to plod again like Stegosaurs used to back in rock's Jurassic Period, and ancient northern European folk jigs and post-rock shoegaze snooze got mixed in somewhere along the line. The endless bifurcation upon bifurcation into minute distinctions got harder and more pointless to keep up with.

Which is by no means to suggest that everybody stopped. There has probably been no more entertaining music publication in the 21st century than the metal magazine *Decibel*. And somewhere along the line, even more lamestream music critics started taking the long-maligned genre seriously: in 2009, three unarguable metal bands (Mastodon, Baroness, Converge) placed albums in the Top 25 of the *Village Voice*'s annual Pazz & Jop critics poll; a fourth—Sunn O)))—finished at a nothing-to-sneeze-at #42. The only previous year that had even come close would've been 1988, when Jane's Addiction, Living Colour, Metallica, and Guns N' Roses—at most one of which the metal audience still tends to consider a metal band in retrospect—all placed in the P&J

Top 40. So somehow, at some point, metal turned respectable. Even to certain aficionados of jazz, or serious minimalist avant-garde composition, which sometimes don't really sound all that different.

You might think that respectability would count as a death knell in metal terms, and maybe that was part of my thinking when I stopped listening to it a few years back—well, that and the fact that I was truly convinced Nashville power country had figured out how to rock harder (a theory certain hair-metal refugees seemed to agree with), and the fact that pirating-paranoid record companies started sending me all these unplayable review discs where some idiot kept announcing "You are listening to the new album by Alestorm" (a pirate-metal band, how appropriate!) every 20 seconds. Of course, in Metal Land, death knells can be a *good* thing. But I can't say I was overjoyed when, last year, my editors at Rhapsody asked me to stop being a jack-of-all-genres utility infielder and start focusing my reviewing skills almost entirely on metal. Frankly, I got pretty neurotic there for a couple weeks about my eventual ability to come up with a year-end list of metal albums I could actually *tolerate*, much less ones I'd like a lot—much less the regular monthly roundups I was being asked to do. Concerned emails were exchanged!

But somehow, my ears were readier than I thought, and metal turned out to be heading in more compelling directions than I'd guessed. A lot of this, it turned out, had to do with attempts to re-create the metal of a less self-conscious, less respectable, less "extreme" time. For instance, new bands exploring the occult acid-rock of the turn of the '70s (Blood Ceremony, Ghost), or that New Wave of Metal moment at the turn of the '80s when hair and thrash hadn't yet fissioned (Cauldron, Midnight Chaser, converters from metalcoredom 3 Inches of Blood), or the dazed-and-confused and biker-boogiefied period in between (Gentlemans Pistols, Freedom Hawk, Gideon Smith and the Dixie Damned), or some mix-and-match mash-up of those historical epochs (Gates of Slumber, Argus, Saviours).

Veteran old-schoolers like Wolf and Manilla Road (from Wichita!) had never stopped attaching memorable melodies to semi-operatic Hagar the Horrible battle metal in the first place; ancient NWOBHMers Angel Witch returned to it, too, after a quarter-century. Arizona's Vektor (and to a lesser extent Stockholm's New Keepers of the Water Towers and Boston's Revocation) reminded me what I used to love about Voivod's strange quantum-caveman science-thrash; Woods of Ypres, Thunderkraft, Opeth, and Korpiklaani raindanced with medieval mugs full of goth-prog mead at the Black Forest Renaissance Faire. Sigh, from Tokyo, managed to extract yet more chewy gorgeousness out of their goofball avant-collage musique concrète black-metal baloney. All that in 2011 and (so far) 2012, plus a pretty good new Van Halen album; what else could I ask for?

Well, all sorts of things. And if you prefer, say, roaring thrash/stoner hybrids like High on Fire and Behold! the Monolith, or theoretical experimentalists like Giant Squid and Wolves in the Throne Room, or swamp-dipped southern sludge-sluggers like Black Tusk and Rwake, or New Agey droners like Blut aus Nord and (2011's big crit-metal hype) Liturgy, or blackdeathcore brutes like All Pigs Must Die and Today Is the Day, more power to you. Point is, there's lots of at least passably intriguing din out there—and no, just like Lester Bangs argued way back when, it still does not all sound the same.

A couple years ago, faced with a similar deluge, I confessed in print to being overwhelmed by "the sheer quantity of marginally decent stuff" that "ultimately all muddles together." So maybe I've brainwashed myself into thinking otherwise for reasons of drawing a regular paycheck. All I know is I'm having fun keeping up with this hubbub in ways that I haven't in, like, forever. For some reason, right now, at this moment, metal sounds like it's managed to retain more sonic integrity, as a genre, than any other music I'm exposed to—by which I guess I just mean it's only full of crap 90% of the time, as opposed to 99%. It's more or less the only music left where self-contained "bands" manage to legitimately "rock" anymore, and it even seems to be relocating its inner rock'n'roll (you know—like, catchy hooks and songs you can tell apart), which it had stupidly put aside as unseemingly cheesy for nigh on a quarter-century. So believe me or don't; no epidermis off my back, either way. But personally, I'm glad I stopped worrying and learned to trust high voltage again.

—rhapsody.com, 25 April 2012

## Voivod: *Target Earth*

· · · · ·

So, you know how heavy metal supposedly suddenly got all avant-garde and high-IQ in the past few years, enabling its embracement by the hippest of the bearded Brooklyn hip? Well, whoever you're banging your microbrewed brainbox to, odds are Voivod beat them to their best ideas by a quarter-century. Weirdness came naturally to four French Canuck street-hockey pucks born around the dawn of the '60s, raised inhaling toxins from earth's most enor-

Voivod liberate Quebec's power grid. (Photo: Ron McGregor)

mous aluminum plant, in Jonquière, in the nexus of Quebec sovereignty country. In 1969—with Away, Blacky, Piggy, and Snake in grade school—Front de
Libération du Québec terrorists bombed the Montreal Stock Exchange; by
1970, in the October Crisis wake of separatist kidnappings and murder, the
province was all but under martial law. The boys soaked it all in and, in 1982,
started a band.

At first Voivod seemed like a joke, apparently not on purpose. They had
those silly nicknames, for one thing, and early on, that's all they went by.
*War and Pain*—released in August 1984, a year or so after Metallica's debut,
eight months after Slayer's—was called "probably the worst record I have
ever heard in my entire life" by Paul Sutter in *Kerrang*: "like a moose being
squashed by a steamroller (the vocals), whilst putting a strong magnetic current through a dustbin half-full of ball bearings (the band)." Their follow-up,
1986's umlautriffically named *Rrröööaaarrr*, was some new species of fallout-
shelter caveman splatter, complete with are-they-kidding song titles on the
order of "Ripping Headaches"; people lumped them in with thrash and/or
speedmetal, but already Voivod sounded like nobody else. They were listening to anarchist Brit hardcore (Rudimentary Peni, Discharge); left-field '70s
Euro-prog (Birth Control, Egg, Amon Düül II, Nektar) that had a surprising
Quebec following; 20th-century classical stuff; goth stuff, horror soundtracks;

biker rock; Sonic Youth and Public Image Ltd.; industrial firms like Einstürzende Neubauten and Laibach, whose T-shirts certain Voivoders wear in '80s gigs captured on 2005's D-V-O-D-1. They had a ridiculous concept—Voivods are a kind of time-hopping Viking vampire, see—but meticulous cover design and calligraphy from not-quite-here (hence his name) drummer Away and vegematic riffs from porcine guitarist Piggy to put it over.

Then on *Killing Technology* (1987—note two-faced title) and *Dimension Hatröss* (1988), they blasted it all into a deep and dense and ulcerous black hole of quantum sound, hanging 10 on the galaxy's outer edge atop a jungle drum rumble and stretching song matter toward ambient antimatter via algebraic equations that later critic-approved metalgaze droners from Neurosis and Isis to Sunn O))) and Liturgy and Pallbearer still haven't figured out how to calculate. Meanwhile, their convoluted structures presaged entire metal subgenres largely preceded by the prefix "tech-," but mainly populated by dorks opting for boilerplate brutality over having personalities.

On *Nothingface* (1989), *Angel Rat* (1991), and *Outer Limits* (1993), Voivod eased their claustrophobic congestion some, letting in more psych/prog/goth beauty, alternate-reality pop hooks, two late-'60s Pink Floyd covers, one 17-minute epic, melodic college radio jangle two decades before Baroness. Years since have been tumultuous: five often grumpy studio albums (plus live and outtake sets) between 1995 and 2009, including two with a vocalist who wasn't Snake, three with a bassist who wasn't Blacky but who used to be in Metallica, and two recorded after colon cancer killed Piggy but featuring guitar parts he'd cranked out before he died. *Voivod* (2003) is one of the band's catchiest records; *Katorz* (2006) one of their most rhythmic.

*Target Earth*, their new one, deserves to be the album whereon social-media-era tastemakers finally anoint them legacy heroes, in the amusingly eons-behind-the-curve tradition of Swans, Nick Cave, and Voivod's own early inspiration Killing Joke. Blacky's back, and if new guitarist Chewy from Quebec tech-deathers Martyr is no Piggy (nobody is), he holds his own—his fills in "Kaleidos" are nutso. As albums by Treponem Pal, Mekong Delta, Angel Witch, and others have demonstrated in the past year, great metal bands have a jellyfish knack for eternal regeneration when lineups change, and Voivod remain as sui generis as, oh, the Fall—their noise still can't be mistaken for anybody else's. *Target Earth*'s self-production is a bit murky, maybe—drums and vocals have seen sharper days. But these dudes still turn sharp corners; 7 of 10 tracks last 5:45 or longer, but not even the 7:35 "Mechanical Mind"—first released last fall, on one-sided, logo-etched 7-inch vinyl—wears out its welcome. It just builds, from wind-chiming start through yawping bad-dream multiverses and impatient time signatures and nyah-nyah-nyahs unto insanity: "Night arrives! The guilt inside! The worms of mind! Scarred me for life!"

There are all sorts of idiosyncrasies tucked into the album's wormholes: Inuit throat singing and an almost lounge-jazzy midsection in the First Nations folklore–derived "Kluskap O'kom"; a Mediterranean intro credited to Greek oudist Perikles Tsoukalas making way for traffic-jam honking and extended staccato rhyming in the black-ice depressive "Empathy for the Enemy"; rain-forest polyrhythms under conspiracy theories of suppressed alien visitation ("skulls with conical shape, a map of outer space") in "Artefact"; intercepted satellite static or aluminum-smelting musique concrète opening several tracks, presumably courtesy of Blacky, who's dabbled in electronic music in recent years. "Corps Etranger," cold and clammy and then raging, is recited in French and seems to concern a parasitic disease—maybe Piggy's cancer.

In the world of extreme metal experimentation, writing songs you'll remember once the album's over isn't cool; either that, or most bands don't know how. Voivod have for ages—environmental horror and nuclear-biological-chemical warfare and chaos theory and drone weapons of the formerly future frontier have been obsessions since *Killing Technology* days. *Target Earth* kicks off with cyberterror—a hacker attacking the power grid. But somehow Snake's nasally accented repetitions, more robotic than monstrous, consistently manage to communicate shades of emotion—worry, despair, but also a hopeful calm—outside metal's usual purview. So a dystopian nuke-wasteland dirge like "Warchaic" ultimately finds him looking to rebuild a "brand new world" like a 16th-century New France settler, then up next is the swinging punk protest "Resistance," not entirely unskeptical yet actively embracing gas-masked street demonstrators toppling champagne-sipping gargoyles from ivory towers—a shout of solidarity with Occupy anarchists or Arab Springsters or Montreal students rioting over tuition hikes or Wal-Mart workers trying to unionize in Jonquière. Eventually, *Target Earth* concludes with an odd, ominous minute-and-a-half snippet called "Defiance": black clouds, world in flames. But it doesn't feel like the end. Just the opposite: it feels *unfinished*. To be continued . . . maybe forever.

—spin.com, 26 January 2013

## Merchandise: *Totale Nite*

· · · · ·

Merchandise are a pair of mild-mannered 20-somethings recording in their house in Tampa (well, actually, *three* guys on record, and now even sorta *four* since they're touring with a drummer, but apparently two guys do most of the work) who've supposedly been building a "buzz" in select circles over the past few years, which means if like me and the vast majority of other earthlings you don't inhabit buzzy orbits you probably never heard of them. They get compared to '80s groups a lot, which makes at least a little bit of sense, since like too many people over the past quarter-century they do the Jesus and Mary Chain (sometimes via Dinosaur Jr.) supersoak-it-all-in-reverb thing, and Carson Cox whines halfway like Morrissey in baritone mode and Ian Curtis in lowing lower registers, and their album *Children of Desire* last year had a thing called "In Nightmare Room" and another that confessed "When I was a boy I would have nightmares in the day," which might well be why somebody at *Dusted* said "They sound like guys with Flock of Seagulls haircuts" (Flock having had their own "Nightmares" song in '83), though really they don't. Also, Depeche Mode get cited a lot, seemingly thanks to cut-rate synth abuse.

One thing this misses is that a lot of that '80s modern-pop dinkiness (certainly Depeche and Flock) was post-disco dance music underneath—well, at least dance music for lonely bedsits—and Merchandise live rhythmically in nowherezville. Their groove-lack also cancels out most Wax Trax, Krautrock, and goth analogies well-wishers make (though Merch do retain much of the latter's wrist-slitting aspects), not to mention Miles Davis / Minutemen / Roxy / Dylan / Haggard (!?) / Boyz II Men (!!??) analogies the band and their publicists *prefer* people were making: it don't mean a thing if it ain't got etc. . . . Well, okay, it might mean *something*, just not that.

On the other hand, Cox has said dub reggae inspired him to record in the first place—he and guitarist/whateverer David Vassalotti and bassist/minority-shareholder Patrick Brady had come out of an early '00s Florida teen hardcore and ska scene they now describe as lifesaving but limiting— and their 2010 cassette *Gone Are the Silk Gardens of Youth* had numbers called "Locked in the Dark (Boulders Meets Merch Rockers Uptown)" (note Augustus Pablo reference) and "Wage Dub," and at least in the latter you could detect sounds dropping out so background became foreground. Two other selections were "Graveyard" (not goth enough) and "Schoolyard" (not "Me and Julio" enough), a nominally intriguing juxtaposition on paper.

Sundry other tapes (niftiest title: *Terminal Jagger Jane's Addiction Boxset*), CD-Rs, Record Store Day 45s with Silver-Jews-covering B-sides, and at least one legit album dotted with your standard recorder grot, heckler spray, and trunk spizzle had seeped out by the time 2012's *Children of Desire* got them noticed by the kind of canny consumers who also order Waxahatchee, Youth Lagoon, and Phosphorescent downloads from Amazon. Drowsy, low-volume, waterlogged, amorphously fading-away-not-burning-out even if Vassalotti is a Neil Young feedback fan, it had six tracks, including two 11-minute marathons, and sounded exactly as exciting as all that suggests, all the way to the drippy church organ at the end. It also got packaged with a booklet of journal entries that corresponded to the lyrics in some way or other.

Well, the good news is that the Merchandisers' new *Totale Nite*, mastered by Sonic Boom from longtime low-calorie Hawkwind-powered generators Spacemen 3 and released on an Iowa City mini-indie called Night People that disappointingly has nothing to do with disco-era Lee Dorsey, does not feel quite so emo and emaciated. Nor quite so generic, either, but please understand we're talking granular degrees of naptime here. Also, this time there's only *five* tracks, four of which are still long (6:36 and up), but none break the dreaded 10-minute barrier. Concision counts! Though amazingly, leadoff batter "Who Are You?" somehow manages to be both the shortest and the most vague, a neat trick on a record so meandering.

Cox has actually expressed concern that Merchandise fans might find the album too challenging, due to perhaps the title cut containing an extremely brief interlude of Sabbathoid funeral plod, then a couple minutes of what passes for faux–Albert Ayler sax blat, or maybe the oppressive 45 seconds of power-violence kerblooey that ends closer "Winter's Dream," which cut had nonetheless kicked off seven minutes before with a snowflake or two of atmosphere right off a late '90s Projekt Records goth Christmas sampler. And "I'll Be Gone" leads propeller-like whirligigging into some momentary rainy-day twang that shambling combos from the north of England might mistake for country music. So, no argument—there is *stuff* here. Now and then.

What *isn't* here is coherently shaped songs, or hooks, or riffs, or melodies that stick—maybe Merch consider all those gauche, or maybe they're still waiting for sedatives to wear off. Cox's vocal grain might have potential if he'd wake up and do more than mumble like a soggy noodle bored by his own noodledom. Between his blank delivery and Vassalotti's blanketing distortomouthwash (which also has moments—fleeting Middle Eastern hookah in "Anxiety's Door," say), lyrics peek out only by accident: "I'm gonna plant myself inside just to be free from all you motherfuckers," Cox seems to mutter once. And "I'd sooner kill myself than be someone else." "Anxiety's Door" has something about walking streets at night in a city you love and dreaming of a perfect country beside the sea where the sun comes out to talk. So okay, sure, Merchandise have *feelings*. Probably intense ones, being young and all. But do they have lunch?

—spin.com, 3 April 2013

## Mumford and Sons: *Babel*

· · · · ·

The first album Marcus Mumford ever paid attention to, he has said, was *Slow Train Coming*, which came out in 1980, seven years before he was born. You know, Bob Dylan's first Christian one: "It may be the devil, or it may be Lord, but you're gonna have to serve somebody." It was Marcus's mom's copy. She and his dad are big on the God thing: when Marcus was half a year old (he'd been born in Anaheim early in 1987), John and Eleanor Mumford returned to England and founded the Vineyard Church of the UK, which they still direct. The Vineyard churches, theoretically nondogmatic if bordering on Pentecostal (lots of Holy Spirit stuff in their Statement of Faith, not to mention "we believe that the world is under the domination of Satan"), had apparently been around in California since the mid-'70s, initially revolving around Bible readings hosted by Jesus-freak-era contemporary Christian music OGs like Larry Norman (whose druid-inspired 1972 album *Only Visiting This Planet* is some excellent hard-boiled singer-songstering), and eventually playing a role in the born-again conversion of, well, Dylan.

That's all just backstory, of course. But even if Mumford and Sons—the now trans-Atlanticly multiplatinum folk-rock foursome Marcus Mumford now fronts—hadn't backed Dylan at the Grammy Awards last year, it would still matter, because that Holy Spirit and Satan stuff is all through Mumford's music. You can take preachers' sons out of religion, but you can't etc.—even ask Kings of Leon, or that guy from Collective Soul. And unsurprisingly, the ultimate objective for musicians of such upbringing is to be the next Bono. Pope rock will never die! Consciously or not, it's all through the Mumfords' bland but biblically titled second album *Babel*—blatantly in the pompous vowel-stretch climaxes of "Whispers in the Dark" and "Lover of the Light," but really wherever keening harmonies reach for heaven in full voice: stretching arms to the sky, as the opening title track puts it. (Though, hmm . . . isn't the Tower of Babel's moral that we *can't* scale heaven?) Several songs feature yelping "woooo!"s, and tests of despair and temptation are triumphed over at every turn: "A brush with the devil can clear your mind and straighten your spine"; "when I'm on my knees I still believe," "hope in the darkness, so that I may hear the light," "ghosts in my head / they run wild and wish me dead," "shake my ash to the wind / Lord forget all my sins," "I was under your spell when I was told by Jesus all was well," thoughts of hell, clouded minds and heavy hearts, fickle flesh keeping heart and soul in place, loving with urgency not haste. Bromides approximately as deep as Matchbox 20, and smug as Dave Matthews. But sincere as all fuck!

Ah, "fuck." Most unbearable part of 2010's breakthrough Grammy record-of-the-year / song-of-the-year nominee "Little Lion Man" was the self-congratulatory way Marcus Mumford delivered that line "I really *fucked* it up this time," like he wanted to make sure we understood just how daring his utterance was. To be fair, the repeated recitation of the same expletive in the new album's "Broken Crown" feels more natural, and in fact, given its foreboding echo and doomful build and especially the hint of Jim Morrison blow-hardiness in the chorus, this is easily the album's most biting track—as tolerable as debut blockbuster *Sigh No More*'s intermittently loud-rock-raving murder ballad "Dust Bowl Dance." Songs drag on longer this time: first time out, none exceeded five minutes; now, four do. But just like on *Sigh*, some of the new material does accrue body and drive as it goes, occasionally slipping into prissy shambling or polite hoedown parts that make the Zac Brown Band seem like the Texas Playboys. Banjos and dobros and mandolins notwithstanding, calling this "bluegrass" is stretching it, though the opening of current single "I Will Wait" does sound vaguely inspired by the theme from *The Beverly Hillbillies*.

Honestly, as folk revivalists, Mumford and Sons don't even come close to ranking, and not just because Marcus Mumford and sideman Ben Lovett's posh education (they met at Kings College School in Wimbledon, alma mater of John Barrymore and Charles Dickens Jr.) might handicap them even more than the faith-based pedigree. West London scenemates Johnny Flynn and Barbara Manning at least incorporate hints of African percussion and Renaissance Faire drone to keep the quaintness passingly interesting. The Mumfords'

American visual antecedents Old Crow Medicine Show have shown a knack for Depression-era hillbilly blues moves. '80s MTV hobos like Men Without Hats and Dexy's Midnight Runners treated dancing around the maypole as a pop goof, with bright and shameless hooks. The Pogues and Dropkick Murphys made it get-drunk-and-fight music; Fairport Convention and Steeleye Span were students of centuries of jigs, reels, waltzes, and Morris dances and figured out how to modernize them, beautifully. Heck, so did Jethro Tull, and this Montreal folk band Elfin Saddle, who put out one of the best albums you never heard of this year (*Devastates*), and several troll-metal combos still wandering through Europe's forests. But lyrical references to Shakespeare and Steinbeck assignments from their sixth-form syllabus or no, the Mumfords barely skim the surface. They don't seem remotely musically curious.

Still, Marcus Mumford ends *Babel* defending himself against charges of inauthenticity and antiquity. "This ain't no sham / I am what I am," he declares, in his mannered puritan burr. "Though I may speak some tongue of old / Or even spit out some holy word." He's setting up straw men, though. Great artists have been incorporating that old-time religion, and old-timey rhythms, ever since old times. It's the way how you do it that matters. A sense of humor helps. There are no roots outside the Gates of Eden.

—spin.com, 24 September 2012

## The Gospel Truth

· · · · ·

Over the past decade or so, gospel music has managed to reach some new ears that probably haven't spent a lot of time in church. In 2003, the small, historically obsessed Atlanta label Dust-to-Digital put together *Goodbye, Babylon*, a Grammy-nominated six-CD box of 135 songs and 25 sermons recorded between 1902 in 1960; six years later, upstart New York boutique imprint Tompkins Square cast forth the triple-disc crate-digger *Fire in My Bones: Raw + Rare + Otherworldly African-American Gospel [1944–2007]*. Venerable Smithsonian Folkways has remained on the case too, in a less collector-obscurantist way (*Classic African American Gospel*, 2008). And meanwhile, the **Five Blind Boys of Alabama**—around in some form since 1939—have continuously upped their heritage-artist visibility, performing with all sorts of prestige adult-alternative acts at the White House and Lincoln Center, showing up frequently on late-night TV, and recording *Take the High Road*, a 2011 album of country gospel duets with people like Willie Nelson, Lee Ann Womack, and Hank Williams Jr.

In 2013, gospel was even harder to miss. The Blind Boys followed up their Jamey Johnson–co-produced Nashville sessions with an indie-collaboration album called *I'll Find a Way*, curated by Bon Iver's Justin Vernon—intriguing since, a half decade ago, Johnson and Vernon came off as flip sides of the same unshaven-guy-with-dark-feelings-emerging-out-of-post-breakup-seclusion-with-an-initially-self-released-album-featuring-gray-foggy-cover-art  coin. Johnson's the livelier of the two depressives, though, and their Blind Boys albums follow suit. *I'll Find a Way* has some fine gospel harmonizing if you can ignore the twee Salvation Army band arrangements, but gets hard to take when mostly traditional worship makes way for Virginia boarding-school folkie Sam Amidon chiming in blankly on a cover of Starbucks-sanctioned Milwaukee folk act Field Report, and even more so when Vernon applies his own wallflower-on-codeine vocal stylings to Bob Dylan's "Every Grain of Sand."

But the Blind Boys were neither the only old gospel group to get indie assistance this year, nor close to the most exciting. **The Relatives**, a band from Dallas who first got together and recorded a few obscure 45s in 1970—rediscovered then compiled on a 2009 reissue called *Don't Let Me Fall*—put out *The Electric Word*, the first real-time full-length of their career, on North Carolina–based, Triple-A-leaning Yep Roc. Spoon drummer Jim Eno produced it, and the support musicians come from Austin's Meters-inspired, Black Joe Lewis–associated Raw Fusion. The singing, from 66-year-old Tommie West's rough low lead growl worrying that people don't pray like they used to pray and his 75-year-old fellow-church-pastor brother Gean on back, is unmistakably gospel—straight a cappella quintet style in "Trouble in My Way" and "I Will Trust in the Lord." But their preferred rhythmic mode partakes in just as much hard-riffing funk, closer to the neighborhood of early Funkadelic or "Psychedelic Shack"–era Temptations: downright acid-rocking in the aptly named, deeper-and-deeper-into-reverb "Bad Trip"; dark like a riot's goin' on in the y'all-better-get-saved admonition "Revelations."

"It's Coming Up Again" is an unabashed James Brown rip, complete with "Say it loud!" exclamations and cities called out like stops on a night train; "Your Love Is Real" and "Speak to Me (What's Wrong with America?)" are rootsier soul blues, the latter fretting about a black man heading off to war

Delta ladies Como Mamas pray for you, sans instruments.
(Photo: Aaron Greenhood)

for "three bloody miserable years and he fought so well they even gave him a medal of bravery," which does him not a lick of good once his boots return to home soil.

The Relatives were one of at least two gospel groups who played SXSW in Austin this year. Another, the less stomping, less urban **Como Mamas**, are three mature women whose home venue is a century-old wooden church in Panola County on the Mississippi Delta, close to where Alan Lomax came across Otha Turner's fife and drum music in the late '50s. Their instrument-free voices aren't big on backbeats, which can make *Get an Understanding*, on soul-revivalist Brooklyn label Daptone, feel field-recording academic—not the easiest listen. But with Esther Mae Smith's frontwoman vocal power holding down a pitch below Angela Taylor and above Taylor's sister Della Daniels, tracks like "Peace of Mind," "One More River to Cross," and especially the inching-toward-100% "Ninety Nine and a Half Won't Do" work a stark, stretched-out mesh of hypnotic variations and ecstatic improvisations on what initially seems a monotonal straight line—suggesting Gregorian chants, almost. Outside of one each by Thomas Dorsey and Rev. James Cleveland, the hymns all come from the public domain; the most jarring, "I Know It Was the Blood," is a crucifixion song that could double as a song about a lynching.

Ghosts from the history of African America drift through this music, obviously. And this year, nobody made that as clear as **Matana Roberts**, the Chicago-born, New York–based alto sax player who identifies as experimental jazz but whose indie post-rock ties date back to '00s work with Godspeed You! Black Emperor and sundry Tortoise and Prefuse 73 members. On *Coin Coin Chapter Two: Mississippi Moonchile*, the multifaceted second volume of a long-term project revolving around her genealogical connections to the 18th-century freedwoman and entrepreneur Marie-Thérèse Coincoin, sung and talked snippets of hymns and spirituals and hollers predating the blues waft in and out: "His Eye Is on the Sparrow," "The Gospel Train," "In the Garden," "Wild Ox Moan (Black Woman)." None of these is named on the cover, which lists 18 tracks by title. But in fact the album is structured as one long suite of music that veers, gradually or abruptly, between swinging Cotton Club jazz (evoking Africa in "Spares of the World," semi-scatted in "Responsory") and more out-there cacophony ("Secret Covens," "The Labor of Their Lips") honked by Roberts and her sax / trumpet / double bass / piano / drums combo.

Male tenor Jeremiah Abiah adds opera interjections composed by one Joseph D. Howard (1873–1952), between spoken recitations from testimony that civil rights activist Fannie Lou Hamer gave at the 1964 Democratic Convention in "Was the Sacred Day," partly about hearing a man get whipped in the next cell over, and interviews with Roberts's maternal grandmother in "Amma Jerusalem School," partly about picking cotton from dawn to dusk in the '40s. But it all feels seamless, circling a grim refrain: "There are some things I just can't tell you about, honey."

Of course, all of these albums—Matana Roberts's avant-garde especially—are a long way from what gets promoted these days as "urban contemporary gospel." Some of which is no doubt excellent—Yarbrough & Peoples' "I'm In . . . I'm All the Way In!," a sanctified comeback by the married Dallas electro-funk duo who've kept a low profile since their R&B-charting early '80s, ranks with the year's most joyful singles in any style, and Mary Mary's "Sunday Morning" and Tye Tribbett's "If He Did It Before (Same God)" are plenty energetic, as well. But 2013's real urban contemporary gospel revelation looks back at a period when that subgenre was only first trying out its wings—namely,

*Overdose of the Holy Ghost*, on UK house producer Joey Negro's Z Records. Subtitled "The Sound of Gospel through the Disco and Boogie Eras," its track-list runs late '70s to mid-'80s, with four cuts—including the earth-shaking, dope-busting, P-Funk-basslined title song—from the camp of influential Detroit family quartet the Clark Sisters.

Several selections—by Ricky Womack & Christian Essence, Elbernita "Twinkie" Clark, Norman Weeks & the Revelations scatting and echoing and keep-on-keeping-on for 14 hugely propulsive minutes—ride the sort of boogie-woogie/salsa piano runs that would soon become a staple of early Chicago house music; a few others saunter closer to smooth jazz. Dan Greer's shiveringly string-orchestrated, gentle-to-tough "Love Is the Message" rails out of Memphis against the pain of poverty, inflation, "wars and rumors of wars." In a right world, D. J. Rogers's call-and-responsive "All I Gave Him Was My Heart" would accelerate aficionado demand for the L.A. soul singer turned choir director's very good late '70s albums. And Kristle's Andrae Crouch–produced "I'll Go" might well count as the first great Prince imitation ever—released in 1980, it almost certainly preceded the purple prodigy's game-changing *Dirty Mind*, which didn't chart until the tail end of that year. That we're only learning of it decades later is yet one more clue that 2013's many-guised gospel emergence signals more good news to come.

—*Wondering Sound*, 10 December 2013

## Southern Soul Keeps On Keepin' On

· · · · ·

A Memphis insurance agent and mother of two with a "sturdy build, big thighs, big hips," a feather boa, and minimal platinum-blond hair, in one of 2010's best singles, reminisced back to when she was 25 and had a crush on a big-time southern soul singer. That'd be Bobby Rush; in "A Girl Like Me," Sweet Angel borrows the incessant, repetitive, knee-deep funk vamp Rush once used in "Sue," a stuttering extended tease from 1982 about being deflowered as a teenager. Around 1990 or so, if her own song is to be believed, Sweet Angel applied to be one of Rush's dancing girls. He told her she was too young, so she tried again 10 years later, at 35—"Ohhh yeah, that's a good age." But 155 pounds? "*Too little.*" Eventually, her singing career takes off instead. She opens for Rush in Mississippi. "You look like one of my dancing girls," he finally concedes. "You just ain't got no hair." Halfway through the song's six minutes, her talking switches to singing, and her register drops to a gloating growl.

Sweet Angel—real name, Clifetta Dobbins—is now 46. Which, in southern soul, still makes her a sweet *young* thing. Bobby Rush himself was born in Louisiana before World War II, played with Elmore James in the mid-'50s, and his deep-fried ham-hock drawl is still going strong; "Night Fishin'," from 2005, even spawned a stack of answer records. Denise LaSalle is 71; her one pop hit, "Trapped by a Thing Called Love," came and went in 1971, but in 2010 she scored on southern soul's chitlin circuit with "Older Woman," about how aging improved her bedroom technique ("like a Whirlpool, I got different speeds"), so now she's looking for a younger man who can keep up. Dirty old Bobby Rush, "over 72," actually gets the final word in LaSalle's song. But 54-year-old white-haired Texan Mel Waiters, probably southern soul's biggest name these days (he even plays up north sometimes), opts out of the competition in 2010's "I Ain't Gone Do It": "Ain't one of them young boys make you scream and shout / You gonna mess me around and make me throw my back out!"

That this self-branded "grown folks music" still flourishes, in an age when mainstream R&B has increasingly become the juvenile province of Beavises babbling about "boobies," is some kind of miracle. Black music, as Nelson George pointed out throughout his 1988 book *The Death of Rhythm & Blues*, was largely an adult commodity in the time of adolescent rock'n'roll. But hip-hop changed that forever, and disco-era assimilation dreams had already begun to sever R&B from the local economics of black communities. When George wrote a 1983 *Voice* roundup of soul journeymen Johnnie Taylor, Tyrone Davis, and Z. Z. Hill—aged 45, 45, and 43 at the time—they were already considered anachronistic relics by major labels too coastal to care, even though raspy Texan Hill's indie-label *Down Home* was then blindsiding northeastern provincials by staying on *Billboard*'s black album chart for almost two years. The piece was titled "Till the Day They Die," as George deduced that middle-aged black men "with no skills other than singing, dancing, and guitar picking" have few financial alternatives other than to keep plugging away until they're gone. And that's pretty much what this trinity did—Hill passed in 1984, Taylor in 2000, Davis in 2005.

Where they live on is in recent southern soul songs, which frequently name-check them as patron saints. Malaco, the grassroots Jackson, Mississippi, company that resuscitated all three singers' careers and old-school soul itself in the '80s and '90s, is still around, too, though it's widely diversified into Christian and catalog items. Daddy B. Nice, whose website at southernsoulrnb.com indispensably chronicles/reviews/aggregates the subculture from the inside, pegs the dominant imprints now, in terms of promoting new talent, as Ecko in Memphis—founded by Malaco expat John Ward, who produces everything and runs the studio—and Carlsbad, California, concern CDs, where New Orleans–via–Nashville vet and former Neville Brothers sideman Carl Marshall has become integral to the creative mix. Other, even tinier companies—in Georgia, Alabama, Louisiana—fill in holes.

These labels will never challenge the overpowering studio bands of deep soul's heyday; Ecko albums inevitably credit Ward with "rhythm tracks," and the arrangements are consistently functional if infrequently ingenious. The spotlight is on the singers, who almost inevitably partake in a church-testifying richness and grit that R&B otherwise abandoned in favor of icy detachment and empty melisma decades ago. In eternal blues-and-country storytelling tradition, the songwriting can get formulaic, especially as themes rework into memes: lots of cheating-with-your-best-friend's-spouse songs, advice from all fronts of the monogamy wars, easy oral-sex jokes way less shocking than they pretend (specialty of Marvin "Candy Licker" Sease, who died at 65 on 8 February), and slides/steps/shuffles/spanks for the family reunion. The CD packaging looks endearingly cut-rate, and quality control often yields to quantity-of-product—Alabama romancer Sir Charles Jones might be blessed with the millennium's most luscious late-night baritone, but his 2010 Mardi Gras Records all-covers set seemed mostly perfunctory.

What's amazing is how much of this music transcends its limitations: Gerod Rayborn's October release *Call Before You Come!!!*—backed by what sounds like a full band, and featuring several men and women sharing Rayborn's last name—is as intense a marriage-soul battle as any since mid-'80s Womack & Womack. *Who's Rockin' You*, new Ecko 10-songer from 51-year-old Texas smoothie Donnie Ray, is every bit as soakable a '70s-throwback quiet-storm bubblebath as the latest (quite good) albums by El Debarge or R. Kelly—neither of which is any more verbally distinctive, but neither of which can touch Ray's most sugar-sweet beach-soul hooks. *That Thang Thang*, out in late 2010 from Ray's more huskily shouting and alcohol-obsessed Clarksdale, Mississippi, labelmate O. B. Buchana, is funkier, funnier, and even catchier, with an excellent Bobby Womack cover and a focus track where a couple expend equal energy fighting and fucking.

*The Preacher's Wife*, last year's unusually lovely and thoughtful album by Buchana's brother Luther Lackey, who writes his own songs and clearly draws

Bigg Robb: *Jerri Curl Muzic* (Over25Sound, 2009)

inspiration from country and gospel as well as Sam Cooke, made my Pazz &
Jop Top 10; belatedly, so did the self-released mid-2009 *Jerri Curl Muzic* by
Bigg Robb, a prolific graduate of Ohio's talkbox-funk scene whom southern
soul partisans have accepted despite the fact that he doesn't exactly sing—
guests like Carl Marshall and Shirley Murdock and "Larry from the Floaters"
mostly do that for him—and his deluge of lengthy albums revolve around a
Gap Band / Cameo default setting. That's as trendy as this genre gets: Robb
learned his trade from Zapp's Roger Troutman, and Kurtis Blow raps on *Jerri
Curl*. So caveat emptor, if "datedness" bugs you.

Give or take the occasional flicker on lower rungs of the blues or "urban
adult" chart, this stuff barely registers in *Billboard* anymore. But to me, it still
feels like 2011 anyway, and presumably it also does to the primarily working-
class, baby-boom-born southern black crowds who pack outskirts-of-town
roadhouses and Elks Lodges every weekend, and arena package tours and
state-park picnic spots every spring and summer, to watch these artists. Mom-
and-pop record stores and local radio (some, like WMPR in Jackson, Mississippi, now web-streamable) get the word out. And if the national recession
and music-biz depression have wreaked havoc on both small neighborhood
businesses and the lives of the fans who rely on them, southern soul doesn't
whitewash hard times, either: Luther Lackey croons about clipping coupons

and shopping at yard sales and shining shoes when unemployment turns permanent; Bigg Robb, who like Lackey sometimes comes off like a small-town minister consoling his down-and-out flock, keeps the party going even when he can't afford the mall. Mel Waiters does "Everything's Going Up (but My Paycheck)"; Sweet Angel does "I Like the Money But I Don't Like the Job," about keeping her daughters fed. "I Lived It All," Carl Marshall's 60-years-on lookback at his impoverished youth, will tear your heart a new ventricle. One of my favorite singles of 2009 was the hilarious plea-to-Obama "I Need a Bailout," by Austin's CDBaby-distributed Larry Shannon Hargrove. This ain't no VIP Room—the action takes place at holes in the wall, or even VFW Halls. Somehow, the singers stay good-humored about it.

And I'm sorry, Aloe Blacc's "I Need a Dollar"—to pick a better-than-average example of the alleged retro-soul typically embraced in indie-adult-alternative circles these days—sounds, in comparison, like the tastefully antiseptic HBO theme it is. And if the museum embalmers at Anti- Records hadn't Anglicized them into arugula suitable to dour and delicate Wilco sensibilities, Mavis Staples and Bettye LaVette could *maybe* still sound half as alive as, say, the call-in-advice-show title-talker on Rubenesque raunch queen Ms. Jody's doubly horny new Ecko album, *Keepin' It Real*. If you're into Sharon Jones or Cee-Lo dressing up vintage, that's your choice. But if so, you really owe it to yourself to acknowledge a thriving world where soul music, as originally understood, never *stopped* being vital—where it's something more than mannerisms reverently simulated from a distance. A place where, as Bigg Robb would say, you can still smell chicken, catfish, and pork chops all cooking in the same grease.

*—Village Voice*, 9 March 2011

## Jamey Johnson Sprawls Out

· · · · ·

Here are some things you'll find on Jamey Johnson's new album: three songs ("Lonely at the Top," "Poor Man Blues," "Can't Cash My Checks") explicitly addressing class differences, the last one featuring a verse about harvesting marijuana even more redolent of *Weeds* than the one on Dierks Bentley's latest. Two songs ("California Riots," "Even the Skies Are Blue") that warn that the world's real bad and getting worse. Two songs (new single "Playing the

Part," "California Riots" again) about faking it in L.A. while wishing you were back in Alabama, and they just happen to be the most '70s-Cali-soft-rock-catchy-singer-songwriter things on the record. Three songs ("That's How I Don't Love You," "Good Morning Sunrise," "My Way to You") that employ alcohol and other poisons for post-breakup self-medication. Two songs in a row with the phrase "good times" in their titles ("Good Times Ain't What They Used to Be," "For the Good Times"). And songs sung from the points of view of God (half of "I Remember You"), two pawnshop guitars (title-track novelty "The Guitar Song"), and "Heartache," which tallies famous folks foiled by said malady throughout history, from cavemen to Antony 'n' Cleopatra to Charles 'n' Diana. (You know, à la "Sympathy for the Devil." Or Motörhead's "Orgas-matron.")

In case you want to pinpoint where this onetime Marine Reserves E-4 mortarman fits on the historical timeline himself, Johnson also interprets oldies by Ray Price, Mel Tillis, alcohol casualty Keith Whitley, and Vern Gos-din (the latter on "Set 'Em Up Joe," a 1988 country #1 about repeatedly putting Ernest Tubb's "Walking the Floor over You" on the jukebox). Which roster, incidentally, shakes out at least as much "countrypolitan" as "outlaw"; "The Guitar Song" itself name-drops Merle, Lefty, Johnny, and Marty Robbins, but Johnson's duet partner is 72-year-old "Whispering Bill" Anderson, who, three decades ago, made a Barry White–influenced country-disco makeout album—and who is, in turn, mentioned in the very next number, which pays generous tribute to Music City's songwriters and shouts out to a few, includ-ing the late Hank Cochran. But just in case that *backdates* Johnson too much, there's also a fairy-tale verse about princes scaring dragons away and saving princesses, concluding a music-box-embellished lullaby apparently directed at his six-year-old daughter—which, who knows, just might be an awkward attempt to keep up with Taylor Swift. And speaking of child-rearing tips, the song that recommends not sparing the rod ("By the Seat of Your Pants") rivals any such pro-spanking gross-out by Montgomery Gentry. So Johnson has got all his bases covered.

*The Guitar Song* spreads 25 songs (five of them over five minutes long, one over seven) onto two discs, labeled "Black" and "White," since the former has marginally darker themes and sonics. (There might also be a white vs. non-white split when Johnson asks, "Where you gonna be when half of California riots?" but he unhelpfully never specifies which half.) The music, at its liveliest, successfully reinvents for studio consumption the tight-but-loose jamming of a working roadhouse band: Johnson's own Kent Hardly Playboys, in this case, though credits suggest occasional pinch-hitting on the drum stool. Piano and Hammond B-3 set the standard; the only time the guitars get real Dixie-rock distorted is on "Macon," as in "Macon love all night," a humid Muscle Shoals–style groover about driving home to Georgia to get laid. And there's still some of the cavernous gloom-metal atmosphere that bled out the pores of Johnson's previous album, maybe most noticeably this time in "Heartache," which echoes and groans like an abandoned asylum deep in the holler, or amid the spacious empty-tavern drift of "My Way to You." For a country album—country being the one musical genre that never much succumbed to ridiculous CD-era album lengths before the bum digital economy brought economy back—this whole project is way beyond ambitious.

It's also a case of a self-conscious artist—an Alabama-fan-turned-renegade who co-wrote "Honky Tonk Badonkadonk," but whose increasingly serial-murderer-scary mountain-goatee serves as an apt metaphor for his aesthetic redefinition—taking advantage of the situation at hand while he can get away with it. Johnson's 2008 *That Lonesome Song*—originally written in backstory-enabling hermit seclusion (beard growth + self-imposed solitude after life-changing breakup + Christgau Dud status = Bon Iver, only good!), then self-released online, then picked up by Mercury in slightly altered form—commercially outdid its considerably more clean-cut 2006 BNA predecessor *The Dollar* despite being concocted with limited biz-suit oversight. *The Guitar Song*'s sprawl alone suggests Mercury gave Johnson something close to free rein. It's got a few clunkers and slow spots, and, especially given the depressive tempos Johnson's so fond of, it's inadvisable to ingest in one sitting. But surprisingly—even without a single track half as monumental or emotionally inescapable as *Lonesome*'s "High Cost of Living," wherein Johnson's marriage and the GNP fell apart in equally inexorable coke-and-whore measure (in a Southern Baptist parking lot no less, and sobriety proved just one more prison)—*Guitar* is packed at least as solid as his last set, and it's less conventional to boot.

For one thing, it doesn't resort to mere high-grade country-popcorn as often. And for another, Johnson is managing more motion in his hungover doomsday baritone: he's downplaying his sluggish mid-'70s Waylon Jennings fixation (responsible for two more-or-less-expendable cover versions and one humorous tribute tune last time), a step in the right direction. Which is saying a lot, given that *Lonesome* was my favorite album of 2008 (it drags more for me recently, but still), not to mention the *only* album (sorry, TV on the Radio and Lil Wayne!) to finish that year on three of four year-end Top 10 lists (Chinen, Pareles, Caramanica) at respected hillbilly circular the *New York Times*. *Lonesome* also dominated 2008's nationwide country critics' poll at *Nashville Scene*—#1 album, single, male singer, songwriter—and wound up long-tailing in the gold range, sales-wise. Got Grammy-nominated, too. This time out, the sky's the limit. Unless, as a couple of *Guitar Song* songs anticipate, the sky falls first.

—*Village Voice*, 15 September 2010

## Country Songs V

· · · · ·

### Lee Brice:
### "Sumter County Friday Night" (2010)

In which a pre–football game *Friday Nights Nights* rumble between rival small-town Carolina schools results in black eyes, and Lee Brice's band sets up an incessant powerchord groove, vicious enough to pass as battle music. Brice, who went to college in South Carolina on a football scholarship himself, has a tendency to slip in more emphatic moments into vocal inflections out of '90s post-grunge rock—he compresses words and stretches them out, turning individual vowels into several syllables or two words into one, in ways country rarely allows. On his 2010 debut *Love Like Crazy*, the track kicks off a brutal three-song midsection—"Carolina Boys" is also *about* potential violence, threatened against a city-slicker yuppie "in his three piece suit and his penny loafer shoes" whose girl Lee, in his "white T-shirt and my cowboy hat and my baby blues," wants to steal. Class warfare of the asshole kind, but efficient. And "Four on the Floor" dives deep into a hybrid of country-rock with post-funk dance while namedropping both Barry White and Waylon Jennings. But "Sumter County Friday Night" is the killer: how Brice impatiently switches tempos to dodge radar traps and swallows his words when he rides those big-tire toys on red-dirt roads out to Sparkleberry Swamp, how he sounds so hungry for blood on the word "fott"—translates as "fight," y'all—even how "50 cellphones ring, and everybody's talking about the same thing." What, no texting?

## Flynnville Train:
## "Sandman" (2010)

I'd been hearing this droning FM staple by America since the early '70s, but managed to ignore it until these super-scraggly Indiana longhairs turned it into the hardest-rocking track I've heard so far this decade. They're a country band, hypothetically (their 2007 debut came out on Toby Keith's Show Dog Nashville imprint), but they're country in the road-tested Kentucky Headhunters real-band sense, and this cut packs at least as high-decibel a wallop as the Headhunters' 2005 take on "Big Boss Man." Total biker jam, exploratory in a Skynyrd sense, with quiet spans and sitar from one Bret Shankar letting rhythm and lead guitars build over monster drums. My colleague George Smith informs me that cover bands frequently handled "Sandman" as "a fuzz-tone proto-metal dirge around '70–'72—it was basically a simple dirge all along, so you could hammer the shit out of it." Amazing if it took 40 years for anyone to finally get that idea recorded, but that's pretty much what Flynn-ville do: dirge into raveup, at least. (Second most menacing stab at the sound on their 2010 *Redemption* album: "Friend of Sinners," about asking Christ's forgiveness since you've flubbed all the commandments.) Anyway, turns out their big inspiration for pummelling the living dickens out of "Sandman" was 9/11: "We prepared ourselves mentally by watching footage of the attack and printing pictures of Bin Laden and placing them all around us in the studio," their press bio reveals. So when Brian Flynn shouts all that cryptic stuff about grounded planes and enlistment and "running from the man who goes by the name of the Sandman," that's what they have in mind. America—two American ex-pats and a Brit who first met on a U.S. Air Force base, allegedly writing about a squadron based in France—had no idea what they were forecasting.

## Toby Keith:
## "Beers Ago" (2012)

For my money, he's the most reliable singles artist, any genre, of the past decade (maybe most reliable album artist, too, even if he's noticeably slipped some lately.) "Beers Ago" gets him in jovial rather than belligerent mode (see "High Maintenance Woman," "As Good as I Once Was," "Whiskey Girl," "I Love This Bar," etc.), and it's got plenty of fast-talked speed-of-sound small-town-decades-ago details ("spent what little bit of money we had on wintergreen Skoal and Main Street gas," "man in the moon works his magic on the second runner-up from the 4H pageant," etc.) and sounds great on a car radio—so, par-for-the-course Toby, pretty much. Kind of confusing, maybe, that he sings some girl "The Homesick Blues"—does he mean "Lovesick Blues" (Emmett Miller via Hank Williams), "Subterranean Homesick Blues" (Bob Dylan) which would be really weird, or what? Only real problem, though, is the beer math: when the song starts, senior year of high school was 1,452 beers ago; when the song ends, 1,653 beers ago. But Toby Keith graduated in Oklahoma in 1979, and even 1,653 divided by 33 years comes out to just over 50 beers per year, which equals less than one beer per week! Wow, what a wild man!

—*Complex*, 5 June 2012

## Bro-Country Isn't as Dumb as It Looks

· · · · ·

Sundry critics have already deemed 2013 an amazing year for country albums by smart young women (Ashley Monroe, Kacey Musgraves, Pistol Annies, Brandy Clark—I'd toss in Cassadee Pope, plus Gretchen Wilson if 40-year-olds are allowed) but an awful year for country radio, which was dominated instead by brainless "bro" songs by pickup-flaunting, beer-swilling young men whose lyrics at best use women as racks to hang Daisy Dukes on. I more or less agree—my *Nashville Scene* poll Top 10 this year will be more female than ever, while the radio format's as unbearable as it's been in ages. That said, I liked a few of the biggest and supposedly dumbest bro-country hits anyway; maybe even think they're smarter than they get credit for.

Zac Brown famously called Luke Bryan's "That's My Kind of Night" the "worst song I ever heard" a few months back, and he's not alone. But Bryan's smash (#1 country, #15 pop) has a funk and push that Brown's own watered-down jam-rock can't touch; beyond signifiers about "rolling on 35s" and making it rain and T-Pain/Conway mixtapes and cornrows (as in hair?), the opening boom-bap beats and Dirty South crunk grunts and eventual internal semi-rhymes ("Flint River" / "catfish dinner" / "winner when I") are evidence that, nearly a decade after the first Big & Rich album, country has absorbed hip-hop to an extent that it's almost an unconscious part of the sound. This is neither a surprise nor as blasphemous as genre segregationists pretend—in fact, it's pretty much what country has *always* done with black pop music. And if the lyric's a sleazy come-on, it's no dumber about it than, say, "Get Lucky" or "Blurred Lines."

Which are admittedly pretty dumb, but admit it—dumb can be fun. And as any Ramones fan understands, self-knowledge helps. For my money, the Best Intentionally Dumb Hook of 2013 trophy goes to Lee Brice's #11 country / #62 pop "Parking Lot Party": "Ain't no party like the pre- [or 'freak,' if you want to hear it that way] party / And after the party is the after-party." Redundancy FTW! Not sure I buy claims that Brice is bumping an R. Kelly groove, though I hope so. Either way, the song's rhythmic energy, goofball asides, drunken backup chatter, and saliva-propelled *p*-pronunciation make for a funnier and more convincing approximation of double-shot '60s frat-rock than anything any so-called indie "garage band" has done in a while, even if this party's particulars involve chicken wings and tailgates, not shing-a-lings and togas.

Brice tells us Marshall Tucker's on the radio, same band some bikini-top-popping lust object sings along to in Florida Georgia Line's country-chart-topping "Cruise," which took forever and a Nelly remix to make it to *Billboard*'s pop Top 5. But neither song *sounds* like Marshall Tucker; if anything, "Cruise (Remix)"—which I've still yet to hear on an actual country station—cruises along with windows down like Nelly's own old country grammar, maybe even in his old Range Rover. Word of Florida Georgia's onstage hip-hop medleys (Lil Troy to Macklemore to 50 Cent to Juvenile to Kanye) suggests untapped potential.

Personally, though, I preferred Jason Aldean's far more ridiculous "1994" (#10 country, #52 pop), which is hip-hoppish in the sense that it's talked on-beat and references "The Real Slim Shady" and advocates imbibing Grey Goose à la the Ying Yang Twins, but which more endearingly rests on the dubious assumptions that (1) it's not too early to get nostalgic for the mid-'90s and (2) the main reason to be nostalgic is that we miss mulletted-and-mustachioed midlevel country lug Joe Diffie, eight of whose oldies get sneakily name-checked, as if Aldean's callow fanbase would even remember them. His best, 1994's "Third Rock from the Sun," the only song about chaos theory's butterfly effect ever to scale the country chart, fortunately gets the most action; hence Aldean's truck turns into a time machine. Plus, "1994"'s throb is limber enough that, for its last minute, we get to bask in an instrumental jam. So stop complaining!

Finally, one last good thing about bro-country is that it hasn't given up yet on trying to be John Cougar. So we got Randy Houser, who just a few years ago was positioning himself for the serious quasi-outlaw role Eric Church wound up in, now settling for the mere windows-down date-fodder "Runnin' Outta Moonlight" (#3 country, #24 pop), salvaged mainly by that indelible "Jack and Diane" riff. Even better, 2013 gave us now-enlightened rogue Toby Keith's "Drinks After Work" (#28 country, #102 pop), which musically is straight-up *Lonesome Jubilee* Mellencamp and lyrically finds a casual sexiness in the after-quitting-time hump-day liaisons of middle-management office workers in "suits and skirts" sipping 7-and-7s: suburban and mature, not "bro" at all really, but Toby's 52 and he's-been-there-done-that and then some (was hick-hopping without making a big deal of it with "I Wanna Talk about Me" way back in 2001), plus he still sings all y'all young bucks under the floor mat. Enjoy your trucks while you can, boys.

—rhapsody.com, 27 December 2013

## Ashley Monroe and Kacey Musgraves Are What They Are

• • • • •

Ashley Monroe and Kacey Musgraves are both Tom Petty fans, and they both covered '30s cowgirl queen Patsy Montana when they were kids (Monroe in a talent contest she won at 11, Musgraves on a CDBaby release at 13), though Musgraves was also the Patsy Montana National Yodeling Champion in 2002 and covered *Hannah* Montana's best song, "See You Again," for an Austin indie label in 2008. (Could French be next?) Monroe and Musgraves are now 26 and 24 respectively, a bit younger than Loretta Lynn when she first hit in the '60s, a bit older than Bobbie Gentry when she did. Like Lynn and Gentry, they are also creative writers—on their excellent new albums out this month, both of which you can sort of call debuts if you have asterisks handy, they both get co-writing credits on every song. They've both written with Miranda Lambert, Trent Dabbs, and Shane McAnally. They both sing more than their doctors might advise about smoking, both tobacco and marijuana, though only Monroe devotes a song specifically to the latter—"Weed Instead of Roses," which additionally advocates whips, whipped cream, and heavy metal as marital aids.

Addiction figures on both albums, too: gambling and cigarettes in Musgraves's stomping "Blowin' Smoke" (one of the best songs about obsessive-compulsive Vegas behavior since Steely Dan's "Do It Again"), unnamed substances and/or unhealthy co-dependency in Monroe's stormy "You Got Me." When Monroe's room starts "spinnin' round faster and faster" before her hangover in "Morning After" and when the broken small-town hamster-wheel carousel metaphor of Musgraves's "Merry Go 'Round" spins us round and round "and where it stops nobody knows and it ain't slowin' down," their dizzy concentric circles both channel the windmills of Dusty Springfield's mind. So even beyond a stark confessionalism that may prove either too pop and not pop enough for country radio, these two young women have a few things in common.

To country radio's credit, it did play "Merry Go 'Round" last year. It peaked at #14 in the format, even though Musgraves's defeated Groundhog Day depiction of boondock life—"just like dust we settle in this town," "tiny little boxes in a row, ain't what you want, it's what you know"—revealed grim truths that Nashville has long preferred to cover up with rural-chauvinist malarkey about not needing to lock doors at night and more-country-than-thou cataloging of fishing lures. To what extent it reflects the life Musgraves knew growing up the child of a couple who ran an independent print shop in a 600-population East Texas town proud of its Sweet Potato Festival is anybody's guess, but the song was as spot-on as any single released by anyone in 2012, and it's tempting to quote the whole thing: Mom hooked on Mary Kay, Bro on Mary Jane, Dad on Mary Two Doors Down (more addiction!); "same checks we're always cashin' to buy a little more distraction" (yet more!—late capitalism division); Mother Goose rhymes going to seed. And there are people who like Musgraves's "Undermine," made famous by Hayden Panettiere on *Nashville*, even more—maybe because "analyzin' everything that ain't worth thinking about" is what we folks who think about such things do.

A line in "Merry Go 'Round" provides *Same Trailer Different Park*'s title, though "My House" actually has more about trailers in it, extending a cordial motorhome invitation like Dionne Warwick's "Hasbrook Heights" for a time of vastly diminished suburban expectations. Musgraves's YouTubable "Trailer Song" didn't make the cut, though a couple of its passably paranoid themes did; i.e., snooping neighbors not minding their own beezwax (in "Step Off"—"don't wreck my reputation, let me wreck my own") and a recurring defensiveness about skipping church, which is overshadowed in the very sweet if slightly precious sisterly advice song "Follow Your Arrow" by a zesty and perhaps zeitgeisty cheerlead chorus that goes "Make lots of noise! Kiss lots of boys! Kiss lots of girls if that's something you're into!" You can quibble that Musgraves never stipulates that last line's directed at girls (though the later "love who you

Ashley Monroe and Hippie Annie, back to back (Photo: Joseph Llanes)

love" is a hint) or that Katy Perry got there forever ago (though Kacey's not just Girls Gone Wilding) or that she even slips in a "you only live once," jeez (though not 'til the end). But for mainstream country, this is up there with Republicans filing an amicus brief advocating gay marriage.

There's a song called "It Is What It Is" at album's end, too—Musgraves loves those catch phrases you're sick of, though at least she didn't call it "It's Complicated," which is what it's about, and her resigning herself to settling for a mediocre partner for the time being might break Lena Dunham's heart. Musgraves opts for sad prettiness more than rocking out—only "Blowin' Smoke" and "Stupid" qualify as the latter—and she's not immune to the little-girl-voiced restraint and nonchalance of '90s college rock. But she's got a superb knack for melodies, even if it means swiping them from Radiohead ("I Miss You"—blatant "Creep" rip, probably another country first) and maybe Jimmy Eat World ("Silver Lining"). "Dandelion" is so gorgeous that anything other than teenage notebook poetry would wreck its mood.

The fuller-drawling Ashley Monroe, by contrast, seems to have gotten most if thankfully not all the moroseness out of her system with *Satisfied*, the debut album Sony was slated to release way back in 2006, then didn't. Review promos went out and everything, then three years later the record sneaked onto digital services. It was serious stuff: Dwight Yoakam duet, Kasey Chambers and Lucinda Williams covers, Ralph Stanley and Hank Williams name-drops, some blues slide and train chug and a needy closer that sounded kind of like Karyn White's "Superwoman," but above all lots of bottomed-out slow ones, all from a 19-year-old convinced that love stinks. She later recorded sundry stray tracks with Wanda Jackson, Train, and Jack White's Raconteurs, and in 2011 resurfaced as part of Miranda Lambert's cowpunkish trio Pistol Annies — nicknamely, "Hippie Annie," the sorority sister in their definitive traveling-girl-band number "Takin' Pills" who opted for prescription antidepressants and pain medicine over booze or chain smoking: "She's on the highest dose of Prozac a woman can take."

Monroe has said sad songs come naturally to her, since she first learned the trade back in Knoxville after her dad died of cancer when she was 13. But though she starts *Like a Rose* singing "I was only 13 when Daddy died" then catching the next bus south from North Dakota, the album is if anything more manic than depressive — or at least considerably more upbeat than *Satisfied*. "Monroe Suede," an eponymous fugitive anthem where Dad dies drunk then Daughter steals a pickup at 14, is downright uproarious. Kinky midnight toker "Weed Instead of Roses" and "You Ain't Dolly (and You Ain't Porter)," a duet with Lambert's hubbie Blake Shelton where he claims to be "the guy they wrote about in *Fifty Shades of Grey*," are comedy not tragedy; "Two Weeks Late," about being unmarried and pregnant with the landlord pestering you for rent you don't have and Mom noticing your weight gain, is both. And all of those songs, "Like a Rose" maybe even more than the louder ones, are immediately, indelibly catchy.

The melancholy tracks are good too — for instance "Used," as in being damaged goods, like an untunable generations-old piano or a house haunted by bodies that died there, which Monroe was smart enough to salvage from *Satisfied*. So, like Musgraves's album, a good balance: classicist in the Lee Ann Womack neo-countrypolitan sense, yet neither stodgy, frail, nor nostalgic, but rather as thoroughly in tune with modern millennial existence as Taylor Swift, who seemingly opened a commercial door for both artists though she makes music more ornately arranged than either. In Nashville, women have long been less stuck than men in the back-40 mud, more on the move. But this genre plows forward only gradually, and Monroe and Musgraves somehow inch country closer to the world it actually lives in.

—spin.com, 12 March 2013

## When the Angels Stopped Watching Mindy McCready

. . . . .

Mindy McCready opened her first album—also her first single, and ultimately one of her biggest hits—tempted by the devil. She'd been singing for 17 years, since she was three in a Pentecostal church in Florida. But now it was 1996, she was 20, and she'd been cavorting for a while with a married baseball star. Satan knew just where to find her, she confessed: "Here we go again."

The song's chorus told us she was counting on 10,000 angels to watch over her. For a while, maybe they did. But within less than a decade, they were letting her down, and you've probably seen the list by now: drug overdoses, abusive boyfriends, arrests, probation violations, repeated suicide attempts, *Celebrity Rehab*, mental illness, custody battles over her kids, the father of her infant son dying of an apparently self-inflicted gunshot on her porch in January. And then, on Sunday, McCready finally turning a gun on herself, successfully this time, on the same porch.

The best song she ever sang—also the only one to cross over to the British charts, where it got to #41, though it went nowhere in the U.S.—talked about suicide: "swallow the poison, pick up the knife." "Oh Romeo" was about a "romantic depressive" who nonetheless decides a guy's not worth dying over, but there's torment in the sound, in the bitter edginess of the singing and the almost gothic space and shadows of David Malloy's production. The rest of McCready's second album, late 1997's *If I Don't Stay the Night*, had more of the same: songs like the title track and "What If I Do," where the devil and angel on her shoulders debated whether going all the way with somebody was worth it, and the singer insisted the storm raging outside was no match for the thunder in her mind; "Cross against the Moon," where a 17-year-old Nebraska preacher's daughter opted for Hollywood and Marilyn Monroe over the gospel tent. An inner battle was leaking in, or so it seemed when I wrote this in the *Village Voice* in early 1998, about McCready interpreting an old Linda Ronstadt classic: "Covering 'Long, Long Time,'" one of the saddest songs on earth, all the extra syllables and serifs and cracks in her voice convince me *she's* about to crack." Where Ronstadt settled for prettiness, McCready got the entire ache: "Time washes clean love's wounds unseen / That's what someone told me, but I don't know what it means."

I heard *If I Don't Stay the Night*, then, as inhabiting "mentally unbalanced terrain"—but if her world had begun to unravel, I had no way of knowing.

Her debut, 1996's *Ten Thousand Angels*, was flirty, upbeat, wholesome, self-assured. In "Guys Do It All the Time," her only song ever to top the country chart, she turned tables on the dudes by staying out 'til 4 A.M. having beers with the girls: a rocking boot-scooter, surrounded on the album with other line-dance-ready two-steps about young ladies out on the town, 'cause it ain't a party 'til they get here. Even that hit about demonic temptation sounded totally optimistic, affirming Nashville's fallback stance that, sure, things might go wrong now and then, but ultimately stuff will work out, because at least if you stick to home and hearth and God and the comfort of your small town, all is right with the world.

McCready probably already knew by then what a crock that is. But she was ambitious — she'd graduated high school early to get her career going — and in the wake of Shania Twain, Nashville had its eyes on photogenic young women. *Ten Thousand Angels*, which went on to sell 2 million copies, came out just a couple months before 14-year-old LeAnn Rimes's *Blue*, which went on to sell 6 million in the U.S. alone. The idea, it seems, was maybe to build a demographic coalition between suburban tween-girl pop fans and their country-fan moms; Lila McCann (1997), Jessica Andrews (1999), Rebecca Lynn Howard (2000), Alecia Elliott (2000), Cyndi Thompson (2001), and others had all come and gone before Taylor Swift finally hit the jackpot starting in 2006.

Which is to say: the industry is hell. Beyond all the tragic tabloid stories, McCready's career trajectory was more or less typical of this bunch: she put out five albums, every subsequent one peaking lower on the country chart than its predecessor. Only her debut, with three, produced any Top 10 country singles. But her first four albums, at least, are all worth hearing, and what makes 1999's BNA Records swan song *I'm Not So Tough* and 2002's Capitol Nashville one-shot *Mindy McCready* intriguing isn't so much the intense emotion of *If I Don't Stay the Night* as a willingness to stir all sorts of left-field '80s pop influences into the country pot: rockabilly-ish big-beat new wave ("All I Want Is Everything"), increasingly lush Stevie Nicks / Quarterflash quasi-soft rock ("I've Got a Feeling"), cute and coy Stacey Q teasing ("Lucky Me"), Spanish-guitared Eurodance grooves ("I Just Want Love"), unbashful womanly belting owing to R&B and Pat Benatar in place of the exaggerated southern drawl McCready had started out with. It sounds like she was being regroomed (as was LeAnn Rimes, around the same time) for either adult contemporary or for a more global, club-minded fanbase. Didn't pan out, though, and country radio had mostly left such theoretically frivolous experimentation behind in Shania's '90s.

One final album, the wishfully titled *I'm Still Here*, came out in 2010, well into the downhill slide of McCready's life, on an obscure Denver indie called Iconic Records. It's difficult to listen to, but notable for being the only album on which McCready gets any co-songwriting credits—namely three, and of those, "I'm Still Here" is the most revelatory. Clearly, she's just barely hanging on: "There was darkness all around me / There were times I was sure I was drowning." Before long, maybe inevitably, she did. As the son of a man who committed suicide when I was 13, four years after my mom died, my thoughts are mostly with 6-year-old Zander and 10-month-old Zane. I should probably be angry, but mostly this just makes me feel sad for them, and thankful Mindy McCready's life isn't mine. Her life makes Hank Williams's sound easy, and who knows what makes life turn that way? "Life is like a box of matches / Sometimes the whole thing catches," she sang way back in "Oh Romeo." "And all you can do is watch it burn."

—spin.com, 19 February 2013

# Conclusion
## I Am the World's Forgettin' Boy

This is absolutely irrational on my part, obviously, and a by-product of paying selective attention to things, but sometimes it feels to me like history just stopped moving at some point, like it fell into a rut and stayed there—not just musically, though that's certainly part of it, but even politically, like how America's adventures in the Middle East have been in a holding pattern ever since 9/11, or even Desert Storm. Which is of course absurd—things are changing all the time, by the minute, and it's not like history progresses "forward" anyway. But somehow, something deep in my gut still believes it. Maybe it's just what happens when people get old.

Anyway, some things do get better! In all sorts of ways, life is safer and more just than when I grew up. Fair housing, marriage equality, theoretically affordable health care, Confederate shame—all upheld in one June week in 2015! Miranda Lambert's "Automatic" to the contrary, I can live without a world where staying in a miserable marriage is the only choice—and I never got the attraction of standard transmission anyway. Still, the idea of society (and since it's the subject at hand, music) somehow constantly maturing and evolving—inevitably getting closer and closer to perfection—is its own myth. It's why certain sounds get lazily dismissed as "dated," and why pop-culture nostalgia so often involves a winking assumption that years ago we sure did look ridiculous. Ultimately, such condescension encompasses every decade. When do we figure out that, no matter how modern we are, somebody 20 years from now will make smug fun of us?

We pretend years and decades end, but they never really do. As Paul Beatty wrote about history in *The Sellout*, his 2015 novel about redacted ghetto communities, the timelessness of minstrelsy, and early-'90s rappers investing in ostriches, "We like to think it's a book—that we can turn the page and move the fuck on. But history isn't the paper it's printed on. It's memory, and memory is time, emotions, and song. History is the things that stay with you." Conversely,

I've been posting lots of my old Pazz & Jop critics poll ballots online in the past few years, and no matter how much I sweated over getting them right at the time, all the way down to dividing 100 points among 10 albums, in retrospect it's clear they're really all still in flux, and maybe always will be—my curiosity about discovering music from 1987 didn't end when 1987 did.

Anyway, people get the idea I have all that information at my fingertips, and in my writing I might come off as somebody who has remarkable memory for obscure musical trivia, which maybe I do sometimes (though maybe I also just keep really good notes). But real life's a different story—please don't ask me what year I saw Sleater-Kinney in Bryn Mawr, or what my all-time favorite *Six Feet Under* episode was. When it comes to movies and TV, I'm totally inept at remembering names and résumés of even reasonably famous actors and directors. And even music-wise, I blow my cover a lot. Back in the '00s the discussion board ilxor.com hosted a trollish thread titled (in typical clumsy-grammar-on-purpose Internet style) "Music Critics Are the Art of Pretend Forgetfulness." I was a regular target, mainly for posts that some people interpreted as idle affectation but I just figured were me thinking on my feet: e.g., "Did Arrested Development even MAKE a second album? I honestly forget." Or "Butch Hancock! He can't sing at ALL! (Unless I'm thinking of Jimmie Dale Gilmore; I totally get those guys mixed up)."

I suppose that's still not really "real life," though. In real life I had a real traumatic childhood (details available elsewhere), and ever since, whenever a chapter of my life was over, I'd shut the memory door and never look back. Or at least, that's the apparent coping mechanism I've discussed with a few therapists since. And it's one reason I'll probably never remember enough about my stint in the army, for instance, to write a memoir about it even though I'm a writer by trade and it might have made for a good one. (Should have kept a journal, but the last thing I wanted to do in my personal officer quarters when a soldiering day was over was relive it in my head.) And believe me, there were incidents growing up that I probably *had* to block out—at least until they re-surfaced decades later—in order to move on and get to where I am now.

On top of everything else, I've never had a sense of smell (don't *remember* ever having one anyway), and evidently smell helps people recall life experiences. D.J. Jazzy Jeff and the Fresh Prince ("the smell from a grill can spark up nostalgia") taught me that; Rudyard Kipling too ("Smells are surer than sounds or sights / To make your heartstrings crack.") So here's a question: Does lacking one of my five senses make me a better music listener because I use ears to compensate, or worse? (Or actually, one and a half—like probably 95% of male music critics, I also wear thick glasses. As for my hearing and taste, judge for yourself and check the title of this book.) Fashion boutique owners in happening neo-hippie tourist spot Asheville, North Carolina, have complained lately that certain unwashed street buskers' odor tends to outdistance their strumming. And to open his EMP Pop Conference presentation a few years back on "the marriage made in hell between folk music, dead cultures, myth, and highly technical modern extreme metal," my pal Scott Seward drew an analogy to how the olfactory brew he endured in his night job as a custodian at a small Martha's Vineyard hospital ("blood, urine, vomit, shit, freshly mown grass, the saltwater spray from the harbor across the street, the oppressive—on hot days almost visible—cloud surrounding the water-treatment plant out back, the cleansers and waxes, the iodine and ammonia") would trigger "Proustian reveries" and elicit "primal, nearly forgotten memories that go back as far as the cradle." Since that's all foreign to me, is my ability to adequately appreciate Ulver's and Týr's solstice metal somehow impaired? As if my lifetime avoidance of horror, fantasy, science fiction, superhero, slasher, and snuff movies, especially the kind with overblown special effects, didn't already disqualify me enough metal-wise!

Then again, for as long as I *can* remember, I've had recurring dreams where I'm navigating on foot through twisted intersections of once-familiar cities and subdivisions, obstacle-course corridors and hospital floors, treacherous terrain guarded by lions and tigers, trying to get back to where I'm supposed to be—which may well be what my writing does sometimes, too. And I can hear Orleans's innocuous 1975 soft-rock hit "Dance With Me"—a song I've never owned in any form or given a second's thought—while shopping for celery at Fresh Plus, and I'm *immediately* flashed back through a mental wormhole to some sunny late afternoon early in tenth grade when I was both mortified and exhilarated by whatever limitless possibilities I associated with asking Shelly or maybe Barb to a high school dance (right, like it was the '50s or something), which I'm not sure I ever even got up the nerve to do. Old songs can do that. But unless urban adult contemporary stations playing '80s quiet-storm hits I ignored in their time count, I never listen to classic or oldies radio in my car. Best to be caught off guard.

Do kids nowadays even *have* high school dances? Maybe apps replaced those, too. And video games like Minecraft. The cliché—which, like all clichés, must have some truth in it—is that they're growing up in a world where several past decades of pop music have all folded in on each other and now happily coexist, since everybody always webstreams and iPod-shuffles them simultaneously. Simon Reynolds suggested in the *New York Times* in 2011 that the 2000s were the first decade without "epoch-defining sounds," the first one that didn't seem "fast-moving and ever-changing." Which is sort of like what I said a few paragraphs back about history stopping.

As for my own history, I wonder how long I can get away with doing what I do. A while, I hope—not sure what I'd do instead. Maybe I could finally write a definitive consumer guide to zoos, though I'd need a travel budget. Or maybe some metal philanthropist will shell out for a *Stairway to Hell, Part II* someday. Might be weird to admit four books and more than three decades into this vocation, but ambition has never been my strong suit. I have never even watched a TED talk, or a webinar even! And though I have little doubt that I could go back and cover sewage boards and zoning commissions in midwestern suburbia if somebody gave me a shot—or edit people who do; heck, I edited the *Village Voice*'s annual Best of New York issue for a few years, and New York's a big place!—I'm well aware that the scope of my writing on back to the '80s has in practice been embarrassingly narrow. I'm rarely even part of the Big Critic Conversation anymore, probably in part because at some point I opted out of it—maybe because deep down I'm not so sure anymore there's much of a conversation going on. Yet, anosmia or no, I've often had a nose for where the action is, and somehow hung in long enough to still put in my two cents now and then. Maybe I'm not quite a victim of natural selection yet.

# Index